The Johnson & Johnson Files

Praise for the Book

'This is the finest of investigative journalism: shoe-leather reporting from hospital wards, company boardrooms and government offices; listening to traumatised patients, deciphering their records; lifting the veil of corporate deceit and untangling the web of regulatory failures. In *The Johnson & Johnson Files*, Kaunain Sheriff tells the remarkable story of how a global giant cynically plays the local game, twists rules, cuts corners and endangers lives – all for profit. Meticulously researched and elegantly written, this must-read book is a cautionary tale for patients and a powerful wake-up call for our health-care system.'

– Raj Kamal Jha, Chief Editor, *The Indian Express*

The Johnson & Johnson Files

The Indian Secrets of a Global Giant

Kaunain Sheriff M.

JUGGERNAUT BOOKS
C-I-128, First Floor, Sangam Vihar, Near Holi Chowk,
New Delhi 110080, India

First published by Juggernaut Books 2025

Copyright © Kaunain Sheriff M. 2025

10 9 8 7 6 5 4 3 2 1

P-ISBN: 9789353453152
E-ISBN: 9789353454524

The views and opinions expressed in this book are the authors' own. The facts contained herein were reported to be true as on the date of publication by the authors to the publishers of the book, and the publishers are not in any way liable for their accuracy or veracity.

All rights reserved. No part of this publication may be reproduced, transmitted, or stored in a retrieval system in any form or by any means without the written permission of the publisher.

Typeset in Adobe Caslon Pro by R. Ajith Kumar, Noida

Printed at Thomson Press India Ltd

*For Ammi and Fareeha,
my constant source of strength*

Contents

Preface   viii

Part I

1. The Billion-Dollar Baby   3
2. The Live Surgery: A Gamble for Life   17
3. Flying Halfway Across the Globe – For an Implant She Never Wanted   38

Part II

4. The First Red Flag   61
5. Exposing the Scandal – Through Science   76
6. Recall and Beyond: Learning from the Crisis   95

Part III

7. A Doctor, Among the Youngest Victims   119
8. Zero Regulation, No Holds Barred   143
9. The Cover-Up   159

Part IV

10. FIR: 435/2011   185
11. The Industry Insider: From Victim to Fighter   215

Part V

12. The Scrutiny   243
13. The Indictment   274
14. The Tide Turns: Patients Fight Back   292

Part VI

15. Courtroom, California – Loren Kransky vs. DePuy   327
16. Courtroom, New Delhi – Daisy Bharucha vs. DePuy   358

Notes   380
A Note on the Author   388

Preface

One evening in February 2018, the city bureau of *The Indian Express* was its usual hive of activity when Ritu Sarin, a legend in investigative journalism, walked in. There's something about her presence that makes people sit up and take notice, even without her saying a word.

She came over to my desk for a quick chat, and honestly, even a short conversation with her feels like a golden opportunity. Having led some of the biggest investigative projects, her insights are pure gold – every word she says is a lesson in journalism you don't want to miss.

That evening, she got straight to the point. 'There's a new project I want to discuss with you,' she said, her voice calm but firm. The topic? The unregulated medical device market.

I blinked, trying to process her words. At that point, my expertise as a health reporter was rooted in city-level stories, patient tales and hospital challenges. The regulatory maze of medical devices? That was uncharted territory. When she asked me how much I knew about the issues in this space, I hesitated, then admitted honestly: 'I have not covered medical devices much, especially the regulatory side, but I'll look into it and get a few leads.'

She smiled and then came the twist. 'This project,' she said, 'is part of a global investigation led by the Pulitzer-winning International Consortium of Investigative Journalists (ICIJ).' Her words hit me like a lightning bolt. A collaboration involving 260 journalists worldwide to expose the flaws in a $400 billion industry? It sounded like the kind of story that could shake the industry and change lives.

The moment I left the bureau, my mind was racing. Where do I start? When it came to health stories, I had a reliable first stop: All India Institute Of Medical Sciences Delhi (AIIMS), India's most prestigious health institution. The sprawling campus, with its maze of corridors and teeming OPDs, was a place where you could find leads on almost any health issue. The very next evening, at 4.30 p.m., I had an appointment with a surgeon who had over 30 years of experience.

Preface

As I entered his office, the air smelled faintly of disinfectant and old paper – a mix that always felt oddly reassuring. The surgeon looked up from a stack of case files. I began explaining the project, but his initial response was a raised eyebrow and a question: 'Why this topic?'

The scepticism in his voice was hard to miss. 'This isn't something we talk about much,' he added, leaning back in his chair. 'Not in conferences, not even in private meetings.' His words painted a picture of an issue buried deep beneath layers of silence. But I wasn't about to give up. I pressed him for leads, though I left that day with little more than his vague interest in the topic.

A week later, the phone rang. It was the surgeon. 'Come by. I have something to share,' he said, his tone now serious. When I walked into his office again, he greeted me with a PowerPoint presentation titled 'Industry Influence in Total Knee Arthroplasty'.

It laid out some glaring facts – there were over 150 types of knee implants on the market and the fierce competition often led to corners being cut. The presentation raised tough questions about the industry's priorities: Were they genuinely innovating or just focused on profits?

I couldn't resist asking, 'Has any device ever performed so badly that it was recalled?'

His response was immediate: 'Yes. The DePuy hip implant. It was a metal-on-metal [MoM] device.'

Now, even as someone new to the medical device industry, I recognized the name DePuy. It's a massive subsidiary of Johnson & Johnson. To explain the problem, the surgeon grabbed a piece of paper and started sketching. He drew a rough diagram of the implant, showing how it had failed.

'What about the patients?' I asked, leaning forward. 'How many were affected?'

He sighed. 'I didn't use that implant myself, so I wouldn't know. That's something you'll have to dig into.'

And just like that, my investigation into the Articular Surface Replacement (ASR) hip implant scandal began – in room 5001 of the AIIMS OPD.

Since the ASR recall was primarily reported by journalists in Mumbai in 2012 – due to actions taken by local government authorities – and later in Delhi during 2017–2018, after the central government formed an expert committee to investigate the issue, revisiting this high-profile medical device recall presented a unique challenge. The goal was to examine the entire event through the lenses of patient safety, regulatory actions and most importantly, whether justice was delivered to the affected patients.

When I began delving into these stories layer by layer, the findings were startling. Starting in August 2018, *The Indian Express* published over half a dozen investigative stories on the ASR recall. Then, in November 2018, *The Indian Express*, in collaboration with the ICIJ, published The Implant Files.

This was another major collaboration with the ICIJ, following explosive investigations like the Panama Papers and Swiss Leaks, which exposed how the world's elite tucked away their riches in offshore havens. But this time, the lens wasn't on money – it was on bodies. And the findings? Disturbing. *The Indian Express* published over twenty-one hard-hitting stories, with the ASR scandal prominently featured in the series.

The first story appeared on 24 August. At exactly 8.23 p.m., as I refreshed my inbox, an email popped up with the subject line: 'Johnson & Johnson faulty implant surgeries'. I clicked it open, and my heart sank. The email was from Lata Pillay, who had read our story and decided to share her husband Dinesh Pillay's ordeal. 'I felt very happy after reading today's article in *The Indian Express*,' she wrote. 'Finally, there's some hope for justice – for compensation for all the suffering.' Her words were laced with equal parts relief and desperation.

Dinesh, she explained, had undergone surgery in Pune and had been battling constant pain and complications ever since. His was just one of the several stories of suffering, but it painted a vivid picture of the human toll behind the statistics. I've included Lata's original email, detailing her and Dinesh's ordeal, below:

```
Subject of the email: Johnson & Johnson faulty implant
surgeries.

Dear Sir,

I am Lata Dinesh Pillay from Pune, Maharashtra.

This has reference to your article on the front page of
Indian Express of today i.e 24th Aug 2018. The article named
'Johnson & Johnson buried key facts on faulty hip implant
surgeries, kept regulator in dark'. I was actually looking
for this opportunity to complaint against Johnson & Johnson.
I have tried calling them at Chennai office in 2016 after
```

Preface

the third operation as my husband was still suffering from
the severe pain.

Let me narrate the whole issue.

My husband Mr Dinesh Pillay, age 50 years was operated for
THR in the year 2007. Even after the operation he was not
okay. He could not walk even for 1 km at a time. Due to
this he could not join any of the job. In the year 2012 he
had a very severe pain in the operated hip and thigh. On
getting the x-ray done, we got to know that the stem of the
implant had broken. Due to which my husband had high fever
and infections. Due to which, he had to undergo the revision
immediately. The revision was done by replacing the ceramic
implant. It was very difficult to remove the broken piece
of the stem. To remove this, surgeon had to make a fracture
in his thigh bone. After which the revision was done by
inserting a long ceramic implant. After the revision, he was
unable to walk until 5 months. Since then he is suffering
with severe pain in the thigh. After again consulting the
surgeon, x-ray was done. Which showed that the pain was
due to the loosening of the stem and the fracture that was
done while removing the broken implant. This is due to the
faulty implant that was supplied by Johnson & Johnson. If
the implant was of the good quality, my husband's operation
would have been succeeded.

Till now he has to get the x-rays followed by bone scan done
twice or thrice a year whenever he has unbearable pain, and
keep a regular follow-up with the surgeon. However, it has
become beyond our affordable status to continue with the
treatment.

I felt very happy after reading today's article in the India
Express today as I can see there are some hope for getting
justice in way of compensation for the sufferings.

Awaiting any update on this matter.

Thanks and regards,

Lata Dinesh Pillay

A few weeks later, on 6 September 2018, another email arrived at 10.26 a.m. This one was gut-wrenching. A husband recounted how his wife had endured a painful revision surgery after her initial implant failed. The tragedy didn't end there – she didn't survive.

During The Implant Files investigation, I highlighted Dinesh's case because it involved a rare instance of 'live surgery' – a questionable practice where medical devices are demonstrated to surgeons during live procedures – raising serious ethical concerns. However, I couldn't highlight the other case because the family couldn't confirm the exact implant used.

It got me thinking: how many families in India are in the same position? Most people trust their doctors completely and don't think to ask questions like, 'Which implant are you using? Why this one? How long does it last? What are the risks?' These aren't questions people are used to asking in the chaos of hospital visits, where decisions are made quickly and consent forms are signed without much thought.

But here's the thing – these questions matter. They demarcate the difference between a successful recovery and years of suffering. Unfortunately, most families don't know this until it's too late. And to make things worse, manufacturers – and even the system as a whole – don't make it easy to get clear answers.

It was during this time that I realized the importance of revisiting my previous journalistic work and compiling it into an investigative book. Patient safety deserved a deeper, more comprehensive examination. And so, this book was born.

When it came to exposing the cracks in our system, no story was more compelling – or urgent – than how the ASR hip implant scandal unfolded in India. It's a tale of trust betrayed and lives upended. What happened – and what should never have happened – must be recounted not just to document the past but to ensure it's not repeated. This story needs to be unravelled layer by layer because it reveals the glaring loopholes in a system that is meant to protect, not harm.

Yet, while revisiting this issue, we cannot ignore an important fact: medical devices, especially hip implants, have been transformative for countless people. These are the miracles of modern medicine. But then there are the exceptions, the outliers – those rare cases where the very device meant to restore a life ends up devastating it instead. Identifying these outliers isn't just important, it's critical. And this book delves into one such case, holding it up as a mirror to the system.

But this isn't just a story about a company or a faulty device. It's about something far bigger. This unprecedented medical device recall offers a stark reminder of the need to put patient safety above profits, bureaucracy and negligence. Through this lens, I examine the broader systemic issues that demand our attention – and action.

Part I

Part 1

1

The Billion-Dollar Baby

It was as if money were falling from the sky, with billions more expected to pour down. The numbers were staggering – $7.3 billion in 1996, climbing to $8.9 billion in 1997.[1] The global orthopaedic product market had morphed into a goldmine, its riches flowing freely into the pockets of eager investors, with profits soaring higher and higher.

But what exactly is the orthopaedic industry? Think about it this way: Your grandma, who used to struggle to walk, now moves around with ease after getting a new hip. Or maybe you know someone who had knee surgery after a sports injury and is back on their feet, running around like nothing happened. And remember that kid in the neighbourhood who broke his arm? The doctors fixed it with metal pins and plates. That's the orthopaedic industry in action – a world of medical devices that help people get back to a normal life after an injury or surgery.

It's about more than just tools and gadgets. These are things that change lives – artificial joints that replace worn-out hips and knees, screws and rods that hold broken bones together. Without these devices, a lot of people would be stuck in bed or living with constant pain. Orthopaedic products might not be flashy, but they're a huge part of modern medicine, quietly helping people get back on their feet every day.

At the helm of this booming industry were four, maybe five, giants of the orthopaedic world. These companies, hailing from the US and Europe, had essentially formed a cartel, controlling the market with an iron grip.

They weren't just players; they *were* the game. They led in design, development, manufacturing and marketing, setting the rules everyone else had to follow. Their products fell into three main categories – orthopaedic implants, surgical products and fracture-management devices. They introduced these products and also created the template for success in the industry. Their marketing and operations were so similar, it was as if they were all working from the same playbook. Imagine a top business school teaching a course on their strategies – you'd be hard-pressed to spot any differences. It was cut–copy–paste.

They commercialized their product lines relentlessly. Every company claimed its products were cutting-edge, revolutionary. The air was thick with bold promises and grandiose claims, with no room for modesty or caution. In this fierce competition, each giant vied for the coveted top spot, desperate to stay ahead of the curve. They penetrated emerging markets and new geographies with the precision of a well-oiled machine.

In these new territories, as in their traditional strongholds in the US and Europe, the orthopaedic companies built vast, seamless distribution networks. The streets of these markets bustled with independent distributors, sales associates and managers – the foot soldiers in this high-stakes battle.

You could find them everywhere – rubbing shoulders with top surgeons at lavish medical conferences, negotiating deals at exclusive dinners with hospital executives or submitting sealed bids worth millions for the latest contracts. In some cases, they even donned scrubs, stepping into operating rooms alongside surgeons to ensure their implants were used correctly. These salespeople weren't just selling; they were living the business, their operations as intricate and far-reaching as a spider's web. They were highly motivated, driven by lofty incentives and laser-focused on smashing their sales targets.

Within this booming billion-dollar market, the reconstructive product line was a lucrative cash cow. By 1997, the global market for these devices had almost reached $3.7 billion in sales. Half of this bounty came from the US, with the other half spread across the globe. But as the year progressed, the numbers climbed even higher, giving birth to a new billion-dollar darling – hip-implant products. By that year's end, the global market for hip implants alone was teetering on the $2 billion mark.

This explosive growth set the industry's wheels spinning. Major manufacturers raced to expand their product lines, eager to seize a bigger slice of this lucrative pie. Strategies were hatched by hushed voices in boardrooms, and the chess pieces of acquisitions and joint ventures were moved with calculated precision.

First to make its move was Warsaw-based Biomet, a global powerhouse distributing its products in more than a hundred countries. In January 1998, they struck a deal with Merck KGaA, a subsidiary of the German giant Merck Group, creating a 50:50 joint venture. This was more than just a partnership; it was Biomet's ticket to conquer the European market.

Meanwhile, across the Atlantic, Michigan-based Stryker Corp. was plotting its own expansion. In December 1998, it snatched up Pfizer's orthopaedic unit, Howmedica, in a $1.65 billion deal.[2] This wasn't just a purchase – it was a power play, giving Stryker control over roughly 20 per cent of the reconstructive-implant-device market. The ink on Stryker's contract had barely dried when Johnson & Johnson swooped in with an even more staggering move.

Known for everything from Band-Aids to baby powder, Johnson & Johnson was already a giant in the medical world. Its worldwide business was divided into three key segments: consumer, pharmaceutical and professional. The professional segment, home to products like orthopaedic replacements, needed a boost. Determined on growth, they set their sights on DePuy Inc., one of the oldest and most respected names in orthopaedic devices. In June 1998, Johnson & Johnson made headlines by acquiring DePuy for a whopping $3.5 billion – double of what Stryker had paid just months earlier.[3]

DePuy, another Warsaw-based titan, was already the second-leading manufacturer of hip and knee implants in the US with impressive global sales of $532 million in 1997 alone.[4] That year, they had also acquired Landanger, a top French hip implant maker, further solidifying their dominance.

For Johnson & Johnson, this was no gamble; it was a calculated move. DePuy's formidable marketing and sales team had already propelled its reach to twenty-three countries, including India, with nearly half of its sales coming from Europe and Asia-Pacific, the hottest markets at the time. By 2003, the results were clear. Johnson & Johnson's ambitious acquisition paid off, with DePuy driving the company's medical device segment to $3 billion in sales, marking a nearly 19 per cent growth.[5]

But then came 2008 – the year the world changed. The global economy crashed, and with it came financial turmoil. Companies buckled under the pressure, but Johnson & Johnson stood tall. It was one of the best-performing stocks on the Dow Jones Industrial Average, and DePuy was its crown jewel.[6] In 2008, DePuy's sales surged past the $5 billion mark, driven by its hip and knee products.[7]

However, even giants feel the tremors of a global crisis. By 2009, Johnson & Johnson's pharmaceutical and consumer segments were reeling, with significant drops in sales. But the medical devices and diagnostics segment, buoyed by DePuy, remained resilient. DePuy's sales continued to grow, reaching $5.4 billion, a testament to the enduring demand for its hip, knee and spine products.[8]

By 2010, DePuy had become the brightest star in Johnson & Johnson's firmament, achieving $5.6 billion in sales and outshining even the company's top pharmaceutical brand, Remicade.[9] The key to DePuy's unabated growth was its strong performance in the US market, where sales of knee and sports medicine products surged, and its success abroad, particularly with its hip implant line.[10] It needed to keep up that pace by driving more sales.

'Despite the trying moments of 2010, our people introduced new products, advanced our pipelines and expanded businesses in emerging markets,' the chairman of Johnson & Johnson told its investors.[11]

One of the major catalysts behind DePuy's hip implant line was the fourth-generation MoM implant – the ASR. This hip implant was introduced with a compelling promise: revolutionary innovations designed to preserve bone during hip-replacement surgery. But the ASR's allure didn't stop there. It boasted high-performance bearings with a larger diameter, which, the company claimed, reduced wear and enhanced joint stability compared to traditional bearings. This superior stability was said to offer patients a newfound confidence as they eased back into their daily routines.

The numbers told their own success story. Between 2005 and 2010, over 90,000 ASR devices were sold worldwide. This impressive figure underscored the ASR's aggressive marketing and its widespread adoption by surgeons globally, painting a picture of a product embraced across continents. Up to 2010, the ASR was a major force behind

DePuy's hip implant line, making it the most profitable subsidiary of Johnson & Johnson.

The billion-dollar hip-implant business, including DePuy's, leveraged three factors to gain maximum success: patients, surgeons and technology.

The hip is like a well-oiled machine that most of us take for granted – until it starts to break down. It's one of the biggest and strongest joints in our body, allowing us to walk, run, sit and move around with ease. Wrapped in a protective layer of muscles and ligaments, it works silently in the background, keeping us mobile. But when something goes wrong, you feel it at every step.

Back in the day, before the 1960s, the orthopaedic world focused mainly on fixing injuries. Broken bones, accidents – doctors relied on tools and devices made by the industry to patch people up. But in the late 1950s and early 1960s, things started to change. New ideas and innovations led to treatments that didn't just fix injuries but tackled long-term issues such as arthritis – a condition that creeps in and slowly wears away the joints.

Arthritis is like rust that sets in when the joints wear out. It's not just one thing – there are different types of arthritis, each with its own way of causing trouble. Sometimes, it runs in the family – passed down from a parent or grandparent. Other times, it's brought on by an old sports injury that never quite healed. The most common type is osteoarthritis, where the protective cartilage in your hip wears away. Once that cushion is gone, the bones start rubbing against each other – imagine sandpaper grinding on wood – and it causes sharp, unrelenting pain.

In more severe cases, there's a condition called avascular necrosis (AVN), which happens when the blood supply to the bone is cut off. Without blood, the bone starts to die. In a healthy hip, the femoral head – the ball part of the joint – is smooth and round, like a brand-new ping-pong ball. But in someone with AVN, that ball starts to collapse and sink in, almost like a crushed ping-pong ball. The bone weakens, the cartilage wears down and soon the hip joint doesn't fit or move the way it should. This causes even more pain and damage.

If you've got arthritis in your hip, life can feel like an uphill struggle. Simple things, like walking, climbing stairs or even lying down at night, become painful struggles. Hip arthritis usually affects people in two ways. Some folks deal with constant pain, even though their hips can still move well enough. Others might not feel as much pain but find that their hip is stiff and won't let them do basic tasks, like bending down to tie their shoes.

At first, doctors will try to manage the pain with anti-inflammatory medications or injections. For milder cases, physical therapy, weight loss and other non-surgical treatments can help for a while. But when arthritis has really set in, and the joint is damaged beyond repair, no amount of medicine or exercise can fix it. At that point, the only option is hip replacement surgery.

Hip replacements have been around for decades and have helped millions regain their mobility. In the beginning, it was thought of as a procedure for the elderly – something for someone's grandma. The early implants were made from tough materials like stainless steel and titanium, but even these could only last about ten years. Think about how many times you move your hip in a single day. Multiply that by 365 days a year, and your hip moves about a million-and-a-half times annually. Even the strongest materials wear down after that kind of use.

As time went on, companies started creating longer-lasting implants, experimenting with materials like metal, ceramic and polyethylene (a type of plastic). These newer implants were designed to last up to approximately twenty years, giving younger patients the chance to stay active for longer without worrying about needing another surgery soon.

On top of that, the surgeries themselves became more advanced. Surgeons developed techniques that allowed them to replace the hip without cutting through as much muscle or tissue, which meant quicker recoveries and less pain. Hip replacements were no longer just for older folks – doctors began recommending them to younger patients who were suffering from severe arthritis and wanted to get back to living their lives.

For many people, a hip replacement isn't just about reducing pain – it's about getting their life back. It means being able to walk without wincing, climb stairs without hesitation, and return to activities they had long given up. Whether it's gardening, hiking or just playing with their kids, a new hip can offer a second chance to enjoy life without pain holding them back.

In 1999, the number of joint replacements performed worldwide hit 1.5 million, with most of them for arthritis. This condition was wreaking havoc on over 200 million people globally, costing more than $100 billion a year in healthcare expenses.[12] Hip replacements weren't just a medical solution – they were a lifeline for people desperate to get their lives back on track.

In Australia, during the early 2000s, the numbers were staggering – 94 per cent of all hip replacement surgeries were due to osteoarthritis.[13] In the US, which had become the main market for hip implants, more than 32 million adults were struggling with the same condition. Clinics across the country were filled with people, many of them contemplating the next step: surgery. Roughly 25 out of every 1,000 patients chose to go under the knife, hoping for relief.[14]

And things were only going to get busier. With people living longer, the demand for hip replacements was set to skyrocket. The world's elderly population was growing twice as fast as the rest of the population, and in developing countries, that number was expected to grow by up to 400 per cent over the next few decades. It wasn't just old age driving this demand, though. Lifestyles were changing fast. People were moving less and eating poorly, which led to more and more cases of obesity. As a result, younger patients – many still in their prime – started showing up at orthopaedic clinics with hip problems.

By the 2000s, the message from doctors and hospitals had shifted. They weren't just offering hip 'replacements'; they were promising that your new hip would be as good as the original, if not better. And people bought into it. The number of hip surgeries climbed higher, especially in wealthier countries such as Australia, where the rate of hip replacements hit 72 per 100,000 people.

The shift was clear in the waiting rooms. It wasn't just the elderly sitting there, but younger patients too – many of them determined not to let a bad hip slow them down. These were people who wanted to stay active, keep up with their demanding jobs and live life to the fullest. They were looking for a fix, not a lifestyle change.

By 2004, the average age for a hip implant patient had dropped to the early fifties. In the United Kingdom (UK), the older generation still dominated traditional hip replacements with an average age of 71.7 years, but hip resurfacing was for the younger crowd – those around 54 years old. And interestingly, nearly 60 per cent of these patients were women.[15]

Prestigious scientific journals published scientific reviews authored by prominent surgeons in the orthopaedic field, who didn't hold back their praise. They declared total hip replacement as the 'operation of the century'.[16]

Companies caught on quickly. Their ads were now targeting vibrant, active people who wanted to live without limits. New hip implants were advertised as being more durable, lasting longer and designed to keep up with an active lifestyle.

And for the most part, these implants worked well. Take for instance, the UK, one of the most influential orthopaedic markets. Between 1 April 2003 and September 2006, the revision rate for primary hip replacement was just around 1.3 per cent after three years, meaning only about 1 out of every 100 patients had to come back for a second surgery within that time frame.[17] That kind of success gave people confidence.

Doctors didn't just offer medical advice – they sold dreams. 'With your new hip, you'll be able to live normally again, no restrictions. Want to run? Jump? Even skydive? No problem!' The message was clear: a new hip wasn't just about walking again; it was about getting your life back.

In waiting rooms, patients watched testimonials from athletes who'd returned to their sports after hip surgery, as well as regular people who'd gone on to run marathons and hike mountains. The idea that you could go from struggling to get up a flight of stairs to crossing the finish line of a triathlon made patients believe anything was possible.

One big selling point was that hip replacement surgery wasn't as painful as people feared. In fact, recovery times had dramatically improved. Twenty years earlier, if you had hip surgery, you'd be stuck in bed for a week. But by the 2000s, things had changed. You'd have surgery in the morning, sit up by next afternoon, and be on your feet in a couple of days. In most cases, patients were discharged in less than a week. Within a month, they'd be back to their daily routines, as if nothing had ever been wrong.

And here's the kicker: hip replacements had become even safer for younger patients. Because they were generally healthier, they healed faster and had fewer complications. With their strength and energy, they could power through the rehabilitation process. Some doctors would have them standing and walking within a few days of the operation.

Even if the worst happened and the implant wore out, it wasn't the end of the world. Surgeons had advanced revision techniques to replace the worn-out implants. While it wasn't a simple fix, it was far more manageable than it used to be, especially with newer, more durable implants.

The surge in patient demand and enthusiastic endorsements from surgeons set the stage for major market leaders to unveil new products.

The year 2003 was a particularly busy one. Zimmer, the top player in the US reconstructive market, showcased Durom Hip Resurfacing to its investors. Branding it as 'a new solution for early-stage hip treatment', the company claimed that it was 'particularly suited to younger patients, allowing them to return to an active lifestyle'.[18]

Resurfacing preserved the femur, capping the head with a prosthetic cover, and fitting a cup in the socket of the hip; the bone was not cut and replaced – the ball-and-socket joint received new surfaces. However, this product was still out of reach in the US, pending FDA approval for hip-resurfacing procedures.

That same year, Stryker generated excitement with the news that the US Food and Drug Administration had given the green light to its ceramic-on-ceramic hip system, known as the Trident. 'This revolutionary product has been helping patients elsewhere in the world, and its enthusiastic reception in the United States demonstrates the potential this innovation holds for the US market,' the company told its investors.[19]

Not to be left behind, DePuy seized the spotlight. In its eagerly awaited annual report, under the section 'What's New?' – a highlight for many investors – the company showcased its rapid adoption of innovations in orthopaedics and spine, promising to 'strengthen leadership positions'.[20] This section featured an impactful image of a prominent joint replacement surgeon from Australia, demonstrating the ASR.

January 2003 marked a pivotal moment when DePuy's ASR earned a CE mark, enabling the sale of both the ASR XL Acetabular System (for conventional total hip replacement) and ASR Hip Resurfacing models in European markets. This approval was significant, as many countries, including India, permitted the sale of products with a CE mark. By October 2003, the ASR models also received approval in Australia.

On 1 March 2004, the DePuy ASR XL (monoblock MoM) made its international debut. 'DePuy International is bringing forward innovation in hip replacement that represents significant advancements for patients with hip arthritis,' the company confidently announced to investors in 2005. That year, DePuy particularly spotlighted the ASR XL, emphasizing, 'DePuy ASR XL metal-on-metal bearings offer larger diameters for improved joint stability and reduced wear.'[21] By 1 December 2005, the ASR XL total hip replacement implant was available in the US after receiving FDA clearance, although the ASR Hip Resurfacing system remained unapproved domestically, it continued to be widely used abroad.

To fuel investor optimism, the company painted a vivid picture of success. They featured remarkable recovery stories, including that of one Christopher, a Swiss DJ, under the headline 'DJ Gets His Groove Back.'[22] The accompanying photo captured Christopher in his element, exuding vitality, while the narrative celebrated the virtues of the DePuy ASR XL MoM bearing. According to the story, Christopher's doctor had selected this implant for its exceptional stability and durability. Just three weeks post-surgery, the DJ was 'already running the show', swiftly returning to his gigs, creating music, driving his car, staying fit and even indulging in sports.

Yet, beneath the surface, it was a calculated marketing ploy. The company strategically enlisted influential surgeons to endorse their new product. In India, the marketing strategy mirrored this approach, employing aggressive advertising techniques – both direct and surrogate. Doctors boasted of performing groundbreaking surgeries with the ASR, illustrating the pervasive influence of big pharma on the medical community.

In 2002, the Medical Council of India (MCI) laid down rules meant to curb the cosy relationships between doctors and pharmaceutical companies. On paper, it sounded foolproof: guidelines about professional conduct and ethics, with even a strict ban on freebies, cash grants or promoting medical devices like hip implants. Doctors could only publish findings on the effectiveness of such devices in scientific journals – no fancy endorsements, no boasting about successful surgeries, nothing that might hint at them pushing a product for personal gain.

But in reality, these rules might as well have been written in invisible ink. Enforcement? Virtually nonexistent. The ASR was one such striking example, pushed so hard by doctors and hospitals that it might as well have had its own commercial jingle, despite rules that were supposed to prevent this exact thing.

In the flashy world of corporate hospitals, the marketing machine runs full throttle. Press releases sing the praises of top surgeons, breakthrough procedures and cutting-edge treatments. Take 4 February 2005, for example. That's when a leading hospital chain in India made a grand announcement, draped in medical jargon: a new and 'superior' hip replacement had hit the Indian market, introduced at their state-of-the-art facility. They went on and on about the implant's design, its high-tech materials and its supposed longevity. But oddly enough, they left out one crucial piece of information – the name of the manufacturer.

This wasn't some innocent oversight.

The omission was deliberate. It was all part of a slick tactic that big corporate hospitals often use – surrogate advertising masquerading as public information. The hospital wasn't just announcing a medical advancement; they were sneakily debuting a new hip implant in the market, calling it 'the Asian hip'. The name alone was enough to grab attention, especially from an audience that's always on the lookout for something custom-made for them.

The hospital framed the implant as if it were tailor-made for the Indian population – like a suit fitted just for the Indian body type. But the reality? It was just another hip implant, specifically the ASR.

This wasn't some revolutionary, India-centric innovation. The ASR, commercially launched by DePuy, had nothing to do with being designed for Asian patients. It hadn't been clinically tested on Asian participants before it was brought to market, nor did it cater specifically to the Asian hip joint. That was just a marketing ploy.

The truth was far less glamorous: DePuy launched the ASR to compete globally in the fiercely competitive orthopaedic market. The hospital's grand announcement was essentially a dressed-up press release from the manufacturer, a clever bit of PR disguised as medical news. What should have been the manufacturer's job – marketing the product – was instead handled by the hospital.

The press release read like a polished ad, the kind that effortlessly grabs attention during a commercial break. Short and sharp, it echoed the style of an advertising agency promoting the latest must-have product.

'Finally managing to do away with the traditional bane associated with hip replacement surgery, this latest technique – the Articular Surface Replacement (ASR) – though a bit expensive, allows the patient to sit, squat, and even engage in sporting and athletic activities, previously unimaginable after a conventional hip surgery,' the hospital proudly claimed.

The tone was brazen, almost like they were stepping in for the company's own sales team. 'Delhi has shared the experience and technique with select Mumbai hospitals that now offer the facility,' they said.

The hospital endorsed the new implant as if they had developed it themselves. 'Titled the "Asian hip", this one claims to be better than the best,' they boasted. But behind the smooth talk, the reality was that these were just claims – not backed by solid evidence. The big claim rested on ten surgeries performed in May 2004. Just ten. There were no details about the patients' ages or medical conditions, as if those crucial factors didn't matter.

The hospital appeared completely convinced, based solely on those ten procedures, that the new implant was flawless. 'Why we did not make a noise about this earlier was because ... we wanted to wait and see the results for ourselves with the new gadgets,' they explained, as if this life-changing surgery was simply another tech experiment.

Then came the bold, sweeping conclusion: 'We are now satisfied with the results and are confident about what the outcome would be.' The confidence was exaggerated, not rooted in clinical trials or even short-term safety data. No independent experts had reviewed or verified the results, yet they were ready to roll out their conclusions as if they were facts.

Even the doctor, normally cautious and measured, seemed swept up in the hype. 'Following ten such successful surgeries that we have performed, we are now sure that the system works for the patients,' he said with conviction.

The press release claimed the ASR hip implant was a marvel of design, standing out for its seamless construction. It featured a large metallic socket and an oversized, metallic head, which they said made it unique and perfect for Indian patients. 'This permits the patients to squat and sit cross-legged, and is hence user-friendly, especially for Indian people, for whom these movements are essential,' the hospital emphasized.

And it wasn't just the design. The new implant came with another supposed perk: it would address the long-standing issue of plastic erosion in older implants, which limited their lifespan to around fifteen years. According to the press release, the ASR was different – built to last.

The good news, or so the hospital claimed, was that this implant would not only last but do so for a very long time. 'What the ASR does is prolong the life of the implants and provide a greater range of functions to patients,' they said, as if promising a miracle cure.

The ASR hip implant was painted as flawless and extraordinary. 'The ASR replacement lines the ball and socket with a metal surface of very high quality and also ensures that very little bone is removed to seat the implant. The size of the ball is very large, and this permits an excellent range of movement,' they concluded, selling the idea that this implant was the perfect solution for anyone seeking mobility and flexibility.

The press release was all about the ASR hip resurfacing – a procedure that, at the time, only a handful of surgeons in India were performing. Most surgeons stuck to the more conventional total hip replacement, making the ASR sound like an elite option, out of reach for many. But the hospital had a trick up its sleeve. Toward the end of the press release, they added a crucial update: the ASR wouldn't just be limited to resurfacing – it would now be available as a total hip replacement too. It was a clever move to widen their audience and reel in more patients, positioning the ASR as an option for everyone, not just a select few.

But what's the difference between the two procedures? Imagine you're told you need a hip replacement. It's a daunting thought, but there are two main options on the table: hip resurfacing or a total hip replacement. In the case of ASR XL total hip replacement, a metal cup will be placed into your hip socket, and the top of your thigh bone replaced with a metal ball connected to a metal stem that's fitted inside your leg.

If you opt for the bone-preserving hip resurfacing, the approach is slightly different. Instead of replacing the whole head of your thigh bone, a metal cap – like a helmet – will be placed over it, while a metal cup still goes into your hip socket. This procedure conserves more of your bone, making it a more appealing option for younger, active patients.

'It is also expected to last longer, and as and when necessary, it is easy to convert this to a conventional hip replacement. It is extremely useful in young patients,' the doctor endorsed how the ASR system offered two distinct options.

This press release was a striking example of the company's overwhelming influence – so powerful that the hospital brazenly promoted its product without hesitation. When patients walked through the doors, it wasn't just treatment they were offered but a dream, a promise of transformation. Forty-year-old Dinesh, with hopes of reclaiming an active life, was one of those who believed it. He was told that a new hip would change everything for the better. But beneath the surface of their optimism lay something far more disturbing.

Dinesh wasn't just another patient. He was a participant in a high-stakes experiment. The hospital would use him as a live demonstration – a spectacle designed to impress and influence surgeons. This wasn't simply about helping Dinesh; it was about showcasing the company's product in the most dramatic way possible. To add credibility, they flew in renowned surgeons from outside India, turning the operating room into a stage, with Dinesh at the centre of a performance.

But little did Dinesh know that the live surgery, and the implant fixed in his body, would turn his life upside down. What was supposed to be a fresh start would turn into a nightmare.

2

The Live Surgery: A Gamble for Life

Most people still recall the famous slogan 'Buland Bharat Ki Buland Tasveer' – the bold words that represented a strong, thriving India, used by Bajaj to promote their iconic Chetak scooter. For many middle-class Indian families, owning a Chetak wasn't just about getting from one place to another – it was a dream, a symbol of pride. The scooter was so popular that people often had to wait for years to get their hands on one, making it all the more special when it finally rolled up to their doorstep.

But what many don't know is where this iconic scooter was made – Pimpri-Chinchwad, a busy industrial hub near Pune, quietly producing the Chetak and turning those dreams into reality.

Picture a city where the hum of engines and the whir of machinery were as common as birdsong. That was Pimpri-Chinchwad in the late 1980s, a vibrant hub at the heart of India's booming automobile industry. In the 1960s, Bajaj produced only two or three scooters a day, but by the 1980s, they were churning out over a thousand daily. The Chetak, with its sleek finish and dependable engine, became a familiar sight on the roads, a testament to the company's growth. Manufactured in Pimpri-Chinchwad, along the bustling Pune–Mumbai highway, the Chetak was more than just a scooter – it was a symbol of a city on the rise.

The transformation of Pimpri-Chinchwad was incredible. What started in the late 1950s with a few companies such as Ruston, Greaves and Formica, quickly grew to include big names like Telco (now Tata Motors).[1] By the 1980s, the area had earned the nickname 'Detroit of the East', showing how important it had become in India's industrial scene.

Growing up in this energetic environment was a unique experience for Dinesh. His childhood was filled with the sounds of machines and the buzz of factories. The air often smelled like motor oil, and the steady clatter of assembly lines was a constant backdrop. On weekends, Dinesh and his friends played near the factories, their games set against the backdrop of the busy industry.

It wasn't just a city; it was a place where dreams were made, both in the factories and beyond. For Dinesh, Pimpri-Chinchwad was the perfect place to find his job, his home and the partner he'd always dreamed of.

In the late 1950s, when Ruston & Hornsby, an England-based manufacturer of diesel engines, set up one of its first factories in Pimpri-Chinchwad, Dinesh's father relocated his family to the new city. The job at the factory, though paid modestly, was more than just employment; it was a symbol of stability. It offered the family a sense of security they had never experienced before, along with access to Ruston Colony, a residential area built in the 1970s specifically for the company's employees.

As Dinesh grew up in this industrial landscape, he witnessed firsthand the transformation of Pimpri-Chinchwad from a sleepy town to a vibrant industrial hub. Factories sprung up, bringing with them essential services like a post office, a bank and a school and creating a bustling community where once there was none.

Amidst this sea of change, Tata Motors made its grand entrance, establishing a massive manufacturing facility that sprawled across 930 acres. The sight of this enormous factory, with its impressive machinery, ignited a spark in young Dinesh's imagination. The factory wasn't just a place where trucks and vans were made; it was a symbol of progress and possibility. The buzz around Tata Motors was palpable – it was not only one of the largest in the country but also a beacon of hope for many.

Dinesh would often gaze at the imposing Tata Motors facility from a distance, dreaming of the day he would be part of that world. The sprawling factory was a dreamscape of ambition for him. He imagined himself walking through its vast halls, contributing to the creation of vehicles and building a future filled with infinite possibilities. The dream of joining Tata Motors became a source of inspiration that fuelled his ambitions.

In 1987, when Dinesh finally secured a job at Tata Motors, it was a moment of immense pride for him and his family. The factory, which had once seemed like a distant dream, had become a crucial part of his journey. Tata Motors was more than a place of employment; it would become intertwined with every significant event in Dinesh's life.

In the 1980s, Dinesh's world had changed dramatically when he met Lata. Her father, who had a good job at the famous HMT watch factory in Karnataka, decided to move his family to Pimpri-Chinchwad for a clerical job at Tata Motors. Lata joined Dinesh's local high school, and suddenly there was a new zest to his life.

Dinesh still gets emotional when he thinks about the day Lata came into his life.

'It was like a scene from a movie,' he says, his voice full of nostalgia. 'We had just started eighth grade, and then she appeared, changing everything.'[2]

Their love story could easily be mistaken for a classic romance film. Their feelings grew stronger in ways neither of them expected. For nearly two years, Dinesh struggled to find the courage to tell Lata how he felt. She was shy and reserved, making him even more nervous. But when he finally asked her out in tenth grade, her response was immediate and heartfelt.

'It was the easiest yes ever,' she says, her smile warm and genuine.

But their journey wasn't smooth. Just months after Lata finished twelfth grade, her parents said they wanted her to get married. Determined to be together, Dinesh and Lata, with the help of a few close friends, planned a secret wedding.

'I knew my family wouldn't approve, so we had a quiet court marriage,' Lata explains.

Their secret didn't stay hidden for long. They finally talked to their families, and the conversations were tense and emotional. Slowly, Lata's sincerity won over Dinesh's parents. Though there were challenges, eventually Lata's family accepted Dinesh. To Dinesh's surprise, months after their secret wedding, Lata's father helped him land his dream job at Tata Motors.

Like his father, Dinesh had a clear, fixed goal: a stable job. And he wanted it fast. Opting against a college degree, Dinesh dove straight into the Industrial Training Institute after high school, driven by a need for immediate stability.

After earning his diploma, he embarked on an apprenticeship at Ruston & Hornsby, where he thrived in the high-heat world of welding. His days were spent immersed in a cacophony of sparks and searing metal.

'I loved my job,' Dinesh recalls.

Dinesh's passion and hard work soon resulted in a higher-paying job with Bajaj Auto. There, he broadened his skills, taking on the assembly and welding of bike chassis. By 1987, with his father-in-law's help, Dinesh landed a position at Tata Motors.

The work at Tata Motors was on a whole new level. The scale was bigger, and the tasks were tougher. Dinesh was part of a team responsible for welding and gas-cutting heavy-duty truck chassis – handling more than fifteen different components. The factory floor was a whirlwind of noise and activity.

Meanwhile, to their joy, a son was born to them in 1993, completing their little family. Dinesh was even more motivated to work and succeed. Lata devoted herself to bringing up their son and making a good home for their family.

Despite the gruelling demands, Dinesh remained undaunted. He channelled every ounce of his physical and mental energy into one singular ambition: achieving permanent status at Tata Motors. This goal wasn't just about a job – it was about providing his family with a sense of security and a stable future.

'I worked under immense pressure. The job was gruelling,' Dinesh says, his voice thick with emotion. 'There were days when the production demands skyrocketed, and I had to push through overtime. I poured sweat, and at times, even blood, to keep up.'

His dedication did not go unnoticed. Within three months, Tata Motors offered him a new contract and elevated him to permanent status. For over a decade, Dinesh's work ethic remained unparalleled, slogging through long hours and demanding tasks.

'It was a risky job,' he reflects. 'At one point, we were churning out a hundred trucks a day – a hundred vehicles in a single shift. Eight hours of non-stop, uncompromising work.'

Dinesh always believed that his hard work would eventually bear fruit. That belief finally brought him closer to his next dream: building a home.

In 1999, he took a significant step by purchasing a small plot of land near his factory. To finance it, Dinesh withdrew Rs 120,000 from his provident fund, painstakingly saved over two decades at Tata Motors. It was a tough choice.

'I knew the stakes were high,' Dinesh admits, his voice tinged with the stress of that period. 'We were anxious about the possibility of needing these savings for emergencies. But we took the plunge. I was still in my late thirties, so I pushed myself to work even harder, believing I could replenish the savings in a few years.'

Dinesh spent half of his provident fund on the land, but the remaining amount fell short for construction. He needed at least Rs 300,000 to build a house – a daunting sum, given his financial constraints.

Determined, Dinesh took incremental steps. For the next three years, he worked tirelessly, often late into the evening. The physical demands of his job were immense. At the factory, he spent long hours lifting and manoeuvring heavy equipment, his body constantly under stress. The repeated strain on his back, shoulders and limbs took a toll, leaving him with aches and the constant threat of injury. The daily grind of heavy-duty work would wear down his body over time.

He started building his home. The company's incentives helped, but they weren't enough. He borrowed from the local cooperative society and received crucial help from his father-in-law.

'We barely scraped together Rs 300,000,' Dinesh says. His face betrays the pressure and exhaustion he felt back then.

Compromises were inevitable. Dinesh scoured the town for used bricks, doors and windows, accepting whatever was available at a discount. Instead of a concrete roof, he opted for asbestos sheets to cut costs. By 2003, the house was finally complete – modest, but a testament to his perseverance.

Standing in front of his completed home, Dinesh now realized that the journey cost him more than just money. The physical strain from his job, the sacrifices and the long hours had taken a significant toll. His dream home came at a price he hadn't expected.

Each day, Dinesh pushed heavy trolleys across the factory floor, the effort of moving their weight pressing down on him like an invisible burden. After welding, his task was to move the scorching, freshly forged products to the paint shop. To get them there, he had to hoist the products onto a trolley and then shove it towards the conveyor. The wheels screeched against the concrete as he strained every muscle.

'I had to throw my entire weight behind the trolley just to get it moving. It felt like my back was being wrenched apart,' Dinesh recalls.

And that wasn't even the worst of it. One day, he was tasked with lifting a massive CO_2 cylinder used for welding – no ordinary load. These cylinders, hulking giants of steel, weighed more than 100 kg each. He had to lift two of them, one after the other. As he bent to lift the first, he felt an ominous twinge in his lower back.

'That was when I knew something was wrong with my disc,' Dinesh says, wincing again at the deeply etched memory. 'Just imagine – holding something that heavy, knowing your body is on the brink of giving out.'

It was a repetitive, exhausting job, but he had always managed – until 2002, when a deep ache started spreading from his hip to his groin and thigh. At first, it was just a nagging pain, something he could shake off. But as the months passed, the sharp pain became more persistent, slowing his movements. Worse, the pain followed him home, at times keeping him awake at night. His work performance plummeted, and he couldn't ignore it any longer.

Frustrated and desperate for answers, Dinesh found himself in the waiting room of a local orthopaedic clinic. When the doctor finally saw him, Dinesh described his symptoms, hoping for some quick fix. But after a series of tests, the diagnosis came like a stunning blow: avascular necrosis (AVN). The doctor explained in sombre tones that the ball of his hip joint, the very core of his mobility, was dying – a slow collapse under the weight of his own body.

'You see this here,' the doctor pointed to an X-ray on the light board, showing Dinesh the damaged hip joint. 'The ball is starting to flatten. That's why it's hurting so much.'

Dinesh stared at the image. He was only in his late thirties.

'Isn't there anything we can do to fix this?' he asked.

The doctor leaned back in his chair.

'At your age, surgery is a last resort. We want to preserve the joint for as long as possible. I recommend starting with conservative treatments – pain management, physiotherapy. Let's try to ease the load on your hip.'

It wasn't the quick solution Dinesh had hoped for, but he nodded, willing to try anything to avoid surgery.

Dinesh vividly recalls sharing his anxiety with his colleagues at the factory.

'You should try homoeopathy,' one of them suggested. 'Worked wonders for my uncle's back pain.' Dinesh decided to give it a shot.

The homoeopathic remedies came in small bottles, each with detailed instructions. To Dinesh's surprise, the pain began to ease over the next few weeks.

'For at least three years, the homoeopathy remedies kept the pain from getting worse,' he says. 'I was doing just fine.'

For a while, it seemed like a miracle solution. Dinesh could move without that searing pain shooting through his hip, and his trips to the factory became less daunting. But deep down, he knew the treatment was more palliative than curative – it eased the pain but didn't fix the underlying problem. His hip was still weakening, and his physically demanding job continued to take its toll. Taking a long break from work wasn't an option. Bills had to be paid, and his employer could only offer him a few days off at a time, here and there, to rest and recover.

But those brief respites weren't enough. After a while, Dinesh's performance at work began to suffer. His movements were slower, and the pain started creeping back into his daily routine. His co-workers noticed his strained expression as he tried to mask the growing discomfort. It became clear that the homoeopathic treatment wasn't enough to keep pace with the demands of his job.

That's when a coworker, in 2006, suggested he check out a new hospital that had just opened in Chinchwad: 'It's huge and modern,' he said. Intrigued, Dinesh decided to visit. When he arrived, the hospital was impressive – a sprawling complex covering sixteen acres.

Inside, the hospital was just as impressive. The floors sparkled, and there was a clean, fresh smell in the air. It felt like a place where you could trust you were getting top-notch care. The orthopaedic team had studied at some of the best schools around the world, and they boasted about their high-quality implants that had been tested globally. He wasn't there for a hip replacement – he was too young for that. But he hoped that the surgeons might offer better treatment options or more effective medication for his issues.

'I just wanted to see if they had something that could help me more,' Dinesh recalls.

After his initial consultation, Dinesh left the hospital feeling hopeful.

'The consultant set me up with a new treatment plan,' he says. 'It went on for weeks, and I had regular follow-ups.' But during one of these visits, out of the blue, his doctor suggested he see the hospital's top surgeon.

'They told me he was a joint replacement specialist, trained in the UK,' Dinesh says. What Dinesh didn't expect was what came next. The senior surgeon recommended a hip replacement surgery.

Though recommending surgery wasn't unusual, the way the senior surgeon pitched it was far from typical. Instead of opting for the established, reliable hip implants, the surgeon proposed a cutting-edge technique with a brand-new product.

This wasn't just any routine procedure – it was a leap into uncharted territory. The hospital's own surgeons would mostly be sidelined. The team would watch or, at best, assist, while an external expert conducted the surgery using this new technology.

In the competitive world of hip implants, influence and relationships play a huge role, much like in high-stakes sports or fashion industries. Imagine a major brand in sports gear sponsoring top athletes to endorse their latest shoes or apparel. In the realm of hip implants, this endorsement and influence come from a select group of surgeons, who are crucial to shaping the success of new products.

DePuy had a strategy similar to that of a top sports brand. Over the years, they have recruited several prominent surgeons – akin to high-profile athletes – as 'surgeon champions'.[3] These individuals are not just top experts; they are highly influential and their endorsement can sway the opinions of other medical professionals. Despite their prestigious roles, their financial dealings with DePuy were often kept under wraps.

These surgeon champions didn't just give a nod to DePuy's

implants; they actively promoted them. DePuy publicly portrayed these champions simply as academic figures who studied and educated other doctors about the new implants. However, their involvement was far deeper.

Even more influential than these surgeon champions were the 'designer surgeons'. Think of them as the star designers behind a groundbreaking line of clothing. These surgeons developed new implant technologies and earned substantial royalties from them. Unlike regular employees, they were vital to the design of these implants and were publicly recognized during product launches.

DePuy's strategy involved not just these key figures but also a sophisticated marketing approach. Picture a brand setting up exclusive distribution channels to ensure their new product reaches every major store. Similarly, DePuy set up specialized distribution networks in crucial markets, aggressively pursuing contracts with top hospitals and offering their implants at discounted prices. Despite the discounts, their strong ties with surgeons and hospitals ensured high sales and profits.

In 2005 and 2006, DePuy introduced two major innovations in the hip implant market, focusing on preserving the bone during surgery. First was the DePuy Proxima hip, designed with a short stem to protect bone and tissue. The second was the ASR XL MoM implant, marketed as providing superior performance for younger patients due to its durable bearings.[4]

When DePuy launched these implants in India, they organized high-profile events. They flew in top designer surgeons and surgeon champions from around the world for a live surgery broadcast. This dramatic presentation was intended to impress and influence local doctors.

The Proxima hip team included five renowned surgeons from leading orthopaedic markets: the UK, Germany, South Korea, Italy and Spain. For the Indian launch, one of these designer surgeons was flown in to perform a live surgery at a modern hospital in Pune. This hospital had a senior surgeon who had previously trained under the designer, making it an ideal location for the event.

Doctors from across India were invited, and the hospital prepared meticulously for the live surgery, setting up everything to create an impeccable spectacle. However, finding a candidate who wouldn't question the safety of the new implant or raise concerns about the informed consent process was challenging. The hospital needed someone unaware of the ethical and legal complexities involved in such live surgeries.

In the end, the hospital's search led them to Dinesh. To entice him, the hospital used deception and dubious tactics.

'At first, they told me that the doctor who invented the implant was coming to India in a month to perform my surgery. They said the company was launching the product here and wanted me as a trial patient because I was an ideal candidate,' Dinesh recalls bitterly.

The hospital's promises were grandiose, claiming the surgery had been flawless every time the new implant was used in the UK.

'They assured me the implant was perfect for patients between thirty and forty,' he says, his voice tinged with the regret of misplaced trust.

With his savings dwindling, Dinesh faced the daunting prospect of abandoning the surgery. But then, the hospital made a compelling offer: a 40 per cent discount if he agreed to the live surgery. It felt like a lifeline amidst financial chaos.

Trusting the doctors, Dinesh didn't question their claims, and he was not in a position to investigate the implant's performance outside India. His hopes for a pain-free future and a swift return to work helped convince him quickly.

Even with the discount, Dinesh lacked health insurance for the remaining cost. Faced with this financial shortfall, he contemplated using his newly built home as collateral for a loan from a local credit cooperative society.

'The house wasn't worth much. I only received Rs 50,000,' he says, the old frustration resurfacing.

With time running out and an additional Rs 70,000 needed for the surgery deposit, the family faced a tough decision. They had to consider taking out a loan against Lata's wedding jewellery.

One evening, as things started looking desperate, Dinesh and Lata sat together in their living room.

'I don't know what to do, Lata,' Dinesh said, his voice filled with uncertainty. 'We're short on money, and the only option left is to take a loan against your wedding jewellery.'

'But ... the jewellery ... It's so special to us. It's not just gold; it's a part of our memories,' Lata said in a trembling voice. She looked into

Dinesh's eyes, which were filled with longing, and took a deep breath.

'Dinesh, I know how much this surgery means for your health and our future. We need this chance for you to get better and return to the factory. That's our ticket to long-term stability. The jewellery can be replaced, but your health and career are irreplaceable.'

Dinesh looked at her, moved by her willingness to sacrifice something so precious.

'Are you sure, Lata? It's a big step.'

'Yes,' she said firmly. 'Jewellery is a part of our past, but securing our future is more important. Once you get back to work, we'll repay the loan and get the jewellery back. I believe that the future is bright.'

The next day, they took out an instant gold loan, pawning the few pieces of jewellery they had left – four bangles and a necklace.

With the loan secured and the surgery date approaching, Dinesh was admitted to the hospital three days before the operation, slated for 27 April 2004. He underwent extensive tests – of his heart, brain and lungs, along with a dozen other diagnostics. Finally, the green light was given for the live surgery.

The hospital was buzzing with anticipation as everyone prepared for the big event: a live broadcast of the hip implant surgery. They set up a high-resolution camera in Operation Theatre Number Four and a huge projector in the auditorium. About 200 doctors filled the hall, chatting and waiting eagerly. Dinesh's family took their seats in the back, their faces betraying a mix of hope and nerves.

At 9.30 a.m., the room went quiet as the surgery started. Dinesh, lying on his side, was determined but nervous, as he waited for the anaesthetist to put him under general anaesthesia for the surgery. The lead surgeon, who was not only performing the surgery but also explaining it through a wireless microphone, talked through every step, trying to make it clear for everyone watching.

As the team used power drills and special tools to work on Dinesh's hip, the sounds and sights were intense. It was like watching a carpenter's workshop, but much more unsettling. Lata, watching from the auditorium, felt her stomach churn. The noise and the sight of metal tools against flesh made her feel sick.

When the surgeons started inserting a 50 mm hip cup, Lata couldn't take it any more. Her heart was racing as she stood up and quietly left the room, needing to escape the overwhelming scene.

The surgery went on for a few more hours. The surgeons carefully implanted the new hip component, sutured the layers of flesh, stapled Dinesh's skin, and finished up. When the live stream ended, the audience left the auditorium, feeling a mix of relief and hope, believing the surgery had gone well and that Dinesh was on the road to recovery.

But things didn't go as planned.

The X-ray showed a serious problem: the ball in the implant had shifted. The team quickly called in more experienced surgeons, and Dinesh had to go back into surgery.

'They had to open everything up again to replace the 50 mm ASR cup with a 49 mm ASR cup. It was a painful redo. But the newspapers made it sound like a huge success,' Dinesh says, clearly frustrated.

A week later, just as Dinesh was about to be discharged, he requested a recording of his surgery. The hospital informed him that the CD had mysteriously disappeared.

'I knew they were hiding something from me,' Dinesh says.

Back at home, the incident weighed heavily on both Dinesh and Lata. Lata sat next to him, concerned.

'Do you really think they lost the CD of your surgery?' she asked, sceptically.

'Well, that's what they told me,' he said dejectedly.

Lata frowned.

'But why would they even broadcast your surgery live in the first place? Doesn't that seem odd?'

Dinesh leaned back, lost in thought.

'That's exactly what I'm wondering. Was I just a test subject? Did they use me to try their new techniques for their own gain?'

Lata's eyes widened.

'You think they treated you like a guinea pig?'

'It certainly feels that way,' Dinesh replied. 'And now, after the redo and all this pain, I'm left wondering if this implant will even hold up. Was all this just a marketing gimmick to make their new implant look good?'

Lata took his hand, squeezing it gently.

'I don't know, Dinesh. But right now, we need to focus on your recovery. Maybe we'll get some answers later. For now, let's stay hopeful and keep moving forward.'

Dinesh nodded, though his worry remained.

'You're right. But these questions won't go away easily. I just hope this implant works and that we weren't misled from the start.'

For two months, Dinesh followed his recovery plan to the letter: eating well, going for physiotherapy and being extra careful. Everything seemed to be going well until suddenly, things took a turn for the worse. By the third month, the femoral stem of his implant started failing. He began limping again, and a check-up showed his movement was severely limited.

Dinesh and Lata vividly remember the evening they returned from the hospital.

They sat in their small living room, their faces etched with worry. The doctor's news had hit them hard.

'They told me I'd be climbing stairs and maybe even riding a horse soon,' Dinesh said, frustrated. 'But now the doctor says the stem has slipped and needs to be replaced. He says my bones are too weak.'

Lata's eyes were filled with tears as she looked at Dinesh.

'I can't believe this is happening,' she told Dinesh, her voice trembling. 'We barely managed to pay for the first surgery. How are we going to afford another one?'

'I don't know,' Dinesh admitted, feeling defeated. 'I thought we were done with this. I thought I'd be getting better, not facing another surgery.'

Lata squeezed his hand, trying to stay strong.

'We'll find a way,' she said, trying to sound hopeful. 'Maybe we can borrow from our family this time. We just need to get through this.'

'But we're running out of time,' Dinesh said, his gaze dropping. 'The hospital needs the money fast. I hate that we're in this mess again.'

In February 2003, as the calendar inched closer to his scheduled hip replacement surgery, Dinesh had made a life-altering decision – he resigned from his job. He took this step because his medical condition made him eligible for the company's Early Separation Scheme. Under this scheme, he would receive 90 per cent of his allowance until the age of sixty, the official retirement age.

'For me, it was like a safety net,' Dinesh recalls, his voice steady but tinged with nostalgia. 'I knew I couldn't continue with the gruelling physical demands of my job. But with my experience, I believed I could find another role – one that wasn't so hard on my body.'

Even as he handed in his resignation, Dinesh had a clear plan. The hip replacement was not the end but a new beginning.

'I saw it as a pause, not a stop,' he says. 'After the surgery, I was determined to step back into the industry – just in a role that matched my new physical capabilities.'

However, Dinesh had never imagined that the surgery would fail so early – just three months after the operation. The lifeline he had counted on now felt like a fragile thread. The monthly allowance he received, though a relief at the time, was far too little to fund the additional surgery needed to fix his hip. In desperation, Dinesh turned to his friends, borrowing money from them to cover the costs of the corrective surgery.

'It wasn't easy to ask for help,' he admits quietly. 'But I had no choice. My plans, my confidence – everything was crumbling. I had to find a way to stand on my feet again, both literally and financially.'

On 6 October 2007, Dinesh finally had his replacement surgery. Lata left their son with her parents while she cared for Dinesh in the hospital after the surgery. He was discharged ten days later – stable but staring down a long, uncertain recovery. The whole ordeal had drained their spirits and emptied their pockets.

When Dinesh and Lata got home, they talked over their situation.

'How did it go?' she asked, referring to his last meeting with his surgeon. She had been absent when he met the doctor the last time.

'It didn't go as planned,' Dinesh replied, his voice heavy with disappointment. 'The doctors said I can't return to regular activities. I have to avoid bending my hip more than 90 degrees. No sitting cross-legged or squatting ...'

Lata's face fell.

'What does that mean for us? Can you go back to work?'

Dinesh shook his head.

'No, it means I can't go back to the factory. The implant didn't work as promised. It's going to be nearly impossible for me to return to a job.'

Tears welled up in Lata's eyes.

'But what will we do now? We've already spent so much. How will we manage?'

'I don't know,' Dinesh said, his voice breaking. 'I thought this surgery was our chance to fix everything. Now it feels like we're back at square one. I'm exhausted from this endless struggle.'

Lata took a deep breath, trying to stay strong.

'We'll figure it out, Dinesh. We have to. Right now, we need to focus on your recovery. We'll face this together, no matter how tough it gets.'

Dinesh nodded, though his heart was heavy.

'I just wish there was something more I could do. This was supposed to be our solution, but now it feels like another setback.'

Dinesh had loans piling up and financial obligations he could no longer meet. Eager to repay his debts, he had expected to get back to work soon after the hip replacement. Instead, he found himself bedridden, the surgery having failed him in the most unexpected way.

'It felt like I'd been in a terrible accident. Trusting the hospital blindly was the biggest mistake of my life,' Dinesh says, disillusioned.

As weeks turned into months, the family's financial stress worsened. Bills piled up, and they defaulted on their gold loan. The jewellery, already handed over as collateral, had been the last thing they could offer. Now, it was clear they couldn't repay the debt, and auctioning it was the only option left.

One evening, Lata and Dinesh sat in their small, dimly lit living room, the weight of their decision pressing down on them.

'It's been seven months, Dinesh. We've missed too many payments,' Lata said, her voice barely a whisper. 'They'll auction the jewellery if we don't do something.'

Dinesh stared at the floor, the thought of losing the wedding jewellery feeling like a punch in the gut. 'I know ... but it's your wedding jewellery, Lata. We promised we'd get it back. How can we let them auction it?'

'We don't have a choice,' Lata sighed. 'The interest keeps growing, and we're barely managing with what Tata Motors is giving us. We can't keep pretending we'll somehow come up with the money.'

She glanced towards the small wooden chest where they used to keep the jewellery, now empty, a constant reminder of what had been sacrificed. The pieces weren't just gold – they were memories, tied to the happiest moments of their lives.

'I never thought it would come to this,' Dinesh muttered, his voice thick with guilt. 'If I hadn't ... if this surgery hadn't failed ...'

Lata reached out, placing a hand on his knee.

'This isn't your fault. You didn't ask for any of this. We've done everything we can. Now we have to let go.'

The next morning, Lata met the lender. Her voice was steady, but inside, it felt like something was breaking.

'Go ahead with the auction,' she told the lender.

But the gold loan was just the beginning. Dinesh's right hip was deteriorating day by day, the pain a constant reminder of his failing body. Fear gnawed at him – fear of losing everything, fear of being a burden.

'I watched my life crumble along with my hip,' he says, eyes downcast. By September 2008, the nightmare deepened when the doctor who performed his second surgery broke the news Dinesh had been dreading: he was left with a permanent disability.

Still, Tata Motors had offered a sliver of hope. The special monthly allowance of Rs 9,600 until he turned sixty was a lifeline, but barely enough to keep them afloat.

Just when they thought they could somehow manage with the little they had, things got even worse. The co-operative society they had borrowed money from wasn't willing to wait any longer. Recovery agents started showing up at their door, relentless and cold. Their knocks felt more like demands, and their presence made the air thick with tension.

'There were days when two agents would stand inside our home, arms crossed, glaring at us like we were criminals, while two more stood outside, waiting for any sign of weakness,' Dinesh recalls.

The first time they showed up, Dinesh tried to reason with them.

'Please, just give me a little more time. I'm trying, I really am,' he pleaded, his voice shaky. But the agent wasn't interested.

'We've heard that before,' one of them said sharply. 'You've already had enough time. Now, we want the money.'

'I'm doing everything I can,' Dinesh replied desperately. 'Just a few more days, I beg you.'

One of the agents stepped closer, threateningly.

'A few more days? You think this is a game? Every day you delay, things will get worse for you.'

'We can come back tomorrow; we can come back the day after that,' added the second agent, still by the door. 'But every time we return, it's going to be harder for you. Don't make this mess any worse.'

Days turned into weeks, and the agents kept showing up, their threats growing harsher with each visit. Dinesh felt like the walls of his home were closing in on him. He couldn't eat, couldn't sleep.

'I felt like I was suffocating,' Dinesh says quietly. 'There was no escape. Every time they left, I knew they'd be back. I was trapped. I even thought ... maybe it would be easier if I wasn't here anymore. That felt like the only way out.'

Lata's burden was no less. The Rs 9,600 they received barely covered the essentials. Food, bills and school fees for their son became a constant worry. Every night, as Dinesh lay silently in bed, she stayed awake, running numbers in her head, trying to figure out how to stretch every rupee. 'We had to pay our son's school fees, and I couldn't let him suffer because of our problems,' Lata explains. 'With the help of a few contacts, I decided to start a tiffin service for some nurses at the local hospital.'

Her days became a blur of exhaustion – waking up before dawn to prepare meals, her back aching as she worked through the long hours. Each meal she delivered was not just food, but an act of survival, her way of fighting for her family.

The suffering had changed Dinesh, not just physically but mentally and emotionally. He wasn't the same man Lata had married. His once hopeful eyes now carried a sadness that words couldn't capture. His life had been shattered in ways he could never have imagined.

In the midst of this turmoil, Lata became the unshakable foundation of their family. Her income, small but constant, began to bring some relief. 'It's only because of her that I'm still here,' Dinesh says, glancing at her with gratitude. 'She's been my pillar of strength, my anchor in the storm. Without her, I don't know if I would have made it through.'

Just as life seemed to be settling back into a routine, Dinesh's health took a dramatic turn. At the beginning of 2012, he was hit by intense pain that returned with a vengeance.

'I remember suffering through three solid months of pain,' he recalls, his face reflecting the suffering he went through.

The pain was more than just physical; it was a daily struggle. On one side, he couldn't put weight on his leg, and on the other, he felt a strange weakness and numbness, like his nerves were malfunctioning. To make matters worse, his feet burned constantly, turning every step into an ordeal.

On 7 April, things took a serious turn when Dinesh developed a high fever, a clear sign of infection. Lata, her heart racing with worry, rushed him to his operating surgeon.

The surgeon took one look at the X-ray and his face grew grave.

'This isn't good,' he said, pointing at the screen.

'Why is this happening?' Dinesh asked shakily.

'The X-ray shows that the stem has broken again, and we'll need to do another revision surgery. It has to be done within a few days.' The surgeon sighed.

Dinesh felt a wave of despair as the surgeon delivered the news, and Lata's mind filled with worry.

'This isn't going to be a simple fix,' the surgeon said. 'Taking out the cup will be very tricky. The hospital where we conducted the first surgery isn't fully equipped to handle a complicated revision surgery.' He paused, then added, 'I'm referring you to another hospital that's equipped for this kind of surgery.'

Dinesh and Lata looked at each other in disbelief. Another painful, costly surgery? They were awash in shock and anxiety, the future looming over them like a dark cloud.

Dinesh checked into the hospital on 10 April 2012. However, the team didn't jump straight into the procedure; instead, they carefully monitored Dinesh's vitals, knowing that blood loss could be significant. They ran several blood tests and X-rays. By 17 April, after making sure everything was stable, they scheduled the revision surgery.

In the operating room, Dinesh was prepped and put under anaesthesia. The team of surgeons, focused and precise, began the procedure. They made a careful incision, removed the damaged stem, and replaced the problematic MoM cup with a new implant. The operation was marked as major in the notes, signalling that recovery would be tough.

On 1 May, Dinesh left the hospital, his body still aching from the complex surgery. The doctors instructed him to follow up in ten days and to stick to gentle bed exercises, relying on a walker for support. The gravity of his situation was unmistakable: after such a harrowing surgery, he had to tread carefully.

But this discharge was different from the two previous times when he had faced the crushing burden of hefty hospital bills for hip-replacement surgery. During the discharge, a peculiar and unexpected twist emerged.

'The hospital told me it was the implant company's fault and that they would cover the entire cost of the surgery,' Dinesh recalled. The relief that washed over his family was palpable; they had already been battered emotionally and financially.

What Dinesh didn't know was that the hospital hadn't actually sought an exception from the company to cover his bills for removing the faulty ASR hip implant. Instead, the company was absorbing the costs of thousands of similar revision surgeries worldwide, running into millions of dollars, as the ASR hip implants had been used in many countries.[5]

The truth, however, was that Dinesh should have been informed about this global recall as early as 24 August 2010, when DePuy issued an unprecedented recall of the ASR hip implant.[6] Yet, neither the hospital nor his doctor had reached out to him.

The ASR recall had sent shockwaves through the hip-replacement industry. A staggering 93,000 of these implants had already been inserted into patients around the globe by the time of the recall.

'We regret that this recall will be concerning for patients, their family members and surgeons,' David Floyd, president of DePuy Orthopaedics, declared on the day of the recall. 'We are committed to assisting patients and healthcare providers by providing information through multiple channels and paying the costs of doctor visits, tests and procedures related to the recall.'[7]

The company presented a facade of transparency, claiming to offer comprehensive information to hospitals, surgeons and patients to guide them through the recall process.

For Dinesh, this reassurance was nothing but an mirage.

The family only learnt of the recall after the hospital unexpectedly announced that Dinesh's bill would be covered by the implant company. At that moment, they were relieved but still in the dark about why the company was footing the bill. Dinesh remained clueless about the serious medical issues driving the recall.

The real story lay buried in his medical records. The doctors had found something unusual when the implant was taken out, but this critical information was never shared with Dinesh – the person most affected. The omission was a silent betrayal, leaving him uninformed and vulnerable.

During the revision surgery, the surgeons found something alarming and wrote it down urgently: 'Finding during surgery – metallosis.' But Dinesh didn't understand that metallosis was a dangerous condition. To put it simply, it was like having metal shavings in his bloodstream. The friction between the parts of the implant had released toxic metal ions into his blood, posing a serious health risk – something that could have been avoided if he had been properly informed.

After the revision surgery, Dinesh found himself unable to walk for five months. The pain in his thigh was relentless and severe, a constant reminder of his ordeal. For the next four years, whenever the pain became unbearable, he had to undergo X-rays and bone scans two or three times a year, all while juggling regular follow-ups with his surgeon. The recall reimbursement didn't cover these mounting costs, and Dinesh was left grappling with a heavy financial burden.

Looking back, Dinesh can't help but feel regret.

'I should never have agreed to that live surgery,' he says, still angry at the injustice of it all. 'They turned it into a show to sell their product. I was just a guinea pig to them. And when the recall happened, I wasn't even informed. They made me a scapegoat.'

Despite over a dozen follow-up visits, his surgeon remained uncommunicative.

'I should have guessed when they wouldn't give me the video of the surgery,' Dinesh reflects. 'It was obvious they were all in it together.'

The ASR implant was supposed to be a game-changer, but it ended up being a nightmare. Dinesh was barely briefed on the risks before the surgery and was never told about the recall years later.

'It's not just me,' he adds, shaking his head. 'Hundreds of others in India had no idea about the recall. We were all left in the dark.'

His life has drastically changed. When he had the surgery, he was earning Rs 18,000 a month. Now, he watches as his peers have advanced in their careers and are earning Rs 85,000.

'I'm left with nothing,' he laments. 'Even to get Rs 9,600, I have to prove I'm still alive.' An August 2021 road accident added more trouble; bedridden for days, Dinesh couldn't provide the necessary certificate and didn't receive the money he was due.

'That's how it is,' he says with a resigned sigh.

Dinesh originally took out a loan for Rs 55,000, but the cycle of missed payments led him to repay Rs 450,000 over the years.

'The doctors told me I'd be back to normal soon, but it was all a lie. I was taken for a ride,' he says bitterly. 'This was the biggest mistake of my life.'

The emotional toll on Dinesh and others like him is immense. They faced repeated hospitalizations, severe financial strain and ongoing pain management, all while their mental and emotional health suffered.

One particularly shocking fact in India is the number of ASR implant recipients who are still untraceable. Many are from India, but a significant number travelled from abroad for the surgery. Like Dinesh, they were also left unaware of the ASR recall, their lives forever altered by a system that failed them when they needed it most. It's a tragic reminder of the personal costs hidden behind corporate negligence.

3

Flying Halfway Across the Globe – For an Implant She Never Wanted

Monica's childhood in Southern Orange County, California, was filled with joy and adventure. While the sun-soaked beaches were always nearby, it was the snow-covered mountains that truly captured her heart. Her most vivid memories weren't of sandy shores but of thrilling weekends spent skiing at Big Bear Mountain Resort, just a short drive away. Her father, eager to share the excitement of winter, bought season passes each year, so every weekend, the whole family would pile into the car, ready for adventure.

'My brother, my sister, my cousins – we all grew up skiing together, every year,' Monica says, her eyes sparkling with nostalgia.[1]

It was during these trips that Monica discovered her love for skiing. The sensation of flying down the snowy slopes, the crisp air stinging her cheeks, and the sound of her family laughing nearby planted a deep passion within her. But what she cherished most was the feeling of freedom and the joy of sharing it with her loved ones.

'There was nothing like it – just me, the snow, and endless possibilities,' she recalls, still savouring the memory of those carefree moments.

As the years went on, skiing became more than just a family tradition – it became Monica's life. Every run down the slope made her feel stronger, more alive. The sport fueled her, giving her confidence and a sense of purpose. She began dedicating herself to perfecting her technique, and in the process, she met others who were just as passionate.

'I decided to move to Park City, Utah – a dream destination for any skier in the US,' Monica says, her excitement still fresh.

Park City was everything she had imagined and more. Tucked into the mountains east of Salt Lake City, this winter wonderland buzzed with life. The slopes stretched endlessly before her, offering cross-country trails, expert runs and a lively atmosphere filled with music and celebration.

'It was like a skier's paradise,' she remembers. But what she didn't expect was how much more the town had in store for her.

One weekend, during Park City's famous Oktoberfest celebration – where the streets overflow with laughter and festive drinks – Monica's life took a new turn.

'The festival was incredible – fun, food and lots of beer. But the best part was meeting him,' she says, her face glowing at the memory. In the midst of the celebration, she noticed a man across the room. They struck up a conversation over a drink, and it wasn't long before they discovered they shared the same love for skiing.

'We instantly hit it off. He had moved to Utah for the same reason as me – to live for the snow,' Monica adds, her smile widening.

The following months were nothing short of magical. Day after day, they hit the slopes together, spending every possible moment skiing and building their relationship. Their connection deepened with every shared adventure, as they raced down the mountains and explored new trails.

'It felt like a dream – we spent that entire season skiing together,' Monica says, her voice filled with warmth and joy.

A few years later, their relationship reached a new milestone. Not only were they still carving their way down the mountains together, but now they had become parents. Their days on the slopes took on a new meaning as they envisioned a future where they could share their love of skiing with their children.

'We knew we wanted our kids to grow up in the mountains, and have the same passion we had for skiing,' Monica explains.

With that dream in mind, they began to explore ways to make skiing a permanent part of their lives, not just a hobby. Eventually, they found the perfect place to start their next chapter: Winthrop, Washington, a small, Old West-themed town where the mountains meet adventure. There, they could build a life filled with skiing, family and the great outdoors, passing on their love of the slopes to the next generation.

Winthrop is the kind of place that feels like a step back in time. Its old-fashioned boardwalks, rustic restaurants and crisp mountain air make it a favourite weekend getaway. In winter, it transforms into a skier's paradise, boasting one of the largest cross-country ski trail networks in the entire country.

'We wanted to raise our kids in Winthrop. Our whole life revolved around the snow and the mountains,' Monica reminisces. Over time, the family became part of the town's growing vacation scene.

'We bought a couple of houses,' she says, 'cosy cottages we rent out to tourists. It's become our little business.'

Living in Winthrop was a dream come true for the family. With mountains in their backyard, they could ski, hike and camp almost every day if they wanted. It was as if nature had laid out a playground just for them. Monica, always up for an adventure, stayed incredibly active. Each winter, she'd cross-country ski three times a week, her breath visible in the cold, her skis cutting through the fresh snow for hours at a time. Downhill skiing became her weekend ritual, with days that stretched into twelve-hour marathons on the slopes. Summers were just as thrilling. The family would hike up to scenic overlooks, the wind brushing against their faces, or raft through rushing rivers, the icy water spraying their skin. They even took up scuba diving, exploring underwater worlds while most people relaxed on the beach.

But as the years rolled on, Monica pushed her body to its limits. In her late forties, an ordinary day took a dangerous turn. She fell from a horse, crashing hard on her right side. Though it wasn't a fracture, the impact left her hip aching, and before long, she found herself in physical therapy with a top specialist who had treated athletes from the US Ski Team. Monica was used to battling the elements, but now she was facing a different challenge.

Despite weeks of therapy, steroid injections and rest, the pain in her hip refused to fade. It clung to her, slowly creeping into her everyday life, turning simple tasks like walking into painful ordeals. Soon, taking even a few steps felt unbearable, and Monica found herself leaning on a cane for support, her once effortless movements now laboured and slow.

For someone who had always been active, the diagnosis didn't come as a complete surprise. Years of high-intensity sports had taken their toll. In 2008, three years after her fall, doctors confirmed what she had feared: primary osteoarthritis in her right hip. The wear and tear were undeniable. X-rays revealed that up to 40 per cent of the cartilage in her femur had eroded, leaving her with bone grinding against bone.

With her adventurous spirit still intact, Monica knew it was time to make a decision. She opted for a hip replacement. Even though she wasn't out on the trails or the slopes like before, Monica wasn't ready to give up her adventurous spirit just yet.

Around the 2000s, India stood out as one of the few countries in the world offering hip resurfacing. The country's top hospitals boasted state-of-the-art equipment, rivalling even the most advanced medical centres in high-income nations. But what truly set India apart was its skilled surgeons – some with nearly a decade of experience in performing complex hip resurfacing procedures, long before the US Food and Drug Administration (USFDA) cleared the first resurfacing implant in 2006. While the world was just catching up, these internationally trained Indian surgeons were already using the hip resurfacing implants with precision and expertise.

Every year, thousands of medical tourists packed their bags and flew in from far-flung corners of the world, seeking not only India's surgical expertise but also the affordable treatment that made it an attractive option. Between 2005 and 2010, when the ASR implant made its debut, India became a magnet for medical tourists, especially those looking for quality care without the hefty price tag. A hip resurfacing procedure in India cost about $8,000, a fraction of what it would cost in Europe or the US – and for many, this was a deal too good to pass up.

By the mid-2000s, India wasn't just another destination; it had become *the* place for younger patients eager to reclaim their mobility with bone-conserving hip resurfacing technology. You could spot them in hospital waiting rooms, nervous but hopeful. They came not just from the US and Canada, but soon from Russia, the Middle East and neighbouring Asian countries, too. And after the 2008 global recession, India's allure only grew stronger, as patients, strapped for cash but desperate for a solution, journeyed halfway across the globe to receive care they could afford.

The experience wasn't just about the surgery, either. These patients, many of whom were venturing outside their home countries for the first time, found themselves swept up in an exotic adventure. Travel packages were curated to offer a cultural experience alongside medical care. Imagine walking about the fabled Taj Mahal before heading to surgery and then a luxurious beach resort in Chennai to recuperate, the salty sea breeze gently blowing as you rested, or visiting sacred temples in southern India, where ancient chants and incense lingered in the air. It wasn't just a medical trip – it was an enriching journey of healing and exploration.

To make things even smoother, large corporate hospital chains in India's biggest cities had formed close partnerships with medical travel agents. These agents acted as guides, carefully organizing every detail, from your initial consultation with the surgeon to your stay at a hotel. They were the patient's bridge between the hospital and a new country, coordinating flights, hospital stays, doctor appointments and sightseeing. All it took was medical clearance from a specialist, and the patient's trip was booked. For many, it felt like they were stepping into a well-oiled machine designed for comfort and care, with the promise of a new hip and a new lease of life waiting at the end.

In 2007, Monica found herself diving into the world of hip resurfacing implants, eager to find a solution that would allow her to stay active. She was still young, full of life and not ready to be slowed down by a failing hip. Her research quickly focused on hip resurfacing, a procedure that stood out to her for one key reason: it didn't involve removing bone, unlike the more invasive total hip replacement. 'I read online that hip resurfacing really works for younger people like me, who want to stay active,' Monica explains.

The testimonials she uncovered were nothing short of inspiring. Patients were back at work just three weeks after surgery, and some were hitting the gym or picking up their tennis rackets within seven or eight weeks. Yet, amidst all the positive stories, Monica found a sobering reality: only a handful of surgeons in the US were performing the procedure at the time. And those who were, had just started using the Birmingham Hip Resurfacing (BHR) System, one of the most trusted hip resurfacing implant manufactured by the British medical device giant Smith & Nephew. The BHR had only received FDA approval in May 2006.

But the cost of the surgery in the US was staggering.

'The cost was $90,000,' Monica says, her voice tinged with disbelief. 'I was self-employed at the time, and my insurance was far from ideal. It would only cover about 50 per cent.' The weight of the financial burden was heavy.

But then, something unexpected happened. A representative from her insurance company suggested she consider an option she hadn't even thought of: surgery outside the US.

'The agent told me they had received reports of successful hip resurfacings being done in other countries,' Monica recalls. It was a turning point.

To sweeten the deal, the insurer promised to cover the entire cost if she chose to have the procedure done abroad. Monica, initially hesitant, soon saw a glimmer of possibility.

'I started looking into it because it was affordable, which was a relief. But affordability wasn't my main concern,' she adds thoughtfully, as though she can still feel the pull between cost and quality.

As she dug deeper, Monica stumbled across blog after blog, each filled with the personal stories of patients who had taken the leap and travelled outside the US for their surgeries. There were tales of relief, of new leases on life. Two countries kept appearing over and over again: Belgium and India. Both offered superior surgery quality at a fraction of the US cost.

But Monica wasn't one to be easily swayed by online reviews. Despite the pain in her hip, she knew this was not a decision to rush. She spent an entire year carefully researching her options, reading everything she could get her hands on.

'India kept coming up as having the best doctors for this kind of surgery,' Monica says. 'A lot of people thought I was a bit crazy for even considering going overseas for such a major procedure. It was a huge step.'

The pain was becoming unbearable, but Monica's focus remained clear. It wasn't just about the money; it was about finding the best surgeon for the job.

'The most important thing was finding a surgeon I could trust,' Monica recalls. 'I did a lot of research on the healthcare system in India and realized it was one of the finest in the world. In the US, we like to think we're the best at everything – but that's not always true. I knew that, and I accepted it.'

Finally, after months of painstaking research, Monica connected with a surgeon in Chennai, India.

'There were other countries that were affordable, but the reputation of Indian surgeons stood out. They were world-class – among the best. I wanted to be able to live an active life afterward, so I made my decision,' she says.

Monica began exchanging emails with the Chennai surgeon, sending him her X-rays for review. The diagnosis? Osteoarthritis in her right hip. But because of her young age and healthy bone stock, the surgeon recommended the BHR procedure. It was the best option to help her maintain her active lifestyle.

'I was overjoyed after our conversations,' Monica says. 'I was convinced I'd be back to skiing in no time. I also knew that eventually, I'd need another surgery since resurfacing isn't a permanent fix. But it would last a long time, and the revision surgery would be much easier.' With renewed hope, Monica set her sights on India, ready to reclaim the active life she had been missing.

―――

In the spring of 2008, Monica and her partner touched down in Mumbai, feeling a mix of excitement and nerves. The next day, they flew to Chennai, where the hospital had arranged a pick-up from the airport. Monica's heart raced – though the surgery was still a few days away, she was already checking into the hospital to complete a series of pre-surgery tests. The moment she stepped into her room in the international patients' division, it felt more like checking into a luxury hotel than a hospital. It had a separate bed for her partner and a cosy little kitchenette, complete with a microwave and a selection of snacks. Everything felt perfectly arranged, and the English-speaking staff made communication a breeze. For a moment, Monica felt herself relax.

But just two days after she settled in, things took an unexpected turn.

'My husband had stepped out for a quick break,' she recalls. 'Then the doctor pulled me into a small room. He calmly said, "I'm going to use this new hip instead of the Birmingham hip,'" she recalls, her voice still carrying the disbelief of that moment.

The surgeon explained that instead of the BHR, he was opting for a newer model, the ASR hip resurfacing. Monica's stomach knotted.

'I had done my homework. I knew everything about the Birmingham hip – what to expect, the risks, the recovery,' she says. 'But he was so confident. He kept saying it was the best choice, a superior product. I trusted him.'

Two days later, after a series of tests and meetings, Monica found herself lying on the operating table, bright lights overhead, ready for the surgery that was supposed to change her life. When the surgeon made the incision, he discovered that her hip joint had suffered almost complete cartilage loss. The surgery itself was smooth, and by the fourth day post-op, Monica, to her amazement, was already climbing stairs using elbow crutches.

'The treatment I got there was like staying in a five-star resort,' Monica recalls. 'The nurses were always smiling, the food was incredible and everything was so well-organized. There's no way you'd get this level of care in the US.'

A week later, Monica was discharged, but she couldn't fly home just yet. The doctor had advised against air travel for at least eleven days after surgery. So, Monica and her partner packed their bags and headed to Taj Fisherman's Cove, a luxury beach resort that hugged the coast of the Bay of Bengal. The waves crashed rhythmically on the shore, and a gentle sea breeze welcomed them to what felt like paradise.

The resort itself was a slice of heaven. Monica's room had a sprawling view of the ocean, with trees swaying gently in the wind and the smell of saltwater filling the air.

'It was the perfect place to recover,' she says. 'The resort catered to all our needs, and the staff was incredibly attentive. I'd sit by the window and just stare out at the Bay of Bengal – it was so peaceful.'

For the next several days, Monica carefully followed all the post-surgery instructions. She placed a pillow between her thighs every time she turned in bed, just as the doctors had advised. She never walked without her crutches and took slow, deliberate steps, even when she explored the lush resort grounds. Everything seemed to be on track – until one evening.

The air was thick with the smell of flowers as Monica walked through the garden towards the hotel's cultural centre, the crutches clicking softly against the ground. She spotted a bench under the canopy of a large tree, shaded and inviting. But when she went to sit down, something went terribly wrong.

'The bench was lower than what I was used to,' she explains. 'I sat down harder than I should have, and in that moment, I felt something snap. I knew instantly – it was my hip. I felt it break right then and there.'

Panic shot through her. Sweat trickled down her back as she grabbed her phone and called her surgeon.

'I was frantic, telling him how bad the pain was,' she says. But his response left her stunned. 'He casually told me, "So what if you're in pain?" as if it was no big deal,' Monica recounts. 'I tried again, explaining that something was seriously wrong, but he just repeated, "Keep doing what you've been doing."'

Monica's heart sank. Against her better judgement, she followed his instructions. She continued walking on a broken hip.

'He didn't even suggest an X-ray,' she says, the frustration still raw in her voice. 'That was his biggest mistake. If he had just ordered an X-ray, everything would've been clear.'

Instead, the surgeon gave her advice for the flight back to the US: sit in an aisle seat, do ankle pumps and walk a few steps every hour. Monica followed his instructions, but all she could think of was that fateful moment under the tree – and the sickening feeling that something had gone terribly, irreversibly wrong.

Monica was scheduled to board a flight from Mumbai to New York City on 8 April. But by the time she touched down in Mumbai from Chennai, she was barely holding herself together, overwhelmed by pain and panic.

'Even now, thinking about that journey makes me break down. The pain was bad when I got on the flight to Mumbai, but by the time we were in the air, it was unbearable. It felt like my bones were being crushed. Still, I forced myself to walk onto the plane with crutches, but the pain was so intense by the time we landed that they had to carry me off.'

Monica had no strength left to board her connecting flight to New York. The idea of setting foot on another plane was unimaginable, and the connection was missed, leaving them stranded.

Hours stretched on as she sat slumped in a chair at the airport, the throbbing pain in her hip relentless, with no relief in sight. She recalls how helpless she felt.

'I was just sitting there, trying not to cry. I had no control over my body; it was like I was falling apart. When we finally got to the Taj hotel at 3.00 a.m., I knew in my heart that something was terribly wrong.'

For three long days in the hotel, Monica couldn't take a single step.

'The pain was so excruciating that I couldn't even lie down. Every movement felt like I was being stabbed. I spent those days propped up in bed, staring at the ceiling, knowing something was broken inside me. By the third day, I couldn't ignore it any longer. I turned to my partner and said, "We need to get to a hospital."'

But they were alone in a foreign city, with no one to turn to. Desperation set in – until a stroke of luck. A friend from the US made a call, connecting them to someone in Mumbai – Anil, a man who ran a small leather shop near the Taj.

When Anil arrived, it was like a lifeline had been thrown to them.

'We were lost, not knowing where to go or what to do. And then there was Anil, like an angel. He brought his friends, too – they all closed their shops just to help us. It was such a kind gesture. They didn't waste a second – they got me into a car. I don't even know whose car it was. By then, I was in shock, barely aware of what was happening.'

Monica was rushed through the chaotic streets of Mumbai, the city alive with noise and movement while she faded in and out of consciousness.

'It felt like a blur. Three hours in that car, drifting in and out of pain. I remember singing hymns and praying, clinging to whatever comfort I could find.'

By the time they reached the hospital, her body had started to betray her. She was violently ill, her system breaking down under the strain. The urgency was clear – she needed immediate medical attention.

A team of doctors sprang into action. She remembers a young doctor, barely older than a student, approaching her. He looked nervous.

'I have some terrible news,' he said, 'You've broken your hip. You'll need surgery immediately.'

The X-ray showed a chilling image – a fracture in the neck of her femur. Monica was rushed to the hospital's intensive care unit, her heart pounding with a mix of fear and disbelief. As she lay there, trying to make sense of what had happened, her surgeon made a call to his colleague in Chennai – the very doctor who had performed her hip resurfacing. Monica could feel the weight of uncertainty pressing down on her as she awaited what was next.

The next morning, her first surgeon flew in from Chennai. Monica had been drowsy from the painkillers, drifting in and out of sleep, when she opened her eyes to find him standing by her bedside. His face was sombre, weighed down with the gravity of the situation.

'I'm very sorry this happened,' he said, regretfully. 'I have no idea why it did. It never should have.'

Monica stared at him, her mind racing. How could this be happening? The surgery that was supposed to change her life for the better had gone terribly wrong. He went on to explain that the resurfacing implant had been perfectly placed, everything had been by the book. But this was an anomaly, a rare failure that none of them had expected.

'He'll never forget me now,' Monica says. 'He told me I was his first real failure. He kept showing me the X-ray, trying to convince me everything had been done right – that the implant was at the perfect angle. But that didn't change the fact that it had broken my femur.'

Later that day, another surgeon in the Mumbai hospital made the decision to convert her hip resurfacing into a total MoM hip replacement. The news hit Monica like a punch in the gut. But her first surgeon stayed on, not leaving her side until the revision surgery was complete. 'I remember being so confused,' Monica says. 'They didn't tell me exactly what they were going to do. I wasn't sure if they were going to fix the resurfacing implant or put something else in entirely. I woke up later and realized my worst fear had come true – they had cut my bone.'

The realization that she no longer had the implant she had so carefully chosen felt like a betrayal. The team had replaced it with the ASR XL total hip replacement – the exact procedure she had spent months researching to avoid.

'During my research, everything pointed to hip resurfacing being my only option. With my age and active lifestyle, it was the only way

I could get back to normal. I knew that if I got the ASR XL, I'd have to live like someone twice my age – no skiing, no risks – just to make sure it didn't dislocate or fail too soon.'

Her frustration boils over as she recounts what had happened.

'I was living in the mountains, skiing, hiking – my life was all about being active. That's why I travelled halfway across the world to get the resurfacing done. I needed it, to keep living the way I was used to. But instead, one surgeon gave me a hip that broke, and another gave me a hip I never wanted. I haven't skied a single day since,' she says, her voice full of regret and anger.

All Monica could do was hope for a quick recovery. The revision surgery had left her drained – emotionally and financially. She had paid for the surgery out of her pocket and flew back to the US just eight days later, feeling utterly defeated. 'The flight home was miserable. Nineteen hours in a cramped seat, and because of the surgical packing, I took up most of it. I felt like I was trapped in a metal box, my hips aching with every passing minute. It was like my whole world had shrunk to that tiny, uncomfortable space.' As she stared out the plane window, watching the clouds pass by, it felt like her old life was slipping away.

It took Monica a couple of months to recover. At first, everything seemed promising. She got back on her feet, easing into a reasonably active life, and for a while, she thought the worst was behind her. But then, her hip began to ache again in 2011 – three years after the surgery. It started as a dull pain, just enough to make her shift her weight and walk with a limp, favouring her right side. But it grew worse. The kind of pain that gnaws at you, sharp and unforgiving, especially when she tried to do something as simple as twist her body quickly.

'For the first two years, I thought everything had gone back to normal. But in that third year, the pain came back and just kept getting worse and worse. I remember thinking, 'What the heck is going on with my hips? I couldn't do anything,' she says, her frustration and confusion still palpable.

The pain took over her life. Every step became an ordeal, and soon it wasn't just her hip – it started radiating into her groin and thigh. Even standing up seemed unbearable. The only escape was to down painkillers at night, the pills dulling her senses just enough for her to sleep through the pain.

'Honestly, I never fully recovered. I just lived with it. It was like this cloud hanging over me. I thought I would never get better. And I was mad – furious – because I had thought I could ski with that first hip. But they took it out, gave me another, and it only made things worse,' she says.

As if the relentless physical pain wasn't enough, Monica's body began throwing more curveballs. Headaches, so piercing they felt like her skull was being crushed. Her mood spiralled into darkness, anxiety clawing at her thoughts, making it hard to focus on anything. She'd forget the simplest of things, leaving her feeling like she was losing control of her own mind.

'I even started seeing a therapist in Twisp,' she recalls. 'Forgetfulness, mood swings – I couldn't convince anyone that my symptoms were real. It felt like I was screaming into a void.'

What made it worse was the trust she had placed in her doctors. After her surgery in Chennai, they had promised to follow up, to check on her after a year and every two years after that. When she returned to Winthrop, she held on to that promise, thinking that either her surgeon from Chennai or the one in Mumbai would reach out. But they didn't. Not once.

'No one followed up on my case. No one even called. I had no idea anything was wrong with the hip. I thought something was wrong with me,' Monica says.

Then, in May 2013, everything changed in an instant. Her nephew casually mentioned that MoM hips were being recalled. It was like a bolt of lightning striking her. She rushed to her long-time general physician.

'I told her about the recall and asked if I should get a metal ion test,' Monica remembers. Her voice cracks slightly at the memory of that panic-stricken moment.

Her doctor took her blood samples and sent them to a lab in Seattle. The week that followed was torture – Monica couldn't shake the anxiety. When the results finally came back, it felt like the missing piece of a twisted puzzle had fallen into place: her blood showed elevated levels of cobalt and chromium.

'It actually made a lot of sense,' Monica says. 'I finally understood why I hadn't been thinking clearly, why I was so sick all the time.'

With the results in hand, her doctor immediately urged her to see a specialist orthopaedic surgeon. The next day, Monica found herself in her physical therapist's office, desperate for a recommendation. Within hours, she was on the road, driving two hours to Wenatchee with her scans and reports piled in the passenger seat, anxiety riding shotgun. When she finally met with the surgeon, she could barely sit still. Her limp had become so severe that even taking a few steps felt like torture.

The surgeon listened carefully, his brow furrowing as he examined her lab results and noted her limp. He didn't mince words: her symptoms were classic signs of a failing ASR implant. Her blood showed elevated levels of metal ions, and her pain was likely due to the local soft tissue reaction. This wasn't surprising – the ASR implant had the potential to release metal ions into the body, triggering inflammation and wreaking havoc on the surrounding tissues. The surgeon also suggested that the pain could be due to micromotion, the slight shifting of the acetabular component, the cup-like part of the implant attached to the hip socket.

'It's painful and it's not going to get better on its own,' he told her. The gravity of the situation hit her like a punch in the gut.

There was no question – the implant had to go. The surgeon didn't even bother recommending an MRI or CT scan.

'We know what we're dealing with here. The implant has to come out,' he said firmly. Monica nodded, her heart pounding. There was no room for delay, no time to second-guess.

She agreed to the revision surgery, though the decision weighed heavily on her. The surgeon sat down with her, going over every detail of the procedure, the long road to recovery, and the possible complications. His words were blunt but necessary: the revision surgery carried a higher risk of dislocation, and her right leg might end up slightly longer than her left to ensure stability. Monica listened, but her mind was already racing ahead, imagining what her life might look like afterward. Would this nightmare finally be over, or would it only bring more pain?

'I remember thinking,' Monica says quietly, '*I don't care what happens – I just need this out of me.*'

On 26 August 2013, Monica underwent another complex revision surgery. Her troublesome DePuy ASR XL implant was swapped out for a Zimmer hip implant, changing from a MoM to a metal-on-polyethylene design. Despite the complexity of the procedure, Monica handled it with impressive strength. The day after surgery, she started her rehab with a determination that was almost palpable. Three days later, she left the hospital, hopeful and ready to move forward.

At home, Monica strictly followed the surgeon's advice: she did her physical therapy exercises and used only a front-wheeled walker. Even so, pain again started to set in, making her feel as if her recovery was slipping through her fingers. During her first follow-up visit, the surgeon reassured her that this pain was normal and would improve in a few weeks. He urged her to keep up with her rehab, promising that better days were ahead.

Six weeks after the surgery, Monica's recovery seemed to be dragging. She was still reliant on her walker, and her physical therapy sessions felt like an endless cycle of hope and frustration. Her walking was awkward and painful, each step a careful manoeuvre to avoid aggravating her discomfort. She vividly remembers breaking down in tears before her surgeon, as she described how pain was taking over her life.

The surgeon examined her with concern. While her wound was healing nicely, Monica was clearly struggling with movement. X-rays showed that the new implants were in place, but they did little to ease her suffering.

'It's normal to be slow to recover,' he said gently. 'Given that this is your third hip surgery in a short time, it's to be expected. Keep using the walker until you're ready for a cane, and stick with your rehab.'

Three months after the revision, Monica was still struggling. She had moved to using a cane, but progress was slow. The groin pain was relentless, affecting every aspect of her life. It wasn't just a minor inconvenience – it was a constant, nagging presence that disrupted her daily routine and sleep. Her rehab efforts were hampered by this persistent pain, and she felt trapped in a never-ending cycle of hope and disappointment.

By five months, the situation seemed even worse. The pain, once a background issue, had become overwhelming. During a follow-up visit, Monica described how the pain had started spreading into her thigh, adding to her misery. The surgeon suggested checking her inflammatory markers and, if they were high, she might need a hip aspiration to relieve the swelling.

Unfortunately, the injections, time and therapy didn't bring the relief Monica desperately needed. Her life had become a daily battle against pain, with her cane and medication as her only tools. Her mental health suffered too, leading to a recommendation for a psychiatric evaluation. The once hopeful journey of recovery now felt like an endless struggle.

In January 2015, nearly two years after her revision surgery, Monica's pain worsened. She visited a new orthopaedic specialist, crying as she described her ongoing issues. The doctor reviewed her records and found inflammation but no infection.

'The injections didn't work,' Monica told him. 'I still feel completely disabled.'

The new doctor couldn't pinpoint a specific cause but suggested the problem might be metallosis – metal ions from the previous implant lingering in her bloodstream. He recommended testing for metal ions once more. 'Recovering after the ASR revision was the hardest thing I've ever gone through,' Monica reflects. 'The pain was unbearable at times, and it took forever to get back to any kind of normal.'

Monica's story is a glaring example of the pain patients endured after revision surgery. It highlights the long-term and often hidden damage metallosis can cause.

Yes, the faulty implant had been removed, but that marked the beginning of her struggle. The medical recall wasn't just a corporate misstep – it was a catastrophe that tore through the lives of real people like Monica. Her anguish, both physical and emotional, was a stark reminder that words alone couldn't capture the full extent of what patients had to go through. It went beyond the surgeries – it was about the crippling pain, the sleepless nights, the endless doctor visits and the haunting thought that things might never return to normal. It was a deeply personal tragedy, one that is impossible to truly measure.

In the US, though, there was a bit of hope when a system was set up to compensate ASR patients for all the suffering they'd gone through. Monica, like thousands of others, felt completely let down by the faulty implant. But she wasn't going to sit quietly. She made up her mind to fight – not just for the money she was owed, but for the justice she knew she deserved.

―⁀―

For years, Monica's life had been an endless search for relief from the nagging pain in her hip. The pain was worsening, her mobility reducing, but the reason remained hidden – until 2013, when her nephew mentioned that the implant had been recalled three years earlier, in August 2010.

Monica was stunned when she heard. How could she not have known? The surgeons in India who performed her operation, who had done no follow-up as promised, also did not inform her. 'Because I got the implant in India, the company didn't reach out to me. The surgeon didn't even tell me it had been recalled,' Monica recalls, shaking her head at the thought of how much time had been lost.

Meanwhile, a much bigger storm had been brewing, one she was completely unaware of. Thousands of patients across the globe were already filing lawsuits against DePuy, desperate for compensation after experiencing injuries similar to hers. By January 2012, the number of lawsuits had ballooned to a staggering 4,700, as victims sought justice for the pain caused by the ASR implant.[2]

These lawsuits accused DePuy of failing to alert patients in time, and worse, not having adequately tested the implant before pushing it into the market. The patients felt betrayed and their attorneys accused the company of negligence.

Later, the cases filed in federal courts in the US were organized as multidistrict litigation in the US District Court for the Northern District of Ohio.[3]

As the lawsuits piled up, the US government began to take notice. In August 2012, DePuy received an informal request from the US Attorney's Office for the District of Massachusetts, demanding materials related to the ASR XL.[4] Monica, living her quiet life, had no idea that the company she was about to go up against was already under intense scrutiny, with the government investigating whether DePuy had submitted false claims or misleading statements related to federal healthcare programmes.

The walls were closing in on DePuy, and the number of plaintiffs in the lawsuits skyrocketed. In less than a year, the number more than doubled – from 4,700 to 10,750.⁵ It wasn't until this point, as Monica prepared for her revision surgery, that she finally heard about the lawsuits and realized she wasn't alone in her struggle.

Suddenly, the thought of taking legal action became a real possibility. The memories of sleepless nights, the countless doctor visits, the frustration – Monica knew she had to act. In May 2013, she picked up the phone and contacted an Atlanta-based personal injury attorney. That call marked the beginning of a new battle.

Her attorney was meticulous. He began piecing together her case like a detective, requesting Monica to fill out detailed questionnaires and gather every scrap of documentation related to her surgeries. Monica, determined to get justice, followed up diligently. In October 2013, she got the news she had been waiting for: her case was officially filed.

Then, with timing that almost felt fated, just one month after Monica's case was submitted, DePuy reached an agreement in November 2013. The company, faced with mounting pressure, established a settlement programme valued at an astounding $2.5 billion, covering around 8,000 patients who had undergone revision surgeries.⁶ For a brief moment, it seemed like Monica's ordeal might be over.

But fate wasn't done with her yet. The settlement didn't apply to US citizens who had received an ASR implant outside the US. 'This means that you are not eligible to participate in this settlement,' Monica's lawyer wrote to her.

Disappointment washed over Monica, but her attorney remained undeterred, reassuring her that they would continue fighting and pushing for a trial for the patients left out in the cold. 'This does not mean that you will not make a recovery against DePuy. We will continue to litigate your case and push for trials in cases that do not settle,' the lawyer emphasized.

Monica's lawyer, a seasoned expert in high-profile product liability cases, didn't sugarcoat the situation. While she was ineligible for compensation at that point in time, they assured her that there was still light at the end of the tunnel.

'We expect that, in the future, DePuy will make settlement offers to all patients who received an ASR hip, which later failed and had to be replaced,' the lawyer wrote to her.

But even as they offered hope, there was no certainty about when – or if – that future would come. The lawyer advised Monica to remain vigilant about her health, and closely monitor the cobalt and chromium levels in her blood every year. 'It is also important for you to report any pain or discomfort you are experiencing with your ASR hip,' they added.

Monica took the advice to heart. Year after year, she underwent tests, watching the numbers, hoping they wouldn't worsen. But alongside the bloodwork, she carried the weight of an exhausting legal battle that showed no signs of ending. What began in 2013 stretched on endlessly, the years blurring together in a relentless cycle of court proceedings and excruciating delays. It felt like running a marathon where the finish line kept moving farther away, always just out of reach.

Then, finally, in 2020 – nearly a decade after the global recall of the ASR hip implant – Monica's long wait came to an end. After years of uncertainty, she reached a settlement, becoming one of seventeen claimants in a settlement. 'I just got so frustrated with the delay,' she admits. 'They would've dragged it on until I was dead. When you fight them, you realize just how deep their pockets are. It's like they don't care how long it takes – they just wear you down.' Her words revealed the exhaustion of someone who had fought for far too long.

But for Monica, the battle was about more than just money.

'I was so angry,' she says. 'They were never going to give me enough to make it right. It wasn't even about that. It was about what they did to us – what they're still doing. We were human beings, but they treated us like numbers.'

The settlement money didn't last long. Like many other patients, Monica watched it slip away, spent on the things she needed just to survive.

'I used it for physical therapy, pain relief and building a new bathroom,' she says with a bitter laugh. 'They didn't give me enough to even take a vacation after everything. Just enough for a safe bathroom.' She pauses. 'After seven years, I can finally get into the shower. Imagine that. I can just walk into it instead of struggling to step over. I couldn't afford it before – handicapped bathrooms are expensive. So, I guess they paid for that.'

Monica's voice shifts, her frustration giving way to disbelief.

'They treated me differently because I had my surgery in India. Like I was some second-class citizen.' She leans forward, her eyes narrowing. 'I found out I got less than half of what patients in the US received. Less than half!' The anger simmers beneath her words. 'They penalized me for trying to save money on the surgery. Treated me like I was trash. My attorney knew it wasn't fair, but his hands were tied. What could he do?'

Monica feels like the system failed her at every turn.

'The company, the doctors, the regulators – they all failed me. If I had kept that implant in any longer, I don't know how much more it would've poisoned me.' Her voice drops. 'I don't even know if the metal ions are gone. Sometimes I feel the same symptoms [anxiety, memory problems and headaches] creeping back.' She pauses, searching for the right words. 'I forget things ... I get confused. I don't think the way I used to.'

More than anything, Monica wants this nightmare to end. But how do you get closure when the people responsible show no remorse?

'My hips don't work like they should. How do you put a price on someone's life, on their existence?' She shakes her head slowly. 'There's no price for that. They took away our quality of life, and they don't care. We're just pawns in their money-making scheme. They used the best doctors, and we were the guinea pigs.'

Even in the toughest times, there were glimpses of hope. Not all doctors stayed quiet. Some had the courage to speak up, refusing to ignore the early problems with the ASR implant. They were the brave ones – the whistle-blowers who noticed the issues long before the recall happened. They were the voices Monica and so many others needed, but for far too long, those voices were muffled by the influence of big pharma.

Part II

Part II

4

The First Red Flag

In the summer of 1996, orthopaedic departments across prominent UK hospitals were thrown into disarray by a shocking revelation: the highly trusted 3M Capital Hip System was failing at an alarming rate. Nearly 40 per cent of patients who had undergone the procedure were back in hospital beds – not for recovery, but because their implants were failing within just five years.[1] Within months, the news quietly spread through the medical community, sparking mutterings of consternation. Surgeons who had once been confident in the device's success found themselves questioning their decisions, while the Medical Devices Agency (MDA) scrambled to investigate the unexpected and widespread failures of the implant, produced by the leading US healthcare company.

The agency continued to monitor the hip implant's clinical performance until January 1998. By then, at least five leading medical centres across the UK were sounding the alarm, reporting a surge in clinically unacceptable complications among patients with these implants. The situation had become so dire that the government was forced to issue a nationwide health warning. The message was clear: every patient with a 3M Capital Hip System implant needed an urgent clinical review.

This was not a small-scale issue. Over a span of six years, more than 4,500 of these potentially dangerous implants had been used in the UK. The day after the government's warning, 3M attempted damage control, promising to cover the cost of all necessary revision surgeries. But the damage was done. The government urged surgeons to comb through their records and contact every affected patient. Yet, shockingly, many patients could not be traced, raising a grave public outcry over the failure to properly track these implants.

The situation demanded a response, and it came from the prestigious Royal College of Surgeons. In July 2001, after an exhaustive investigation, they delivered damning findings: had a national hip registry been in place, this catastrophe could have been averted. Such a registry would have flagged the failing implants early on and ensured that no patient slipped through the cracks. It was a wake-up call that couldn't be ignored.

The outcry and the findings of the Royal College of Surgeons finally led to the establishment of the National Joint Registry (NJR) for hip and knee replacements in the UK in 2002. This wasn't just about tracking data; it was about safeguarding lives. The NJR became a crucial step forward, ensuring that no patient would ever again be lost in the system, and no faulty device would remain undetected until it was too late.

The NJR launched its data collection efforts in April 2003, marking a significant milestone in tracking joint replacements across the UK. At the outset, over 400 hospitals were enlisted in the NJR system, ready to contribute valuable data. However, before the NJR could commence operations, considerable preparations were made to ensure its success. The government crafted a unique financing plan: a levy on the sale of hip implants was introduced to fund the registry. This innovative approach not only supported the NJR but also demonstrated a commitment to improving patient safety and advancing medical research.

In the early stages, the NJR diligently fed data on several popular hip implants into its system. However, a significant event occurred in July 2003, just three months after the NJR's launch. It was then that the registry received its first record of the ASR implant – a moment that would later prove to be pivotal. The submission of this data marked the beginning of what would become a crucial chapter in the NJR's history, as the ASR implant would soon come under intense scrutiny for its performance and safety.

―⁓―

The NJR was established as a crucial tool for identifying early warnings of patient safety issues. Over time, it began to uncover essential insights into revision rates, revealing whether implants were failing prematurely or proving durable. To investigate higher-than-expected failure rates, the NJR held discussions with key stakeholders, including leading orthopaedic associations, the UK regulator and implant manufacturers. By 2007, the NJR had developed a robust scientific methodology to accurately identify and monitor these failure rates across various brands – a methodology that became vital for safeguarding patient outcomes.

After every joint replacement surgery, diligent surgeons didn't just send their patients home and move on to the next case. Instead, they closely monitored their patients' recovery, noting every detail of their postoperative experience. These surgeons, committed to improving future outcomes, fed this valuable data into the NJR. With each entry, the NJR grew into a powerful tool, offering critical insights into revision rates based on various bearing surfaces and implant sizes. Simultaneously, the NJR took a closer look at the performance of the top eight brands making resurfacing implants. By 2008, it was ready to publicly release these significant findings on the resurfacing cup brands implanted between 1 April 2003 and 30 November 2008. The results were telling.

The NJR shared data on thousands of patients who had undergone hip resurfacing, a procedure where the damaged surface of the hip joint is covered with a metal shell. But the real story was in what happened afterwards – how often these implants failed and had to be replaced – known as the revision rate. For the BHR, the market leader, data from 6,746 patients showed a 3.3 per cent revision rate at three years after surgery. In simpler terms, out of every 100 people who received this implant, about 3 needed a follow-up surgery within three years because their original implant didn't hold up. Then there was the Cormet 2000, made by the UK-based company Corin. Among the 1,697 patients who got the Cormet, the revision rate was higher – 6 per cent, or roughly 6 out of every 100 patients.[2]

The ASR resurfacing, another popular choice, fared worse. Out of 1,332 patients, 7.5 per cent needed their implants replaced within three years. Conserve, yet another brand, wasn't much better, with a 7.4 per cent revision rate among 521 patients.

By 2008, the NJR made a critical observation: the BHR had the lowest revision rate, while the ASR and Conserve implants had the highest. But beyond just numbers, the NJR sounded an alarm. For the first time, they found strong statistical evidence linking the specific brand of implant to how likely it was to fail. This was a significant breakthrough, revealing that while some hip resurfacing models like the BHR were performing exceptionally well, others, such as the ASR, were far more prone to problems, leading to more surgeries and complications for patients.

In the following two years, unsettling news about the ASR's performance began to emerge quietly among surgeons. Early failures were becoming evident, yet there was a pervasive silence – likely due to the industry's close-knit nature and the high stakes involved. By September 2010, the NJR was set to reveal a troubling discovery: its five-year revision rates for leading hip resurfacing brands. The BHR, a market leader, had a revision rate of 4.3 per cent, a figure considered relatively standard. In stark contrast, the ASR's five-year revision rate was a staggering 12 per cent – three times higher than its competitor's.[3]

The inner workings of the NJR were no secret. Several members had connections to DePuy: one was employed by the company, and a few others had received funding or royalties for developing hip implants. It was evident that DePuy was bracing for trouble as soon as it became clear that the ASR implants were under intense scrutiny. As the NJR's report neared publication, the pressure on DePuy mounted. Not surprisingly, just as the NJR was about to disclose its findings, DePuy issued a global voluntary recall of both ASR models. The timing was no coincidence; DePuy's recall came as the NJR's data was poised to unveil the severe issues with the ASR implants.

At the forefront of diligent monitoring was the University Hospital of North Tees, where surgeons took an extraordinary approach to patient care. They did more than oversee surgeries; they became vigilant stewards of their patients' health. Every patient's progress was meticulously tracked and every detail carefully recorded. This data was not left to gather dust in hospital archives; it was swiftly shared with the NJR. This proactive approach ensured that the performance of the ASR implants was under constant review, providing crucial insights and allowing for quick responses to emerging issues.

University Hospital of North Tees, located in the vibrant market town of Stockton-on-Tees along the picturesque River Tees, is more than just a local landmark. Stockton, with its bustling shopping centre and historic buildings, exudes a charming local spirit. Conveniently located just two miles from Stockton railway station – only a ten-minute drive or a quick bus ride away – the hospital is easily accessible for patients. Its central location and comprehensive health services make it a crucial hub in northeast England's medical landscape. But the hospital's reputation extends far beyond the local community. Patients from around the world, including from India, travel here specifically for its renowned treatment of hip conditions. The reason? The hospital's trauma and orthopaedic services are among the best in the UK. Since 2008, its specialized unit for MoM hip joints has attracted patients seeking cutting-edge care and expertise.

The hospital's team of seasoned surgeons, over the years, have successfully replaced failed MoM hip joints. Their expertise has also contributed significantly to the broader medical community. The insights gained from their extensive experience have sparked important conversations at international medical conferences and have been instrumental in guiding other centres facing similar challenges. Their work, published in prestigious journals, has offered valuable understanding that has helped enhance patient safety.

Spearheading this specialized service is Antoni Nargol, a distinguished orthopaedic consultant. His surname is rich with history. Nargol is a small coastal village in the Valsad district of Gujarat, nestled near the Maharashtra border. This village, with its sun-soaked shores and bustling fishing boats, is considered the first place where the Parsis landed when they fled persecution in Persia, making it their ancestral home in India. Over generations, many of them have spread to distant corners of the world. His connection to this tiny Gujarati village is more than just ancestral; it's a testament to the global journey of a community that, like him, has made its mark far beyond its humble origins.

Nargol is a maestro in the operating room, where his hands move with a precision that seems almost effortless, as if guided by instinct. For nearly a decade, he has been the clinical lead for lower limb surgeries, a role in which he has not just led but excelled, performing over 3,000 hip replacements and 1,500 knee replacements. Beyond the operating room, Nargol's name carries weight. As a distinguished member of the prestigious British Hip Society, he's recognized among the elite in his field. Since February 2002, he has been practising at the University Hospital of North Tees, where his reputation as a skilled joint replacement surgeon makes both his patients and colleagues trust and admire him.

As a teenager, Nargol would spend his holidays in India, visiting his uncle in Mumbai and exploring other parts of the country. In 2008, he visited his family in Mumbai again, but this time, the visit was far from leisurely. He was a busy surgeon, pressed for time, with only a brief window to catch up with loved ones.

Nargol's schedule was relentless. He hopped from one Indian city to another, performing multiple hip replacement surgeries each day. His mornings began at dawn, often before the sun had fully risen, and he didn't stop until well past 9.00 p.m. Each surgery was broadcast live to a wide audience, adding to the pressure. Between surgeries, he dashed into conference rooms, engaging in detailed, interactive discussions with Indian surgeons about the new implant in the market – the ASR.

At that time, Nargol maintained a close professional relationship with DePuy. In fact, his practice at the University Hospital of North Tees was conveniently located near another key landmark: DePuy International Limited in Leeds. When DePuy launched the ASR models, they didn't just supply the hospital with these new implants – they also tapped into both the hospital's and Nargol's expertise for a critical role. The company sought out leading surgeons from Australia, Germany, the US, Ireland and the UK to assess the ASR's clinical performance, and in the UK, Nargol was selected as the chief investigator.

In the early years after the ASR implants' launch, Nargol stood out as one of the few European surgeons with extensive experience in both ASR models. His intimate knowledge of the implants made him a key figure in their evaluation. Recognizing his exceptional surgical skills, DePuy flew him to India in 2008 to share his insights on the intricate surgical techniques required for the ASR procedure. At his centre, Nargol managed a bustling schedule, with patients often lining up for his specialized care. From 2004 to 2007, he performed nearly 200 ASR implant surgeries, handling a high volume of complex cases.[4]

When companies launch new hip implants, they often flood the market with bold claims and glossy ads, promising top-tier performance and a lifespan that seems almost too good to be true. But before any implant reaches a patient, it must undergo rigorous preclinical testing. Why? Because these implants, like custom-tailored suits, need to fit perfectly – not only for the individual patient but also for the specific movements they'll make every day.

Picture a hip implant: it's made up of different parts, such as the acetabular and femoral components. As you move, these parts rub against each other, producing tiny particles called wear debris over time. And that wear? It's a big deal. If the implant wears out too quickly, it could fail, leaving the patient in unbearable pain. That's why minimising wear is a top priority for engineers, clinicians and manufacturers. It depends on the materials, the mechanics and how well the pieces fit – with each other and with the recipient.

To address this issue, implants undergo extensive testing in high-tech labs. Special machines replicate real-life movements and stress – like putting the implant on a treadmill, running nonstop. These machines simulate everything your hip would experience in the real world, collecting vital data on friction and wear. It's like giving the implant a test run to ensure it can handle the daily grind without breaking down.

In the end, this testing isn't just about numbers and data – it's about ensuring that when you receive a new hip, it's built to last. Because no one wants to endure that kind of surgery twice.

In 2004, DePuy targeted Nargol, a surgeon known to prefer tried-and-tested implants, to endorse their latest hip implant, the ASR. Recognizing Nargol as a prized target, DePuy pulled out all the stops. They didn't just send a few brochures or an email; they flew a team of representatives to his hospital, armed with glossy presentation decks, high-definition videos and the charm of seasoned salespeople.

The DePuy representatives brought a carefully curated arsenal of marketing materials designed to make a powerful impression. They began their pitch with the precision of a well-rehearsed play, starting with a simulator study that highlighted the supposed benefits of the ASR. Knowing that Nargol had consistently used the BHR implant – a product trusted by top surgeons worldwide – they decided to directly challenge the competition.

The sales team played a compelling video that pitted the ASR against the BHR in a head-to-head comparison. The screen showed two simulators side by side, each testing the endurance of the implants under stress. As the video played, the sales representatives narrated every detail, emphasising the potential pitfalls of the BHR.

'Look here, Dr Nargol,' one of them said, pointing at the BHR simulator. 'See how the metal ions are released? In a few years, the Birmingham implant is likely to fail. But look at our ASR – it's clean, stable, with no sign of ion release. Plus, it preserves more bone. This is the future of hip resurfacing.'[5]

Their strategy was clear: if they could plant a seed of doubt about the BHR – an implant that had been used in over 27,000 patients since 1997 – they might persuade Nargol to switch.[6] They knew they were up against a long-standing preference and the collective trust of the surgical community. Yet, they were confident. They had seen how the promise of cutting-edge technology and minor design tweaks could win over even the most cautious surgeons. After all, in the highly competitive hip implant industry, newer often meant better – or so the narrative went.

The company representatives leaned in, their voices dropping to a confidential whisper.

'Dr Nargol, we understand your commitment to your patients. This is about giving them the best. The BHR may have a strong reputation, but it's ageing. The ASR is the next generation, designed to outperform and outlast.'

Nargol listened, intrigued but cautious. He knew the risks of jumping onto the bandwagon of new implants without substantial evidence. Yet, the allure of being at the forefront of innovation, coupled with DePuy's persuasive pitch, began to take hold.

'The trouble with orthopaedics is that manufacturers don't often have pre-clinical studies,' Nargol thought to himself. 'If you wait for five years for these studies, you end up missing out.'

'Surgeons make this mistake: they like new things,' says Nargol in hindsight. 'Patients also like new things.'

In April 2004, after much deliberation and fuelled by the optimism of the sales pitch, Nargol decided to switch to the ASR. There were no pre-clinical studies yet, however, the simulator study was convincing.

'Because it was new, from seeing the simulators, it was thought to work better, and it preserved a little more bone,' he explains.

When Johnson & Johnson decided to launch their new ASR hip implant, they orchestrated a marketing blitz. Slick videos, polished to perfection, were dispatched to surgeons around the world, promising a revolutionary breakthrough in hip replacement.

'It's amazing how everyone falls for their marketing,' Nargol recalls, shaking his head. 'They are very, very good at it.'

Nargol was one of the chosen few, a top surgeon whisked away to Rome for an exclusive training event during the launch. Held in one of the city's most luxurious hotels, the event combined high-tech learning with high-end living. Surgeons from across the globe arrived, to be regaled with lectures and demonstrations garnished with generous helpings of the good life. Fine wines, gourmet meals and the chance to explore Rome's iconic landmarks awaited them after hours.

Days were packed with activities. After introductory talks and discussions, the organizers divided the participants into groups. Nargol's group was ushered into a sleek, modern room where company representatives showed them exactly how to implant the ASR device. The real showstopper came later: a live surgery demonstration by the designer surgeons themselves. Like magicians revealing their tricks, they showcased the precise technique needed to implant the ASR, leaving the audience of surgeons in awe.

They didn't stop at educating their guests. Johnson & Johnson knew that winning over these influential surgeons meant pulling out all the stops. In the evenings, over lavish dinners, they wined and dined the attendees, building connections and generating buzz. Nargol, already marked as a key figure in the UK, found himself in a private meeting with counterparts from other countries, where there were intimate discussions with the influential design surgeons.

'It was a good meeting,' he remembers. Dr Nargol and his peers went home, convinced of the superiority of the ASR implant.

But then, in 2007, the first cracks in this promising narrative began to show. Three female patients came to Nargol, their faces drawn with pain, complaining of unusual and persistent groin pain.

'They all said the same thing: "I start getting groin pain when I'm getting in and out of a car or when I walk,"' Nargol recalls, the look of pain in their eyes still vivid in his memory.

Nargol's optimism was replaced by a creeping sense of unease. These complaints were unexpected. His mind raced through possibilities as he examined the patients. The pain could not be ignored – it was real and consistent across all three cases. He decided to investigate further. He withdrew fluid from their hips, expecting to see the clear fluid typical of healthy joints. Instead, he was taken aback. The fluid was milky, abnormal in appearance.

'I sent the samples to the lab. I thought they were infected,' he says. This should have been a straightforward infection, he thought. But then the lab results came back with no signs of infection. Puzzled, Nargol wrote to the microbiology department, demanding answers: 'Come on, guys. I have given you all this pus – how can you say it is not infected?'

The results forced Nargol to reconsider his initial assumptions. What if this wasn't an infection? What if it was something entirely new? His medical instincts kicked in. He decided to operate on one of the patients to get a closer look.

'All this gluey, milky-white fluid was in the hip. The tissue was damaged,' he recalls, his voice taut with frustration. It was like nothing he had seen before. Realizing the need for more expertise, he brought in a pathologist. Together, they conducted another analysis. The findings were startling.

'We discovered that the condition is called ALVAL (aseptic lymphocyte-dominated vasculitis-associated lesions), which is when the lymphocytes try to "eat" the soft tissue,' Nargol explains.

Determined to get to the bottom of this, Nargol arranged for representatives from DePuy to witness the revision surgery. It was a strategic move. The team didn't include anyone from DePuy's clinical department, but a key marketing representative was present – a figure who had sold the implants and was influential within the company. As Nargol opened the hip, the milky fluid spilled out, confirming his worst fears. He turned to the DePuy representative.

'What the hell is this?' he asked.

The marketing representative stood there, bewildered. He had no answers. The sight of the fluid left him just as baffled.

'That milky white fluid is typical of the problem we now recognize. Back then, I only knew that it didn't look very good. I showed it to the DePuy representative and asked him: "Is this meant to come out of one of his hips?" He shook his head and said "no". He admitted that this was not right. It was a surprise to him.'

Nargol's team was now fully engaged, their initial confusion giving way to determination. They decided to test for metal ions in the blood to understand the nature of the complication.

'We thought, "Is this metal debris or is this an allergic reaction?" We started doing tests to check the cobalt–chromium levels. This was in 2007, before anyone ever heard of these metal ions being in the body,' Nargol says.

The test results came back, showing elevated levels of metal ions, but this only led to more questions.

'We didn't know what a normal level of cobalt and chromium in the blood was,' Nargol admits. So his team conducted blood tests on non-patients to compare the metal ion levels. The findings were conclusive.

'We immediately recognized that there was a problem with excessive metal leaking out of the implants,' Nargol says. The discovery sent a ripple through the team – a mixture of shock and a steely resolve to find out how and why these implants were failing.

In November 2007, Nargol travelled to Texas for the annual meeting of the American Association of Hip and Knee Surgeons. This seventeenth meeting, held in Dallas, remains clearly etched in his memory.

'It was a big deal,' Nargol recalls. 'I remember it vividly because the next day, I ended up in a Texas hospital, feeling quite unwell. Thankfully, I recovered.'

But his hospitalization wasn't the only reason the event was unforgettable. At this meeting, Nargol presented his findings on the ASR implant, exposing the troubling issues he had encountered at his hospital. This was his first public warning about the implant's potential for early failure.

As Nargol took the stage, the room fell silent, all eyes focused on him. He detailed the three major problems that he had observed: high cup angles in women that could lead to excessive metal wear, persistent pain and early implant failure.

'I told them the implant seemed decent overall, but we had three patients whose conditions we couldn't explain. I began showing photos of the troubling white fluid we had discovered,' he says.

The unusual findings captured the audience's attention, with many listening intently and visibly concerned. Nargol could sense the unease in the room as questions began to swirl. A few surgeons even stood up to share their own similar observations.

'But there were only a few of us,' Nargol notes.

In the audience were some of the company's top designer surgeons and leading engineers – individuals prominently featured in the ASR's promotional materials and instruction manuals. They listened intently as Nargol laid out the crucial evidence of early ASR failures.

'In 2007, despite my presentation, I still believed the ASR was a good product overall. This was when everyone should have urgently investigated what was going wrong. Instead, the implant continued its trajectory,' Nargol reflects.

After Nargol's presentation, DePuy officials took the stage to present the early results from their metal ion study involving ASR patients. However, this presentation contrasted sharply with Nargol's. Their study tracked eighty-nine patients – sixty-six males and twenty-three females – from four centres across the UK, South Africa, Australia and Germany.

The data they presented was significant: among fifty patients followed for two years, three females and three males had cobalt or chromium levels exceeding 10 micrograms per litre. Yet, the company dismissed these cases as outliers, attributing the high metal ion levels to issues with acetabular component placement. Their graph suggested that while large diameter cups might result in low metal ion levels, improper placement could cause significant wear and elevate metal ion levels in the blood.

In essence, DePuy implicitly placed the blame on surgical technique rather than the implant itself. They argued that while the ASR cups were adequate, they needed to be implanted at a precise 45-degree angle – a standard inclination.

'In Texas, DePuy maintained that everything was generally okay,' Nargol says. 'I countered, "Yes, it's okay, but we have these three patients for whom it's not working."'

Despite the mounting evidence and the company's attempts to shift the blame, Nargol was left with a lingering sense of unease. The presentation left him with no clear answers.

'That's where it all started – where we first told DePuy something was seriously amiss, yet clarity on the problem remained elusive,' he says.

After the Texas meeting, DePuy representatives met with Nargol regularly, each time more eager than the last to demonstrate their so-called commitment to solving the problems with the ASR hip implants. On the surface, their concern seemed genuine, even admirable. But beneath the facade, Nargol could sense their true priority: not patient safety, but damage control.

'It was about how they could market the product and turn it around,' he observes, recognizing the company's real agenda.

To sway Nargol, DePuy went all out. They assured him they had different strategies that would help him implant the ASR cups more effectively.

'They kept telling me, "Because you are struggling, we'll help you put them in better. Then everything will be fine,"' Nargol recalls. It was a clever ploy, one that disguised a sales pitch as a solution.

The company spared no expense to back up their claims. They rented a lavish hotel, flew in their top engineers and staged a grand demonstration of alternative implant techniques. The presentations were slick, the explanations polished, making it easy to believe that the problem lay in the hands of the surgeons, not the product.

'They really emphasized improving the surgical technique,' Nargol says. They were adamant that the issue was technique and patient selection, not a fault in the ASR implants. 'They insisted it was the surgeons' fault, not the implant. This narrative was pushed globally,' Nargol recalls.

They projected unshakeable confidence, and they used it to make Nargol doubt his own abilities. They told him that no one else in the world was reporting the issues he was seeing. 'Trust the product,' they urged. Their words were so firm, their tone so self-assured that Nargol began to question himself.

'You start thinking, "It can't be the implant – it must be me." They make you doubt your skills, playing with your mind,' he says.

By November 2007, Nargol was convinced the fault lay with him. He continued using the ASR implants, believing that his surgical technique was the problem. In response to the company's suggestions, he adjusted his approach.

'I started placing the cups at lower angles,' he says, ensuring they never went above 45 degrees, hoping this change would solve the problem.

When DePuy asked Nargol to tour India in early 2008, he went along with their narrative, echoing the company's claims. He informed doctors about the three early ASR failures but reassured them that positioning the cups lower would prevent such issues.

'That's what we did in 2008 – we changed the way we implanted ASR hips,' Nargol says.

Yet despite his adjustments, the problems persisted. Slowly, it became impossible to ignore the reality: the issue wasn't with the surgical technique – it was the implant itself. By the summer of 2008, Nargol knew this for sure.

Initially, he had concerns only about the ASR hip resurfacing model. But by mid-2008, he noticed serious problems with the ASR XL implants as well.

'It was evident it had nothing to do with the cup position. Patients were experiencing issues even with perfect placement. That's when I truly started to worry,' he says.

By late 2008, his fears had been confirmed. No matter how well the ASR was implanted – even with precision at the recommended 45-degree angle – it still failed. The evidence was undeniable.

By Christmas, Nargol had seen failures in both the resurfacing model and the ASR XL. He began analysing the failure rate and realized just how dire the situation was.

'I told DePuy, "This is terrible. There's something wrong with your implants, not my technique,"' he recalls. In January 2009, he finally made a decisive move. He informed DePuy that the problem was serious and that his team would no longer use the ASR implants.

By then, in January 2009, Nargol had implanted several hundred ASR devices. His decision to stop using them was based on a thorough and scientific analysis of his patients' clinical data. This conclusion was not reached alone. Nargol had already started a clinical research project in 2007 to audit his patients; he had hired a full-time researcher, using the funds DePuy had provided to evaluate the performance of its ASR hip implants.

This unprecedented collaboration would become a turning point, uncovering undeniable scientific evidence of the ASR's early failures – evidence so compelling that it couldn't be ignored. As the findings spread, the medical community could no longer afford to overlook them, sparking debates and raising serious questions about the safety of the ASR. What started as a quiet internal audit soon became a powerful force, bringing a dark truth to light that the world could no longer ignore.

5

Exposing the Scandal – Through Science

In September 2007, a young and eager David Langton stepped into the University Hospital of North Tees, thrilled to begin his career in orthopaedics as a researcher under a top surgeon. This was no ordinary hospital; every day, a high volume of patients passed through its doors, many desperate for the promise of pain-free mobility through hip replacements. Langton was ready to prove himself in this high-pressure environment, where each case had the potential to change a life. However, he had no idea that he was about to become part of a unique and significant scientific collaboration – one whose impact would resonate far beyond the hospital walls. Through this endeavour, the team would challenge the practices of one of the industry's biggest names.

Langton was handed a unique challenge aimed at reshaping how hip surgeries were monitored. At the time, DePuy had a strong foothold in the hospital.

'I think they were putting money into the hospital to employ a research assistant,' Langton recalls.

Langton would be reporting to Antoni Nargol, a consultant who demanded excellence and left nothing to chance. Nargol's commitment to his patients was his hallmark – he scrutinized every recovery and every data point with a laser focus. For Nargol and his team, patient safety wasn't just a part of the job – it was the job. And when Langton joined him, he quickly realized that Nargol's meticulous approach was driven by something more than routine diligence.

Nargol had noticed troubling patterns among patients with ASR hip implants. Reports of unexplained pain were becoming too frequent to ignore. These patients, promised a new lease of life, were instead facing discomfort and uncertainty. Nargol's instincts told him something was wrong, prompting him to start an exhaustive audit of his cases. He needed help – someone who could match his dedication to uncovering the truth. And so, with the support of DePuy's research funds, he hired Langton as a full-time researcher.

Nargol left no room for error, insisting on rigorous follow-ups and exacting standards. Inspired, Langton immersed himself in the new role, aware that every chart he updated and every patient he monitored could be the key to improving lives.

At first, Langton found the work intellectually fascinating – a puzzle to solve, each patient's recovery chart a clue – a scientific scrutiny of the new product they were using. But as he delved deeper, he began to see patterns that unsettled him. Patients who had undergone the ASR hip resurfacing procedure were coming back with complaints of severe pain, far beyond what should be expected from normal post-operative recovery. The pain was often sharp and unrelenting, leaving patients frustrated and desperate for answers. Langton's initial excitement gave way to a growing sense of unease. The more data he collected, the more he realized that something was terribly wrong.

A few months in, Langton and Nargol compiled the initial data and began examining the issue more systematically. They decided to get to the bottom of what was causing these unusual symptoms. They started poring over spreadsheets late into the night, cross-referencing patients' medical records. They were like detectives, piecing together a mystery. Every day brought new findings, each one adding another layer to the emerging picture.

'Soon after Texas in November, Dave started to look at the implants to find out what was wrong with them,' Nargol said. 'Because in 2007, the debate was: Is what we see an allergy to normal wear? Or is this normal wear in patients who are not allergic?'

Starting in June 2007, the team had begun routinely analysing metal ion levels in each patient at least one year after the primary ASR surgery. Langton recalls that the early data showed very high levels of metal ions in the patients' bloodstreams. The numbers jumped off the charts, far exceeding safe thresholds.

'We didn't know why the cobalt–chromium levels were so high, and we didn't know why our patients were in so much pain,' he said.

Langton was buried in data – tables, graphs and test results. Each new entry felt like an added weight on his shoulders. Patients reported more pain, metal ion levels kept rising and Langton's anxiety grew. The young researcher could feel the walls closing in, the silent pressure of knowing that lives were at stake. As the weeks went by, Langton found himself swamped with alarming results. Each test seemed to confirm the last – skyrocketing metal ion levels, patients complaining of pain, swelling and a lack of mobility. Every new file he opened felt like another warning sign, another piece of evidence that something was seriously amiss.

Langton, still just a junior researcher, felt overwhelmed. Questions swirled in his mind. Were these implants harming patients? Were the findings right? Doubt gnawed at him, but so did a creeping sense of responsibility. Was he sure of his results, sure enough to raise the alarm? Should he do it?

'I was just twenty-eight. You would never, ever question the functioning of the implant as a junior,' Langton said, recalling the internal struggle. 'As a junior, you cannot even question the concerns linked to the performance of the device. Many of us don't even know what the implants are made of. We just blindly trust the senior doctors.' But he knew he had been meticulous, and his senior surgeon had been overseeing the research; people's well-being was at stake.

As the data piled up, so did the anxiety. Langton and Nargol decided it was time to confront DePuy with their findings. They met the DePuy officials, armed with their notes and a sense of urgency that was hard to mask.

'We've been seeing incredibly high levels of metal ions in patients,' Nargol began, his voice calm but firm. Langton nodded, showing data that illustrated the alarming trends. However, the company officials listened with polite smiles but offered little more than nods and vague assurances.

'They would just say, "You know, we haven't seen this anywhere else in the world. We don't know what it means,"' Langton recalls. The words stung, a dismissive wave that brushed aside their growing concerns. Despite the regular communications and urgent data, the company did not respond with any concrete action. It was like hitting a wall of indifference, each meeting a replay of the last, the same polite stonewalling.

Langton wanted to believe the company had his patients' best interests at heart.

'They were really nice. I kind of liked them at the time. I thought Antoni was crazy for doubting them. I thought medical devices could not go wrong.' Yet, every time he left a meeting, a sense of disillusionment crept in. It was as if his concerns were being brushed aside, his findings dismissed without a second thought.

However, as time went on, Langton's perception of the company began to shift. He started noticing things – little things at first, but unsettling nonetheless. The chief engineer's evasive answers, the way he would sidestep direct questions.

'I grew to particularly dislike their chief engineer. I could tell he was holding things back, that he was lying. That just became more and more apparent as the months went by.'

The team's unease turned into a quiet determination. Nargol and Langton sensed they were onto something significant, and they weren't about to let it go. The thought of patients suffering, of lives being ruined by a faulty implant, weighed heavily on them.

It wasn't just about data anymore – it was about patient safety. They knew they had to do everything in their power to ensure that the scientific community was made aware of their findings. But before that, they decided to inject an extra layer of rigour, ensuring their scientific scrutiny was not just thorough but undeniably compelling.

―――

In 2008, Nargol's team knew they were onto something bigger than just a few faulty hip implants. They suspected the issue wasn't isolated to their hospital but could be a widespread ticking time bomb. Determined to get to the bottom of it, they took the next step: compare the metal ion levels in the blood of patients with ASR implants to those with other hip devices. If ASR patients had higher levels, it would confirm their worst fears.

As soon as the results came in, the evidence was undeniable. Langton recalls the moment of realization vividly.

'When we plotted the graph,' Langton says, 'the results were shocking. ASR patients had significantly higher levels of metal ions in their blood than those with other devices. We thought, "Oh no, this is a serious problem."'

Alarm bells went off. Langton knew they couldn't keep this within their team. They needed answers fast and not just from orthopaedic surgeons. They reached out to toxicologists and rheumatologists, experts who could shed light on what these dangerous levels of metal ions could do to the human body. These specialists, used to dealing with toxins and immune responses, were stunned.

'When we showed them the data, they were in disbelief,' Langton says. 'They assumed we'd made some sort of error. No one believed that people could still be walking around, alive, with this much metal in their blood.'

The team knew they needed to dig deeper. Hence, they examined implants from patients who had complained of worsening groin pain at various stages after their ASR surgeries. What they found was nothing short of alarming: the condition of the hips and surrounding tissues was dreadful.

'Patients would come in with unbearable pain, and when we removed the implants, it was like a nightmare – pus and fluid everywhere,' Langton says.

Determined to find answers, they turned to DePuy, handing over the explants (extracted implants) with the hope that the company would provide clarity. Yet, DePuy's response was infuriatingly evasive.

'We presented the components to the company, asking for their analysis,' Langton recalls. 'Each time, they dismissed our concerns, claiming there was nothing wrong. They insisted, "The issue was with the surgery." They blamed us, saying, "You guys put it in wrong."'

Faced with a lack of support and no means to independently examine the explant, the team was at a crossroads. They needed to act swiftly and decisively. Langton, driven by a sense of urgency, reached out to experts in tribology – the study of wear, friction, lubrication. This was their last hope for uncovering the truth.

Their persistence paid off in a dramatic turn of events. Out of the blue, a professor of orthopaedic engineering responded to Langton's email. This response set the ball rolling and offered a glimmer of hope in their quest for answers.

Tom Joyce is a professor of orthopaedic engineering at the School of Mechanical and Systems Engineering at Newcastle University in the UK, a world where cutting-edge technology meets the critical quest to ensure patient safety. For nearly three decades, Joyce has dedicated his career to the intricate process of designing, testing and analysing artificial joints. His collaborative efforts with others in the field ensure that the medical devices millions of people rely on every day are safe and reliable. In this high-stakes and complex field, detecting even a tiny design flaw can be the difference between a patient walking pain-free or enduring discomfort.

His journey into this crucial yet often overlooked allied area of medical science began during his days as a mechanical engineering student at the University of Leeds. Back then, Joyce was like any other student – searching for a purpose, a spark to ignite his passion. It wasn't until his final year that he stumbled upon the subject that would change everything: tribology.

'It was the first subject in engineering that really clicked with me – I immediately loved it,' he remembers, his eyes lighting up with the enthusiasm of that younger self.

Intrigued by how these principles could be applied to real-world problems, Joyce pursued a master's degree in tribology, immersing himself in the science of surfaces and movement. While the discipline seemed niche at first glance, it was crucial for the safe and effective function of artificial joints and other medical devices. After completing his master's, Joyce took a job in the industry, hoping to make a tangible impact. However, he soon found himself frustrated, questioning the direction of his career.

'I got fed up with it. I kept wondering what I was doing with my life. So I went on to pursue a PhD in bioengineering,' he explains.

That decision marked a turning point, propelling Joyce into the specialized world of medical device testing. Here, every day brought new challenges – ensuring that artificial hips, knees and other implants could withstand the daily grind of human life. In this field, patient safety is paramount, and Joyce's meticulous work helps to prevent the kind of catastrophic failures that can lead to recalls and life-threatening complications. It's a realm where engineering precision directly translates into human well-being, and Joyce has made it his life's mission to bridge the gap between technology and patient care.

His work took a defining turn during his doctoral research, where Joyce focused on artificial finger joints. This was more than a mere academic exercise; it was a deep dive into understanding why some medical devices failed. Joyce meticulously studied artificial joints removed from patients due to failure, gaining invaluable insights.

'For me, the key thing is, always has been and still is: how do you know your results are clinically valid? Clinical validation is generally found from explants. That is why I have always been interested in explants,' Joyce says. This hands-on, evidence-based approach became the cornerstone of his career, cementing his reputation as an expert in scientifically analysing failed medical devices.

In late 2007, Joyce's expertise was put to the test during a wear analysis of failed MoM joints linked to toes. The process required careful attention to detail. This kind of work is not glamorous – hours are spent in labs, examining wear patterns under microscopes, seeking the tiniest clues that could explain a failure. But it is this painstaking work that ensures future patients are spared from the pain of malfunctioning implants.

It was around this time that Joyce's career took an unexpected turn. David Langton reached out to him with concerns about the ASR MoM hip implants, which were already showing troubling signs of failure in patients. Joyce's curiosity was piqued.

'So when David Langton contacted me about the ASR, I was curious. I asked, "Can we have the explanted devices? We can do engineering measurements that give some really good insights." Everything snowballed from there,' Joyce recalls. This simple question sparked a chain of events that would lead to groundbreaking scientific research about the dangers of certain types of MoM implants.

Finally, the team at the University Hospital of North Tees had found a facility to examine the removed ASR devices and determine the cause of their early failure. The doctors partnered with Joyce at Newcastle University, setting the stage for a crucial scientific investigation – piecing together the puzzle of why the ASR implants had failed prematurely.

When Langton arrived with the first few ASR explants, Joyce and his team only had a basic machine at their disposal – one designed to measure surface roughness. It wasn't state-of-the-art, but it was enough to get started. The team gathered around the machine, their faces a mix of curiosity and anxiety, eager to see what they might uncover. The implants, removed from patients' bodies, were carefully placed under the machine's sensor, which began to analyse the texture of their surfaces.

Despite its simplicity, this device could reveal important clues. By quantifying tiny variations in the implant's surface texture, the team could start to understand how well the implants bonded with bone and how much wear they had endured. These measurements could indirectly indicate how long the implants might last inside the body.

'We measured the roughness of these ASRs, and they had roughened up inside the body,' Joyce recalls. 'This was the first evidence that the high levels of metal ions Dave was finding in his patients were due to the rough surfaces. The implants were rubbing together, generating metal debris that was coming off.'

In 2008, the team acquired more sophisticated instruments, adding a new dimension to their scientific scrutiny.

'We got our first coordinate measuring machine [CMM],' Joyce remembers. A CMM functions like a super-precise digital ruler for measuring objects. Imagine a robotic arm with a probe that delicately touches every part of an object to record its exact shape and size. This arm moves with incredible accuracy in three dimensions – up and down, side to side, and forward and backward – capturing a detailed map of the object's surface.

Consider a complex medical implant, like a knee or hip replacement. These implants aren't simple shapes; they have intricate curves and details to fit perfectly within the human body. The CMM can handle these challenging shapes effortlessly, scanning every groove and contour. For failing MoM hip implants, wear is often localized, affecting specific areas while leaving the rest of the implant relatively unworn. By using the CMM for explant analysis, the team could reverse-engineer the original surface, comparing the worn areas to where the surface used to be.

'It's like saying, "It used to be here, now it's there," and we know that this ball must have lost material. We can even determine what size it was when it left the factory,' Langton explains.

However, the process is complex.

'The machine was incredibly sophisticated. It was a brilliant piece of kit that is computer-controlled. But it takes a lot of effort,' Joyce recalls. He highlights that this is where his team's expertise came into play. 'You have to write the program. You have to validate that. That's where cleverness comes in, and it takes time. And that time, you cannot buy off the shelf. You have to develop it,' Joyce says.

In fact, one of his PhD students focused his research on this very topic.

'There was a dedicated PhD candidate working on the program. His entire PhD was about writing this program and understanding how it works. So you can imagine the time and skills involved, and the cost too. But many of us are passionate about this because we saw so many patients suffering,' Joyce emphasizes. As a result of their analysis, the team measured wear for the first time. 'We found that these ASR resurfacings had worn out,' Joyce points out. Within months, they pieced together the puzzle, understanding how the implant's surface was originally intended to fit and how it had changed over time.

The team meticulously pieced together their findings. They worked late into the night, driven by a sense of urgency. They pored over patient records, analysed metal ion levels and compared their results. Every figure was checked, every conclusion cross-referenced with data from other scientific papers. With painstaking effort, they crafted a compelling narrative that pointed to one alarming conclusion: the MoM implants were failing far faster than expected, leaving patients with dangerously high levels of metal ions in their blood.

'We showed the increased failure rates in our papers. In patients whose implants failed, the metal ion levels were through the roof. We argued that these implants were deteriorating much faster than anyone anticipated,' Langton explains.

But as soon as the papers were submitted to scientific journals, the team's excitement quickly turned into frustration.

'All the papers got rejected for eighteen months to two years,' Langton recalls. 'The real problem still stands: you can have your findings, but no one will act on them until they are peer-reviewed and published. And even if your paper is accepted, it can still take up to a year to see it in print.'

Despite their rigorous scientific work, the team found themselves stuck in a disheartening cycle of delays. The mounting frustration was palpable.

'You pour your heart into this research, only to be stonewalled. If you publish the dataset on failures, all you do is risk hurting the profits of manufacturers,' Langton says, shaking his head. 'Everything is aligned with the interests of the manufacturers. You have to proceed with caution.'

Langton likens the situation to a pilot warning of technical problems long before a crash, only for those warnings to be ignored – till disaster strikes.

'It's like the pilot saying, "There's a problem with the aeroplane. Everyone survived, but we should be worried." And the experts respond, "We're not convinced by your report. We'll reject it until the plane actually crashes. Only then will we take you seriously." That's what it felt like dealing with the journals,' Langton says, his frustration evident.

Despite the early setbacks, the team's persistence began to pay off as they gathered more data on implant failures. They decided to take their findings directly to the medical community by presenting them at prestigious scientific forums. This was a significant move because, up until then, their work on early implant failures had largely gone unnoticed. All that changed when they stepped onto the stage. The valuable scientific data they presented captured the attention of top surgeons, sparking immediate interest.

St Andrew's Hall, located in the heart of Norwich, England, is a venue rich in history and grandeur. Known for hosting everything from royal banquets to classical music concerts, the hall attracts jazz, pop and folk artists from around the world during the annual Norfolk and Norwich Festival. However, in February 2008, the hall took on a new role, transforming into a vibrant hub for discussions on cutting-edge orthopaedic techniques and research. It was the venue for the Annual Scientific Meeting organized by the prestigious British Hip Society, drawing top surgeons and medical experts eager to share their latest findings and debate the future of hip surgery.

Weeks before the conference, Langton had discovered that another surgeon from the UK was scheduled to present his findings on the

ASR at the conference. This piqued Langton's curiosity – he wondered if other hospitals were encountering similar early failures of the device. 'So I got on the train and went down to meet this guy,' Langton recounts, who was eager to uncover more.

When Langton met the other surgeon, they were both keen to exchange insights about the ASR.

'First, he asked me what I had found,' Langton recalls. 'I told him the women did terribly and that the metal ion levels were linked to cup inclination.' Just as Langton was about to ask about the surgeon's findings, the conversation took an unexpected turn.

'Could you just go across the hospital, to the bar floor?' the surgeon said with a wide smile. 'Give them my name. You'll get a beer. I'll meet you there in a bit.' Langton followed the instructions.

As he reached the designated spot, Langton was baffled. The bar floor wasn't a bar at all – it was a florist.

'I walked around again. It was a big hospital. I couldn't find the bar floor anywhere,' he recounts. He thought it might have been a prank. In a moment of confusion, he even asked the florist for a beer. The scene took a bizarre turn when the florist, with a knowing look, moved aside two flower pots, retrieved a box and handed Langton a beer.

It wasn't a joke.

'The florist pointed to a lounge downstairs. I went down with my beer. It was a big, beautiful lounge. Completely empty. It had a huge TV on one wall and a leather sofa,' Langton describes. Half an hour later, the surgeon finally appeared, complimenting Langton on his excellent data.

'He comes in and tells me that I had some excellent data on the ASR,' Langton recalls.

Langton assumed the other hospital had similar findings. He was taken aback at what the surgeon said next.

'Don't present the data on the early failures of the ASR at the meeting,' the surgeon advised him.

Confused, Langton pressed for clarification. The surgeon's reply was straightforward but unexpected: 'If I were you, I would stop at Leeds on your way home tomorrow. Go to DePuy and get a consultancy agreement. You could make a few thousand pounds a week for doing nothing. A much easier life. Much more money.'

Langton was stunned. The ease with which the surgeon brushed off the idea of reporting adverse effects of a medical device was chilling.

But things got even murkier. Langton later discovered that this surgeon was among the select few consultants handpicked by the company to investigate implants at the London Implant Retrieval Centre, a facility supposedly dedicated to uncovering the real reasons behind ASR implant failures. The irony was staggering. Surgeons with clear biases, already favouring the company's interests, were being entrusted with so-called objective scientific scrutiny. This left Langton wondering how many other truths were being buried in the name of corporate loyalty.

However, the team from the University Hospital of North Tees, did not get swayed.

Over three days, the grand hall echoed with presentations that highlighted the latest advancements and ongoing challenges in the field. Surgeons discussed case studies, offering candid insights into the complications they encountered in the operating room. Top surgeons took to the podium to present their findings on various topics, ranging from primary hip replacements to updates on MoM implants and the intricacies of hip resurfacing. These presentations were more than just routine updates; they were crucial exchanges that could shape the future of treatment and surgical methods.

Among the many presentations at the conference, all eyes were drawn to the team from the University Hospital of North Tees. They were set to make an important revelation about the early failures of the ASR hip implant, a topic that had long been shrouded in quiet speculation. It appeared surgeons had been underdiagnosing pain in women who had undergone MoM hip resurfacing procedures.

At the annual meeting, the North Tees team chose to confront head-on the industry's reluctance to reveal the troubling truth about ASR. Their research posed a critical question: whether surgeons were systematically underdiagnosing metal ion hypersensitivity in patients with failed hip resurfacing procedures involving the ASR. The team was prepared to present follow-up data on eighty-one women who had experienced the ASR hip resurfacing procedure.

The team presented compelling data: the University Hospital of North Tees had recorded a troubling 7.4 per cent revision rate in patients who underwent the ASR hip resurfacing procedure. What made this study stand out was its focus – it was among the first to include extensive data on women.

They then drew attention to three particularly alarming cases. These patients had reported persistent groin pain and struggled to lift their legs a year after their surgeries, signalling that something was clearly amiss. Blood tests showed no signs of infection, yet when the team aspirated the hip joints, they discovered a curious, milky green-grey fluid – a finding that raised more questions than it answered.

Based on their observations, the team suggested that complications from metal hypersensitivity might be more common than previously thought. This led them to a critical conclusion: older female patients experiencing ongoing pain after ASR resurfacing procedures at other hospitals might be suffering from undiagnosed metal hypersensitivity.

The presentation sparked considerable interest among senior surgeons at the event. Nargol vividly recalls a particular conversation he had at the bar afterwards. A distinguished surgeon from Norwich leaned in, his voice tinged with frustration. He revealed that his hospital, too, was grappling with severe issues related to the ASR implants. Initially, he had suspected that the problems were due to surgical errors rather than flaws in the implants themselves.

'His reasoning was typical,' Nargol recounts. 'He was convinced that his colleagues had not positioned the hips correctly. It was a telling moment – one that illustrated just how deeply embedded these assumptions were in the surgical community, even as the evidence pointed elsewhere.'

Months later, after an exhaustive and painstaking investigation, the team proved beyond a shadow of a doubt that the early failures were not the result of surgical errors but stemmed directly from the flawed design of the ASR.

―

In March 2009, the annual meeting of the British Hip Society brought together leading surgeons, researchers and medical professionals in the bustling city of Manchester. This year, Nargol and his team were set to deliver not one, but three scientific presentations about the ASR implants. By then, Nargol's team wasn't merely speculating anymore – they were convinced they had cracked the mystery behind the alarming failure rates of these implants and were ready to reveal their findings to a room full of their peers, confident that their evidence would finally spark the urgency the issue deserved.

Their first presentation focused on early clinical and radiological results from 214 patients who had undergone ASR hip resurfacing. Radiological results are a great tool to show if the implant is in the right place, if it's coming loose or wearing out, if there's bone loss around it, if there are unusual growths or swelling, or if there are fractures or abnormal reactions in the bone. They were presented data on patients tracked for nearly three-and-a-half years after their ASR hip resurfacing. The follow-up results were clearly undesirable: twelve hips had already been revised, translating to a 5.6 per cent revision rate. As this number echoed through the room, murmurs rippled through the audience.

'This rate,' Nargol's team emphasized, 'is a cause for concern.'

But it wasn't just about numbers. The team directed the audience's attention to five specific cases – five women who had undergone revision surgery. Each case shared a disturbing commonality. The women had experienced relentless, severe pain. Their outcome scores were poor, all pointing to a single culprit: metallosis. The room fell silent as the disturbing data were projected onto the screen, showing the telltale signs of metal wear debris around the implants.

Nargol's voice cut through the silence, clear.

'We believe,' he said, 'that the persistent, undiagnosed pain is due to excessive inflammatory fluid buildup, a reaction to metal particles released from the implant.'

The audience sat riveted. Nargol and his team didn't just bring data to the table – they brought a wake-up call. They also showed the findings from the Australian Orthopaedic Association National Joint Replacement Registry (AOANJRR), which had already flagged the ASR resurfacing as having twice the risk of needing revision surgery compared to other implants.[1]

In their next presentation, they presented a comparison of metal ion levels in patients with ASR implants versus those with BHR implants. This was a game-changing study, as it was the first to examine how the implants of two rival brands performed; especially when it came to the amount of metal ion levels being released into the bloodstream.

The spotlight was on the smaller hip implants, commonly used for women. The team emphasized that these implants performed best when positioned at specific angles – between 35 and 55 degrees. Implants outside this optimal range were deemed poorly placed and were referred to as 'sub-optimally placed small implants'.[2] For poorly positioned BHR implants, chromium levels in the blood were 6.56 micrograms per litre. However, for ASR implants in the same sub-optimal positions, chromium levels shot up to 17.51 micrograms per litre.

But it was the cobalt levels that were truly alarming. For poorly positioned BHR implants, cobalt levels were 5.26 micrograms per litre. In stark contrast, cobalt levels for poorly positioned ASR implants soared to an astonishing 27.90 micrograms per litre. The team's conclusion was clear: ASR implants released far more metal ions into the bloodstream, depending on the size of the implant and its positioning. This wasn't just data; it was a dire warning about the escalating risks posed by these implants.

The team concluded that the ASR resurfacing's release of metal ions was significantly linked to the size of the hip and the three-dimensional orientation of the acetabular component. They had shone a spotlight on the potential dangers lurking in operating rooms across the UK.

The team's scientific work wasn't just acknowledged; it was celebrated at the conference when Langton was honoured with the prestigious McKee Prize for the incisive paper on blood metal ion concentrations after hip resurfacing surgery – a testament to the paper's impact.

'Everyone at the meeting saw it clearly – the ASR was flawed, and the BHR was the superior choice,' Nargol reminisces with a satisfied grin. 'Receiving the award was not just a personal triumph but a unanimous endorsement from the scientific community, affirming that our findings resonated with everyone in that room.'

Receiving an endorsement for their scientific work at the conference was a tremendous validation for Nargol and his team. However, when they had made a deliberate stop before the conference at DePuy's headquarters in Leeds to present the same data to the company, there was no such endorsement. Instead, the company tried to brush it aside, though it was clear they knew a storm was brewing regarding the ASR.

'We showed them the results. I told them, "You should review our presentation before we present it,"' Nargol recalls.

Nargol also vividly remembers two senior engineers, both deeply involved in designing the ASR cups, looking visibly rattled.

'The severity of the situation hit them hard. One engineer, overwhelmed, placed his head in his hands and said, "We're screwed." As we were leaving to catch our train, the other engineer, trying to deflect the tension, sarcastically joked, "I hope your train crashes on the way to the meeting." The gravity of their reaction was unmistakable. They knew our findings spelled serious trouble, and their nervous attempt at humour only highlighted their deep concern.'

That was the beginning of 2009.

During the ASR launch, DePuy made sweeping claims, promoting two unique design features over previous generations of hip implants: one, a sub-hemispherical acetabular component, and two, an optimal clearance between the large-diameter head and the cup. DePuy asserted that this innovative clearance would establish a fluid film interface, dramatically reducing wear rates and enhancing implant durability. In essence, they promised patients a longer-lasting solution and relief.

Yet, by April 2009, Nargol's team was ready to reveal a far different narrative. What had initially been celebrated as groundbreaking design soon revealed itself as deeply flawed. The team's investigation exposed significant issues with the ASR, leading them to challenge the very advantages that DePuy had championed. They submitted their findings to scientific journals, presenting results from the ASR resurfacing in 214 hips with a mean follow-up of forty-three months. The mean age of patients was fifty-six years, and a striking 40 per cent were women.

The Journal of Bone & Joint Surgery (British Volume) received their paper, titled as 'Articular Surface Replacement of the Hip: A Prospective Single-Surgeon Series',[3] in April 2009. After rigorous revisions, it was accepted in August 2009, and by January 2010, just six months before the recall, their peer-reviewed paper – flagging critical design flaws – was published in the leading orthopaedic journal.

The data starkly contradicted DePuy's claims. The revision rate was alarmingly high at 5.6 per cent, and 2.8 per cent of cases showed failures related to metal wear debris. Most critically, the team revealed that the very features touted as design innovations were, in fact, contributing to the implant's failure. The sub-hemispherical acetabular component and the supposed optimal clearance were, in reality, creating issues rather than solving them.

Their paper publicly disclosed that they had stopped using the smaller components – primarily employed in women – due to poor performance. The researchers did not mince words in their conclusion:

'The ASR implant has a lower diametrical clearance and a sub hemispherical acetabular component when compared with other more frequently implanted MoM hip resurfacings. These changes may contribute to the higher failure rate than in other series, compared with other designs. Given our poor results with the small components, we are no longer implanting the smaller size.'

One of DePuy's main design objectives was to avoid edge loading. The idea was simple: if the ASR could ensure that the articulation – the movement of the ball within the socket – occurred only on the smooth articular surface, rather than on the edge, it would minimise wear. But in practice, things were far from perfect. Nargol and his team discovered that the unique sub-hemispherical design, instead of preventing edge loading, might actually encourage it. Edge loading typically occurs when the femoral head presses against the edge of the acetabular cup rather than staying within the smooth, intended zone of contact. This pressure can cause excessive wear, much like a car tyre that rubs against the curb while driving. Over time, this edge friction can lead to the release of tiny metal particles, which could cause inflammation and pain.

'The latest generation of resurfacing devices, such as ASR, have a number of perceived advantages of design,' they wrote, highlighting sub-hemispherical acetabular component and lower clearance between the components. However, they raised a red flag, highlighting that this low clearance 'may actually increase metal wear and the sub hemispherical design could increase edge loading'.

Nargol also vividly recalls raising concerns with DePuy about a crucial aspect of the design: the arc of cover. Imagine your hip as a perfectly coordinated team, with the ball and socket working together in harmony – like a baseball fitting snugly into a well-worn glove. The more of the ball that's covered by the glove, the smoother and more reliable the movements.

Now, picture the ASR MoM hip implant. It was designed differently from its competitors. Instead of ensuring a snug fit, like a glove fully cradling a baseball, the ASR ended up with less coverage. The designers made the glove portion – the cup – in a way that pushed the ball outwards. Nargol says this design flaw, known as a lower arc of cover, left the ASR implant with less coverage on the ball.

A lower arc of cover meant that instead of the ball moving smoothly within the cup, it tends to hit the edges more often. Nargol also recalls that he pointed to DePuy that the arc of cover varied significantly between smaller and larger cups, leaving smaller cups with less coverage. 'We said: look, the smaller the cup, the less its arc of cover. And this is why we were seeing the small cups failing,' Nargol recalls. 'That's the big reason: the arc of cover is smaller in the smallest cups. The smallest cups are typically used in women, which explains why failures were more common in them. The arc of cover was the biggest factor for early failures.'

As mentioned earlier, just months before the recall, the team sounded the alarm in a scientific paper titled as *Early Failure of Metal-on-Metal Bearings in Hip Resurfacing and Large-Diameter Total Hip Replacement* (2010), exposing this critical design flaw.[4]

This research paper offered the first glimpse into nearly three years of intensive work that combined cutting-edge engineering with critical clinical insights. The message was clear: the ASR hip implant, once hailed as a breakthrough in orthopaedic surgery, was failing patients in ways that could no longer be ignored. The evidence presented was not just compelling – it was undeniable.

Since 2007, they had been meticulously analysing explants using state-of-the-art technology that could detect changes smaller than a grain of dust. By measuring the roundness of the implant's components at three different points, they revealed a startling truth: many of these implants were wearing down inside patients' bodies. And this was no minor defect. Implants that should have remained almost perfectly round were showing significant out-of-roundness, a sign of wear.

What did this mean for patients? Imagine a hip implant that grinds away at its own structure with every movement, releasing tiny metal particles into the body. The study showed that implants removed due to adverse reactions to metal debris had much higher out-of-roundness values compared to those removed for other reasons. In simple terms, these implants were wearing out and breaking down at an alarming rate, posing serious risks to patients' health.

The study went on to offer a possible explanation for why the ASR implants were failing – it brought up the design flaw Nargol had pointed out to DePuy. The ASR hip implant, unlike the BHR model, provided less coverage over the femoral head. While the BHR covers 162°, the ASR only covers 151°. This seemingly small difference had huge implications. Less coverage meant that the implant's contact point was dangerously close to the edge, leading to edge loading. The team flagged that this is where most of the wear occurred, causing the implant to shed metal particles into the body, increasing the risk of complications.

'Surgeons must consider implant design … in order to reduce early failures when performing large-bearing metal-on-metal hip resurfacing and replacement,' the team recommended.

Adding to these concerns, Nargol was troubled by another critical design feature: the recessed rim of the acetabular component in the ASR implant, where the edge of the cup was cut back outwards, sloping down and away from the inner edge. This meant the head of the femur played against a sharper edge as it moved around, instead of having a good, solid, flat and even edge that would provide better support.

This design can lead to uneven weight distribution. In an implant, the more the edge comes into play, the more wear we see, leading to early failure. And in ASR, this design feature took away more of the articulating surface that was supposed to facilitate smooth movement. Instead, it led to even more edge loading, increasing the risk of wear.

'Edge loading is the effect of all this,' Nargol concludes.

In 2009, and gaining momentum into 2010, the team made a bold move that changed everything. They reached out to two critical players: the NJR and the UK Medicines and Healthcare products Regulatory Agency (MHRA). These weren't just routine discussions; they were the kind of high-stakes conversations that ignited real change. These interactions sparked a chain reaction, leading the UK to become one of the first countries to issue a medical device alert, sounding the alarm on the early failures of the device. This wasn't just a step forward – it was a giant leap that sent ripples through the entire orthopaedic industry in the UK.

6

Recall and Beyond: Learning from the Crisis

As 2010 approached, Nargol's alarm had reached a fever pitch. The hospital saw a steady increase in patients desperately seeking revisions to remove the failing ASR implants. Their pain and distress were constant, heart-wrenching reminders of the crisis at hand. Every ASR patient who walked through the hospital doors added to the growing urgency.

Each revision case deepened Nargol's fear that many other patients might be unknowingly suffering. The implant's alarmingly high early failure rates were not just a clinical statistic – they were evidence of a crisis unfolding before his eyes, with real lives at stake. Determined to act before it was too late, Nargol reached out to the implant division of the MHRA.

The division head assembled a team and they arrived at the hospital, their demeanour showing it was clearly a serious matter. The room was taut with anticipation as Nargol and Langton began their presentation, which would stretch for nearly two intense hours. Their display was meticulously detailed: patient records, clinical data, striking surgical photographs, blood test results and histology analyses. But the centrepiece was Dave Langton's revealing explant analysis of the ASR, laid out with a sense of urgency.

The MHRA team listened with rapt attention. Each piece of data added to the mounting gravity, and the room's atmosphere grew heavier with the realization of the implications. Questions flew thick and fast, probing every detail, but the evidence was irrefutable.

'There was no argument,' Nargol recounts. 'At the end of the presentation, the head of the implant division stood up, visibly shaken, and said, "Oh my God! We have a problem."'

This dramatic reaction marked a turning point, compelling the MHRA to take decisive action. They did not waste time. The agency quickly invited Nargol and Langton to London for a critical presentation before its advisory group of top consultant surgeons. The room was filled with the most prestigious names in orthopaedics: the president of the British Hip Society, the head of the London Implant Retrieval Centre and other leading experts. As Nargol and Langton presented their findings once again, the tension in the room was palpable. Every surgeon present understood the magnitude of the crisis, their seriousness underscored by the hushed intensity of the meeting.

The next day, Nargol's phone rang incessantly. The British Hip Society and the NJR were calling, astonished.

'They told us they hadn't seen this problem before,' Nargol recalls. 'It was our alert that finally brought the issue to light.'

However, the troubles weren't confined to the University Hospital of North Tees.

By the summer of 2010, Nargol began to hear about distressing patterns unfolding in other hospitals. He says the MHRA began raising alarms about problems with the ASR implants in the UK to the company. Another major centre, Norfolk and Norwich University Hospital, reported similar issues, revealing that two prominent hospitals were now documenting alarming early failures of the ASR.

The situation had first become apparent in 2008 at the Annual Scientific Meeting of the British Hip Society. A leading surgeon had disclosed troubling early failures at Norwich, raising concerns among his peers. Initially, the surgeon speculated that the problems were related to surgical technique rather than the implants themselves. However, as reports accumulated, it became clear that the issue was far more systemic.

By 2010, the alarm bells grew louder. Surgeons from Norfolk and Norwich University Hospital travelled to Sheffield to present their findings at the Annual Scientific Meeting. Their presentation was a revelation – the ASR XL was exhibiting shockingly high early failure rates. Nargol vividly recalls texting the company in distress: 'I've just come out of a BHS gathering, and Norfolk has presented even worse results than our hospital. That's two major centres now with a problem.'

In Cardiff, the situation was equally dire, Nargol recalls. He described the growing crisis as catastrophic:

'It was disastrous. Three centres in the UK were now reporting severe problems. This was no longer a minor issue – it was a full-blown crisis. By early 2010, the alarm was spreading far and wide.'

The mounting concerns were sharply at odds with DePuy's dismissive stance. The company insisted that only Nargol faced issues with the ASR, attributing the failures to localized factors such as water quality, patient genetics or surgical technique. Their explanations seemed increasingly inadequate as evidence of widespread problems surfaced.

Around this time, Nargol received a valuable tip to contact a renowned Irish surgeon – a high-volume practitioner closely associated with the company and a close friend of one of the ASR's chief engineers. During their phone conversation, the Irish surgeon revealed that he too had encountered severe problems with the ASR. His patients were suffering from persistent groin pain, forcing him to abandon the implant in 2007. Nargol was shocked to learn that this Irish surgeon had been among the first prominent doctors to cease using the ASR due to patient suffering.

'He stopped early because his patients were experiencing debilitating pain. I reported similar issues, but he didn't have any answers either,' Nargol recounts.

Nargol says the company had misleadingly assured the Irish surgeon that he was an isolated case.

'I was also told I was the only surgeon facing these issues,' Nargol says. 'Yet, as we dug deeper, we discovered other troubled centres: Northern Ireland, northeast England, Norfolk, southeast England and even Australia.'

With complaints pouring in from various corners of the UK, the situation had escalated to a critical level. It became evident that action from the regulatory bodies was imminent. On 22 April 2010, the MHRA issued a medical device alert, acknowledging the widespread and serious issues surrounding the ASR implants, marking an important milestone in the crisis.

At exactly 2.00 p.m. on 22 April 2010, the MHRA issued a medical device alert regarding MoM hip replacements. The alert zeroed in on four key aspects: the nature of the problem, the actions that needed to be taken, the stakeholders responsible for those actions and the strict deadline for compliance.

The alert highlighted reports of MoM hip replacements needing revisions due to soft tissue reactions. 'These reactions may be associated with unexplained hip pain,' the alert said. At the same time, the MHRA was quick to reassure that most patients with MoM hip replacements had well-functioning hips and were considered at low risk for serious complications. This balanced message would prevent needless alarm, acknowledging that, while many MoM hip replacements had been successful, there were still issues that warranted attention.

The alert then addressed the specific problem in detail. It warned that a small number of patients might experience ongoing damage to the soft tissues around the hip joint due to tiny metal particles breaking off from the implant. This debris could cause the surrounding muscle and tissue to die, making future surgeries more difficult and less likely to succeed. The MHRA emphasized that catching these issues early and opting for a timely revision surgery would significantly improve the chances of a successful outcome. In other words, the sooner a faulty hip is replaced, the better the results, reducing the risk of long-term damage and giving patients a better shot at recovery.

The regulator clarified that it was issuing this interim advice to healthcare professionals after extensive consultation with orthopaedic experts and analysis of data from the NJR for England and Wales. This backing by expert advice and scientific evidence lent significant weight to the alert.

Then came the action steps, the most critical part of the alert. Doctors were instructed to follow up with patients at least once a year for the first five years after their surgery and more frequently if patients showed any symptoms. The alert also advised doctors to investigate patients with painful MoM hip replacements using specific tests, including checking levels of cobalt and chromium in the blood, along with imaging techniques like MRI or ultrasound scans to get a detailed view of the hip joint.

Doctors were particularly urged to conduct these tests and scans on four specific groups of patients: those showing warning signs on

X-rays; those with smaller hip components, which often included women; patients who had concerns about the implant or patients of surgeons who were concerned; and groups of patients experiencing higher than expected failure rates of their MoM hips.

Most importantly, the alert highlighted a critical number: if cobalt or chromium levels in the blood exceeded seven parts per billion (ppb), a second test should be conducted three months later to determine if the patient needed closer monitoring. The alert concluded that if these scans detected any abnormal soft tissue reactions, fluid build-ups or tissue masses, then doctors should seriously consider revision surgery to replace the implant.

In simpler terms, if the tests showed high or rising metal levels in the blood, or if scans revealed damage around the hip, it was a sign that the implant might be causing harm and needed to be replaced sooner rather than later. This early action could prevent more serious problems down the line and give patients a better chance at a full recovery.

The recommendations were strikingly similar to what Nargol was already doing at his hospital, especially for patients with smaller ASR component sizes.

'So we helped the MHRA, and they came out with solid guidance. But even then, a lot of people were never recalled,' Nargol says, his frustration evident.

There was something intriguing about the MHRA's first medical device alert, Nargol remembers. The regulator had issued a detailed alert, highlighting the mounting problems with the ASR implants. Yet, strangely, it didn't name the ASR specifically. Instead, the MHRA took a broad approach, saying the alert was related to 'all' MoM hip replacements. For Nargol, this felt like a missed opportunity, a half-measure that diluted the urgency of the situation.

A year or two later, the pieces started to fall into place. Nargol remembers a conversation with a senior doctor who advises the MHRA. The doctor pulled him aside, away from the bustling hospital corridors, and explained why the ASR had not been named in the first alert. Nargol recounts what the doctor said:

'Antoni, after you raised the alarm, the MHRA found themselves in a tough spot. They wanted to warn everyone that DePuy's MoM ASR hip implant was causing problems. But if DePuy decided to sue the MHRA, they were advised that they wouldn't be covered – no indemnity. They didn't know what to do. So, they opted for a generic warning, avoiding any mention of DePuy's ASR.'

Nargol could hardly believe what he was hearing. It all made sense now – the vague language, the reluctance to call out the ASR by name. But change was on the horizon. Just months after the first alert, a new government came into power.

'The new government provided the MHRA with the indemnity they needed. They had the backing now,' Nargol says, relief in his voice. 'So the MHRA finally updated the alert and explicitly named DePuy and the ASR.'

On 25 May 2010, the MHRA issued another alert that directly named the ASR hip replacement cups. This was a red flag that couldn't be ignored. The alert included compelling evidence from the NJR.[1] According to the NJR's data, the ASR cups were failing at alarmingly high rates, requiring more patients to undergo painful revision surgeries than initially expected.

The MHRA put out NJR data of 2,769 hip replacements using ASR cups with surface replacement heads, performed between 1 April 2001 and 31 March 2010. Normally, for a device like this, it said, the NJR predicted around 80 out of 2,769 patients might need revision surgery to fix issues. However, the actual number was much higher: 130 patients had already needed revision surgery.

The alert also highlighted problems with larger femoral heads. In the same time frame, 3,155 hip replacements using DePuy ASR acetabular cups with extra-large femoral heads were reported to the NJR. The expected number of revision surgeries was 85, but the real figure was 126.

Up until this point, the concerns raised by orthopaedic surgeon Nargol and his team about the ASR's high failure rate had mostly been discussed behind closed doors, among experts and in scientific forums. Now, the MHRA made it clear that their concerns were valid. Without naming specific hospitals, the agency admitted that 2 of the 257 clinics in the UK using ASR devices had reported similar high failure rates. This was the first time the MHRA explicitly acknowledged the issues raised by Nargol, Langton and the University Hospital of North Tees.

This public disclosure was a significant development. It signalled that the problems with the ASR devices were not just isolated incidents but part of a broader issue that could no longer be swept under the rug. Patients and doctors alike had every reason to be worried. The data was now out in the open, and the implications were clear: the ASR hip replacements were more prone to failure than anyone had previously acknowledged, putting several patients at risk.

In this alert, the regulator uncovered a crucial issue: a mismatch between two key instruction documents for the ASR hip implants. The confusion centred around the recommended cup inclination angle for implantation. According to the surgical technique manual and the instructions for use (IFU) supplied with the device, a cup inclination angle of 45° was suggested. But the MHRA pointed out that the original IFU did not specify any cup placement angles at all.

Here's where it gets interesting: 'Based on post-market experience, in October 2008, the manufacturer added to their IFU (Revision C) a recommended cup inclination angle of between 40° and 45° and distributed a document entitled "The importance of correct acetabular component positioning", highlighting the importance of cup angles to implanting surgeons from February 2009,' the alert noted. This was the same time that Nargol was flagging issues with the implant, while the company dismissed his concerns, claiming, 'It's not us; it's your surgical technique.'

Almost a month before the MHRA's first medical device alert, DePuy sent out an urgent field safety notice (FSN) to surgeons using the ASR Hip Systems. This notice was the company's first attempt to mention any concerns about the ASR to surgeons. However, it missed a crucial point: it did not ask surgeons to check for high levels of cobalt and chromium in the blood of ASR patients. Instead, the FSN merely instructed surgeons to implant the devices at a specific angle, saying, 'Ensure the cups are implanted with an inclination of between 40 to 45 degrees.'[2]

The second MHRA alert took a closer look at this FSN, highlighting that it focused only on 'correct cup angles'. The alert raised two important concerns. First, the FSN didn't recommend any follow-up for patients without symptoms, potentially leaving issues unnoticed. Second, it was unclear how devices implanted outside the recommended angle range (40°–45°) would perform, since no data was available.

The MHRA alert made two key recommendations. One, for ASR patients who showed symptoms or had cups implanted at angles greater than 45° – especially those with smaller components – surgeons should consider checking metal ion levels in their blood and/or performing imaging tests like MRI or ultrasound scans. If metal ion levels exceed 120 nmol/L (nanomoles per litre) for cobalt or 135 nmol/L for chromium, which translates to seven parts per billion, a second test should be done three months later to monitor any issues. If the imaging revealed problems such as soft tissue reactions or fluid collections, revision surgery might be necessary.

Two, for new patients, the alert advised surgeons to adhere to the manufacturer's most recent IFU and surgical technique, ensuring that the cup inclination angle remained between 40° and 45°.

The company's tactic of deflecting blame onto the surgeons and their surgical techniques was now glaringly apparent. Nargol, a seasoned expert in complex hip replacements, underscores a harsh truth: even the most skilled surgeons cannot consistently hit that exact 40° to 45° mark. It's an impossibility, no matter how precise they are.

He vividly recalls another important event. Just a day before these changes were announced, Nargol was in the US, presenting at the prestigious American Academy of Orthopaedic Surgeons. His presentation starkly revealed the ASR's poor performance in patients. With a mix of frustration and irony, he projected an image depicting the exact placement surgeons were instructed to aim for.

'That's the tiny spot you have to hit,' he told the audience. The reaction was a wave of laughter. 'The implant had been in the market for almost six years, and now they suddenly tell us, "Oh, you have to put it in that tiny space,"' Nargol said.

Above all, the alert from the MHRA set a crucial deadline: by 25 August 2010, every UK hospital needed to have a system in place for the follow-up of ASR patients. The clock was ticking. Once these systems were in place, surgeons and administrators were expected to rush to contact patients, notifying them that their hip implants might be causing serious issues. Clinics would then buzz with activity – medical teams scrambling to perform tests and check for abnormal levels of metal ions in patients' bloodstreams.

The data in the alert painted a grim picture. There were far more unexpected revision surgeries than the NJR data had previously shown.

Recall and Beyond: Learning from the Crisis

As more patients were systematically tracked, it was anticipated that these numbers would climb higher, adding to the mounting sense of catastrophe.

Back at company headquarters, executives could feel the heat intensifying. The news spread quickly. In a desperate move to manage the fallout, the company issued another urgent FSN just twenty-four hours before the MHRA's deadline for hospitals. But it was clear that more drastic action was needed. With regulatory scrutiny tightening, the company finally made the inevitable decision: it announced a voluntary global recall of all ASR products, hoping to contain the storm.

Following the global recall of the ASR hip implants, the University Hospital of North Tees became a lifeline for hundreds of ASR patients. People from different parts of the globe walked into the hospital, seeking the specialized care of Nargol and his team, whose reputation for expertise had spread far and wide.

To meet this urgent need, the hospital set up a specialized screening and treatment programme that was second to none. This initiative wasn't limited to patients treated at North Tees; it extended a helping hand to anyone affected by the ASR implants, regardless of where their original surgery had been performed. The team employed advanced tests to meticulously examine the joint and the surrounding tissues, ensuring no detail was overlooked. They also screened for elevated metal ion levels in the blood – critical indicators of implant failure.

They developed internal protocols for precise monitoring, charting a new course in early detection and intervention. Through these screenings, the team could pinpoint exactly which patients needed immediate medical attention. Nargol noted from his vast experience that if a patient had a fully functioning metal hip, the cobalt levels would usually be up to two parts per billion (ppb).

'However, if it is above two, it likely indicates the metal implant is wearing a bit too much. When it reaches four, we know there's a problem. If it gets up to ten, it's a serious issue,' Nargol explains.

He emphasizes that the real danger lay in the damage to the surrounding hip tissue, a consequence of high metal ion levels.

'In our hospital, if the cobalt level is above 4 ppb, we immediately send patients for a detailed scan. Four is our threshold,' Nargol says. When cobalt levels skyrocketed to 50 ppb, the risks of cobalt poisoning became undeniable.

'Scientific evidence shows that poisoning can start at 50 ppb, but I've seen it happen even at 25 ppb,' Nargol warns. This is why whenever he encountered patients with cobalt levels of over 25 ppb, he sounded the alarm.

'If a patient's level is above 25, there's a very real risk of damage to the heart, thyroid or brain. At 25 and above, we don't take chances – we remove the implant, even if the patient shows no symptoms of pain or hip problems.' The severity of the situation was underscored by cases where Nargol had seen cobalt levels soar to an astonishing 250 ppb, a figure that seemed almost surreal.

It was in this aspect of their work that Nargol and his team truly began to shine. The numbers were staggering: Nargol and his team alone conducted over 500 complex revision surgeries at the hospital, many involving the ASR and other MoM hip implant models. With each patient they operated, their understanding deepened, revealing a more complex and disturbing picture of how these metal implants affected the human body. And the insights he gained from inside the operation, while conducting the complex revision surgery theatre, were revealing.

Revision surgery of the hip is a long, complex process, a tightrope walk where one wrong move can lead to severe health problems. Every moment in the operating room demands precision, as surgeons work to save as much healthy bone as they can. But when Nargol started operating on patients with the ASR, a MoM hip implant, he realized that this wasn't the same as the typical hip revisions he was used to. 'You see, most hip replacements use a metal head and a plastic cup,' he said. 'Normally, when plastic particles wear off, macrophages – these white blood cells that act like the body's cleanup crew – react and damage the bone, and you start seeing holes in the bone. You know what to expect.'

Recall and Beyond: Learning from the Crisis

With conventional metal-on-plastic implants, Nargol had a predictable routine. When these implants failed, the solution was straightforward: a bit of bone grafting to fill in the damaged areas, much like fixing a crack in the wall.

'I would tell patients, "Your hip is wearing out. See how it's getting close to the bone?" We could both see the problem clearly,' Nargol recalls. The solution was simple, the path forward obvious.

But the ASR revisions were a different beast entirely. The failure of these implants introduced Nargol to a new kind of challenge.

'But the metal from the ASR implants didn't trigger the macrophages like plastic does. Instead, it set off the lymphocytes, another type of white blood cell, and the results were devastating.'

What Nargol found inside patients' bodies was more like a horror show than a surgical routine. Instead of finding eroded bone, he often saw muscles that had literally turned to mush, as if they'd been eaten away from the inside out. 'With a regular hip replacement, if there's a hole in the bone, you just fill it in with a bone graft,' Nargol said. 'But when a metal implant fails and the muscles are gone, there's nothing you can do. You can't just regrow muscle.'

This reality made the ASR revision surgeries incredibly complicated and far more painful for patients. Many were left with permanent damage, limping through the rest of their lives with muscles that could never be fully repaired.

'For us surgeons, it was like venturing into unknown territory,' Nargol admits. 'You open up a patient, see the hip and realize you've never seen anything like it before. It's terrifying. You're left wondering what you can possibly do to help.'

The situation was so severe that the UK's medical regulators stepped in, understanding that only highly experienced surgeons should handle these cases.

'That's why the MHRA recommended that only surgeons experienced in metal hip revisions take on these surgeries,' Nargol said. 'The stakes are just too high for anything less.'

There was another challenge that haunted Nargol during the ASR revision surgeries: breaking the news to his patients about the true state of their hips and preparing them for the reality that they might not feel much better after surgery. But what set the ASR patients apart from others was the strange fact that many of them hardly felt any pain, even though their bodies were being poisoned by extremely high levels of metal ions leaking into their blood from the failed implants. This was both alarming and puzzling.

Nargol, following conventional wisdom, expected that the patients with the most tissue damage would also be the ones experiencing the most pain. That's usually how it worked with other implants. But in the case of ASR, things were different.

'We found that quite a few patients had very little pain but severe tissue damage,' Nargol says, the disbelief he felt still evident. 'So, if you waited until the patient complained of a lot of pain, it was already too late. The damage had been done.'

Some of Nargol's patients, who came in feeling almost normal, had blood tests that told a different story. Their metal ion levels were through the roof.

'This was the worst,' Nargol recalled. 'I'd see patients who didn't have much pain, but their cobalt levels were fifty times higher than normal. In those cases, you're not just taking out the implant because it's failing – you're doing it to prevent cobalt poisoning.'

Nargol vividly remembers one case that left him appalled. He treated a seemingly healthy middle-aged man who had metal ions in his blood a hundred times above the normal amount.

'I said to the man, "You need to take your hip out," Nargol recounted. 'He looked at me, confused, and said, "Why? I can walk miles. I have no pain."'

But Nargol insisted, knowing the danger lurking beneath the surface. When they opened him up for surgery, what they found was shocking. 'His pelvis looked like metal,' Nargol said, shaking his head at the memory. 'It was all grey, as if someone had poured molten steel inside him. It was horrendous.'

But convincing these patients to undergo painful revision surgeries was a whole other battle. Many were mentally unprepared for what was coming. They didn't understand why they needed to go through such an ordeal when they weren't feeling much pain.

'Telling a patient they need major surgery because their cobalt levels are too high is a very difficult conversation to have,' Nargol admits. 'Many didn't want to get their hips changed, especially when they felt fine. But the truth was, their bodies were being silently poisoned.'

Another significant revelation came when Nargol and his team realized that traditional diagnostic tools, like X-rays, were almost useless in identifying which patients needed urgent medical intervention.

'Orthopaedic surgeons used to rely on X-rays to tell us if something was wrong,' Nargol explains. 'But now, if you wait for an X-ray to show a problem, it's already too late. That was a hard lesson for many orthopaedic surgeons to learn. You have to use more advanced scans and blood tests – those are far more reliable than looking at X-rays or asking patients if they're in pain. We quickly realized that we had to act sooner than we used to think. Operating earlier helps to lessen the damage.'

This shift in approach was crucial. Nargol and his team learned to read the signs that weren't immediately visible. They had to trust the silent alarms – the abnormal blood tests, the scans that showed tiny changes invisible to the naked eye. These methods became their new compass, guiding them to make decisions that could prevent catastrophic damage before it happened. As a result, the team's contributions to addressing the issue of failed MoM implants have been immense.

Nargol's unit was made the national lead on research into causes and management of these surgical failures. The specialized unit continues to provide screening, monitoring and revision surgeries to patients with MoM implants. However, the lessons learned during this fiasco extended beyond clinical practice. Their interactions with patient groups exposed glaring loopholes in medical device regulations – issues that needed urgent attention.

An important parliamentary committee, alarmed by the scale of the issue, extended an invitation to Joyce, a close collaborator of Nargol who had worked tirelessly on the explant analysis. The committee needed answers, and Joyce was there to provide them.

And his deposition was telling.

In 2010, the medical device industry was rocked by a double whammy of scandals. The first shock came from the recall of the ASR hip implants. Almost simultaneously, another scandal erupted involving breast implants manufactured by the French company Poly Implant Prothèse (PIP). These implants, used in a staggering 47,000 women across Britain, were found to be filled with unapproved silicone gel – cheap, industrial-grade materials that had no place inside the human body.³ As these stories made headlines, panic spread among thousands of patients. Once again, these high-profile medical device recalls exposed glaring flaws in the regulation of medical implants, raising urgent questions about the processes that had allowed these faulty products to flood the market.

The aftershocks of these scandals were still being felt.

In response to the growing patient outcry, the Science and Technology Committee of the UK's House of Commons took up the matter in 2012. They examined whether the UK's existing laws on the safety and efficacy of medical implants were rigorous enough to protect patients. The committee also scrutinized the functioning of regulatory bodies, asking tough questions about how these organizations could have missed the red flags. Finally, they sought expert advice on how to tighten regulations and prevent future disasters.

Over two evidence sessions, the committee heard from four specialist panels. There was significant convergence in the use of cutting-edge technology in the medical device manufacturing industry, with engineering playing a vital role, especially in orthopaedics. Tom Joyce, a leading engineering expert from Newcastle University, had meticulously studied failed MoM hips, including the ASR. His groundbreaking research made him one of the top experts summoned to share his insights.

On 23 May 2012, Joyce took the floor. He described how, time and again, he had seen MoM hips, including the ASR, fail inside patients, despite being cleared by regulatory authorities. These implants, Joyce pointed out, had been marked and checked, '…but when it comes to pass, they have failed a massive amount,' he told the committee.⁴

Joyce zeroed in on the ASR scandal, making it clear that the problems could have been avoided.

'That could have been identified through pre-market testing,' he told the committee. His words were a call to arms, underlining the critical importance of testing implants before they ever reach patients. 'They had the machines and the equipment, and those tests could have been done,' he emphasized.

But pre-market testing alone, Joyce cautioned, was not enough. It wasn't just about conducting tests; it was about ensuring that the data from these tests were subjected to independent scrutiny.

'We need an independent centre examining them,' he insisted, 'and sharing that information, saying, "We think there is a problem here."'

Joyce says that the key recommendation to the committee on independent pre-market testing of implants was drawn from lessons learned from the ASR.

'I attended numerous orthopaedic conferences. Surgeons affiliated with the company repeatedly claimed that the ASR was the most tested hip implant in history. My response was always the same: *It might be the most tested hip ever, but where is the data?* They've never shared it.'

Despite the recall and widespread concerns about the ASR's performance, Joyce points out that its pre-marketing test data is still shrouded in secrecy.

'This was true back in 2003, and it was still true in 2012 when I addressed the select committee. Even now, trying to get hold of that data is like chasing shadows.'

Joyce stresses that manufacturers treat this critical data related to patient safety as if it were a state secret, arguing that disclosure could hurt their commercial interests.

'The rules conveniently classify pre-market testing data as "commercial in confidence", meaning it can't be shared. This creates a significant barrier. The company may conduct all the tests in the world, even adhering to international standards. But when it comes to revealing the results, they lock them away.'

While Joyce acknowledges the need for post-marketing surveillance, he voices concerns that even with new legislation for medical devices and increased emphasis on post-market checks, pre-market testing still isn't getting the attention it deserves.

'Once an implant is inside a patient, it's like setting a ship to sea – what's done is done. The real opportunity to prevent harm is *before* that, during pre-market testing. It's about conducting robust tests with advanced equipment and making those results publicly available. That way, independent experts can scrutinize the data and flag any potential red flags. Pre-market testing is a crucial piece of the puzzle.'

Joyce is convinced that the gaps in pre-market testing aren't due to a lack of technology.

'The first hip simulator was built in the UK in 1966. Over the years, these simulators have become more sophisticated.' He points out that companies can now test multiple hips – five, six, even twelve – simultaneously. 'These advanced machines are widely available, developed by commercial companies. So, when it comes to testing capabilities, there's no shortage of technological advancement.'

He notes that robust international standards were in place during the ASR's development.

'We have the necessary machinery, established international standards and access to skilled engineers. DePuy employs hundreds of talented engineers. So all the building blocks are there.'

In fact, Joyce emphasizes that hip simulators typically do a good job of mimicking real-life conditions.

'We tested metal-on-poly hips for years in these simulators, and the results were generally applicable,' he says, recalling hours spent in the lab with these high-tech machines. However, he acknowledges the unpredictable nature of human behaviour. 'People aren't robots,' he admits. 'One patient might spend most of their day on the couch, binge-watching TV, while another might be out jogging at the crack of dawn. The activity levels between people can vary drastically, and then there are different body weights to consider too.'

This variability is why Joyce insists that assumptions must be made before testing new hips in the simulators. These assumptions are grounded in international standards.

'Most people take about a million steps a year,' he explains, 'but many do closer to two million. I probably clock in around four million steps annually.' He smiles, thinking of his own routine of morning walks. 'So, there's quite a range, but on average, hip simulators work. They give us a valuable insight into how these implants will perform.'

So why did ASR hips fail despite having sophisticated stimulator tests? Joyce has the answer: the company failed to test a wide range of ASR cup sizes before introducing them into the market.

Before the committee, he made two crucial recommendations. First, international standards must require testing acetabular cups at various angles of inclination before they ever reach the market. Second, these standards should mandate that manufacturers test both the smallest and largest sizes of cups in artificial hips. Had such pre-clinical tests been undertaken on the ASR, the current disaster might have been averted, he told the committee.

At the same time, Joyce highlighted another critical concern: the integrity of the testing process.

'We must ensure these tests are conducted independently, free from any influence or manipulation,' he insists.

Joyce had good reasons for making these recommendations, reasons rooted in the murky history of the ASR's launch. He had seen firsthand how the marketing of the ASR had been built on misleading claims and half-truths. Around 2000–2004, hip resurfacing had signalled a shift in the orthopaedic industry, promising a new era of improved patient outcomes.

'This was a pivotal moment in hip joint replacement,' Joyce explains. 'In the early 2000s, the BHR [Birmingham Hip Resurfacing system] was hailed as the future. Metal-on-metal technology was supposed to eliminate the wear and tear seen in traditional metal-on-plastic hips.'

He then emphasizes:

'ASR resurfacing was rushed to market, not because it was ready, but to compete with the BHR. When companies are more focused on beating their rivals than on patient safety, we have to question the credibility of their testing data.'

Joyce vividly recalls how during the ASR's launch, DePuy, eager to make a splash in the market, had brandished publications showing vials filled with ominous dark particles. This, they claimed, was metal debris allegedly from BHR hips. The image was meant to stir fear, to cast doubt on their competitor's product. But it was all a mere façade. In reality, long-term clinical data painted a very different picture. 'So, we have the machines. But is that testing truly independent? Because beneath the surface lies a fierce battle for market dominance. These companies are locked in a high-stakes game, and sometimes, patient safety is the price.'

Joyce and his team were like medical detectives on a mission – the only independent researchers in the UK, and perhaps even the world, who thoroughly investigated the mystery of the failed ASR hip implants. They didn't rely on guesses; they conducted an extensive explant analysis, carefully examining the defective implants. What set them apart was their willingness to publish critical, evidence-backed data on the ASR even before the product was recalled in August 2010. At that time, they had something others didn't: access to the explants, the discarded implants that held the key to understanding why these devices were failing.

Joyce knew the power of these explants.

'Think of a plane crash,' he explains. 'Investigators look for the black box to determine what went wrong. The explants are the black box for these hip implants. They reveal exactly how and why the implant failed. Without them, people can make any claim or excuse they want. But explants provide definitive proof.' Thus, Joyce emphasized to the committee the 'value of keeping explanted joints'.

Joyce feels fortunate to collaborate with Nargol and his team, who already had a collection of explants.

'We started running our tests, and the insights were eye-opening,' Joyce says. 'But obtaining these explants isn't easy.' He highlighted a critical problem to the committee – some surgeons and hospitals were discarding these valuable pieces of evidence, even when patients requested them to be preserved. 'Nine times out of ten, they end up in the clinical waste bin. Destroyed. That's just wrong – completely wrong.'

This raises another crucial issue: Is clinical data always necessary for analyzing explants? Ideally, yes, Joyce admits. That was how he started researching the MoM hip joints – after Langton reached out to him when his clinical data on the ASR revealed a problem with the implants. Matching the clinical data with implant analysis – at least at the start of research – helps connect cause and effect, and set benchmarks. However, he argues that even with minimal clinical data, skilled experts can still uncover important information about why an implant failed, vis-à-vis the critical engineering aspect.

'I often hear, "Sure, this explant analysis is interesting, but you need clinical data to back it up." In an ideal world, you'd have both. But if you have to choose between nothing and just the explant, I'd choose the explant every time. It still provides valuable insights.' Joyce believes that extensive data or complete clinical records aren't always required to understand explant analysis. 'You can still uncover key truths with what you have. What we need are quality explants and skilled, independent engineers. It's challenging work. It requires time, effort and funding. But it's worth it.'

Above all, Joyce wants to clarify that their research isn't about attacking specific companies or brands. 'If an implant works exceptionally well, that's fantastic. We should celebrate and share what makes it successful. This isn't about assigning blame. The goal is to improve medical devices for patients. It's about understanding what works in the human body, and what doesn't. That's the information we need to share.'

Even DePuy, the manufacturer of the ASR, had access to explants collected with patients' consent after revision surgeries. These were sent for analysis to determine why their implants were failing, but the findings remain largely undisclosed.

Before the committee, Joyce made another crucial recommendation: explant analysis should be conducted by independent, not-for-profit experts.

'Currently, explants are sent to the company, and they perform the analysis. But we need to consider what happens to that information. Companies are inherently biased. I'm not suggesting they are dishonest, but they are in the business of making and selling products. It's natural for them to want to defend their product,' Joyce explains. He supports a system where companies subcontract independent retrieval centres to conduct explant analysis.

'We need to ask ourselves: Who controls the science? Independence is essential for ensuring honest, unbiased scientific reviews.'

Joyce made another important recommendation: to make conservation and analysis of explants mandatory. That hasn't happened. However, an equally pressing question remains: how to fund this crucial explant analysis? Joyce reflects on the debate.

'Some argue that it's too expensive and not worth the cost. But remember the metal-on-metal hip disaster? We don't know what might happen in the future.' Penny-pinching today can have huge costs tomorrow.

Joyce vividly recalls a conversation from the 1990s with a senior surgeon who outright dismissed the need for wear tests on MoM hips. Almost a decade later, those implants failed catastrophically. Joyce remembers the conversation:

'When I was a PhD student, he told me, "Why are you doing wear tests, Tom? There's no issue here. We have metal-on-metal hips that don't wear down." Many shared that belief at the time. Unfortunately, he was wrong.'

Imagine an ideal scenario where Joyce had access to the faulty ASR explants when the very first failures were reported: he could have delved into them like a detective piecing together a mystery – carefully examining the implants, uncovering tiny clues that pointed to a design flaw. With a thorough explant analysis, he could have sounded the alarm early, backed by solid data proving the device had a serious problem. This is the kind of game-changing insight explant analysis provides, especially when hip implants hit the market with little to no pre-clinical testing.

This experience is why Joyce insists on the importance of mandatory explant analysis. Without pre-test clinical data on implants, we risk another disaster. 'Even with newer devices, which we hope are better, how can we be sure? We don't have access to pre-test [simulator test] data. Thousands of these implants are being used right now. We're left waiting and hoping everything will turn out fine, but the truth is, we just don't know.'

The most important part of Joyce's deposition before the committee was his focus on patients' experiences. At the time, the MHRA managed an online reporting system known as the Yellow Card Scheme, designed for tracking adverse incidents with medical devices. This system allowed users to report side effects directly to the MHRA, although it was primarily used for reporting adverse drug reactions back then.

Joyce's testimony was particularly striking as he highlighted a troubling pattern: patients repeatedly reported that their concerns about symptoms from their hip implants were often dismissed or ignored by medical professionals. 'We believe that the Yellow Card System, whereby a user of medication can report side effects directly to the MHRA, could be usefully expanded to include users of medical devices,' it was suggested. He raised this point during a discussion on the importance of effective post-market surveillance, stressing that both patients and clinicians need to report problems as soon as they occur.

Despite the existence of this system, Joyce revealed a sobering reality: many patients and even some surgeons in the UK were unaware of it.

'It's a great concept,' he said, 'where you can report issues online directly to the MHRA. But in practice, most patients have never heard of it. They know there's a regulator, but they're oblivious to the reporting system.'

Joyce also underscored a related problem: the overwhelming positive marketing that surrounded hip replacements. He recalls how a 2007 scientific paper hailed them as the 'operation of the century'.

'Metal-on-metal hips were marketed as the cutting-edge solution, with no hint of potential failure,' Joyce notes. 'But as with any technology, things can go wrong.'

This overly optimistic marketing created a false sense of security. When patients started experiencing various health-related problems, they often first visited their general practitioners. Joyce described a common scenario:

'Patients might think, 'Maybe it's just a bad back or some other minor issue. I'll just take some painkillers and see if it gets better.'

The assumption that the implant was flawless led patients to seek help from their surgeons only when the pain became unbearable. Given that most implants were mostly painless and seemed to perform well, neither doctors nor patients considered the possibility that the implants themselves could be the source of the problem.

Joyce emphasizes the critical need for doctors to believe their patients, a sentiment that was often missing with the ASR.

'We've seen numerous failures with medical devices. Take the vaginal mesh, which was banned by the US FDA in 2019. Women, unfortunately, were frequently dismissed and not believed.' The bottom line, Joyce says, is that if a large group of patients have raised concerns, the stakeholders need to investigate the issue.

At the close of the committee consultation, an additional written submission cut through the room like a razor.

'The last word in our submission goes to the patients, who are astute in summarizing what action they would like to see taken,' Joyce and another specialist wrote.

'We are just saying that the MHRA needs to learn and listen to the experts and take action without the fear of being sued, and the government needs to step in to confront the apparent corrupt practices and the hidden, unacknowledged evidence,' a focus group patient's testimony declared, the words reflecting frustration.

'We here on the shop floor* are suffering, so everybody should be responsible for bringing this out into the open and making sure it doesn't happen again,' another testimony added – the patient's anger and desperation is evident.

These heartfelt testimonies might have come from two ASR patients in the UK, but every word carried the weight of pain and suffering that Indian patients felt as acutely, and is a desperate cry for accountability on their behalf ,too.

While other nations were learning from the ASR debacle, in India, an extensive cover-up of the scandal was underway.

---

* In this context, 'shop floor' is used metaphorically to describe the experiences of patients. As in a factory setting, where workers on the shop floor deal directly with production issues, the patients are the ones affected by the failure of the implant, rather than the corporate executives or decision-makers.

Part III

7

A Doctor, Among the Youngest Victims

For as long as Vijaya could remember, she had always dreamed of becoming a doctor. Her teenage years were filled with late-night reveries where she imagined herself in a crisp white coat, striding through emergency rooms, healing patients with a steady hand and a compassionate heart. Every time she saw a stethoscope, her heart raced with excitement.

The path, however, was gruelling, and she knew that relentless hard work was the only way to her dream. Every morning, as the first light of dawn pierced through her curtains at 5.00 a.m., she was already at her desk, her textbooks spread out like a battlefield map. She never missed a day of school and sacrificed countless evenings to study late into the night. Her excellent grades were her fuel, keeping her eyes set firmly on her ultimate goal – admission to medical school.

In 2005, her relentless efforts began to pay off. After weeks of anxious anticipation, the results were finally announced. Vijaya's heart soared as she saw her name on the list of accepted students. She was accepted into a medical college in Coimbatore, Tamil Nadu's second-largest city. It was a moment of triumph – her years of dedication and sacrifice had culminated in this exhilarating success, marking the beginning of a new chapter in her life.

The first year was a whirlwind of hard work and emotions. The pace was relentless – full days of lectures, and nights spent buried in coursework about human physiology and anatomy. Vijaya spent countless hours in the lab, her hands trembling with both excitement and trepidation as she dissected cadavers. The smell of formaldehyde mixed with the crisp, sterile environment of the lab only heightened her fascination with surgery. Yet, the road ahead was anything but smooth.

'I was just starting my journey in medical school,' Vijaya recalls, her voice trembling with grief and disbelief.[1] 'One day, while fooling around with a friend in the lab, I accidentally slammed into a desk.'

What seemed like a minor mishap soon spiralled into a major concern. A few days later, she began to limp, each step radiating a dull, persistent pain. Balancing her pain with the pressure of looming lab exams, Vijaya took painkillers and soldiered on. An X-ray showed nothing alarming, but the pain was unbearable. Vijaya sought the help of a renowned orthopaedic specialist.

She never anticipated that her specialist visit would unveil anything serious, for his attitude was pretty indifferent and casual. When the specialist suggested a CT scan, Vijaya was initially sceptical.

'Given the hospital's reputation, I thought he was just trying to extract more money from me,' she says.

CT scans are a vital tool in diagnosing conditions like fractures, arthritis and tumours. When the results came back, the specialist recommended an MRI, giving her no reasons.

'I was furious and shocked. He didn't offer any explanations, assuming I was too young to understand,' she says, her frustration evident. She thought the battery of tests were just a money-making ploy.

The prospect of an MRI, with its hefty price tag of nearly Rs 7,000, was daunting for a student. Vijaya called her father, who was working in Nigeria.

'He told me to get the MRI and sent me the money right away. I took the test but tried not to worry. I was active and believed the results would be manageable.'

However, when Vijaya returned to the hospital, accompanied by a friend from medical school, the scene was surreal. She was asked to get into a wheelchair and was wheeled into a room. The specialist's grave demeanour was a stark contrast to his earlier indifference.

'He said he suspected a tumour, and told me not to move or walk. I was stunned!'

The specialist then requested permission to perform a bone biopsy, seeking to determine if the tumour was benign or something more sinister. Vijaya was at a loss.

'I felt like I was being kept in the dark. I explained that my mother was far away in Andhra Pradesh and couldn't come. I insisted on understanding what was happening,' she recalls.

Despite her pleas, the doctor remained vague, offering only reassurance that her youth was in her favour. As Vijaya waited, her friend scoured through her report, but with smartphones not yet in common use and their limited medical knowledge, they only grasped that something was terribly wrong.

When the specialist finally revealed the diagnosis, the weight of the news was crushing. Vijaya had a rare bone tumour and needed surgery.

'He didn't specify if it would be a hip replacement or bone grafting,' she says, reliving her frustration at being kept in the dark.

The report indicated a giant cell tumour on the left femoral head of her hip – benign but locally aggressive. Initial consultations warned of potential complications from surgery. Desperate, Vijaya sought a surgeon with the expertise required.

'No specialist in Coimbatore was willing to take my case,' she admits.

Determined not to be defeated, on her doctor's advice, Vijaya took seven months' leave from college. She went home to Kurnool to her family, while they searched for the best hospital for her surgery. Weeks later, she arrived at a top hospital in Hyderabad, accompanied by her mother and brother. By then, the pain had immobilized her left hip for nearly a month.

An examination revealed a loss of two-thirds of the femur due to the tumour. The surgeon, renowned for his skill, decided on a total hip replacement.

'He was brilliant. He explained that bone grafting wasn't advisable due to my young age and the rarity of the condition. A metal implant was the best choice to avoid being bedridden for months,' Vijaya recounts, recalling the relief she felt.

The surgeon assured her that the ASR hip replacement would facilitate a quicker recovery and allow her to resume an active lifestyle.

'I was thrilled. I wanted to get back to college and continue pursuing my dream of becoming a surgeon. He assured me that this surgery wouldn't derail my career.' Vijaya felt optimistic at this assurance.

On 3 July 2006, Vijaya, only eighteen years old, faced a situation that no teenager should have to go through. As she prepared for a total hip replacement, becoming one of the youngest recipients of the ASR implant in India, she was not just dealing with the physical challenges of the surgery but also the emotional weight of her future. Balancing the demands of recovering from surgery while still needing to finish medical school felt overwhelming. It was a turning point that tested her strength and resilience, as she faced the dual pressures of her health and her ambition.

Vijaya's recovery began on a hopeful note. Just a week after her hip replacement surgery, she was discharged from the hospital. Her steps were unsteady, but the promise of a fresh start pushed her forward. She went to her mother in Kurnool. Armed with a walker, she moved through her home, which now felt like a place of cautious optimism.

Then came the months of physical therapy, each session more gruelling than the last. The pain and exhaustion were relentless. Her muscles ached, her joints protested, and on some days, even the simplest exercises felt impossible. She found herself pushing through the pain, fuelled by determination, though the process was draining. Her friends from medical school were in distant Coimbatore, and old high school friends had all gone their own way. She was mostly alone at home, with usually only her mother for company. The isolation weighed heavily on her, and the feeling of missing out on valuable time, each moment alone serving as a stark reminder of how much her life had changed.

When she finally made it back to medical school, it felt like a dream she had clung to through every gruelling therapy session.

'For the first year and a half after the surgery, everything seemed to fall into place,' she recalls. 'Being back in college was something I thought I'd never achieve when I was first diagnosed.'

But soon, reality caught up with her. The discomfort she had learned to tolerate began to intensify. What had once been a dull ache turned into sharp, shooting pains that made her wince with each step. It was as if her body was sending urgent signals, each twinge a plea for attention. Fear gnawed at the back of her mind, whispering that her recovery might be falling apart.

Despite the pain, Vijaya pressed on, pouring herself into her studies. She began her final year, diving into the demanding world of clinical rotations. Long hours on her feet, rushing from one patient to the next, left her physically exhausted. But her determination was stronger than the pain. She had worked too hard to let anything get in the way of her dream of becoming a doctor.

It was during these busy rotations that the pain became impossible to ignore. Standing for hours, she'd feel a strange numbness creeping into her leg. Then there was the clunking noise – the sound of metal shifting within her hip. It was unnerving, like carrying a ticking clock inside her body.

Her friends noticed it too.

'They'd ask, "What's that sound?" and I'd just say, "It's the metal inside me,"' Vijaya remembers. 'I got used to it, but deep down, I always thought it was bizarre, even wrong, for an implant to make that kind of noise.' She knew something wasn't right, but she was too overwhelmed by her studies to deal with it. So, she pushed the thoughts aside, hoping the problem would disappear on its own.

But the pain only grew worse.

'One night, my leg just wouldn't move. It felt like it was frozen solid,' she recounts. Her roommate, seeing her in agony, rushed to give her a painkiller. After what felt like an eternity, Vijaya could finally stretch her leg, but the fear lingered. 'That was when I knew things were getting out of control,' she says.

She sought advice from her surgeon, who told her to lose weight to reduce the strain on her implant. Vijaya started a strict diet, but it only added to her exhaustion.

'I was constantly tired, couldn't walk long distances,' she says dejectedly.

Through it all, Vijaya refused to let the pain define her.

'Every time I got stressed, my leg would swell up. Pain was just part of my life now,' she recalls.

Eventually, she stopped taking painkillers, telling herself this was her new normal.

'I had to adapt, make the best of it and keep moving forward,' she says, quiet resolve like steel in her voice. Despite everything, Vijaya kept going. Each day was a test of her strength, balancing the pain with the drive to succeed in her career.

In 2011, Vijaya finished her bachelor's degree in medicine and moved to Delhi to prepare for her postgraduate studies.

'It was eight months of gruelling coaching. I would stay up all night, sometimes studying for eighteen hours straight. The pressure from the competitive exams was overwhelming.'

But as she threw herself into her studies, Vijaya started noticing something wasn't right. The pain had started spreading to other parts of her body.

'I began having severe headaches. At first, I blamed it on lack of sleep, but soon it wasn't just my head. My thumb started hurting all the time, and my toes swelled up like balloons.'

Things got even stranger. Vijaya, who had always been sharp and focused, found herself struggling to concentrate. It felt like her mind was trapped in a thick fog.

'I couldn't think clearly. It was a weird, foggy feeling, something I'd never experienced before, even after all those years of studying long hours,' she recalls. This time, she failed to pass the master's entrance exam.

Despite the growing pain and the nagging feeling that something was seriously wrong, Vijaya pushed on. She was determined not to let these strange symptoms mess with her career.

By 2013, she made an important decision – she moved to Hyderabad to start practising as a doctor. She was determined not to let health interfere with her career, no matter how much it tried to hold her back.

In 2015, Vijaya, an intern in the obstetrics department, stepped into Osmania General Hospital, one of the oldest medical institutions in India. Located in the heart of Hyderabad, Osmania was a lifeline for thousands of patients, where hope and desperation collided daily. At one of the largest government hospitals in Telangana, the sight was overwhelming – patients lined the corridors, and the number of beds was dwarfed by the number of patients in desperate need.

For Vijaya, working as an intern meant confronting this reality every day. Her team was constantly on edge, racing against time and fighting exhaustion. The job was a relentless endurance test. Forty-eight-hour shifts were the norm, not the exception. Each day, nearly seventy labour admissions came through the department's doors, with women in various stages of childbirth requiring immediate attention. The air was thick with urgency, filled with the frantic energy of doctors and nurses. The cries of newborns and the anxious whispers of families only heightened the sense of urgency.

The heavy workload didn't deter her. She felt it was her duty to ensure every mother and child received the best care.

'I was actually losing weight because of the physical demands,' she recalls wryly. 'And while the doctors had advised me to shed some kilos to make my hip implant last longer, the pain was becoming unbearable.'

The dull ache in her hip became a constant companion. Vijaya vividly recalls the gruelling days during a doctors' strike. The hospital, refusing to close its emergency services, left the burden on the interns.

'I remember those days all too well,' she says. 'We were just three on duty, and I ended up handling thirty labour cases back-to-back. The pain in my hip was unbearable, like a heavy weight lodged deep inside me, refusing to let go. But there was no time to pause; every case was an emergency, and I had to push through, no matter what.'

The long hours on her feet, the strain of difficult deliveries, and the endless bending and working took their toll. Vijaya's pain started to affect her work, slowing her down and making each movement a calculated risk.

'Sleep or any form of rest offered no relief,' she says.

She turned to painkillers again, swallowing them like candy just to get through the day. But the relief was fleeting, like trying to cover a deep wound with a small band-aid. Her colleagues noticed the change – how she winced when she thought no one was looking or took moments to lean against the wall for support.

'Some days, I had to force myself to go to work,' she says.

Despite these challenges, Vijaya's dedication never wavered. She completed her stint at Osmania General Hospital, where she absorbed invaluable lessons amidst the relentless pace. But she needed a change, a new chapter. She set up her own clinic in Hyderabad.

'It was a new phase, a little less hectic than Osmania,' she recalls with a faint smile. But even with a lighter workload, the toll on her body was undeniable. Even cutting back on her workload didn't stop the constant pain and fatigue that followed her everywhere.

'I knew I needed to step back and figure out what was happening to my body before it completely ruined my health,' she says. Concerned, she confided in her family, and they were distraught with worry. They urged her to return to Kurnool, where the familiarity of her childhood home offered comfort, and where practising medicine in a smaller, quieter city might be kinder to her weary body.

'I moved back to Kurnool,' she says, remembering her sense of relief. 'I started practising at a friend's hospital. It was less hectic, yes, but it wasn't that I didn't want to work – I just had to reduce the intensity. And with family close by, I hoped to regain the mental peace that had been eluding me.'

In an attempt to regain control over her health, Vijaya joined a gym, signing up for a weight reduction programme. She hoped the routine would bring back a semblance of normalcy.

'I started with simple cardio and exercises using super-light dumbbells,' she says. The clank of weights and the hum of treadmills surrounded her, but even these modest efforts left her drained.

At the gym, she met a paediatrician, a man who exuded energy and optimism. Coincidentally, he had undergone a total hip replacement just two years before. They soon became friends.

'He was in his forties,' Vijaya says, with a mix of admiration and envy, 'but unlike me, he was incredibly active.'

It didn't take long for the paediatrician to notice something was amiss. Vijaya would often finish a workout looking utterly spent, her face flushed, her breath coming in ragged gasps. She'd retreat to a corner, drenched in sweat, or stand motionless in front of the air conditioner, trying to cool down her overheated body.

'He could tell that something was really wrong,' she admits.

Concerned, he took her aside one day. His words were kind but firm, like a doctor delivering a difficult diagnosis.

'You should be more active at your age,' he told her, his eyes searching hers for understanding. 'I'm forty-five, and despite a hectic hospital schedule, I feel completely normal with my hip implant. Even with my weight, I can work out far more comfortably than you can.'

For Vijaya, these words hit hard – a jarring reminder that something was seriously off. But she pushed the thoughts away, tucking them into a corner of her mind where they wouldn't disturb her carefully constructed plans.

'I was getting married soon,' she says, a hint of defiance in her tone. 'I told myself that things are different for men and women, and that everything was under control.'

But deep down, a seed of doubt had been planted, one that would soon demand her attention, whether she was ready or not.

In 2017, Vijaya's wedding was a beautiful moment, a fresh start filled with hope and excitement. But even as she celebrated, she couldn't shake off the worry that the faulty implant inside her might overshadow the happiness of her new life.

'At that time, the pain almost took a backseat,' she remembers. 'Starting a marriage means there's a natural closeness and intimacy expected. But I was constantly anxious about how the implant, which was already causing so much trouble, would affect our relationship,' she says.

Two months into their marriage, the couple faced an unexpected challenge. 'I had a miscarriage – it was spontaneous,' she says, reflecting on that tough moment. Even though it was hard, they chose not to let it get them down. They stayed hopeful for the future, not letting this setback overshadow their dreams.

A few weeks later, Vijaya's life took a turn for the worse. She had a minor slip, just a little stumble – something that would normally go unnoticed. But within minutes, a sharp pain shot through her leg – the same side where she had her hip implant.

'The pain was unbearable,' Vijaya recalls. She was rushed to a nearby surgeon, every bump in the road making the pain even worse.

'It was such a small fall,' she says, still in disbelief. 'But it felt like something serious was happening inside. I was scared it might be the implant.' Each minute felt like an hour as she held her leg, trying to stay calm.

At the hospital, Vijaya was helped onto the examination table, her face pale with pain. The doctor came in, looking calm and collected, as if nothing was wrong. He examined her quickly and asked a few questions. When he finally finished, his words were shockingly casual.

'It's nothing serious,' he said with a shrug. 'The implant is fine. I don't really know why you're in so much pain.' His words hit Vijaya hard. She felt her genuine concerns about the implant were being dismissed, as if they were all in her head.

Desperate for answers, Vijaya didn't waste a second. At the crack of dawn, she was already on her way to Hyderabad to meet her surgeon. When she arrived at the clinic, she was immediately guided to the examination room, the X-ray machine looming like a judge waiting to deliver its verdict. Once the X-ray was complete, she entered the consultation room. The surgeon's face remained unreadable as he reviewed her X-rays. Moments later, the truth was revealed. As the X-ray results flashed on the screen, Vijaya's breath caught in her throat. The image was a nightmare: the ASR implant was slipping out of its socket.

Her heart raced, and she felt a cold sweat break out on her forehead.

'The surgeon said the implant needed to be replaced,' Vijaya says, her voice breaking. The idea of enduring another surgery was almost too much to bear.

Then, out of nowhere, the surgeon asked with a hint of uncertainty: 'Did I use a DePuy implant for your original hip replacement?' Vijaya's anxiety spiked.

'I don't know anything about DePuy. I remember you said it was a Johnson & Johnson implant,' she replied.

'Has anyone reached out to you about the implant?' The surgeon looked puzzled, but did not explain any further.

'No,' Vijaya answered, feeling a growing sense of unease.

The surgeon's sudden, almost casual questions about whether her implant was from DePuy or if anyone from the company had contacted her seemed to come out of nowhere. The questions hung in the air, filled with hidden meaning, but Vijaya didn't see them as anything to worry about. For whatever reasons, her surgeon did not mention the recall. Even though she worked in the medical field herself, this brief conversation showed just how unaware Indian patients were of serious issues like medical device recalls and that doctors were not talking about it either. It was a clear sign of the unquestioning trust patients placed in their doctors, never doubting them, even when there might be a real danger hiding in plain sight. This was a pattern – in Dinesh's case, too, the surgeon did not explicitly mention that the implant had been recalled. The doctors and the company were secretive about the issue, and doctors would only bring up the recall if they were certain the patient urgently needed revision surgery.

However, Vijaya had another pressing concern. Just a few weeks earlier, she had suffered a miscarriage. Despite the setback, the couple's dream of becoming parents remained bright in their minds – a future filled with laughter, love and the joyful sound of a baby's footsteps. But now, hearing that her implant was loosening felt like the rug had been pulled out from under her.

Her mind was spinning. If the implant wasn't holding up, what would that mean for her ability to move around? What about the future she had always pictured – the one with a child's laughter filling their home? A knot of fear formed in her stomach. Could she even think about becoming a mom with this going on?

Feeling overwhelmed, Vijaya asked her surgeon the question that weighed heavily on her mind. 'Is it safe to plan for a pregnancy?' she asked, hoping to hear that everything would be okay, that she could still have the life she dreamed of.

The surgeon assured her it was fine to get pregnant, even with the pain she was in.

'But he advised me to prepare for the pregnancy quickly,' she recalls.

Even at this stage, the idea of recommending a cobalt–chromium blood test never crossed the surgeon's mind. A simple test could have determined whether toxic metal ions were leaking into her bloodstream, posing a serious threat to her health. Instead, the surgeon was nonchalant.

'If you end up needing another surgery, it will be easier on you if you've already had the baby,' he said.

This starkly illustrated how, in India, metal ion testing remained largely unknown and overlooked as a diagnostic tool. It wasn't like the familiar protocol for common health issues – when you gain weight or exhibit symptoms of diabetes, even a general physician is quick to suggest basic blood glucose and lipid profile tests. In those cases, preventive tests were almost second nature. But here, even when faced with a recalled MoM implant, surgeons rarely took the straightforward step of recommending a metal ion blood test.

Vijaya became pregnant again. However, this time, she recalls how the excitement of expecting a child was at times, overshadowed by the fear that her faulty hip might complicate everything. She adhered strictly to every health guideline: eating well, taking gentle walks and avoiding any activities that might strain her. Each step she took was burdened by the worry that any misstep could harm either her baby or herself.

As her pregnancy advanced, the stress seemed to compound. By the second month, things were spiralling out of control. 'I was vomiting incessantly, up to sixteen times a day. As a doctor, I knew hyperemesis could be severe, but this was far beyond what I'd ever seen. I had to see the surgeon again.'

Vijaya vividly recalls how during this visit to the surgeon, she couldn't hide her fear any longer.

'Should I consider an abortion?' she asked, her voice trembling.

'Trust me. Don't worry. Continue with the pregnancy,' the surgeon said confidently. He still didn't suggest a cobalt–chromium test, focusing instead on wanting her to deliver before any potential revision surgery, because post-op recovery would be a challenging road.

Throughout her pregnancy, Vijaya's mind was a whirlwind of thoughts and fears. The thought of undergoing a possible surgery during the pregnancy was terrifying. 'Each day was a battle between hope and anxiety. My only fear was the impact it might have on the baby's health,' she recalls.

Vijaya prepared for childbirth while managing the relentless stress of her situation. Finally, in May 2018, after months of intense worry and physical strain, she gave birth to a healthy baby girl. Holding her daughter for the first time was a huge relief, a shining moment that brought light to her tough journey.

In the months that followed, Vijaya was so wrapped up in caring for her newborn that she hardly noticed her pain or fatigue.

'Sure, there was pain after giving birth,' she says, 'but holding my baby and seeing her sweet face made all the discomfort fade away. The joy and peace of being a mom just made everything else seem unimportant.'

In November 2019, Vijaya was in the living room, playing tag with her one-year-old daughter. The sound of her little girl's giggles filled the air, making Vijaya's heart swell with happiness. She watched as her daughter stumbled around on her tiny legs, trying to stay just out of reach. Vijaya laughed and lunged forward to catch her, but her foot slipped on a wet spot on the floor. In an instant, she was on the ground, a sharp pain shooting through her leg. She struggled to stand, her leg pounding with pain. The next morning, she was limping, barely able to walk. Vijaya knew she couldn't ignore it; she needed to see the surgeon again.

During the consultation, the surgeon's eyes darted between Vijaya and the X-ray on the screen, his face clouding with concern. He knew her case inside-out – the implant, which was supposed to be a long-term fix, was failing far sooner than anyone had expected. Vijaya had come in limping and wincing with each step. Things were clearly going downhill. It didn't take long for him to deliver the diagnosis.

'You have aseptic loosening of the ASR hip,' he said, his tone sombre. Vijaya's heart sank. She had feared bad news, but hearing it confirmed felt like a punch to the gut.

'This time,' he said, 'you need immediate revision surgery.' He also told her she needed a cobalt–chromium test to see if metal particles were leaching into her blood.

The results of the cobalt–chromium test were expected within a month, but before that, the hospital team dropped another bombshell: the cost of the revision surgery. It was a staggering Rs 700,000 for the painful and complex procedure. Vijaya's heart sank. The reality of her situation was sinking in fast – she and her husband had to fight an uphill battle against time and finances. She went to see her surgeon.

'I told the surgeon I needed at least two months to gather the funds. Until then, I would be cautious about the hip,' she recalls.

Unexpectedly, the surgeon told Vijaya that she wouldn't have to pay for the revision surgery, after all. DePuy would cover the hospital costs.

'Naturally, I didn't mind not having to pay,' Vijaya said, 'but I was shocked that the company would cover it.'

Nine years after the global recall, Vijaya finally learned the unsettling truth. The surgeon revealed that the metal hip implant she had had been recalled because it had caused an unusually high number of revision surgeries. The company was now covering her revision surgery through reimbursement. Despite her medical background, Vijaya had been kept in the dark about the recall. It was a clear sign of how closely the information was guarded. Patients weren't informed until things got really bad – sometimes years later, as in Vijaya's case, nearly a decade.

In an attempt to cushion the blow and make her feel less alone, the surgeon shared that another patient had undergone a similar revision almost ten years after the recall and had also had the costs covered by DePuy.

'He said all I needed to do was submit my medical records,' Vijaya recalls. This reassurance seemed to downplay the magnitude of the delayed notification, almost as if it were just a minor oversight. It painted the company in a favourable light, suggesting that despite their lapse in informing patients, they still had a safety net in place.

'The day the surgeon finally admitted it was a faulty product,' Vijaya says, her voice trembling with a mix of anger and disbelief, 'I was completely stunned. The idea that they had kept so much from us and that it took nearly a decade for the truth to surface was deeply unsettling. It felt like a betrayal,' she says.

As Vijaya limped out of the consultation room, her mind was buzzing with anxiety. The thought of the upcoming revision surgery weighed heavily on her, but she couldn't shake the nagging worry about the cobalt–chromium test results. Her heart pounded with each step, hoping for good news.

'Not knowing my cobalt–chromium levels made me feel like I was in the dark. I had no clue how serious things might be.'

When the test results finally came in January 2020, they were jaw-dropping: her cobalt–chromium levels were 200 times higher than what was considered safe. Vijaya was floored. It felt like a punch to the gut. She reached out to her medical friends, trying to piece together the puzzle of what these alarming levels could mean.

'I learned that my situation was incredibly rare. The levels of metal ions in my blood were off the charts compared to others who had the ASR hip replacement. It was like I was facing a unique crisis that no one else seemed to experience.'

The surgeon made it clear: the revision surgery couldn't wait. Vijaya agreed, her mind racing with fears of brain damage. 'The thought of such high metallosis was terrifying. I knew metal poisoning could cause terrible headaches, but my biggest fear was that it could mess with my nervous system or harm my kidneys. It was like a dark cloud hanging over me, threatening everything.'

Just when things seemed bleak, another orthopaedic surgeon came to the rescue. He moved quickly to sort out the details for the revision surgery which would be a full hip replacement this time.

'He didn't just handle the logistics; he also got in touch with DePuy and filled me in on the recall,' Vijaya says. 'He encouraged me to fight back, reminding me that I had already been through so much and deserved justice.'

Over the years, Vijaya, the once-sharp young doctor, had noticed something unsettling creeping into her mind – a vague feeling that she was losing her ability to concentrate. The razor-sharp focus she had always relied on had started blurring. At times, it felt as though whole chunks of knowledge had simply evaporated from her memory. And then there were the headaches – severe, throbbing pains that would grip her skull like a vice, often leaving her unable to function.

The answer to the cognitive decline came when at last she had the cobalt–chromium test done that January 2020 before her revision surgery, casting a stark light on her deteriorating condition. The results explained many of her other symptoms, too.

'High, toxic levels of cobalt and chromium can lead to concentration problems and short-term memory loss,' Vijaya explains.

'At first, when I couldn't remember things, everyone around me brushed it off. "It's just stress," they said. "You're overworked." They all dismissed it as a minor issue, something to laugh off. But I knew something was terribly wrong. I could feel it in my bones, even if I couldn't put it into words.'

Vijaya is convinced that it all began while she was preparing for her postgraduate exams.

'I'd spend hours with my books, writing and rewriting notes, sticking reminders everywhere. But after a few days, it was like my mind was a blank canvas again. All my hard work vanished into thin air.'

She recalls with vivid clarity the first time anxiety seized her body like a violent storm.

'It was a quiet evening, and I was driving back to college from my hometown. The journey was just 200 kilometres, but I stopped sixteen times. My heart was pounding in my chest, and my mind was racing with thoughts I couldn't control. I wasn't even sure why I was feeling this way, only that my brain felt trapped in a fog.'

As time went on, her symptoms became more bizarre.

'I'd get these uncontrollable shivers in my legs, as if my muscles were revolting against me. Standing for long periods became impossible. I even started having trouble holding my urine. Suddenly, I couldn't trust my own body. It was humiliating.'

Desperate for answers, Vijaya consulted a parade of doctors, hoping someone could make sense of her plight.

'They told me maybe my eyesight was failing, but every test came back normal. My vision was perfect. With no other options, I turned to caffeine, drowning my anxiety in cup after cup of coffee. I'd never touched the stuff before, but now I was drinking six to seven cups a day, just to make it through the relentless headaches. It only made things worse.'

In a final attempt to find relief, Vijaya visited a neurologist. The specialist, concerned by the severity of her symptoms, recommended a brain MRI.

'I held my breath, hoping they'd find something, anything to explain what was happening to me,' she says. 'But the MRI showed no abnormalities. No need for neurological intervention.'

Vijaya was in perfect health on paper – no comorbidities, no underlying conditions. Her symptoms remained a mystery, a cruel puzzle no one could solve.

By the end of 2019, however, the truth began to emerge, dark and undeniable. Her symptoms were classic signs of metallosis, which was confirmed in January 2020, when she got her blood cobalt–chromium test results. But till then, no one joined the dots between these symptoms and the state of her ASR implant.

'Poor memory, mental fog, those were just the beginning,' Vijaya says, her voice tinged with bitterness. 'Anxiety, relentless headaches, the feeling that I couldn't catch my breath – all of it pointed to metallosis. When the blood test results came back, that's when the pieces finally fell into place. My implant was leaking metal ions into my blood, poisoning me from the inside out.'

Her experience mirrored that of several others with ASR implants. Their symptoms, so often dismissed by doctors as trivial or psychological, were in fact the body's desperate cry for help. The reality was far more sinister than anyone had imagined. This wasn't just a story of physical pain, but of a silent, metal-induced agony that twisted the mind and body alike – an ordeal so profound, its true depth is almost impossible to capture.

There was another part of the patient's struggle, something most didn't see or even hear about: dealing with the company that was supposed to cover the costs of their revision surgeries. Even before patients like Vijaya could be wheeled into the operating room for the complicated revision surgery, they had to navigate a maze of frustrating paperwork and endless phone calls. The company responsible for reimbursing these surgeries made the whole process feel like a cruel game, as if they'd forgotten they were dealing with real people whose lives had been turned upside down.

―○―

Vijaya's anxiety about the upcoming revision surgery grew with every passing minute. Her mind was whirling with questions: *How long would the surgery take? What problems might come up? Would the recovery be a tough battle?* The uncertainty was paralysing, and she couldn't escape the fear of what lay ahead.

It was only natural for her to expect some compassion from the firm appointed by the company to handle the reimbursement for the revision surgery – a crucial step before the surgery could even take place. But, unfortunately, that was not the case.

'It felt like DePuy was doing me a favour,' she recalls, her resentment resurfacing.

On 8 January 2020, the hospital pegged the cost of the revision surgery at Rs 795,000. By February, Vijaya was directed by the company to consult with the surgeon and book the surgery for 6 March. But as the date approached, a new complication emerged. Puri Crawford Insurance Surveyors & Loss Assessors India Pvt. Ltd., the private agency in charge of reimbursement, suddenly baulked at the expense. 'The provided estimation is above our historic limit,' the claims manager wrote. Vijaya was now required to submit a clinical justification letter explaining the cost, which would then be reviewed by a medical panel. 'We will let you know their response,' the manager said.

Vijaya's frustration grew with each new delay, and her father was just as upset. However, he chose to address the situation with a calm demeanour.

The claims manager's email arrived at 5.27 p.m., and despite his annoyance, her father responded calmly and reasonably, though it took him till 11.30 p.m. to write and send the email.

In his reply, he expressed concern about the sudden focus on the surgery's cost. He pointed out that raising this issue just days before the surgery was not only discouraging but also a serious obstacle. 'It's really unfortunate that after all this time, your company's management is only now communicating with the patient,' he noted, highlighting that the company had initially approved the revision.

He clarified that their interactions with the hospital and surgeon had shown no change in the cost estimate. He tactfully then suggested that the company should deal directly with the hospital for a proper cost comparison, rather than involving patients. 'In some cities, hospitals might charge less ... but when it comes to my daughter's health and future, we won't compromise on quality and expertise,' he wrote.

He concluded with a heartfelt appeal: 'I ask your medical team to understand this from the patient and her parents' point of view.' His words were a sincere plea for empathy in a seemingly indifferent system. 'She's already struggling with high levels of chromium and cobalt in her blood, constant discomfort and sleepless nights filled with pain,' he added, hoping to convey the deep emotional toll they were experiencing.

As the company's cost-saving attempts became more apparent, Vijaya's frustration boiled over.

'First, they questioned why I hadn't chosen a cheaper hospital in Hyderabad,' she says. When she didn't respond, they suggested she travel to Chennai, where the costs were lower. 'They insisted that the hospital's quote was excessive and that they had never paid so much for an ASR revision.'

Determined not to compromise on her care, Vijaya stood her ground.

'I told them I wouldn't settle for a hospital they chose. I was resolved to have my surgery where I felt it was right, regardless of the company's financial considerations. Eventually, I lost my temper, telling them they had ruined my life. I insisted I would only go to a hospital of my choice, even if I had to pay for it myself. I told them that because of metallosis, my body could develop tumours and that I might not have long to live.'

Despite her pleas, the company's response remained mechanical.

'They never engaged with my concerns. There wasn't a single conversation about how we were coping, even with a faulty implant causing so much suffering.'

After much struggle, the company finally agreed to reimburse Vijaya for the hospital of her choice. Yet, a sense of dissatisfaction lingered. As a doctor, Vijaya believes in the importance of compassionate communication, especially in high-risk situations.

'But the company's policy was impersonal. They simply passed reports to doctors on a panel without direct patient interaction. The process shouldn't be mechanical; it should involve real conversations with the patient,' she says.

'Because I am a doctor, I understand the complexities. But for someone without that background, navigating these risks without reassurance is overwhelming. All they needed to say was, "We are here for you. We stand by you."'

On 9 March 2020, Vijaya underwent what was supposed to be a life-changing revision surgery. The procedure itself went off without a hitch, and she was discharged in stable condition, with strict instructions to use a walker.

'After I came back home, I was on bed rest. I felt a sense of relief and optimism. Everything seemed fine, and I was actually happy.'

Determined to regain her mobility, Vijaya committed to her physiotherapy sessions. Vijaya's journey back to normalcy initially seemed to be on track. In just a few weeks, she was walking again, albeit with the support of a stick. The simple act of placing one foot in front of the other, even with the stick's help, felt like a small victory. As the days went by, her confidence grew. By early summer, she was moving around her house, getting involved in daily chores and even daring to walk without the stick. For a moment, it felt like the dark days were behind her.

But by August, the familiar ache returned, creeping into her bones like an unwanted ghost. At first, it was a dull, nagging sensation. But soon the limp came back, more pronounced this time, each step a reminder of her fragility. Four long months dragged on, filled with sleepless nights. However, she did not give up.

By late November, Vijaya clung to the hope of a fresh start. She was thrilled to have been selected by a multinational company, ready to take on the role of a medical officer – a job she had always dreamed of. It felt like the universe was finally aligning in her favour. But as the days to her new job drew closer, the pain tightened its grip. Her limp became more pronounced, turning her steps into a struggle. Then, one day, out of nowhere, the pain erupted with a vengeance, sharp and unforgiving. Her left hip throbbed, swelling visibly, a cruel twist of fate.

'I could feel it again – the cup inside my hip shifting, moving out of place. The pain was vicious. I couldn't walk; I was completely helpless,' Vijaya recalls, her voice thick with the memory of despair.

Desperate, Vijaya returned to her surgeon. He ordered an X-ray of her pelvis, and the results were devastating: the new acetabular cup in her left hip had come loose. It was the last thing she expected. Her surgeon's words were like a hammer blow: another revision surgery was needed.

'The surgeon told me the metal from the ASR implant had damaged the bone. The bone wasn't strong enough to support the new implant. Imagine trying to hang a heavy picture frame on a crumbling wall – it's bound to fall. That's what happened to me. The ASR implant had wrecked my bone.'

She was just thirty-three, far too young to face such a relentless cycle of surgeries and pain.

On 1 December 2020, Vijaya reached out to the company, her words brimming with desperation. She needed a second revision surgery. The pain was unbearable. The cup was loosening again, despite the first revision surgery that she had hoped would put an end to her agony.

'This is due to implantation of the ASR cup in the first instance,' she wrote to them, each word laced with frustration. She then laid bare her anguish. Another surgery meant facing high risks, risks she knew all too well. 'This is all because of the failure of the faulty ASR cup, which raised a high level of chromium and cobalt in my blood. It is due to the erosion of the metal. I am facing many side effects with these high chromium and cobalt levels,' she told the company.

For Vijaya, this nightmare felt like it would never end. Her career as a doctor and her family life hung in the balance, all because of a piece of metal that had failed her body. The thought of undergoing another major surgery, barely seven months after the last, filled her with dread. 'I have a little child of two years,' she confided in the email. 'I'm unable to take care of her. I'm totally disappointed and again, going for revision surgery. This is a very painful situation for me.'

The timing couldn't have been worse. Vijaya was in the thick of the COVID-19 pandemic, a time when her skills as a doctor were needed more than ever. Yet, instead of saving lives, she found herself trapped in a personal battle, sidelined by a failing hip and mounting health issues. The feeling of helplessness clawed at her every day.

'Being a doctor, I'm not able to do anything that a doctor should actually do. I'm paying with my life for someone else's mistake, which is totally an injustice, especially in this COVID-19 period,' she told the company. Her words carried a mix of anger and despair. All she wanted was for the company to acknowledge her pain, to take responsibility and to cover the cost of the second revision surgery. It was the least they could do for the ordeal she was enduring.

The hospital had set 7 December 2020, as the date for Vijaya's surgery. That date hung over the family like a ticking clock, each passing day filled with a mix of hope and dread. But while the days flew by, the company handling her case seemed in no rush to help, showing no sense of urgency. Feeling desperate, Vijaya's father took matters into his own hands, writing an email to the company to speed up the reimbursement process.

'... They (treating surgeons) have advised for immediate response revision of surgery ... Please don't neglect this issue,' he wrote on 3 December.

He didn't hold back, explaining that any delay could turn this already critical situation into an emergency. He also painted a stark picture of what Vijaya would face even if the surgery went ahead. 'Again she has to undergo all procedures and for another nine months she has to stay home and walk with support or a stick,' he wrote, describing how his daughter, who once had a bright future, would be stuck at home, struggling to get through each day, just like she had the first time. The thought of seeing her endure another long, painful recovery, feeling trapped and dependent, was heartbreaking.

In a final plea, he appealed to their sense of compassion, hoping they would see his daughter's situation as more than just another case file. 'She is a medical doctor, and is lying in bed, helpless, unable to take care of herself or her child. Kindly consider her condition and take necessary action in time to avoid a last-minute rush and more damage to her health,' he wrote, hoping that these words would strike a chord and prompt immediate action.

Typically, DePuy only reimbursed patients for their first revision surgery. But Vijaya's case was different. There was clear evidence that metal debris from her hip implant had damaged her bones for years, causing the first surgery to fail. Acknowledging this, the company informed Vijaya they were reviewing her situation. Finally, on

7 December 2020 – the very day she was supposed to have the surgery – the company informed her they would cover the costs for this second revision surgery too. It was a last-minute decision, offering some relief.

―⁂―

Vijaya was discharged on 19 December 2020, but her return home marked the beginning of an agonizing chapter. She was confined to her bed for four long months, a prisoner of her own body.

'The recovery was excruciating,' she recalls. 'After the second revision, I was overwhelmed with lethargy. For two months, I couldn't even put my leg down. I was completely immobile. It was only in the fifth month that I finally mustered the courage to try walking again.'

Her journey had been anything but ordinary. Vijaya had endured a complex revision surgery, followed by another revision just a few months later – a gruelling ordeal that would test even the strongest of wills. Her body, already worn from the surgeries, was left vulnerable. It wasn't long before her fragile immunity faltered. Just as she began to regain a semblance of normalcy, she was struck by a severe case of COVID-19.

'I had to be rushed to the hospital. I was so immunocompromised from the back-to-back surgeries that my condition quickly became critical. At one point, it was so bad that my family was told to prepare for the worst,' she recalls, the fear still fresh in her voice. Though she eventually recovered, it came at a great cost, both physically and emotionally.

To an outside observer, it's clear that something isn't right with Vijaya. Her gait is uneven and her steps uncertain.

'There's a reason for that,' she explains, a trace of sadness in her voice. 'With so many revisions – which are incredibly rare – there's now almost a one-inch difference in length between my healthy leg and the operated side. I lost muscle and bone during these surgeries. The impact is still visible. I can no longer walk like a normal person.'

But what truly terrifies Vijaya is something invisible – something lurking beneath the surface.

'I had my blood tested twice after the second revision. You'll be shocked to know that even though the implant was removed, my blood still shows high levels of metal ions. This is what the implant did. The implant is gone, but the metal ions remain,' she says, her dread of the future colours her voice.

These lingering traces of metal have left Vijaya grappling with mysterious, unnerving symptoms.

'That implant was inside my body for fourteen years. I don't think anyone in the country – or probably in the world – has had it inside them for so long. Just imagine the impact,' she says, her voice trembling with emotion. 'The symptoms I face are so elusive, so hard to define. But I can tell when something's not right. Sometimes, even the smallest stress makes me go numb. There's this strange tingling at the back of my head. It's weird, but that's just one example,' she says, trying to convey the inexplicable.

The trauma didn't just take a toll on her body; it derailed her career. Once a thriving professional, Vijaya found herself sidelined. She managed to hold onto her job at a corporate organization after the second revision, but her ambitions had to be put on hold. Yet, in the past year, something shifted. Bolstered by her family's unwavering support, Vijaya has been slowly gathering the strength to pursue an unfinished dream: completing her post-graduation.

'With my family's encouragement, I've returned to what I love most – specializing and returning to a hospital to treat patients,' she says in ringing tones of determination.

But the journey is far from easy.

'One thing I'm certain of is the fogginess in my mind,' she admits. 'There's a feeling of cognitive decline. My mind isn't as sharp as it used to be. Even small tasks, like completing the syllabus, feel monumental now. This is what I mean when I say the aftereffects are so unusual – they're hard to pin down.

Amidst all this pain and struggle, one thing continues to haunt Vijaya: the lengths to which the company went to keep the ASR recall in India hidden.

'If they treated a doctor like this, I shudder to think what happened to others,' she says.

In time, Vijaya discovered that even many surgeons were in the dark about the recall's details. She suspects that several smaller hospitals might still be unaware, even today. Her thoughts often drift to the untraced Indian patients who unknowingly continue to carry the same faulty implant inside them.

'It's not that hard to track patients. Even small companies have records of their sold products. Implants like these have one big dealer. It's not like chocolates being distributed to many vendors. If they really wanted to, the company could have tracked down all its Indian patients,' she says.

What's even more shocking is that it wasn't just the patients, doctors and hospital administrations who were kept in the dark. In India, even the regulator, the very authority that granted the company the licence to sell the product, was kept unaware for years. The realization that so many lives were affected, including her own, is something Vijaya is still coming to terms with.

If Vijaya had been informed in time about the recall, she could have quickly undergone metal ion tests and avoided nearly a decade of pain and suffering. The nearly ten-year delay wasn't just a minor inconvenience – it was a huge setback that affected her body, mind and family. The damage caused by the faulty implant was severe, and every bit of delay had only made things worse, leading to life-altering complications. Vijaya's story shows just how devastating it can be when companies fail to track patients properly, leaving them to face risks that could affect their lives forever.

8

Zero Regulation, No Holds Barred

Medical device giants are notorious for their aggressive marketing strategies, often using high-profile scientific conferences as a key tactic. Picture this: extravagant events hosted in lavish five-star hotels, complete with glittering gala dinners and luxurious overseas trips for surgeons and their spouses. The millions spent on these affairs aren't just for show; they're a calculated ploy to sway the medical community.[1]

At these grand conferences, companies pull out all the stops. They stage live surgeries and product launches that feel more like theatrical performances. Surgeons and their peers are dazzled by these high-tech showcases, subtly nudged towards adopting and promoting the latest devices. The opulence and spectacle are meticulously designed to leave a lasting impression. The goal? To ensure that when a patient walks into the operating room, the surgeon is more likely to choose and recommend these expensive, cutting-edge devices. The boundary between genuine scientific discourse and corporate influence becomes increasingly blurred.

Even before the August 2010 voluntary recall, DePuy, a subsidiary of Johnson & Johnson, was already under scrutiny for its ASR implant – particularly in Australia and the UK. Orthopaedic registries had begun reporting troublingly high revision rates, raising red flags.

In India, a year before the recall, the Indian subsidiary, Johnson & Johnson Ltd. – 75 per cent of which was owned by Johnson & Johnson Inc. (US) and the remaining 25 per cent was owned by DePuy Medical Pvt. Ltd. (India) – was facing its own issues, but not with the drug regulators over safety concerns linked to the ASR. Instead, it was the Income Tax Department (ITD) that was taking a closer look.

Johnson & Johnson had claimed a hefty tax benefit of Rs 231.1 million for 'professional sponsorship' expenses for the assessment year

2006–07.[2] When the ITD questioned these claims in December 2009, Johnson & Johnson responded by saying it had sponsored top doctors to attend international conferences, offering them firsthand information and live surgery demonstrations. At the same time, Johnson & Johnson was hosting its own live surgeries in India, including those featuring the ASR implant.

However, the details provided about these international trips were scant, and it wasn't clear how these sponsorships were tied to the company's business. The ITD found the explanation lacking and disallowed the entire Rs 231.1 million claim. As expected, Johnson & Johnson challenged this ruling before the Income Tax Appellate Tribunal.

Johnson & Johnson wasn't alone in facing such scrutiny. Over the years, the ITD had flagged similar tax benefits claimed by other major pharmaceutical companies. The ITD's stance was clear: companies can offer doctors freebies, but they can't claim tax benefits on these expenditures.

Despite this, companies continued to exploit a loophole in Indian law. While the Medical Council of India (MCI) regulations govern doctors, they don't apply to the companies making the expenditures. This legal gap has allowed these companies to push the boundaries, making the most of every opportunity to influence and impress.

This was in stark contrast to the situation in other countries.

By March 2005, DePuy was under the microscope. The US Attorney's Office for the District of New Jersey had sent them a subpoena, demanding records of their deals with surgeons involved in hip and knee surgeries. The company faced scrutiny over their business practices.

DePuy wasn't the only one in hot water. The investigation targeted the big names in the hip and knee implant market: Zimmer, DePuy, Biomet, Stryker and Smith & Nephew, which together made up nearly 95 per cent of the market. All five companies were under intense scrutiny, with their financial dealings and contracts closely examined.

In September 2007, the five companies avoided criminal prosecution over financial inducements paid to surgeons by agreeing to a new corporate compliance programme.

They agreed to pay a combined total of $311 million to settle the claims, with DePuy alone paying $84.7 million. This agreement was a significant shift, forcing the companies to change their ways.

While announcing the agreement, US Attorney Christopher J. Christie did not shy away from saying that the industry routinely violated the country's anti-kickback statute by paying physicians to exclusively use their products.

'Prior to our investigation, many orthopaedic surgeons in this country made decisions predicated on how much money they could make – choosing which device to implant by going to the highest bidder. With these agreements in place, we expect doctors to make decisions based on what is in the best interests of their patients – not the best interests of their bank accounts,' Christie emphasized.[3]

In India, there was no such investigation into the questionable marketing practices of big medical device companies. Instead, these companies enjoyed tax benefits for their marketing practices. Expecting Indian enforcement authorities to dig into these practices was almost too much to ask.

In many countries, regulators kept a close watch over medical devices even after they hit the market, like a hawk circling its prey. There were already strict rules for post-market surveillance to ensure the devices performed as promised. Systems were firmly in place for adverse event reporting, making it mandatory for manufacturers to promptly report any issues. These reports were then made public on dedicated websites, like warning signs flashing in plain view, so patients could see which devices might fail them.

But in India, the scene was very different. Even the most basic patient safety concerns were left in the hands of powerful manufacturers, as if the fox were guarding the henhouse. The regulatory system meant to monitor the safety and effectiveness of medical devices – a system that should have been strong – was practically non-existent, leaving patients vulnerable and uninformed.

Devices critical to health, such as coronary stents, pacemakers, pelvic meshes, intrauterine devices, and breast and hip implants, were circulating with little to no oversight. Imagine a marketplace where these crucial medical devices were aggressively marketed and sold, often with promises that outpaced their real efficacy, and implanted into patients' bodies with scant regulatory review. It was against the backdrop of this regulatory ecosystem that the ASR was launched in India.

Life expectancy in India has seen a remarkable rise. Back in 2001, it stood at 63.4 years. By 2010, it had soared to 67 years, thanks to strides in healthcare and medical technology that have allowed many to live longer, healthier lives.[4]

But all this progress has not been without its drawbacks. As people live longer, the rise in sedentary lifestyles has led to increased rates of obesity, diabetes and heart disease. For many, this has meant turning to private hospitals, driving a surge in the private healthcare sector.

Imagine walking into a sleek, modern private hospital, where the costs are eye-wateringly high. In 2004 and 2005, expenditure in the private sector accounted for a staggering 78 per cent of health expenses in India. This suggests either a sharp rise in people opting for private care or that these hospitals were charging far more than public institutions. A substantial 65 per cent of a patient's bill often went towards medicines and consultations.[5]

The impact of these rising costs was profound. Private hospitals thrived as out-of-pocket expenses surged. Families spent crores on private care, and investors eagerly poured money into these facilities, making India a hotspot for global medical device manufacturers. New products were hitting the market almost every year.

Take the orthopaedic field, for instance: in 2003 and 2004, India imported artificial joints worth Rs 28.8 million. By 2010, this figure had skyrocketed to Rs 2.23 billion.[6]

But amidst this booming industry, a darker side lurked. Despite the Drugs and Cosmetics Act being in place for over fifty years, it did little to regulate the influx of medical devices. Implants entered the market with scant oversight, putting patient safety at risk.

Regulators found themselves in a tight spot. Devices were approved on paper and flooded the market, each promising a better quality of life. Yet, the real challenge was not just in approval but in monitoring their performance and identifying flaws. Unfortunately, this crucial step was often neglected.

As these issues began to surface, alarm bells started ringing at the highest levels of the government, signalling the need for urgent action.

The Indian Parliament isn't just a place where laws are made; it's the nation's grand stage for debate where the spotlight often falls on pressing national concerns. Members of Parliament wield the power to ask probing questions that hold the government accountable, illuminating matters of public interest. During almost every parliamentary session, the first hour is reserved for 'Question Hour', a time when the chamber buzzes with activity. Questions fly across the floor, challenging ministers, uncovering truths and sometimes stirring up controversy. These questions fall into two main categories: starred questions, which demand oral answers and allow for immediate follow-up queries, and unstarred questions, which require written responses and do not permit supplementary questions.

On 22 December 2003, as the winter session of the Parliament was nearing its end, the Rajya Sabha saw a flood of fifty-eight unstarred questions, all focusing on critical health issues. These questions covered a range of topics, from the harmful effects of fast food and the rising costs of anti-cancer drugs to the problems in healthcare caused by increasing privatization. These were not just theoretical issues; they touched on real, everyday concerns affecting millions of people across India.

Amidst this, one question stood out. Rajya Sabha member Eknath Thakur, representing the Shiv Sena, addressed a critical issue that had long been overlooked: the lack of regulation in India's medical devices market. He filed a set of written questions, hoping to get clear answers.

Thakur's questions cut straight to the heart of the matter. In his first question, he asked, 'Whether [the] Government are aware of the fact that a large number of doctors in the country choose medical devices for their kickbacks rather than quality, while [the] Government do not even pretend to regulate [the] manufacture and sale of medical equipments?' These words laid bare a harsh reality – suggesting that financial incentives, rather than the quality of care, often dictated the medical devices used in treatments.

His next question pushed further into uncomfortable territory: 'Whether it is a fact that one cannot sell an aspirin without a licence but one can sell coronary stents, hips and knees without meeting a single regulation?' This pointed out a glaring inconsistency in the regulatory landscape: while common over-the-counter medications faced scrutiny, complex and potentially life-saving medical devices were allowed into the market with little to no oversight.

Thakur's final question sought a commitment from the government: 'If so, the steps Government propose to take to ensure the safety of patients undergoing operations for life threatening diseases?'

Rather than addressing each question individually, the government issued a single, broad answer. First, it referenced existing regulations under The Indian Medical Council (Professional Conduct, Etiquette and Ethics) Regulations, 2002, which prohibits doctors from engaging in unethical activities like endorsing medical products. The implication was that if a doctor were found guilty of such practices, action could be taken against them. However, this response missed a crucial point: while regulations existed to control doctors' behaviour, there were no such rules for the companies aggressively marketing these products. This oversight left a significant loophole that companies could exploit freely.

The government added that no cases of doctors receiving kickbacks for choosing medical devices had been reported in central government hospitals, suggesting that devices in these institutions were selected based on quality and according to established procedures. Yet, this response only covered government hospitals, leaving the vast and largely unregulated private healthcare sector out of the equation.

It also offered little clarity on broader regulatory actions. The government failed to specify whether it required companies to monitor the safety of new devices after they entered the market or if there were any pre-market safety checks at all. The lack of specifics highlighted a troubling reality: such measures were likely non-existent.

In concluding its response, the government listed the types of medical devices that were regulated: sterile disposable perfusion sets for administering IV fluids, sterile disposable hypodermic syringes and needles for single use, and in vitro diagnostic devices for detecting infections like HIV, Hepatitis B and Hepatitis C.

But then came a startling admission that seemed to have slipped under the radar: 'Coronary stents, hips and knees are not notified under the said Act.' This meant that these critical devices were not regulated under the Drugs and Cosmetics Act. The implications were clear – there was no oversight, no safety checks and no accountability for these complex medical devices. This lack of regulation gave manufacturers a free pass to market and sell these products on their own terms, with patient safety taking a back seat.

This response exposed the deep flaws in India's regulatory system for medical devices. While basic items like syringes were under regulation, sophisticated devices that were implanted into people's bodies, like hip replacements and heart stents, were left unregulated. In such an environment, companies could freely enter the market and sway doctors and hospitals with incentives, with little concern for the potential risks to patients. The Indian healthcare system, facing a surge of new technologies and products, was like a ship navigating the rough seas without a compass.

It was in this regulatory void that DePuy introduced its ASR hip implants in India. With no system requiring safety data before new products could be marketed, hundreds of critical medical devices flooded the market without oversight. The risks to patient safety were all too real.

Coincidentally, just a month before Thakur raised the issue of regulating medical devices in the Parliament, a government-appointed committee had already sounded the alarm to the health ministry about the same matter.

Amidst growing concerns over the quality and effectiveness of drugs available in the market, and the pressing need for a world-class drug regulatory system, the health ministry set up an expert committee. This committee, formed on 21 May 2003, was led by R.A. Mashelkar[7] – a distinguished figure who had been a visiting professor at Harvard University and served as director-general of the Council of Scientific and Industrial Research (CSIR). Its mandate was clear: to recommend measures that would strengthen the control and management of drug administration across India.

By November 2003, the committee had submitted an exhaustive report packed with recommendations aimed at overhauling the country's drug regulatory framework. It was perhaps the first time a government-appointed body had unequivocally called for regulation specifically targeting medical devices. The timing of these recommendations was crucial, as many innovative medical devices were flooding the market. Yet, as the committee pointed out, 'only a few of such products are regulated by central and state drug control agencies under the Drugs and Cosmetics Act.' The report underscored that despite the growing use of medical devices in healthcare, only seven types were actually being regulated. 'Any devices, other than those mentioned above, whether imported or manufactured in the country, are not regulated at present,' the report noted, highlighting a gaping hole in the system.

The committee didn't stop there. It went on to criticize the lack of specialized bodies to manage the regulation of these devices. It pointed out that while the Bureau of Indian Standards (BIS) did regulate low-technology devices, it fell short when it came to high-tech medical equipment. 'However, the current procedures are not adequate to assure the quality of high technology medical devices,' the report emphasized. It was a chilling reminder that India was heavily reliant on foreign regulators' approvals, such as those from the US FDA, for high-tech devices. 'Currently, no regulatory mechanism exists for certification, quality assurance and post-marketing surveillance of imported and locally made medical devices except for the notified devices and diagnostics,' the committee stated.

The report also raised serious concerns about the expertise – or rather, the lack of it – among those handling medical device regulation. Despite the critical nature of these devices, most regulatory officials came from a drug-focused background, with virtually no specialized knowledge of medical devices. 'There is varying degree of control over medical devices and enforcement procedures in different countries. However, the regulatory responsibilities and modalities are seen to be mostly managed by the respective Drug Administrations through dedicated divisions under their overall set-up,' the committee observed. However, India lacked specialized divisions, which was a glaring vulnerability.

The committee didn't shy away from identifying the root causes of the problem. 'It is the responsibility of the Government to regulate and assure the quality of any product marketed in the country. In the case of medical devices, which have potential health risks, this responsibility becomes even greater,' the report stated. The main reasons for the inadequate regulation were laid bare: insufficient manpower and a lack of proper infrastructure. The committee put forth three pivotal recommendations: first, to specifically define 'Medical Devices' under the Drugs and Cosmetics Act and develop relevant rules and guidelines for their regulation; second, to establish a dedicated Medical Devices Division within the newly structured Central Drug Authority (CDA) to oversee the approval, certification and quality control of these devices; and third, to create a regulatory framework for certification, quality assurance and post-marketing surveillance of both imported and domestically manufactured medical devices.

These three recommendations could have been game-changers, setting a new standard for medical device regulation in India and putting patient safety front and centre. By focusing on both regulatory approval and rigorous post-marketing surveillance, the committee aimed to ensure that any medical device, especially implants, showing signs of early failure could be swiftly recalled, protecting patients from harm.

Yet, despite the urgency of these recommendations, the government seemed unmoved. The committee's findings gathered dust, and it took nearly two years before the government health system even acknowledged a problem that affected the health and safety of millions of patients.

On 23 and 24 June 2005, the Drugs Consultative Committee (DCC) convened at the India Habitat Centre, in the heart of New Delhi. Inside a conference room filled with murmurs and the rustling of papers, a group of officials had gathered from across India's states. These officials, mostly state drug controllers, had travelled here to discuss the pressing issues related to drug and medical device regulation. The DCC, a crucial advisory body, played a vital role in guiding the central government and another key group, the Drugs Technical Advisory Board (DTAB). Their primary function: to ensure the consistent enforcement of the Drugs and Cosmetics Act and related rules across the nation.

This June meeting was especially important. The then union health minister, Dr Anbumani Ramadoss, stood before the gathered officials.

'The drug regulatory system ... has to be dynamic ... We have to keep pace with the international developments,' he said, emphasizing the huge responsibility that lay before the officials. 'We need a lot of changes. We have to be serious.'

Dr Ramadoss highlighted the recommendations of the Mashelkar committee, which had called for major reforms in medical device regulations. 'There are practical problems,' he continued. 'You are going to deliberate on all these aspects ... Then, there is the issue regarding control over medical devices,' he said.

The officials knew the decisions made in this room would impact people all over the country, from small-town clinics to big city hospitals. This meeting wasn't just about new rules; it was about protecting the health of millions of people.

The DCC's agenda was packed, but one item stood out: the regulation of medical devices. The DCC members acknowledged what had long been whispered among the medical fraternity: India was facing a significant regulatory gap in medical device oversight.

'As the members are aware, currently there is no separate regulation to control manufacture and marketing of medical devices in the country ... There is an increasing concern to regulate medical devices,' the DCC said in the minutes of the meeting, citing the recommendations of the Mashelkar committee.

The members then held a detailed deliberation on medical device regulations.

'... presently there is a vacuum in the country in respect of regulation over import, manufacture and sale of most medical devices,' they emphasized.

'In most of the developed countries the respective drug regulatory agencies are performing such function[s] and have created separate capacities in terms of trained manpower for evaluation of a wide range of medical devices,' the DCC stated in its minutes, reflecting the growing concern about the situation in India.

The members also discussed the existing drug regulation laws. They stressed that lawmakers had given the central government the authority to bring medical devices under regulatory oversight by notifying them under relevant sections of the Drugs and Cosmetics Act. The members unanimously supported a proposal to regulate a broad category of critical medical devices by classifying them as 'sterile medical devices' under the same section.

They noted that the government must immediately strengthen its infrastructure to handle the expected increase in regulatory workload effectively. This included expanding manpower and building a network of subject-matter experts within the drug regulator. This small yet significant step was a clear signal that things were about to change.

———

Two months later, the DTAB, a more specialized and technically skilled advisory body, picked up the issue. Known for its expert panel of top-tier specialists – from the Director-General of Health Services to representatives of the Indian Medical Association and leading scientists – the DTAB convened on 2 August 2005.

The agenda for this crucial meeting was also packed, listing twenty-four items, each as critical as the next. But it was the third item – concerning medical device regulations – that was at the top on everyone's mind. When it came up for discussion, the Member Secretary first briefed the attendees. He painted a picture of the current regulatory landscape, pointing out that only sterile disposable syringes, needles and in-vitro diagnostic devices were currently notified under the law. He spoke of the urgent need 'to regulate, in general, a number of other medical devices which are sterile and are for critical use'.[8]

The members were also updated on the DCC's recommendations from June. 'There is an urgent need to exercise control over medical devices in the country,' the DTAB noted in the minutes of the meeting, a statement that rang a warning bell.

The conversation then shifted to specific examples that underscored the dire need for regulation. The chairman addressed the gathering. He brought up the issue of stents – those tiny, life-saving devices used to keep blood flowing through clogged arteries. He highlighted drug-eluting stents (DESs), which are coated with medication to prevent scar tissue formation and reduce the chances of arteries re-clogging. 'Even though DES contains a drug, it is considered a medical device because of its basic function and the classification internationally followed,' he stated. He then emphasized the alarming number of DES variants flooding the market, many of which were unchecked and unregulated, because '... no regulatory control is presently being exercised on these products. Apart from stents, there are a large number of medical devices which need to be controlled under the Act.

It would, therefore, be desirable to include all sterile medical devices under the Act through notification,' he said.

Another expert echoed a sentiment that many shared but had yet to articulate so clearly:

'Anything which enters the human body – be [it] a drug or a device, implant or prosthesis – needs to be regulated.'

He zeroed in on orthopaedic implants, arguing convincingly that they, too, should be regulated under the Drugs and Cosmetics Act to safeguard quality and safety.

A representative from the Indian Council of Medical Research added a new layer of concern to the ongoing discussion. He stressed the importance of examining the biocompatibility of materials used in implants. '... Their standards prescribed in various countries would require to be examined,' he noted. His words underscored the complexity of the issue, pointing out that more than merely imposing regulations, it was necessary to ensure that these devices were safe and effective for Indian patients. The room was filled with an unspoken understanding that this was a task that required diligence and international benchmarking.

As the hours wore on, the deliberation came to a conclusion. The DTAB reached a consensus, emerging with three key recommendations. First, they proposed that ten specific 'sterile' medical devices such as cardiac stents and heart valves – and orthopaedic implants – be brought under the Drugs and Cosmetics Act. Second, they called for the formation of expert committees to assess and define standards for each category of device, to ensure that no stone was left unturned. Third, they stressed the need for the government to provide the necessary manpower and budget, so as to enable collaboration with experts and support drug regulators in managing this critical responsibility.

'The Board also decided that in view of the urgency of the matter, the Chairman may move the proposal to the Ministry at the earliest,' the minutes of the meeting noted. The statement underscored the pressing nature of the issue, and indeed, every moment of delay could risk lives.

These decisions marked a turning point in India's medical device regulatory affairs. On 6 October 2005, the government officially notified ten specific medical devices, bringing them under regulatory scrutiny for the first time. This move, long overdue, marked the beginning of medical device regulations.

On 20 June 2006, DePuy applied to register its ASR hip implants and other devices in India, listing DePuy UK as the legal manufacturer. On 29 November 2006, the Drugs Controller General of India granted DePuy International Ltd in Leeds a registration certificate, allowing the ASR hip implants to be imported into India.

In theory, this regulatory oversight meant that ASR implants were now under strict watch. DePuy was legally bound to inform the Indian regulator of any adverse reactions linked to the implant and to disclose any regulatory actions taken in other countries. But in reality, these regulations were little more than ink on paper.

Despite the statutory requirements, the actual enforcement of medical device regulations in India fell far short, leaving patients vulnerable, with little action on ensuring safety and transparency. The disconnect between regulation and practice was a glaring issue, one that would have significant implications.

On 21 August 2007, the Rajya Sabha was engulfed in a furore over the Indo–US nuclear deal. Amidst the high-decibel interruptions, Dr Panabaka Lakshmi, a Congress leader from Andhra Pradesh who also held the portfolio of Minister of State in the health ministry, introduced an important piece of legislation: the Drugs and Cosmetics (Amendment) Bill, 2007.

This bill was rooted in the Mashelkar report from 2003, which had urgently called for the government to establish robust guidelines for regulating medical devices – guidelines that had remained conspicuously absent.

Just two days later, the bill was referred to the Parliamentary Standing Committee on Health and Family Welfare. Chaired by senior parliamentarian Amar Singh of the Samajwadi Party, this committee was given three months to dissect and scrutinize the proposed law.

The committee embarked on its task with a series of intense discussions, peeling back the layers of a regulatory framework that had long been creaking under its own inadequacies. They went on study visits, interacting directly with the medical device industry – an industry of rapid technological advancements that were miles ahead of the outdated laws aiming to regulate them.

On 21 October 2008, the committee presented its findings to the Rajya Sabha – a report that delved deep into the glaring gaps within the system. It was a report filled with revelations, observations and a roadmap for change.

Representatives from the medical device industry had appeared before the committee. The stakes were high, and they didn't hold back. They argued passionately that medical devices, with their distinct manufacturing processes, applications and outcomes, should never be lumped with drugs. The committee also flagged the industry's experience with current medical device law regulation: the regulation of medical devices in India was inadequate.

Not surprisingly, the industry flagged to the committee that as more sophisticated devices enter the market, the old standards that only related to drugs and simple devices were not relevant to them; so adhering to them was increasingly moot.

The committee put it on record, plain and clear: 'The Committee finds logic in the views aired by the medical devices industry that the current system is inadequate in regulating certification, quality assurance and post-marketing surveillance of both imported and locally made medical devices.'[9]

This was no small statement. For the first time, an official body of lawmakers was acknowledging a critical flaw in the system – the almost complete absence of post-marketing surveillance. Post-marketing surveillance is like a watchdog – ensuring that once a device hits the market, it continues to perform safely and effectively. Without it, the consequences can be dire.

As far back as 2003, the Mashelkar report had sounded the alarm, calling for the creation of a specialized Medical Devices Division to manage approvals, certifications and regulatory mechanisms for post-marketing surveillance. Yet, five years later, these recommendations were still gathering dust. The proposed 2007 bill had failed to incorporate these critical changes – a glaring omission that could have serious consequences.

The committee expressed its astonishment at this oversight, noting that the only significant change in the bill was a more detailed definition of medical devices. There was no effort to distinguish them from drugs or to address their unique regulatory needs. It was like trying to fix a leaking roof by repainting the walls – completely missing the point.

In their inquiry, the committee pressed the health ministry on why regulation, surveillance and monitoring of medical devices weren't included in the proposed law. The ministry conceded that separate provisions were necessary, acknowledging that medical devices required distinct definitions and specific regulatory frameworks. This led the committee to recommend a dedicated chapter in the bill, addressing all aspects related to the regulation of medical devices – a move that underscored the government's acceptance of the critical role surveillance plays in safeguarding public health.

'The Committee also strongly feels that a dedicated division as recommended by the Mashelkar Committee may be set up to deal with regulation, licensing, surveillance and monitoring of the uniform implementation of the laws on medical devices in the country,' the committee recommended.

In a rare moment of candour, a senior health ministry official laid bare the system's deficiencies. He spoke of a regulatory framework plagued by a shortage of drug inspectors, inadequate infrastructure, insufficient testing facilities and a lack of specially trained personnel. Data banks didn't exist, and accurate information was hard to come by – a perfect storm of inefficiencies that could have disastrous consequences.

Picture this: a patient is in desperate need of a life-saving device, but is unaware that the implant they're receiving has not been properly vetted. Without trained inspectors, issues with the device might go unnoticed until it's too late. If something goes wrong – if the device fails prematurely – the consequences could be catastrophic. And without proper data or communication channels, patients might never know they're at risk.

The 2008 parliamentary report was telling. For the first time, it officially documented the reality on the ground. While some critical medical devices, like orthopaedic implants, had theoretically been brought under regulation in 2006, the system had failed to adapt to the evolving landscape. There was no comprehensive registry, like those in the UK or Australia, to track early product failures. This lack of oversight meant that patient safety was compromised.

Not surprisingly, when the global recall of the ASR device hit in August 2010, India's regulatory system was caught flat-footed. The Indian regulator, CDSCO, had no clue about the early warning signs raised elsewhere. And when it did finally learn of the recall, the company managed to conceal data on Indian ASR patients, exploiting the weaknesses in the system. It took the regulatory body for a ride – a stark reminder that in the complex world of medical devices, if the regulations are not robust, it's the patients who pay the price.

9

The Cover-Up

In 2009, as worries slowly rippled across the globe about unusually high revision surgeries tied to the ASR – particularly hitting hard in places like Australia and the United Kingdom – India's regulatory radar remained surprisingly oblivious.

A peculiar set of events unfolded on the regulatory front in India.

Back in 2006, when India implemented new regulations for medical devices, DePuy had to obtain a registration certification to import ASR devices. They received it in October 2006, but its validity extended only from 1 November 2006 to 31 October 2009.[1]

Now, here's where it gets interesting.

In early March 2009, things heated up in the US as law firms representing afflicted patients started filing product liability cases against the company linked to the problematic ASR implant.[2] Reports of cup loosening emerged, compelling many to undergo premature and agonizing revision surgery.

Meanwhile, across the globe, countries like Australia and the United Kingdom, keeping a hawkish eye on the performance of hip implants through orthopaedic registries, witnessed a surge in unexpected revision surgeries among ASR patients, sounding alarm bells far and wide.

As troubles with the ASR surfaced globally, in India, the company, DePuy, painted a perfect picture for the regulator, the CDSCO. Between April and December 2009, the exchanges between DePuys and CDSCO reveal how the company concealed the early warning signs of the implant's flaws reported elsewhere. It was truly a case of ignorance is bliss for the regulators, until reality came crashing down.

On 3 April 2009, anticipating the need to keep ASR imports flowing, the company applied for renewal.[3] On 1 September, the regulator demanded an undertaking assuring a squeaky-clean track record – no complaints about the device's quality over the past three years. Responding on 23 September 2009, the company confidently assured them of a spotless track record linked to the ASR.

Based on this exchange, on 23 December 2009, the regulator handed out a fresh certificate for the ASR, valid from 1 November 2009 to 31 October 2012. The regulator, without batting an eye, nodded along to the company's narrative, swallowing it hook, line and sinker – a clear indication that the regulator was made to believe that the device was as safe as could be. This renewal, however, was based on unfounded claims.

Implant manufacturers conduct post-market surveillance to monitor the performance of their products. They scour data from diverse channels, such as orthopaedic registries, published literature, in-house trials, internal complaints data and unpublished clinical research reports. When any of these sources raise concerns about a device's performance, the manufacturer issues an FSN – a vital communication regarding the device's safety.

Just seventy-six days after DePuy received a fresh license to import the ASR into India, an important message reached the regulator's desk on 8 March 2010.[4] The message contained an FSN linked to the performance issues associated with the ASR. The FSN was based on an analysis of the company's data sources – which revealed an unexpectedly high revision rate for the ASR system, specifically in smaller heads less than 50 mm in diameter.

The communication contained two important pieces of information. First, a clear directive to the surgeons: to make sure those ASR cups are set with a 40 to 45-degree tilt – the sweet spot for peak performance and survivorship. The company subtly hinted at a crucial message: ASR patients might be experiencing higher revision surgeries than anticipated, but the root cause was likely how surgeons implant the devices, not the implant design itself. So, it was up to the surgeons to master an optimal surgical technique, particularly with smaller heads commonly used in women.

Second, through this official communication, DePuy revealed startling information from the Australian National Joint Replacement Registry. They disclosed a 5.4 per cent revision rate at three years for ASR patients undergoing total hip replacements. The message to clinicians hinted at a startling trend, suggesting that the spike in revision surgeries might be concentrated among female cohorts.

Adding to the shock, the data highlighted a concerning correlation: heads with a diameter less than 50 mm were linked to a significantly higher revision rate, reaching a staggering 8–9 per cent at three years. This unveiled the harsh truth that nearly 9 per cent of patients with these smaller heads faced the ordeal of painful revision surgeries within just three years of their primary total hip replacement.

The revision surgery statistics raised serious concerns, and the company's response was to refine its communication strategy. The company began emphasizing two key priorities in its guidance to surgeons: ensuring optimal surgical technique, particularly avoiding excessive cup inclination beyond 45 degrees, which could contribute to early revisions, and careful patient selection and rehabilitation. It highlighted that individuals with bone quality issues might require additional evaluation to determine their suitability for this procedure.

For the Indian regulator CDSCO, this was no mundane communication. It marked the first time the Indian regulator became aware of the ASR's early performance issues that were being reported outside the country. This revelation was disconcerting, especially because the regulator had recently granted a new license to import the same device a few days earlier, and they were unaware of these issues during that decision-making process.

What transpired in India – the lack of full disclosure on the performance of the device to the regulator – was truly disturbing. Unfortunately, this wasn't the only such instance. The pattern persisted for several months, revealing a troubling state of regulatory affairs for medical devices in India.

In fact, during the initial sixteen months following the worldwide recall, away from the spotlight, DePuy and the regulatory body exchanged numerous communications addressing various aspects of the recall. These exchanges uncovered a troubling pattern: the company furnished incomplete information on critical matters, concealing the true magnitude of the issue within the country. This lack of transparency left Indian patients unaware and vulnerable, jeopardizing their safety.

On 24 August 2010, DePuy dispatched a brief message to the regulator CDSCO, marking the start of the ASR recall saga in India. DePuy's Vice President of Medical Affairs in Mumbai communicated that the company was voluntarily recalling its two ASR hip implant models, with the Indian subsidiary preparing for necessary action.[5]

Despite its brevity, this message held significant revelations for India. In this message, the company sent two vital documents as attachments, containing information previously undisclosed to the regulator.

The first document was a 'report form' outlining the field safety corrective action (FSCA), a technical term denoting medical device recall. Through this report form, the regulator gained its first ever insight into the alarming unpublished 2010 data from the National Joint Registry (NJR) of England and Wales: the five year revision rate of ASR Hip Resurfacing System was roughly 12 per cent and for the ASR XL about 13 per cent. Crucially, the highest risk was found in ASR head sizes below 50 mm and among female patients.

The second document was the 'Urgent Field Safety Notice', through which the company conveyed the message to the clinicians that ASR patients needed to be informed about the recall, stressing the importance of scheduling a follow-up visit. Additionally, through this communication the company conveyed to the surgeons that they could reach out to its medical director based in India for any clinical queries regarding the recalled device.

When outlining the steps for patient follow-up, the company highlighted crucial information from the medical device alerts of 22 April 2010 and 25 May 2010. These alerts, issued by the UK regulator, specifically pertained to the ASR.

Significantly, it marked the first time the Indian regulator officially learned of the UK's medical device alert. This was an unmistakable breach of the conditions set by the Indian regulator. Because when the Indian regulator granted certification for importing and marketing the ASR device, it included a condition that the manufacturer must immediately inform them about any regulatory restrictions imposed by countries where the device is marketed. By failing to promptly inform the Indian regulator about the UK's medical device alert, the company had in a way breached this condition.

The two medical device alerts by the UK regulator contained important information related to patient follow-up and safety. First, it raised a red flag that a small number of patients may develop a soft tissue reaction to metal wear debris being released by the faulty device. Second, it highlighted the risk that this debris could compromise the outcomes of any necessary revision surgeries. Third, most crucially, it stressed the higher probability of success if early revisions were done for poorly performing hip replacements that were leaking metal ions. This underscored the urgency of tracking and testing patients promptly to reduce the risk of painful revision surgeries.

This clearly showed that these alerts were not routine notifications that DePuy could afford to overlook; rather, the company had a significant responsibility to promptly communicate this critical information to the Indian regulator. Unfortunately, it failed to do so in April and May 2010, and only indirectly informed the Indian regulator in August 2010.

In fact, from a regulatory perspective, the contents of the second document were unsettling, because its message to doctors made it clear that the device had the potential to release abnormal levels of metal ions into the bloodstream. To address this problem, the doctors were asked to closely monitor such patients who used the implant, particularly through cobalt–chromium blood tests.

Furthermore, the letter instructed surgeons to be vigilant if metal ion levels in whole blood exceeded 7 parts per billion. It advised conducting a second test three months after the initial one, if a patient reported metal ions at this level, with the aim of identifying those requiring closer surveillance. In essence, this message subtly highlighted the vital importance of conducting cobalt–chromium testing for patient follow-up.

The message to the surgeons about the significance of cobalt–chromium testing may appear clear-cut, but for India, it was a different ball game altogether. It was a red flag that should have set the regulator on edge – because back in 2010, metal ion testing of patients was virtually unheard of in India. Rarely would a patient in India undergo a cobalt–chromium test while grappling with health concerns linked to their implant, given the limited awareness surrounding these tests.

Additionally, during that period, doctors rarely recommended these tests. In such a challenging situation, there was a high possibility that many patients implanted with the recalled device could be silently suffering without actually getting tested.

Hence, as far as India was concerned, it was quite clear that the only way to determine the extent of damage the implant was causing was to actually track patients and ask them to undergo metal ion testing. And to achieve this, not only the manufacturer, but the hospital, the doctors and the regulator needed to take proactive steps to trace patients and swiftly conduct these tests before their health conditions took a turn for the worse.

But before anything else, the absolute first thing the company needed to shout from the rooftops and swiftly disclose to the regulator was the count of Indian patients implanted with the recalled devices. Yet, surprisingly, the company didn't. Not disclosing the number of affected patients in the very first communication highlighted how manufacturers could exploit a lax regulatory system and escape accountability during a medical device recall.

In fact, in 2010, the system for medical device recalls was virtually non-existent. So much so that the regulator had not established any statutory guidelines mandating a specific time limit for companies to inform Indian patients and issue public announcements when recalling a medical device. Everything hinged on how proactive, sensitive and transparent the company wanted to be during the recall of its device.

To make matters worse, back in 2010, the concept of recalled medical devices was little known, seldom making headlines or raising concerns even within the healthcare industry. So, when the company had to alert the regulator about such an important medical device recall, it conveniently chose not to mention any details about the number of affected Indian patients.

In August 2010, after receiving the first communication on the device recall, the regulator clearly found itself in a challenging position. First, the company stayed mum about the number of Indian patients implanted with the recalled devices, leaving the regulator unaware of the magnitude of the problem. Additionally, the challenge of tracing, testing and treating the patients seemed like a daunting journey through uncharted terrain, adding an extra layer of complexity to the task at hand.

Consequently, one would have expected the regulator to seek crucial details, such as the count of Indian patients, within a day or two, but it failed to do so. In an astonishing delay, it took the regulator eighty days to communicate to the company its decision to take 'further necessary action' related to the recall, requesting the company to provide documentation.[6] The delayed response from the regulator, typical of bureaucratic setups in India, highlighted a concerning lack of urgency, especially when dealing with the issue of patient safety – an unfortunate illustration of a weak regulatory oversight of medical devices in the country at that time.

When the regulator received the first message about the recall in August 2010, it was obvious this wasn't going to be a simple task. It wasn't just about telling surgeons to stop implanting the device. It was way more complicated.

Surgeons and hospitals faced a tough task: tracing patients, checking their health and dealing with the risk of metal ion leakage. It went beyond paperwork; it was about real people and protecting their lives. Complicating matters further, many patients might not exhibit symptoms of adverse reactions to metal ions, yet the implant could be quietly causing harm internally. In such cases, it was crucial to locate these seemingly healthy patients who unknowingly had their bodies at risk.

In navigating this complex recall, proactive measures from the Indian regulator were paramount. Therefore, it needed to be aware of the company's plan of action. Consequently, on 12 November 2010, the needle began to shift in that direction with the Assistant Drugs Controller of India requesting vital documents related to the ASR implant recall.

The documents sought by the regulator pertained to the total quantity of ASR implants imported into India, the quantity of implants both used and recalled within the country, the proposed plan for recalling the product from the Indian market, the status of the recall in India and the tentative completion date for the recall. By seeking this essential information on the recalled product, it implied that the regulator was going to assess the extent of any potential issues, ensure accountability from manufacturers and distributors, and take appropriate actions to protect patient interest.

There was a breakthrough on 27 December 2010, when DePuy's Vice President of Strategic Regulatory Affairs and Quality Compliance disclosed the number of ASR surgeries performed in India prior to the global recall. It was revealed that its Indian subsidiary had imported a total of 15,829 ASR XL and ASR Hip Resurfacing Systems.[7] It is important to note that the number of systems imported did not equate to the exact number of patients, as each procedure required the use of multiple components from ASR XL and ASR Hip Resurfacing Systems. Consequently, the company estimated that approximately 4,700 procedures had taken place since 2004.

Finally, the most fundamental statistic regarding the recall, the number of ASR procedures, was shared with the regulator. Furthermore, the company stated that they had returned 1,295 unused product units.

The data on the number of ASR systems imported and the estimated procedures, uncovered the scale of the issue: thousands of Indians had been implanted with the recalled device. However, a critical gap remained as the company failed to disclose their plan of action for the Indian market – the pivotal question posed to the company.

What was the company's plan of action for tracing and testing Indian patients? There were no answers. Tied to this issue was some other crucial information that the regulator was still unaware of.

For instance, in the first communication, the company had informed the regulator about inviting Indian surgeons to connect with their medical director in India to delve into why certain patients experienced soft tissue reactions due to metal wear debris from the implant. Following this outreach, the company failed to disclose how many Indian surgeons responded.

There were other questions: Were there any inquiries from the company regarding patients in India exhibiting metal ion levels surpassing 7 ppb? Did any surgeon report instances of fluid accumulation and tissue masses detected through ultrasound or MRI scans in patients undergoing unexpected revision surgeries? On these critical patient safety concerns, the company maintained a conspicuous silence, providing no insight into these pressing questions. Instead, it made a superficial claim to the regulator that the recall had concluded in September 2010.

The regulator knew the company's claim was implausible. Concluding a recall wasn't merely about notifying surgeons; it involved meticulously tracking, testing and assessing affected patients. There was no way this critical process was wrapped up in September 2010.

Even more alarming, the regulator remained oblivious to a crucial detail: the company's internal probe into the surge of ASR revision surgeries. It was perplexing that the Indian regulator didn't get wind of this, especially considering that no company would pull a product off the shelves without first detecting warning signs in its performance monitoring system, particularly when it concerns patient safety.

The company's internal investigation, an important process usually undertaken during a product recall, could have shed light on what drove the recall – whether it stemmed from flaws in the implant's design, the surgical procedure or patient selection. But the regulator didn't know any of this. In this situation, the only way for the regulator to access this vital information would have been through seeking details of the corrective and preventive actions (CAPA).

So what is a CAPA? When a product is sold commercially, the likelihood of customer complaints increases. In case of medical devices, a series of complaints prompts manufacturers to swiftly address the issue. Regulatory agencies mandate a thorough investigation to prevent similar issues from happening again.

In response to situations where there are multiple complaints on the functioning of a medical device, manufacturers swiftly activate a CAPA – a crucial system designed to pinpoint quality-related concerns, understand their root causes and implement measures to prevent reoccurrence. In the context of the 2010 recall, when the company began receiving complaints about a higher-than-expected number of revision surgeries, an immediate CAPA was initiated. Leveraging this system, the company was expected to investigate and solve the patient safety issues concerning the hip implant.

Most importantly, the CAPA's findings offer crucial insights to regulators regarding the root cause of medical device recalls. Hence, on 18 February 2011, the regulator reached out to the company to access one of the most important pieces of information on the recall. 'You are hereby requested to submit the details of corrective and preventive actions taken by the manufacturer so that such types of recalls would not occur in future, to this office for taking further necessary action in this matter,' the regulator wrote to the company.[8]

The UK and Australia had established orthopaedic registries to keep tabs on implant performance independently. But in India, such a mechanism was non-existent. Consequently, regulators were left in the dark regarding implant performance, especially those that were pulled from the market by manufacturers, leaving them flying blind.

In India, unless patients or doctors complained about a device's shortcomings, there was no way to monitor its performance systematically. However, once a company recalled its device, regulators could uncover the reasons behind its poor performance by requesting the CAPA findings.

In India, the regulator wasn't just in the dark about the technical aspects of the product recall. More than six months after the August 2010 recall, the regulator found itself grappling with limited details on Indian patients. In these circumstances, the findings of the CAPA became paramount, offering regulators the sole means to comprehend the magnitude of the problem.

Therefore, when the regulator actively sought key information on the CAPA, it proved to be the silver lining in an otherwise uncertain situation. On 28 March 2011, the vice president of Strategic Regulatory Affairs and Quality Compliance finally responded to the Assistant Drugs Controller's communication from 18 February.

This was a worldwide recall that impacted thousands of patients. It was reasonable to expect that the company had ample data on the device's performance, which likely informed their CAPA process. With the company presumably having a wealth of data on the device's performance, it was also logical to assume that they had conducted a thorough investigation before initiating the recall. Therefore, when the regulator requested details on the CAPA, the anticipation was high for a comprehensive explanation. Unfortunately, the actual response was brief and couched in vague terms. It fell far short of expectations.

The company's information on the CAPA to the regulator merely opened the door to a maze of uncertainty. Instead of a single culprit for the ASR product line's alarming revision rates, the company hinted at a complex web of factors. 'The root-cause of the higher than expected revision rate of the ASR product line is multifactorial and not completely understood at this stage,' the official communicated.[9]

The company failed to explain what these various factors were. Was it linked to implant design, surgical technique or patient selection? Or perhaps it was due to inadequate testing of the implant before market launch? The root cause behind the heightened revision rate of the ASR implant remained a mystery.

From the company's response on CAPA, it appeared that the company hadn't yet fully understood the reasons behind unexpected revisions to the implant even in March 2011. No reasons were offered regarding the delay in reaching a conclusion. Did the company lack sufficient data for conclusive scientific insights, or was it examining country-specific data on the poor performance of the recalled device? The company gave no clarifications.

Moreover, it remained unclear if this statement pertained to Indian patients, leaving the Indian regulator in the dark about crucial details on patient safety. Instead, in its brief reply, the company told the regulator that the response requested by it on 18 February 2011, had also been submitted to the competent authority in the UK.

However, within this short communication lay a critical piece of information: the company had launched an 'extensive investigation'. The company revealed they were diving deep into two crucial areas. First, this investigation would uncover the factors behind the higher-than-anticipated revision rate seen in the recalled devices. Second, this investigation would connect the dots to understand the relationships between these factors. But the company chose not to disclose the investigation's blueprint, leaving unanswered questions about its scope, especially whether it was investigating Indian cases.

Instead, the official vaguely stated, 'The investigation has identified areas of focus that now require further verification testing to confirm or discount these factors during the root cause identification process and the final conclusion.'[10] The official further stated that this investigation would provide valuable insights into the company's quality management system.

It was evident that the regulator gained no new insights into the CAPA from DePuy's communication of 28 March 2011. The only update was the confirmation of the ongoing extensive investigation by the company, but without a complete and detailed overview of even this ongoing investigation. As they say, the devil is in the details, and it was high time for the company to provide clear-cut answers in the face of this extensive investigation.

Consequently, almost two months later, on 24 May 2011, the

assistant drug controller wrote to the company: 'You are hereby requested to submit the protocol followed for carrying out the investigation, along with the results of the investigation, to find out the root cause of the said recall, to this office for taking further necessary action in this matter.'[11]

Amidst a flurry of lawsuits that were being filed against the company in the US, by the first quarter of 2011, the company urgently briefed its investors on the looming financial repercussions of the ASR recall. It informed them that a significant $800 million had already been drained on litigation and ASR hip recall expenses, hinting at deeper financial woes ahead.[12]

As the company navigated these financial uncertainties in the US, a world away in India, a different uncertainty unfolded. Here, the regulators, even nine months after the recall, struggled to grasp even the fundamental details, such as the root cause of the recall, highlighting the stark contrast in the global response to the unfolding crisis.

Ultimately, on 24 May 2011 the regulator wrote to DePuy, seeking clarity on the actual root cause of the product recall. The objective was to understand the precise nature of the issues that lead to the recall and illuminate how the flawed implant had the potential to jeopardize patient safety.

Armed with this insight, the regulator would gain clarity on two fronts. First, it would provide crucial insights about how the company had investigated the root cause of the implant failure. Second, the results of the investigation would reveal how adverse the data was, and decide if they needed to act more quickly to keep Indian patients safe.

The answer to these pressing questions ultimately – though not completely – were disclosed to the regulator on 8 June 2011, when the Vice President of Strategic Regulatory Affairs and Quality Compliance sent a crucial communication replying to the specific queries on the investigation being carried out by it. The significance of this communication cannot be overstated. Because the company for the first time divulged to the regulator that it possessed a critical piece of evidence – the explant.

But why focus on explants? During the revision surgery for ASR patients, surgeons removed the problematic MoM hip implant, which was causing the leakage of metal ions into the bloodstream. In several cases, these removed implants, referred to as explants, were not simply discarded. Instead, the company took possession of them post the revision surgery. The rationale behind this practice was that explants offered valuable insights into the performance of hip implants while inside the patient's body.

In the case of recalled devices like the ASR, manufacturers examined the explants meticulously to pinpoint the exact reasons for failures. This process is a critical exercise undertaken by the manufacturers for ensuring patient safety. This examination is also done by government-funded centres.

On 8 June 2011, the official informed the Indian regulator that the company was transferring all 'available explants' to the London Implant Retrieval Centre (LIRC).[13] The purpose behind this move was to subject the ASR explants to analysis, with the results contributing to the company's 'over-arching ASR failure investigation'.

The company also divulged that it would undertake four types of examinations to evaluate the explants removed from the patients. First, was the macro examination: it is like looking at the big picture; you are checking the entire explant with your eyes for any obvious issues or damage.

Second, was the stereomicroscopic examination: this is like zooming in closer; you use a special microscope to look at the surface of the explant in more detail, seeing things like scratches or tiny cracks.

Third, was the CMM surface profiling: this is about measuring the surface of the explant really accurately; it helps to map out the exact shape and features of the surface, like bumps or hollows.

Fourth, surface finish measurements: this is about checking how smooth or rough the surface is, done with precise measurements.

Overall, these processes were being undertaken to provide a comprehensive understanding of the implant's condition, helping the company identify discrepancies in the implant's design or manufacturing process, and also reveal anomalies in the manufacturing process or material quality, which could have affected the implant performance or longevity.

Amidst all the uncertainty, the company's communication to the regulator about a failure investigation into the recalled device sparked a glimmer of hope. It seemed like a chance to clear things up. But, as the regulator waited, the company didn't share all the details on this investigation. They told the regulator about their protocol but kept important findings secret. The regulator didn't know how many devices the company was investigating or what they had found so far or when they would finish.

Instead, the company gave a technical explanation that its investigation would be performed in line with the European Commission's guidelines on medical device vigilance system – a broad framework for detecting, assessing and addressing risks associated with medical devices.

Most importantly, without knowing how many devices from India were being looked at, the regulator would not get a full picture. People in different parts of the world might have different reactions to the implants, so it was crucial to understand how they worked in different populations. For instance, smaller implants might cause more problems for certain groups, like women. But did the same happen in India? The regulator couldn't tell because the company didn't say how many Indian implants they were studying. Without this information, it was hard for the regulator to know the full extent of harm Indian patients might face.

As they waited for vital data from the company about the findings of the investigation, a surprising turn of events unfolded. On 22 June 2011, a staggering 303 days after the recall announcement, the company reached out to the regulator with an update.

'We would like to update you on the progress to date regarding the voluntary recall ... This report is meant to provide you with information on the systems put in place since then to handle patient and surgeon claims resulting from the recall and the result of our communications to surgeons,' the company wrote to the regulator.[14] At first glance, the correspondence seemed routine, but it held a startling revelation concerning Indian patients.

In December 2010, nearly four months after the announcement of a global recall for its ASR hip implant, the company assured regulators that the recall had been successfully completed. However, reality painted a different picture. Fast-forward to 22 June 2011, when the company issued an update on the recall – the communication revealed a startling truth: the previous claim of completion, made in December 2010, merely meant that the company had only contacted the surgeons who had implanted the device – an admission that the recall process was far from over.

Not only this, the June 2011 communication revealed that India was trailing far behind on another key front: tracking down the patients impacted by the recalled implant.

Consider this.

On 22 June 2011, the company sent an update to the regulator, seemingly to reassure them about their efforts in managing patient and surgeon claims following a product recall. They boasted about engaging an independent claims processor, Puri Crawford and Associates India Pvt. Ltd., to handle claims efficiently. The company claimed the processor would have a dedicated team to manage calls and process claims promptly, ensuring patients and surgeons received accurate information and timely reimbursements. While this communication painted a picture of proactive customer care, the reality was far from it.

Buried within this communication lay the revelation of direct outreach to surgeons, twice – first between 26 August 2010 and 8 October 2010, and then again from 1 March 2011 to 6 June 2011. The sales force managed to track down 337 surgeons in the first round and 227 in the second round – 7 were not traceable, and 3 were out of town. These figures held significance beyond mere statistics. They unveiled approximately 300 surgeons utilizing ASR implants in India, suggesting ease in locating affected patients, especially in major hospitals.

At first glance, it seemed like the company had nailed it, hitting up every surgeon and one should expect a flood of over 4,000 Indian patients calling up the ASR helpline, racing to start those all-important metal ion blood tests. However, only a measly forty-five patients rang up the helpline by 15 June 2011. Surprisingly, the company did not even break a sweat, shrugging off the disappointing reachout like it was no big deal.

This number should have rung the alarm bell loud and clear. Because, according to the company's own submission, through this process, ASR patients were registering to get tests and doctor's visits to ascertain if revision surgery was needed. So, if the company was not able to get all the patients on board for blood tests, then the outreach and the helpline were just smoke and mirrors, not a serious recall to identify the patients whose lives were at significant risk.

The company should have been concerned about the substandard effort made to trace patients in India. Instead, the company decided to even downplay the poor showing of just forty-five patients registering. Right away, it was ready with a vague defence.

'It is important to note that the number of patients registered [on the helpline] as having had ASR implants is not indicative of the number who will need revision surgery,' the company told the regulator.[15]

'It should also be noted that in our estimate, about 4,700 ASR implants were conducted in India, although the total number of patients will be much less than this number due to some patients having had both hips replaced with ASR implants,' the company told the regulator.[16]

In essence, the company's response missed the mark, diverting attention from the glaring shortfall in patient engagement. But the most astonishing and distressing fact that emerged out of the 22 June 2011 communication by the company to the regulator was the double standards of the company on patient safety. The data revealed that the company's talk on patients' safety smacked of hypocrisy. The company said one thing and did another.

In the 22 June communication, the company unapologetically placed shocking data before the regulator: in the US alone, they had registered 23,366 patients, nearly 60 per cent of the nation's ASR patients. In Australia, DePuy had registered 2,970 patients, almost 50 per cent of the total; in South Africa, 2,098 were registered, or nearly 55 per cent; and in the United Kingdom, the company had registered 1,968 patients, almost 20 per cent of the total ASR patients.

However, in India, the company had registered only forty-five patients, a mere 1 per cent of the ASR patients in the country. Only neighbouring China fared worse than India, with a dismal 0.5 per cent registration rate.

The company offered no satisfactory explanation for this vast disparity. Despite possessing comparable resources and systems, their efforts in India paled in comparison to their endeavours elsewhere.

Instead of addressing this discrepancy head-on, they offered a shoddy and half-baked response to the Indian regulator. 'We want to assure you that DePuy Medical Pvt. Ltd. remains committed to supporting patients and surgeons through the recall process, and we maintain our commitment to the provision of quality medical devices and care.'[17]

The company extended an invitation to the regulator to discuss additional measures. 'If there are any additional efforts that you believe should be undertaken to ensure the process moves forward to benefit ASR patients, we would like to meet to discuss these efforts further,' it said.[18]

Another startling revelation lay hidden in the update, shedding light on the plight of Indian patients affected by the recall. The company, almost reluctantly, disclosed that by 15 June 2011, just nineteen revision surgeries had been conducted in the country.

Despite the urgency of the situation, in India, a glaring gap had emerged: no scientific studies had been undertaken to evaluate the performance of the recalled product in the Indian context. To add to the concern, there was a conspicuous absence of post-marketing surveillance data tailored to India when the recall was announced. Or if there was any, the company kept it under wraps. Thus, it was the data from these limited revision surgeries that finally shed light on the early failures of the ASR in India.

Consider this: an Indian patient underwent primary hip replacement on 4 July 2006, only to face revision surgery for the ASR on 2 April 2007 – more than three years before the global recall. Coincidentally, this timeline mirrored the early alarms raised by a few surgeons outside India about the ASR's premature failure.

Within this sparse data on revision surgeries lay stark evidence of early failures of ASR. For instance, eight patients underwent primary ASR surgery in 2008; among them, four required revision surgery in 2010, with the remaining four following suit in 2011 – signifying failure within a mere two to three years.

Even more alarming was the fate of two patients implanted with ASR in 2009, forced into revision surgery by 2010 – an aberrantly high failure rate becoming apparent.

The data also revealed one patient, implanted in 2004, undergoing revision in 2011, and three others from 2005 facing revision that same year, highlighting that even those who fared relatively better endured revision surgery after six to seven years – a failure rate deemed unacceptable in the orthopaedic industry.

As India's limited revision surgeries data was placed before the regulator, it showed just how important it was for the company to have shared whatever data they had about Indian ASR-related problems with the regulator way back in August 2010, when they decided to recall the device. Fast-forward to June 2011, with the company ultimately divulging this data through an update – suddenly, the potential health risk for Indian patients undergoing revision surgeries began to be revealed, giving a clearer understanding of the situation.

This update must have sparked a flurry of concern, because it highlighted glaring issues with tracing Indian patients and alarming data on the early failures of ASR implants. The data showed that any delay in addressing health risks associated with the recalled device might expose patients to unnecessary complications, highlighting the importance of timely regulatory intervention.

But most importantly, the limited revision surgery data indicated the premature revision surgeries were an indicator of life-changing complications due to the faulty implant in some affected patients. In such a scenario, compensation to these affected patients was imperative. However, until now, the regulator had not officially initiated any conversation on the important issue of compensation.

One would assume that swift action would follow, with the regulator promptly seeking further data and clarification. However, to the dismay of many, urgency seemed to be sorely lacking. Not surprisingly, it took a staggering ninety-nine days for the regulator to respond. The only glimmer of hope was that the June 2011 update prompted the regulator to finally summon company officials for a much-needed discussion on the issue of compensation to the Indian patients. 'You are hereby requested to give a technical presentation dated 13 October 2011,' the regulator wrote to the company.[19]

One year and five days after the global ASR recall of 24 August 2010, the Indian regulatory authority finally summoned DePuy to present crucial data regarding the recall. It was a meeting long overdue, considering the urgency of the matter. Set for 13 October 2011, at 4.00 p.m, the stage was the Food and Drugs Administration Bhawan on Kotla Road in the heart of the national capital.

The regulator outlined five key areas for presentation, most notably, the issue of compensation for affected Indian patients. However, prior to this meeting, the company had already touched upon four of these topics in various communications, albeit not comprehensively. These four issues included the recall procedure, reasons behind the recall, actions taken and the international regulatory status.

As the presentation unfolded, the company began by making broad claims about its values and commitments to quality and service to patients and healthcare professionals. 'We believe our first responsibility is to the doctors, nurses and patients, to mothers and fathers, and all others who use our products and services. In meeting their needs, everything we do must be of high quality,' it said in its presentation.[20]

Then the company gave a full rundown of the recall details regarding these four issues. It was essentially a recap of what the company had already communicated. The anticipation mounted as the regulators eagerly awaited the crucial discussion on compensation, a topic of paramount importance for ASR patients in India.

However, they were disappointed because the company's presentation failed to address this pressing concern. Instead, attempts were made to divert attention, with vague references to ongoing support for needy patients worldwide. Yet, the relevance of this statement to Indian patients remained unexplained. The presentation concluded with not a single word uttered regarding compensation, leaving many questions unanswered and frustrations unresolved.

The day following the presentation, the company wasted no time in reaching out to the regulator. In a swift and courteous message, they expressed gratitude for the opportunity to make a presentation on the recall. It was a good interaction with your team,' they wrote, and said they were eager to provide additional global data as requested.[21]

The company disclosed that 93,000 patients worldwide had received the implant in question. They also provided an update on another MoM hip implant, the Pinnacle Acetabular Cup System model. They also reassured the regulator of their commitment to patient safety and promised to keep them informed of any developments. However, they remained silent on the matter of compensation for Indian patients, leaving that aspect undisclosed once again.

For the next two months, a peculiar quiet settled between the regulator and the company: there was no official communication between the two on the issue of compensation. It appeared as though the company had skillfully diverted attention away from the pressing matter of compensation, keeping it safely tucked away on the back burner. But that changed. Fifty-seven days later, the regulator sent a message – marking perhaps the most significant development since the device recall in August 2010.

On 9 December 2011, the assistant drug controller wrote to the company, demanding detailed documents on three crucial matters regarding compensation for Indian patients. Each word in this communication carried weight, signalling a turning point. For the first time, the regulator hinted that Indian patients had borne the brunt of the recalled device's faults.

Questions were set out: What compensation had been offered to affected patients? Who were these patients, and what injuries had they suffered due to the ASR? And most crucially, it sought details of patients who had undergone surgery since 2004. 'You are hereby requested to submit ... documents to this office for taking further necessary action in the matter,' the regulator told the company.[22]

This communication marked a significant shift in tone. At least on paper, the regulator sounded more assertive. It seemed as though the regulator wanted to delve deep into the heart of the matter and understand how the company intended to address the concerns of Indian patients affected by the device's shortcomings. This shift was underscored by a crucial request: patient details. It looked like the regulator was no longer satisfied with mere numbers. By seeking details of Indian patients, it was indirectly asking the company to furnish details that would reveal the patient names, their locations, details on hospital visits and follow-up treatment, and their current state. It looked like the stakes had been raised, and the regulator seemed determined to get to the bottom of things.

The company replied quickly on 21 December 2011, on the detailed query by the regulator regarding compensating Indian patients. In its communication, the company carefully avoided using the word 'compensation'. For instance, the question posed by the regulator was about details of compensation given to each patient.

Replying to this question, the company artfully sidestepped the term 'compensation', opting instead to emphasize the 'remedial and reimbursement process'.[23] They said they had a process to reimburse patients for tests, revision surgeries, essential expenses such as travel and hospital stay for the patient as well as the attendant, alongside reimbursement for loss of wages. They also listed what they had reimbursed patients for until 12 December 2011.

The regulator had asked the company to furnish details of patients who were paid compensation for the injury caused to them by the ASR. The inquiry hinted at the regulator's expectation that the company take responsibility and compensate those who suffered severe health issues due to the defective implant. However, in response, the company didn't even touch upon the topic of compensation. Instead, it made a bold assertion, exonerating itself completely: 'We would like to bring to your notice that no injury was caused to any patient by ASR devices.'[24]

Lastly and most importantly, the regulator had pressed for details regarding patients who had undergone surgery dating back to 2004. It seemed like a simple inquiry, one that the company should readily address. However, instead of a straightforward response, they offered a murky explanation. Claiming confidentiality, they insisted that only surgeons and hospitals held such records, leaving them unable to disclose any details to any third party. 'We do not have the details of the patients who have undergone surgery since the year 2004 till 24 August 2010, the date of the voluntary recall,' it said.[25]

The company made two statements. But they didn't add up. First, they claimed no patients were hurt by their recalled device. Then, they claimed they did not have details about the patients. The stark contradiction between these two statements exposed a glaring inconsistency – raising doubts about the true extent of the situation. By making these two contradictory statements to the regulator in the same communication, it appeared like the company was caught in a web of its own lies. In fact, the company did know a lot about at least a few Indian patients.

Here's why.

While confidentiality clauses typically shield patient data, the voluntary recall of the ASR demanded a different approach. In such unusual circumstances, the company, hospitals and surgeons bore a moral responsibility to track every affected patient, potentially in need of revision surgery. This necessitated sharing patient information with the company undertaking the recall.

The company's excuse of confidentiality preventing access to patient details was contradicted by their own actions. As a matter of fact, on 22 June 2011, communicating to the regulator, the company had given out the details of patients registered through its helpline in India. It did not explicitly reveal each patient's personal identity and only shared relevant information regarding the safety of the product – that is, if the patient required revision surgery or not.

For that matter, the company provided the patient details to the team conducting the ASR explant analysis in London, as part of its ASR failure investigation. This fact was also earlier communicated to the regulator. Moreover, the voluntary recall stemmed from data on high revision rates reported in the UK registry. This meant doctors and hospitals were feeding patients details to the company to inform them about the product's performance. Of course, while doing this to ensure patient safety, doctors were not revealing the personal details of their patients. Furthermore, the company's claim of continuous post-marketing surveillance hinted at a deeper level of access to patient data.

In fact, the company was not revealing the full truth. Every time Puri Crawford processed patient claims, it asked patients to sign a consent form for disclosure of all medical records. The patients consented to provide the company copies of all medical records, including those after the revision surgery: discharge summary, physician progress notes, operative procedure records and follow-up visit documents.

The company used this information to ascertain who were eligible for reimbursement and the cost related to medical treatment associated with the recall of the ASR.

In essence, while the company professed confidentiality constraints, they were actually privy to extensive data of some patients. This raised questions about the company's transparency and motives. It also made you wonder what else they might be hiding.

However, the most striking revelation from the 21 December communication was the deliberate silence of the company on the issue of compensation for Indian patients. Rather than addressing the issue head-on, the company instead spoke about reimbursement that covered testing, monitoring, revision surgery, travel expenses and other allied costs. It became apparent that this information didn't shed any light on how Indian patients would be compensated. Instead, the information only served to muddle the waters, leaving the regulators feeling like they were chasing their own tail.

However, in the US, at least to its investors, the company was maintaining full transparency on how it was facing a barrage of product liability claims and lawsuits, particularly concerning its ASR. It informed investors that by the end of 2011, there were approximately 4,700 claimants with pending lawsuits linked to alleged injuries from ASR.[26]

It gave another update to its investors about a significant move they made during the final months of 2011. It revealed that the company had decided to put aside more money for the DePuy ASR Hip recall programme and any related product liability issues. But this decision didn't come out of thin air. The company carefully looked at new data, like how many claims they expected, updated revision rates of the ASR and product liability expense per case. Through this communication, they assured the investors that they aimed to make sure they were ready for any financial bumps in the road.

But most importantly, it told its investors about the possibility of 'ultimate resolution' of these ongoing lawsuits. With confidence, it conveyed its belief that these issues would find a conclusive resolution, assuring minimal impact on its financial stability and cash flow in the near future. The term 'resolution' hinted at the prospect of a settlement or resolution in the future to compensate the affected US patients. However, amidst this narrative of reassurance in the US, the company maintained a conspicuous silence regarding the topic of compensation in India.

Meanwhile, another parallel story was unfolding. As the year 2011 was drawing to an end, all eyes were on the regulator, awaiting its next move after the 9 December letter regarding compensation for Indian patients. But on 20 December 2011, the script took a sharp turn. A different bombshell rocked the scene. The regulator's next communication wasn't about compensation – it was about a whole new crisis. The Mumbai police had filed a criminal case against DePuy in connection with the recalled device. This was unprecedented in India's medical device regulatory landscape.

'This is to inform you that this office has received a letter from Sr. Inspector of Police, Mahim Police Station, Mumbai,' the regulator communicated to the company on 20 December.[27] In its communication, the regulator sought a detailed response on the serious allegations levelled against the company in the criminal case filed by the Mumbai police. First, it sought the company's response to the allegation that the company harboured the knowledge of the defective nature of their recalled device yet failed to disclose this crucial detail to the unsuspecting patients. Second, the regulator asked the company to reply to the allegation that it was responsible for the pain and suffering inflicted upon the affected patients.

This communication, one of the most important ones from the regulator, revealed that the company found itself at a crossroads in India, where stakes were high and uncertainty loomed large – marking a significant shift in focus since the device recall. The DePuy's 21 December response did not refer to this new communication and restricted itself to responding to the 9 December one, asserting that no patient was injured by the ASR. This development suggested serious legal implications for the company, as it was now accused of withholding crucial information about the device's defects from patients and causing them harm.

Almost sixteen months after the global recall, the company in India found itself entangled in a crisis. It was no longer just about regulatory scrutiny; it was about navigating legal waters and salvaging its public image. The stakes couldn't be higher as the company braced itself for the storm ahead. And the unprecedented criminal case initiated against the company was primarily driven by the steadfast efforts of an honest and upright officer at the helm of the drug regulatory body in Maharashtra, working tirelessly to unearth the truth related to the health status of the patients and hold the company accountable – a task that should have been undertaken from day one of the recall announcement.

Part IV

10

FIR: 435/2011

Enter the world of Mahesh Zagade, a senior bureaucrat, whose career shines with determination and honesty. Since joining the Indian Administrative Service (IAS) in 1993, he served for nearly three decades, fearlessly navigating the intricate web of bureaucracy in the politically influential state of Maharashtra. His actions echoed through the corridors of power, where he confronted the mighty. In May 2009, Zagade assumed the role of Pune's municipal commissioner, with a big job ahead: transforming the Pune landscape and ensuring the city becomes a great place to live, where everyone follows the rules.

During this period, Pune found itself at a crossroads of transformation. As the second-largest city in Maharashtra, it had experienced the highest migration rate over the past decade in India.[1] The city's booming information technology industry was set to touch a staggering Rs 30 billion in exports.[2] Simultaneously, the city's real estate market flourished, boasting one of the highest rates of property price escalation nationwide. However, amidst this prosperity lurked the spectre of illegal construction.

In response, Zagade initiated a rigorous crackdown on illegal construction activities, drawing upon his reputation for integrity and past experiences in exposing corruption.[3] His prior tenure as the district magistrate of Nashik had seen him expose a major land scandal, exposing the darker facets of urban development. Despite facing formidable opposition from the powerful real estate lobby in Pune, Zagade remained steadfast in his resolve.

However, his tenure in Pune was abruptly cut short after just over two years when he was reassigned to Mussoorie for official training at the Lal Bahadur Shastri National Academy of Administration (LBSNAA). This move sparked a political firestorm, with opposition parties protesting Zagade's transfer and accusing the ruling government of yielding to the demands of the real estate lobby.[4]

Amidst the controversy, concerns arose regarding Zagade's future in Pune. These concerns proved valid when Zagade, still in training, was replaced by another officer in Pune.

'While I was still training, they transferred me and posted somebody else in Pune,' Zagade recalls.[5]

After completing his training, Zagade came back, expecting a new posting as is customary for IAS officers, especially those of secretary rank, shortly after their transfer. However, contrary to this norm, Zagade didn't receive a new assignment for three months. During this time, he engaged with top officials, from the chief secretary to the chief minister, all of whom assured him that they were working on finding him a suitable posting.

Despite assurances, the wait stretched on for weeks. Then came the midnight call, while Zagade and his wife were visiting a friend in Mumbai. The additional chief secretary, who handled service matters, placed two options before Zagade: secretary of medical education, or commissioner of the state food and drug administration (FDA).

'I had no time to think. I just told them that I was picking the post of secretary of medical education,' Zagade says.

But his wife, sitting right there, wasn't so sure. She challenged his choice with a foresight born of experience.

'She said that as secretary of medical education, I would end up fighting every other day with the minister. She told me to relax, because I still had a few years left in the IAS.'

Zagade thought it over and changed his mind.

'I called the senior officer back and said, "I've changed my mind. I'll take up the assignment as the FDA commissioner,"' Zagade recalls. And so, on that fateful March night in 2011, Zagade embarked on a new journey, steering the course of Maharasthra's FDA.

Mahesh Zagade arrived at his new post in August 2011. Until then, Zagade was largely unaware of the inner workings of the FDA. He assumed his new staff would bring him up to speed. Instead, they merely hinted at the cushy nature of his new job – just a few days a week, a handful of hours. Word had it that his predecessor, who resided comfortably in South Mumbai, treated the office like a leisurely affair, clocking in at 10.00 a.m. and out by lunch.

'It was considered to be a very, very cosy posting,' Zagade says.

Yet, Zagade's curiosity got the better of him, and he wasted no time in immersing himself in the myriad files and documents. He knew that a thorough examination of these key files would provide him with invaluable insights into the department's operations. His sudden deep dive into the department's affairs injected urgency into the usually routine environment. Papers shuffled, computers hummed softly, juniors scurried with files to the commissioner's room. Department colleagues exchanged cautious glances, unsure how Zagade's scrutiny might affect things.

As his office waited nervously, Zagade next ordered a review of all pending matters, catching the department off guard. As he probed deeper, he found the workload remarkably light, with the only pending issues being related to leave approvals. It seemed too good to be true. Determined to get to the bottom of this unique scenario, he convened a meeting with his officers to ascertain the true status of pending matters.

'They came up with the defence that everything happens at the district level – which was not true. In fact, by this time, I had understood that the previous commissioner was pretty much unaware of what was happening inside the department,' Zagade recalls.

At this juncture, Zagade intensified his efforts, adopting a rigorous schedule. Commencing work at 9.30 a.m., he conducted numerous review meetings extending into the evenings, departing the office as late as 8.00 p.m. This shift signified a significant departure from the previous relaxed atmosphere within the department, particularly for those directly reporting to him. They were now part of a detailed review process touching every aspect of the department. He also asked senior officials to schedule a meeting to discuss another important issue: complaints received by the FDA.

'To gauge the pulse of any department, I always scanned all the complaints. Audit reports and the complaints reveal what the bureaucratic machinery is doing and the mistakes they are making.

Reviewing complaints gave me a fair idea about their nature,' Zagade says.

After a thorough review meeting, Zagade delved into a pile of complaints, only to discover that many had been gathering dust for a staggering five to ten years. He took the decision to address this backlog and tasked his personal assistant with keeping a register for quicker resolution.

In all the complaints, two stood out.

'The complaint dated back to 2009. It spoke about suffering due to a wrong product,' Zagade recalls. Strikingly, he found another complaint with almost identical facts. 'The other complainant said he had lost his father due to a faulty product.' Struck by the eerie parallels between these cases, he felt compelled to bring them to the attention of his junior.

'Despite the gravity of the complaints, the joint commissioner dismissed them, attributing them to common patient grievances,' Zagade recalls.

Zagade was not convinced. He informed the joint commissioner that the complaints were serious and that the department could not simply dismiss or ignore them.

'However, the officer brushed them off, once again claiming that patients routinely send complaints like these, even for mild pain,' says Zagade. At this point, the junior officer made another statement that startled Zagade.

'This is a huge company – a hundred-billion-dollar company,' the officer told Zagade. The junior commissioner's casual mention of the big pharma's massive financial clout hinted at the undue influence these giants wielded over regulatory officials.

But Zagade ignored the dissuading voices around him and kept pushing forward.

'I noticed a few more complaints of similar nature. I was curious,' he says. Finally, he initiated an internal exercise and instructed his team to dissect a specific grievance originating from Mumbai, regarding implant-related pain. The officials submitted a report, but their stance didn't change a bit. They gave a clean chit to the company, recommending that the complaint be closed.

But Zagade refused to be quieted. He rallied his officers once more, declaring his intent to dig deeper, this time under the scrutiny of a new team, handpicked from the vigilance wing.

'No field officers this time,' he asserted firmly. However, changing the officers didn't elicit a different response.

'The vigilance officer also resisted. First, the officer said it was an old complaint. Then the officer pointed out that no reminders had been sent. Then they tried to convince me that it is field officers, not vigilance officers, who are involved in investigating these types of complaints,' Zagade recalls.

Zagade didn't give up. He kept pushing, determined to get to the truth, no matter what. However, days later, the officers came up with another excuse.

'They said that state departments' hands are tied because we weren't the ones to issue a license to the company. They kept arguing that only the national regulator DCGI [Drugs Controller General of India] could do anything in the case because the implant had been imported based on their license,' Zagade says.

Tension hung thick at the FDA office as Zagade and the officers found themselves at odds over the direction of the investigation, casting a pall of unease among the team. However, Zagade was adamant about preserving harmony within the team.

'So I told them they had my support,' says Zagade. Quietly, without causing a stir, he started investigating the matter – on his own.

At the Maharashtra FDA headquarters, as Zagade began to uncover the truth behind the written complaints linked to the recalled medical device, a palpable sense of purpose filled his room. With a stack of documents sprawled across his desk, he dove headfirst into the medical literature on hip implants, methodically sifting through each page, taking printouts to dissect the intricate details. He turned to the internet, searching for clinical literature on the implant – exploring how it works, the potential adverse events and the firsthand experiences of users. Each mouse click and every turned page brought him closer to solving the mystery of why patients were complaining about the device.

Navigating through complex scientific issues was second nature to Zagade, a testament to his mastery in phytopathology, the study of plant diseases. His journey into the bureaucracy had been preceded by years of research in a leading multinational corporation, where his expertise was instrumental in unravelling the intricacies of plant diseases. Besides, Zagade's involvement in understanding medical adverse reactions was more than professional; it was deeply personal. A brush with cerebral malaria in 2002 exposed him to the harsh realities of adverse drug reactions when he was prescribed Mefloquine.

'The experience left its mark,' he reflects, recalling the severe reaction that fuelled his resolve to delve into the side effects of medications.

The meticulous research conducted by Zagade, utilizing the internet, led to a significant breakthrough. He uncovered orthopaedic registry data concerning the ASR from Australia and the United Kingdom, which proved to be a vital source of information to his investigation. This dataset provided invaluable insights into the actual performance of the product, as documented by doctors in the registry. Moreover, it helped him compare the ASR's performance with other similar products.

As Zagade combed through the extensive data from the Australian orthopaedic registry, another startling revelation leaped off the screen: the ASR had been discontinued in the country in 2009, a year before the voluntary global recall. Immediately, Zagade rallied his team for an urgent meeting to discuss this issue.

'I told them that there was a huge problem. We needed to relook at the issue.' In the ensuing days, his research unearthed further unsettling truths. 'I found out that in the US, the FDA had never approved the resurfacing model of the ASR. But we continued to use it here in India. I was perplexed.'

The Maharashtra FDA office was charged with a mix of surprise and shock as Zagade revealed crucial data on the recalled device that had previously eluded their knowledge. He, himself, had been taken aback at the magnitude of the problem when he uncovered its facets. However, despite the mounting evidence against the company, some officials remained hesitant and were reluctant to take decisive action.

'Some officials kept insisting that only the national regulator was empowered to act against the company,' Zagade recalls.

At this juncture, a clear disagreement was brewing between Zagade and his officers. However, this time Zagade stood firm in his belief that the office's foremost duty was to protect the safety of patients.

His voice resonant with conviction, he spoke to his gathered officers.

'I told them that patient safety is the responsibility of the drug controller of the state. That's what the law states. No one could disagree on this point. So they asked me how to proceed in such unique circumstances,' Zagade says.

A sense of suspense filled the Maharashtra FDA office as Zagade calmly addressed his team. It was rare for a state regulator to consider taking direct action related to a medical device recall. His subordinates listened with a mix of astonishment and unease as he outlined a unique solution to address the issue at hand. First, he decided to make an official note about the limitations of the powers of the state regulator which hampered efforts in tracing all affected patients of the recalled device. Then, he made a decisive move: organizing a press conference with the aim to reach out to the patients.

Zagade's team huddled together and began preparing for the press conference. This wasn't just an ordinary press briefing; he, in particular, understood the weight of the responsibility resting on his shoulders. It was a rare opportunity where a state-level drug regulator would discuss and share with local journalists the complexities of a medical device recall.

It was a warm, humid day in Mumbai. The important day had finally arrived for the drug regulator to meet the press: the room buzzed with anticipation as journalists from various newspapers and television networks filled the room, their pens poised and cameras rolling. As Zagade took the stand, he didn't hesitate to name the company at the centre of the controversy, articulating the importance of the issue.

'I made it unequivocally clear,' Zagade recalls, 'there were more patients out there experiencing problems linked to the implant. Those facing similar challenges could turn to us for assistance. I cited the case from Australia as an example. Furthermore, I recounted another complaint, detailing how a patient's concerns were ignored by their physician. Essentially, I underscored that the sole purpose of the press conference was to safeguard the interests of patients.'

As Zagade concluded the press conference, he harboured a glimmer of hope – a hope that his words would resonate far beyond the walls of the room, igniting a chain reaction of awareness and action. His anticipation was soon met with reality, as the days following the press conference saw an influx of complaints flooding into the department.

From the urban hub of Mumbai to the rural areas of Nashik, patients emerged, the mark of their suffering visible on their faces. Every story of pain acted as a powerful reminder of the seriousness of the situation, strengthening Zagade's belief in the urgent need for intervention.

'At this point, I was convinced that this was a matter of serious concern,' Zagade recalls.

Following the conclusion of the press conference, the atmosphere at the Maharashtra FDA office was divided. On one side, a palpable sense of satisfaction lingered. Zagade believed that his team had done their duty in protecting the patients' interests by disclosing crucial information about a medical device recall. For him, transparency was paramount, and he felt a measure of satisfaction in having fulfilled that obligation. Yet, across the room, there were some officers at the Maharashtra FDA who remained obdurate, their faces hard with quiet resistance.

Despite the public disclosure, they held reservations about taking further action, especially when Zagade decided to collect more specific details on the implant. He couldn't help but wonder if there was a hidden agenda at play. The reason behind their opposition remained shrouded in mystery. Whatever the reason, their resistance highlighted the complexities inherent in regulatory decision-making in India.

'They said we shouldn't continue doing this. I didn't know why they resisted collecting data. Maybe they were cosy with the company. I just didn't know,' Zagade recalls.

Zagade recounts facing bizarre arguments against taking further action.

'The list of arguments was endless: not all implants always offer a full or definitive solution to a patient's health issue; if we start doing this, too many patients will come to us; we will create havoc in the industry; so on and so forth. I heard it all,' he recalls. However, he boldly took the lead, urging his officers to move ahead and intensify their efforts in tracing more affected patients in the state.

Zagade was known for his meticulous adherence to regulations. He always ensured that he familiarized himself with the pertinent law before authorizing any action. Hence, even in this case, before issuing instructions to his officials to trace patients in the state, he ensured that all actions aligned with the established protocols.

'In fact, I read out to the team the specific provisions under the law that allow us to take action to trace patients,' Zagade recalls.

However, among a few officers, a dissenting murmur arose against Zagade's interpretation of law for tracing patients.

'There were some officers, with thirty years of experience in the FDA commissioner's office, who argued that there are no such provisions,' Zagade recalls. Yet, this was insufficient to sway him from his course. Instead, he rationally explained to these officers the law's applicability in extraordinary circumstances.

'I told them an implant is a form of prescription drug, so the distribution is under licence. The hospitals would have the names of the patients. I told them it would only take a few days to trace each patient.' And thus, the department embarked on tracking the patients.

Almost at the same time, another kind of pressure began to mount. Company bigwigs hurried to the regulator's office, feeling anxious about what was to come. It was an unusual sight at the local regulator's office, one that hinted at the gravity of the situation at hand. The spotlight was on the company now, and Zagade was getting ready to talk about his concerns to them directly. It was like two sides getting ready for a showdown, each fully aware of the high stakes involved.

The atmosphere crackled with tension as the company vehemently expressed its discontent with Zagade's decision to hold a press conference. Voices rose, punctuated by sharp exchanges as both parties defended their positions. The company argued for a more discreet approach. But Zagade stood firm, citing public safety concerns and the need for transparency.

'The company officials argued that I should not have held a press conference. They implied that they could sue me for dragging their name [into it]. I made my point clear. I told them that I was only making a public appeal to the patients. In fact, I told them I would have done the same if patients were suffering because of another hip joint,' Zagade recalls.

In particular, tension simmered as differences arose between the two parties over the issue of disclosing the complete patient data. The company attempted to navigate the discussion with a strategy to downplay the necessity of disclosing complete data. In contrast,

Zagade, firm and unyielding, insisted on receiving complete and transparent information linked to patient data.

'However, the company disagreed with this demand. They took a legal stand, citing patient confidentiality. I told them patients' confidentiality is invoked for misuse. But as the regulator – and I'm asking for patient data to protect them – their vague defence wouldn't hold water with me,' he recalls.

The company refrained from making any concrete commitment regarding provision of complete patient data. Instead, it expressed the intention to delve into this matter, studying the legal issue of patient confidentiality – a cautious approach to buy time.

'I told their representatives that they could study as much as they wanted to, but they could not delay on this issue,' Zagade recalls.

For over a month, Zagade and his team waited impatiently: would the company provide the crucial patient data they had sought? This uncertainty complicated the already daunting task of tracing the affected patients.

The last meeting had ended with a clear directive from Zagade: submit patient details.

At the next meeting, as the company officials arrived, Zagade waited in anticipation. But instead of producing the requested patient details, the officials launched into a polished speech about the company's dedication to patient safety. They painted a picture of a company deeply committed to safeguarding patients.

'They also spoke about the developments overseas,' Zagade recalls.

However, as Zagade listened intently, his patience waned. He sternly reminded them of the meeting's purpose.

'I told them that I knew every single thing about what was happening outside India and that we need not waste our time discussing it,' he recalls. Realizing their diversionary tactic had failed, the officials quickly adjusted their approach and unveiled a new plan: the company would appoint a coordinator to closely monitor the progress of patients registering with Puri Crawford. This, they asserted, would significantly enhance their ability to reach out to patients. But this offer seemed like an attempt to brush aside the discussion on providing complete patient data.

At this point, some of Zagade's officers leaned forward eagerly, their voices animated with enthusiasm as they welcomed the company's new proposal, as an excellent idea.

'My officers started saying that the company was now fully cooperating, even spending money to trace patients,' Zagade recalls.

However, Zagade remained silent for a few minutes, his face unreadable. Finally, his dispassionate voice broke through the fawning babble.

'I asked them why an implant company would require another company to trace patients.' He specifically gave them the example of a car manufacturer who has the complete details of customers when vehicles are registered. On similar lines, in the case of an implant, the distributor and hospitals have complete patient data. No other agent or middleman was needed.

As the crucial meeting neared its conclusion, Zagade pondered over how India's situation differed from that of other wealthy countries. Unlike the seamless patient tracing abroad, India grappled with significant hurdles. He was determined to overcome them. Hence, despite his colleagues' best efforts to sway him, Zagade remained unmoved – insisting that the company provide him with the complete list of patients so that they could be traced.

'I told them this was the same product that had been sold in several high-income countries. Indians are not different from white-skinned people. We are the same. What happens there should happen here,' Zagade says.

After a few days of going back and forth, Zagade's department and the company had a final meeting to discuss the issue of providing the data to trace patients. This final meeting however, felt different – there was an unspoken understanding that the stakes were higher, the consequences even severe. With measured steps, they took their seats, exchanging wary glances. The topic of providing full patient data loomed over them like a dark cloud. Again, the same sorts of arguments were being trotted out. Suddenly, in the midst of the tense discussion, Zagade issued a warning.

'I told the company that if they didn't provide the information, I would file an FIR against the company. That made them blow their top,' Zagade recalls.

This sent shockwaves through the room, leaving the company officials visibly unsettled. The atmosphere grew increasingly heated as a contentious exchange erupted between the two sides. Zagade recalls the company officials accusing him of harassment.

'I said I wasn't interested in harassing them. I reiterated that Indian patients should be treated on par with international patients. I just told them that they should do the same here with sincerity,' Zagade says.

Amidst the escalating confrontation, the company questioned Zagade, demanding under which specific provisions he could criminally prosecute the company for its actions on the implant. He guessed that the company officials were again reaching into their bag of tricks. He knew they were digressing to avoid addressing the real issue of providing the complete patient data.

'I know how to file the FIR, I told them,' Zagade recalls.

After the meeting, Zagade wasted no time. Determined to walk the talk, he dove headfirst into collecting more data on the implant. He meticulously organized the evidence. Patient testimonies, medical reports and expert analyses began to pile up on his desk, forming a solid foundation for his case. Late nights and early mornings became his routine as he combed through documents, cross-referenced data and consulted with legal experts. His resolve was unshakable; he knew the stakes were high, not just for him but for all the patients who were quietly suffering unknowingly.

Zagade was aware that the battle ahead would be tough, but he was prepared. Within days, he stood ready to file the case. The local law dictated a formal process: drafting a complaint and presenting it to the police to kickstart the FIR registration. The draft of the complaint for filing an FIR was prepared with meticulous attention to detail, leaving no room for ambiguity. Recognizing the gravity of the situation, Zagade assigned a team of officers from both the headquarters and the Mumbai regional office to submit the complaint at the Mahim police station.

This station has jurisdiction over one of the important zones of the central region of Mumbai. It is a modest-looking building with rough old stone walls painted pale blue and yellow. On any given day, officers in uniform can be found seated behind their desks, listening to and registering complainants on local crimes – everything from thefts and assaults to the occasional murder investigation. Behind these officers, there is a large board displaying various official details in Marathi, likely about duties, assignments or case statuses.

With the arrival of the FDA team sent by Zagade, the police found themselves on the cusp of a rare and intricate investigation. It wasn't the usual run-of-the-mill crime they were accustomed to. This time, they were entering uncharted territory: the complex world of medical device recalls. Across a wooden table sat Zagade's team. Opposite them was the local sub-inspector, flanked by his own team, their faces reflecting a blend of curiosity and anticipation.

This meeting was unusual but critical; the police needed to understand the complexities of the case to build a solid criminal case under the Indian Penal Code. As the team began their briefing, the police officers leaned in, absorbing every word. The team meticulously outlined the background of the medical device recall, emphasizing the potential harm caused by the defective devices and the urgent need for swift action.

At the same time, murmurs about an impending criminal complaint began to circulate within the Maharashtra FDA corridors. Sensing the imminent storm brewing, company officials sprang into action, urgently arranging a meeting with Zagade. Both parties were aware that the atmosphere would be far from cordial due to the issue at stake. They eventually met after a few weeks. The company officials, while attempting to maintain composure, could not hide the tension in their voice as they spoke.

'This is not done, Mr Zagade. No country has lodged an FIR in the matter,' the company official told Zagade, he recalls.

Zagade was undeterred; he was prepared to push hard on accountability and compliance. He sternly emphasized the urgency of tracing all affected patients, making it abundantly clear that this was non-negotiable. Any semblance of complacency in this matter would not be tolerated.

'I told them that since 2010 the company had not done anything to trace patients. However, they vehemently argued that I could not name the company directors in the FIR,' Zagade says.

The threat of a criminal case was a constant undercurrent, influencing every exchange and making it clear that the stakes were extraordinarily high. Accusations and rebuttals flew across the table. The meeting ended with no clear resolution. Both sides knew that the path forward would be fraught with further disputes.

After this meeting, Zagade was determined to proceed with the case. His department came together to finalize the blueprint of the complaint. Intense debates and discussions ensued. They reviewed legal precedents, examined the regulatory framework and scrutinized the company actions. They debated the specific provisions applicable in the extraordinary case of a medical device recall, considering factors such as patient safety, corporate responsibility and legal accountability. Every angle was explored to ensure the complaint was comprehensive and unassailable.

'Honestly, I was not fighting with the company. I was fighting with the system. The officials in the department had been trained for decades to remain silent. We collected all the relevant data. I studied everything in detail. Finally, I had to dictate every section we would use in the case. It was an exhaustive process,' Zagade recalls.

Weeks before the registration of the FIR, Zagade, his assistant commissioner who was conducting an internal department inquiry into the case and other key members gathered for a series of meetings. Everyone knew that the decision made in these moments could have far-reaching legal consequences, and they all felt the weight of responsibility.

During these final meetings, where he invited them to speak up, all their doubts and uncertainties were raised and addressed. These discussions went beyond the issues related to recalled devices; they delved into the responsibilities of the manufacturers and distributors. With each query, Zagade responded with precision, offering detailed technical insights and presenting evidence to back his claims.

The cross-questioning was intense, with concerns about the applicability of specific sections of the Indian Penal Code (IPC), Zagade, anticipating them, provided legal interpretations. This back-and-forth was crucial; his team needed to fully grasp the case's complexities.

Days later, the Maharashtra FDA, now armed with a clearer understanding of the case, was ready to proceed with the necessary legal actions. Zagade had done more than just brief them; he had built a foundation for a strong, informed collaboration to tackle this unique challenge. Zagade once again sent his team to the Mahim police station to check on the progress of converting the complaint into an FIR. When they returned in the evening, they informed him that the uniqueness of the complaint had prompted the police to request additional time to examine the document before deciding whether to register an FIR. This response struck Zagade as peculiar.

Unwilling to let bureaucratic inertia delay the matter, he waited a couple of days before instructing his team to revisit the police station and follow up. The team returned with disheartening news – the police were still 'in the process' of making a decision. Realizing the need for firmer intervention, Zagade contacted the deputy commissioner of police (DCP) for the zone and urged him to expedite the matter. The DCP promptly acted on his instructions, dispatching a senior police inspector to meet Zagade and gain a deeper understanding of the case.

During their meeting, Zagade provided a detailed account, emphasizing the case's international implications, the suffering of the affected patients, and the urgent need to register the FIR without further delay. The inspector, who appeared both knowledgeable and empathetic, assured him of his personal commitment to addressing the issue. 'True to his word, he took swift action,' Zagade recalls.

Within a couple of days, the FDA team revisited the police station, and this time, their perseverance paid off – the FIR was finally filed. This outcome was not just a testament to Zagade's persistence but also to the collaborative efforts of conscientious officers who recognized the significance of justice in this case. 'It underscored a powerful truth: when diligence meets determination, even the most complex hurdles can be surmounted,' Zagade says.

General Diary Entry, 19 November 2011
Location: Mahim Police Station
Time: 9.30 p.m.

At this date and hour, a unique complaint was lodged. A drug inspector from the Maharashtra FDA headquarters arrived, his demeanour resolute. Despite the late hour, the station buzzed with an unusual energy. The drug inspector approached the senior sub-inspector to file the complaint, who immediately noted the complaint and oversaw the process of registering the FIR.

As the complaint was formally recorded, it was clear that it was no ordinary general diary entry. This complaint was designated as

FIR: 435/11, filed by the Maharashtra FDA. DePuy Medical Private Limited was named as the accused. As a result, the police were set to delve into a domain rarely treaded, ready to uncover the truth behind a medical device recall.

The complaint that served as the basis of the FIR offered a glimpse into the findings of the department's internal investigation. It compellingly justified the invocation of specific sections of the IPC and laid out a clear path forward, highlighting crucial areas that still required further investigation.

At the heart of the FIR was the company's urgent field safety notices issued to surgeons – the first one on 8 March 2010 and the second one on 24 August 2010. This crucial document was the complaint's backbone, to get across the message that the company was aware about elevated levels of metal ions being released into the blood; that the implants could release metal ions in dangerous amounts; and that this directly harms patients, often forcing them to undergo revision surgery to remove the implant. This alarming possibility underscored the urgent need for action and further investigation. Furthermore, it raised a red flag that even if some patients had no complaints now, the implant could still corrode over time and create metal debris in the patient's body.

Relying on these documents, the complaint's first pillar was the seven potential health risks that patients might face due to the implant. The first issue encountered was component loosening. Those who had hoped the implant would restore their mobility instead found themselves feeling the implant shift and loosen within their hip, causing instability. Each painful step was a stark reminder that the surgery intended to help them had, in some cases, turned daily activities into daunting challenges.

Infection was the second issue, characterized by symptoms such as fever, redness and swelling. In severe cases, this could lead to hospital stays, revision surgeries and prolonged, painful recoveries.

Pain was the third issue. Persistent discomfort could disrupt sleep, affect mental health and significantly diminish quality of life, leaving patients frustrated and desperate for relief.

Fracture and dislocation were the fourth and fifth. These not only caused pain but also rendered the implant useless, often necessitating emergency surgery. Consequently, patients faced the ordeal of recovering from yet another invasive procedure.

The last two issues were component malignancy, a severe complication that could upend a patient's life, and metal sensitivity, which could result in severe allergic reactions, manifesting as rashes, swelling and joint pain.

The second pillar of the complaint centred on the crucial issue of tracing patients. The complaint first brought to light some alarming numbers: just under one year after the recall, only forty-three patients informed the company that they had the ASR. Out of those, twenty-six had to undergo the painful revision surgery. A vast majority of patients had not been traced.

Then the complaint painted a stark picture of the company struggling to manage a crisis, highlighting the gaps in its response in tracing the patients. It specifically noted that on 11 October 2011, the FDA department communicated an urgent directive, instructing DePuy to gather information about all affected patients. On 2 November 2011, the company replied that to handle this issue efficiently, a new plan was set in motion: a coordinator would be appointed to closely monitor the progress of patient registration on the helpline and provide any necessary assistance to expedite the remedial measures.

The complaint raised a red-flag that despite these reassurances, a troubling oversight emerged. The company had failed to conduct crucial metal ion tests on each patient who had contacted it. This neglect did not go unnoticed. '... It is clear that the company ... has shown a lackadaisical approach,' the Maharashtra FDA said in the complaint.[6]

The final pillar of the complaint was on the critical issue of timely revision surgeries. The complaint highlighted a troublingly high rate of revision surgeries linked to the implant. The department could not present the full scope of the problem due to incomplete patient data. Undeterred, the complaint pivoted to a different strategy: utilizing the available data from forty-three patients. This data starkly revealed that approximately six out of ten patients needed a revision surgery. '... As the treatment is delayed ... there would [be] side effects on the patient's health ... [A]nd if revision surgery is not done by reviewing the case in proper time ... it may cause harm ... [S]erious note should be taken about this failure to act,' the complaint asserted.[7]

This statement highlighted the agency's argument: despite the alarming revision rates evident even in a small patient sample, the company had inexplicably failed to ensure that all Indian patients with the implant were tested. 'Despite this, the company is not bothered to undertake testing of each patient ... As the toxic substance ... starts releasing in the body of patients in whom these faulty devices are implanted, it would pose a serious risk ... the company has [a] lackadaisical approach ... about enquiring with each patient,' the complaint said.[8]

In the end, the most crucial part of the FIR was revealed – the specific sections of the IPC invoked in this unprecedented case of a medical device recall. The first was Section 320 of the IPC. This section deals with grievous hurt, which includes severe injuries such as fractures or dislocation of bones. The invocation of this section indicated that the faulty implant allegedly caused significant physical harm to the affected patients.

Then came Section 321 of the IPC, invoked in criminal cases for voluntarily causing hurt. It implied that the harm was deliberate or that the company allegedly acted with knowledge that the device would cause physical harm. The complaint, specifically, alleged that the company, knowing the risks, failed to take necessary actions like medical tests or revision surgeries to mitigate the damage, thereby committing a criminal offence under this section.

Third, Section 328 of the IPC was invoked. It is typically used in criminal cases where harmful substances are administered with the intent to cause harm. The complaint argued that the company was aware that the devices were allegedly harmful – likened to 'unwholesome drugs' – but still did not act to prevent harm to patients, thus violating the law.

The complaint wasn't limited to just invoking the sections of the IPC; it took things further. The department levelled a serious accusation against the company, alleging a violation of Section 18(a)(1) of the Drugs and Cosmetics Act. This particular charge suggested that the company had been allegedly distributing medical devices that failed to meet the necessary quality standards.

But the implications were even more severe: if the company were found guilty, it would face punishment under Section 27(a) of the same Act. At the time the complaint was filed, this section mandated a minimum imprisonment of five years, potentially extending to life.

'This really created the flurry,' Zagade recalls.

FIR: 435/11 ignited an unprecedented investigation into a medical device recall case. It marked an important event in India's medical device regulatory landscape. Both the police and the Maharashtra FDA, just days after the launch of the probe, faced the risk of unforeseen hurdles. Especially for the local police, this was an entirely new world. They had to navigate unfamiliar investigative procedures and grapple with the complexities of a medical device recall.

For the Maharashtra FDA, the probe pushed the members of the department out of their comfort zones – learn quickly, absorb vast amounts of new information and collaborate in unprecedented ways. In many ways, the probe served as a template for regulators both at the national and state levels – one that they should have implemented the day the ASR recall was announced in August 2010 – for greater transparency and enhanced patient safety.

―――

The investigation began with a crucial first step: tracing the patients implanted with the device. This task was essential to uncovering the truth. How many patients were suffering from adverse reactions? How many had already endured painful revision surgeries? Finding these answers demanded locating the patients themselves.

What seemed like a straightforward task quickly became challenging. The police interrogated the company's sales team, hoping to trace the affected patients, but found no registry of those who had received the implants. The sales team had only called the supplier about the recall and informed the surgeons directly, without contacting the patients. This fragmented communication between the company and the hospitals complicated the police's work, and patient confidentiality issues further muddled the situation.

Faced with these obstacles, the police then turned to the medical supplier. As a key player in the distribution network, the Mumbai-based supplier held invaluable information about the hospitals that had used the implants. Reaching out to the implant supplier marked an important moment in the investigation. With the supplier's cooperation, new avenues of information opened up. The police gained access to the list of hospitals who had used the implants. Armed with this crucial information, the police reached out to the hospitals.

The patients' details had the potential to break the case wide open – this information was not just a catalogue of the patients affected by the implants, but also a window into the experiences of the doctors who had treated them. This insight was a goldmine for the police, presenting a prime opportunity to build a strong case. With each doctor's statement potentially serving as a stepping stone in their investigation, the police decided to move forward with meeting the surgeons.

The police began recording firsthand accounts from a few doctors who had used these implants. These surgeons held a unique perspective, having witnessed firsthand the adverse impacts on their patients' health. Their testimonies painted a vivid picture of the potential problems caused by the faulty implants.

The third leg of the investigation was centred around collecting the irrefutable scientific evidence. Here, investigators examined two sources. First, they collected blood test reports to prove the presence of high levels of metals ions in the patients' blood. Second, after searching for blood test reports, they collected samples of faulty implants removed from the body, and dispatched them for a detailed forensic examination. This was essential to expose the full extent of the potential damage inflicted by the implant.

At first glance, these three facets of investigation seemed straightforward: access patients' details, record statements from doctors and collect scientific evidence. It looked like a case that could be neatly wrapped up in no time. However, reality had other plans.

In the initial ten months of the investigation, the team reached out to over 100 patients via phone. While the sheer number was promising, there was a snag. Many of these individuals hadn't undergone their crucial blood tests, and wanted to do so before giving their formal statements. This added a layer of complexity to the case, as they would have to come back to these patients later. However, amidst this, there was some positive breakthrough: approximately thirty patients who had suffered post-surgery pain had their statements recorded.

To bridge the gap created by the unavailability of blood test results, the police then decided to send notices under criminal procedure code. They asked the company to submit blood test reports from all those patients who had undergone revision surgery. The company, represented by Puri Crawford, cooperated to a certain extent. They provided some details while coyly revealing that metal ion tests were conducted only in select cases.

Consequently, in the initial ten months, the police managed to unearth details of sixty-three patients grappling with pain. However, the scarcity of blood test reports proved to be a formidable obstacle, allowing access to metal ion test results in a mere seven cases. Alarmingly, in this sample of seven cases, four revealed high metal ion concentrations, exceeding 7 ppb.

However, the police could not overlook patients suffering from acute pain despite lacking metal ion test results. The stakes were high, and the urgency great. For the first time in the investigation, the local police collected explants as evidence and sent them for scientific examination to the local forensic department. Two shining circular metallic objects, the two components of an explant set, were placed in a polythene bag, sealed and carefully dispatched to the experts. The examination results confirmed suspicions: the explants contained alarmingly high levels of both cobalt and chromium.

Amidst these challenges, another issue surfaced. The police uncovered two or three rare cases of deceased patients, with grieving families insisting that the faulty implants were to blame. This development made the police's task even more daunting: they now had to meticulously establish a possible causal link between these tragic deaths and the adverse reactions allegedly triggered by the implants in these cases.

The probe agencies were engrossed in investigating a complex medical device recall, grappling with numerous challenges due to the unprecedented nature of the case. Even as they put their best foot forward to navigate the intricacies of the investigation, the company filed a high-stakes legal case before the Bombay High Court, aiming to quash the entire investigation. This new legal battle added another layer of complexity, throwing a spanner in the works.

―――

When the FIR was filed, there were immediate concerns about the potential arrest of the company's directors during the investigation. Here's why: the import license was issued to the company as an entity, not to any individual. However, under the Drugs and Cosmetics Act, if a company violates the law and it is proven that a director, manager or any other officer either endorsed the violation, facilitated it or failed to prevent it, that individual will also be held accountable. They will face legal consequences and punishment, just like the company.

Hence, the company strategically devised a two-pronged legal approach to tackle this issue: one, quashing the FIR, and two, requesting interim relief to prevent any arrest, till the petition was disposed of. On 17 December 2011, nearly a month after the criminal prosecution began, it petitioned the Bombay High Court to quash the FIR. Understanding the complexities of the case and the inevitable delay in reaching a final verdict, the company wisely requested interim relief to prevent any coercive measures against it. Just two days later, on 19 December 2011, the High Court granted this crucial interim relief. This decisive move safeguarded the company's immediate interests – protecting its top officials from any coercive action while the case was still pending. This move by the company showed that their legal strategy was very well conceived.

After the grant of interim relief, the company's legal battle entered the next crucial phase. In the initial stage of a legal scenario where a party seeks to quash an FIR, the court first decides whether to admit the petition or not. To make this crucial determination, the court commenced hearings to assess the petition's legal validity. During these hearings, the police and the Maharashtra FDA submitted comprehensive affidavits and presented thorough arguments against the company's plea and the interim relief previously granted by the court. These included detailed evidence, extensive scientific literature on the implants and insights into the ongoing police investigation. The probe agencies argued that with such substantial evidence and the ongoing nature of the investigation, clearly there were no legal grounds to admit the petition to quash the FIR.

The exchange of legal arguments between the police, the Maharashtra FDA and the company unfolded over many months. Each submitted responses and counter-responses, which illustrated the complexity of the case. As the process continued back and forth, a year after the petition was filed, on 4 January 2013, the high court issued an important order. The court permitted the Mumbai police to continue their investigation but with a crucial condition: the charge sheet could only be filed after securing prior approval from the court. Moreover, the court ordered that if the investigating officer planned to arrest any directors or officers of the company, they must first provide a seventy-two-hour notice. This safeguard was designed to ensure that company officials had adequate time to seek legal recourse before any potential arrest.

In February, the company filed a rejoinder to the government's reply opposing the petition, addressing crucial issues. The Maharashtra FDA, the probe agency, requested more time to respond, because its investigations were still underway. Listed once in April, the plea saw no hearing and was postponed, with the court setting a new date. Again in July, the matter was listed but faced a similar fate, being postponed yet again.

By the next hearing, on 3 September 2013, both the parties had meticulously submitted all necessary affidavits and supporting documents, ensuring the case file was complete. Recognizing the thorough preparation, the court issued an order to place the plea for disposal at the admission stage, signalling a strong inclination to resolve the matter at the stage of admission itself. The next hearing was scheduled for October.

Entrenched in their respective offices, both the legal teams pored over documents, crafted airtight arguments and diligently prepared refining strategies for the crucial courtroom battle ahead. It was also anticipated that the company, armed with a formidable team of lawyers, would vociferously argue to quash the FIR.

Yet, what unfolded was a startling turn of events: the DePuy legal team informed the court that, following instructions from the company, they would withdraw the plea entirely.

This move meant that the interim protection from arrest would end, leaving the company directors vulnerable to immediate arrest without prior notice. Anticipating this risk, the DePuy team of lawyers voiced their concerns and requested limited protection from the court, similar to the one before: they proposed that if the police intended to arrest any directors, they should provide seventy-two hours' notice, allowing the company time to apply for anticipatory bail.

However, the government lawyer argued that such an order favouring the company might hamper their investigations. After weighing both sides, the court issued a balanced order. It said that the police must provide the applicants with seventy-two hours' notice before any arrests of officials were made. However, it clarified that while this provision offered company officials a measure of protection against arrests, in no way would it hamper the ongoing investigation. Authorities would retain complete power to summon officials for interrogation or other investigative procedures as needed, ensuring that justice and public welfare remain paramount.

With the company opting to withdraw its plea from the high court, a major obstacle in the Mumbai police's case was finally cleared, paving the way for further progress in the case. However, almost at the same time, Zagade found himself facing another daunting challenge, adding a new twist to the unfolding probe.

In mid-2013, as the Maharashtra FDA advanced its investigation, a patient in his thirties reached out to the agency with a desperate plea for justice. This man, burdened by the pain of failed ASR hip implants, had received them in both hips in December 2005 and January 2006. By September 2009, he found himself undergoing a painful total hip replacement revision surgery. Despite the recall of March 2010, the company failed to contact him until January 2013, leaving him in prolonged agony and uncertainty.

The patient shared his harrowing story with the agency. For nearly three years, he had endured relentless pain, with the defective implants causing severe infections and pus formation around the femur head. The revision surgery, far more complicated than expected, was a testament to his suffering. His frustration was palpable as he recounted how the company in India left patients like him to fend for themselves. With his medical records in hand, he urged the agency to take decisive action against the company, arguing that if compensation was granted in US courts, the same should hold true in India, if not more.

His narrative struck a chord with the agency officials, resonating with several other patients who had shared their stories. Yet, his case had a unique twist: he was from outside Maharashtra, and all his surgeries had been performed in a southern Indian hospital. This case highlighted a new challenge facing the Maharashtra FDA. Despite being a state-level investigation, it had drawn patients from across the country to its doorstep. The complexity of such widespread cases demanded more than state resources; it required the intervention of a central agency. Recognizing this, Zagade was ready with his next big move in the case.

In August 2013, Zagade sent a communication to the additional chief secretary. What initially appeared to be a routine update on the ongoing Maharashtra FDA investigation – a summary of the case's background and the current status of the legal battle in the high court – was, in fact, a call to action. Zagade's message was anything but ordinary. With a sense of urgency, he made an unprecedented plea: to hand over the entire case to the country's premier investigation agency – the Central Bureau of Investigation (CBI).

Zagade wrote that since these implants were imported and used for patients across India, the scope of the investigation was not limited to the state but was nationwide. Considering the critical and serious nature of this case from a national public interest perspective and the threat to patients' lives, it would be easier to prosecute the crime if the investigation were handed over to the CBI. Therefore, he requested that this matter be transferred to the CBI through the home department for further action.

This was not a decision made lightly; it was a strategic and necessary step to ensure the highest level of scrutiny. The stakes were too high for anything less, and Zagade's appeal highlighted the critical need for the CBI's involvement to uncover the truth and deliver justice. However, recommending a CBI probe created panic within his own department.

'People in the department were scared. "Sir, please don't involve the CBI. They will also question us. They'll ask us about the delay in taking action. They can grill us on why patients' complaints remained pending for so long," they said. But I wanted a CBI probe to help trace patients across India. I was not scared of answering to any agency,' Zagade recalls.

Zagade's determination to uncover the truth, even at the cost of internal discord, highlighted the critical nature of the case and his commitment to justice. This move was more than just a procedural step. If the case was taken up by the CBI, it would pave the way for a comprehensive, nationwide investigation – setting the stage for a deeper probe into the far-reaching implications of this unique case involving thousands of patients. However, for months, the government's lack of urgency left the recommendation languishing.

Zagade's team was still anxiously waiting to see if the case would be transferred to the CBI. Despite the uncertainty, they pressed on with their own investigation, navigating a maze of challenges. The hurdles were many, mainly stemming from the fact that a state agency was trying to unravel a case with nationwide implications. Jurisdictional boundaries further compounded their difficulties.

These challenges faced by the Maharashtra FDA did not go unnoticed. A few journalists, with a keen eye on the case, started to highlight the growing concerns. India's leading newspaper, *The Times of India*, published an important report on 23 July 2014.[9] It revealed that, despite the recall being announced in August 2010, only 850 Indian patients were traceable. The report further exposed a troubling issue: many hospitals had failed to provide the product codes of the implants when discharging patients, further complicating the task for authorities trying to trace them.

Most strikingly, the news report highlighted the glaring inaction by the central government. Despite patients being spread across the country, there had been no effort to request an investigation by the CBI, as recommended by the Maharashtra FDA headed by Zagade. This lack of response raised serious questions about regulatory oversight and put immense pressure on the authorities to act.

There was still no movement on transferring the case to the CBI; however, in a rare turn of events, this news report compelled the national regulator, the Drugs Controller General of India (DCGI), to once again confront the company with some tough questions. Central to this renewed scrutiny was the most crucial issue of all: ensuring fair and adequate compensation for Indian patients.

On 23 July 2014, *The Times of India*'s journalists Rema Nagarajan and Sumitra Debroy published a hard-hitting exposé. Their report revealed two deeply troubling issues: despite the 2010 recall, a staggering 82 per cent of ASR patients in India remained untraced. Moreover, several Indian patients lacked access to their complete medical records related to the implant.

The report jolted the national regulator, the DCGI, into action. It demanded accountability from the company by seeking full information on patients who had registered with the ASR helpline, and details of the company's efforts to identify all affected individuals in India. Most crucially, the regulator demanded updates on the status of patients who had undergone revision surgery and the current health conditions of the 850 patients the company had managed to trace. Furthermore, they pressed the company for details on compensation to Indian patients.

In an uncharacteristic show of urgency, the regulator set an extremely tight deadline. 'Keeping in view the serious nature of the complaint, you are directed to submit the reply to this directorate within 7 days,' the DCGI wrote to the company on 24 July 2014.[10]

Despite the gravity of the directive, the company missed the deadline, responding instead on 4 August 2014. In its reply, the company boldly claimed to have reached out to more than 2,300 patients. They described a comprehensive outreach strategy: establishing the ASR helpline, dispatching letters to surgeons, sending follow-up reminders and employing third-party firms to connect with surgeons, facilitating patient registration on the helpline. Yet, even with these measures, the company failed to explain why it could not reach out to the remaining 2,400 patients implanted with ASR devices.

The company's communication included details about patient registration on the ASR helpline. One might reasonably expect that, with such a supposedly extensive outreach, the number of patients who registered would be approximately the 2,300 mentioned. However, the actual figures were startlingly low. The company revealed that only 903 patients in India had registered through the ASR helpline, and out of these, only 882 were confirmed as ASR patients through medical records. These 882 patients accounted for 1,056 ASR hip implant surgeries in India, with some patients having both hips replaced.

This stark reality highlighted the company's failure to trace all the affected Indian patients: four years after the recall, approximately eight out of every ten ASR surgeries in India remained untraced. The discrepancy between the company's claims and the actual outcomes was alarming.

As usual, the company subtly shifted the blame onto doctors and hospitals. 'ASR patient data is available only from surgeons and hospitals. DePuy has been actively requesting that surgeons and hospitals reach out to their ASR patients,' the company told the regulator.[11] Yet, the company failed to address a crucial question: Why did these doctors, who supposedly held all the information on ASR patients, choose to withhold critical details and not assist the company in locating untraced patients? This silence left a significant gap in the narrative, casting doubt on the company's transparency.

The company divulged another key detail: that 162 out of the 882 patients registered through the ASR helpline had needed revision surgery. Despite this, the company reiterated its stance, emphasizing that not all patients with ASR hip implants would require a second procedure. As they put it, 'Please kindly note that not all patients who have undergone ASR hip implant surgery will need revision surgery.'[12] They were playing down the enormity of issue.

DePuy was confidently asserting that the ASRs were functioning as intended. However, this confidence was not accompanied by concrete evidence. The company failed to provide data on how many patients had normal metal ion levels in their blood, leaving a gap in their argument. Instead, they claimed that the ASR helpline regularly followed up with patients who had not undergone revision surgery, suggesting ongoing support but offering little in the way of tangible proof.

However, in its response of 4 August 2014, the company finally unveiled its stance on compensation for Indian patients, shedding light on this important matter that had long been shrouded in ambiguity. In this communication, the company reiterated its commitment to covering reasonable and customary costs, including testing, monitoring, revision surgery and loss of wages. For the first time, it specified the range of this expenditure: Rs 500,000 to 2.5 million.

In a surprising revelation, the company informed the regulator that it had already 'settled' three cases involving Indian ASR patients. However, this wasn't out of sheer goodwill; the compensation was provided only after these patients 'directly approached' DePuy. The company opted for legal settlements rather than voluntary compensation, highlighting a reactive rather than proactive approach.

'It may be kindly noted that whenever an ASR patient brings a claim for compensation, DePuy will assess the specific facts and background with its legal advisors based in India based on prevailing local laws by taking into account all applicable factors and, where appropriate, seek to reach a reasonable settlement by mutual agreement with the patient,' the company explained to the regulator.

The company was also unequivocal in stating that it would not replicate the US compensation process in India. First, it highlighted that the US settlement did not automatically compensate all ASR patients; rather, it was a settlement reached through a legal process with litigants who had pursued their claims in US courts.

Moreover, the company highlighted that several terms and conditions applied in the US, necessitating thorough scrutiny and examination of each case under 'specific and relevant parameters' for settlement purposes.

Importantly, the company pointed out that compensation for ASR patients would not be based on a uniform formula due to the variances in local consumer protection laws. 'Legal systems in different countries function differently according to their own applicable laws and the individual facts and circumstances of a specific case. In India and other countries outside the US where ASR litigation is pending, the company is continuing to appropriately address the litigation in a manner that is consistent with the country's legal system,' the company told the regulator. This communication marked a significant moment, providing long-awaited clarity on the issue of compensation to the Indian patients.

As the company faced intense scrutiny from the national regulator over glaring recall issues, it seemed like the Maharashtra FDA probe would gain momentum, and the recommendation to transfer the case to the CBI would finally come to fruition.

The ASR saga seemed poised for a breakthrough, suggesting that long-awaited answers, especially on the untraced patients, might soon be uncovered. However, fate had other plans. In August 2014, Zagade was suddenly and unexpectedly transferred, casting uncertainty over the future of the probe.

More often than not, in the Indian bureaucracy, sudden transfers occur when an individual is making significant positive strides or when an officer disrupts the long-standing status quo within a department. In Zagade's case, his bold efforts and willingness to shake things up led directly to his abrupt transfer – illustrating the unpredictable nature of bureaucratic politics. Not only did he launch a probe into an unprecedented medical device recall, but he also banned gutkha, seized stocks worth tens of millions and spearheaded a relentless crackdown against rule-violating chemists (as pharmacies are called in India).

Remarkably, a month before his transfer, he was selected to make an important presentation before the union health minister on the various reforms introduced by the state drug administration under his tenure.

As the saying goes, 'his work spoke volumes', and the recognition Zagade received from the health ministry – being selected to make a crucial presentation on public health – was a testament to the significant reforms he had implemented.

However, as anticipated, his departure led to the gradual fading of the criminal case concerning the ASR in Maharashtra. After his exit, even his recommendation for a CBI probe into the case was buried deep in government files. The central government decided against launching such an investigation, claiming that involving the CBI might not facilitate patients' compensation claims.[13] The system had won, again.

Yet, the probe remains a watershed moment in India's medical device regulatory landscape, as it highlighted the critical issue of product recalls. For the first time, because of this probe, the media brought concerns into the public eye, igniting scrutiny that compelled the national regulator to demand answers from the company involved. This wasn't just another investigation; it was a turning point. There was a palpable sense of hope that, finally, the voices of affected patients would be heard and justice would be served. While that hope was disappointing, Zagade's gallant battle inspired people.

Above all, critical revelations gained from this investigation empowered some patients to persistently pressure both the company and the government. This resilience ignited a new chapter in the ASR saga in India.

'My motto in public service is: I act because I must,' Zagade reflects. 'However, when I was transferred, my successors showed little interest. There was a complete lack of action on the case. Fortunately, some patients chose to carry on this battle on their own.'

11

The Industry Insider: From Victim to Fighter

Medical device sales is a lucrative career, but it's far from straightforward. In a field where cutting-edge technology meets the realities of healthcare, the path to success demands more than just a good product. It requires skill in building relationships in a highly competitive market.

The stakes are high. Successful medical device reps wield significant influence, often steering decisions that affect hospital budgets, running into hundreds of thousands of rupees. Their role goes beyond sales; they become trusted advisors, helping doctors decide which implants to use, impacting patient care.

In this high-pressure environment, top medical device reps sell, persuade and support their clients. This role places them at the centre of an influential industry, where every decision can significantly affect patients' lives. In early 2003, Vijay, based in Mumbai, was leading one such sales and marketing team while working as a regional product manager at Philips India.

Vijay specialized in selling four key super-specialities: general surgery, cardiology, radiology and orthopaedics. Being a product manager at one of the country's top health technology companies was challenging and intense but rewarding. As he entered his early thirties and advanced as a mid-career professional, he faced a demanding regime that was both mentally and physically challenging. His day typically began with setting up meetings with doctors, followed by making persuasive pitches to get the company's medical devices into their hands. From Monday through Friday, this was his relentless routine, with most of his time spent travelling.

Vijay's motivation was impressive. He set ambitious targets and juggled multiple customers simultaneously. On average, he visited three to four accounts daily, often journeying to different parts of the country. His team had woven an extensive sales network across the region and Vijay was its star player, consistently hitting his sales targets. His exceptional performance didn't go unnoticed; the company rewarded him handsomely.

In the world of medical device sales, market knowledge is crucial, but forging strong client relationships is paramount. Vijay was a master of both. He stayed ahead of the curve, constantly updating his knowledge to provide surgeons with the most competitive information. At the same time, he built a strong rapport with these medical professionals, ensuring they felt valued and informed. Vijay's innate negotiation skills often left his peers trailing. Each triumph over his targets brought him additional sales incentives, fuelling his drive even further.

Within a few years, Vijay steadily climbed the corporate ladder. With each account he secured and every doctor he convinced, Vijay moved closer to his goal, building a bright future in the competitive field of medical device sales. However, in 2006, at the age of thirty-six, his professional rise came to an abrupt halt. The setback had nothing to do with missing company targets, fierce corporate rivalry or a lack of skill. Instead, it was a cruel twist of fate – an unforeseen health complication – that derailed his professional growth.

―――

In 2006, at the age of thirty-six, Vijay's life took an unexpected turn when he began experiencing persistent lower back pain. He couldn't recall any injury that might have caused it, so he assumed it was due to a muscle sprain or a sudden physical movement at work. Up until that point, he had been leading a healthy and active life, free from any major health issues.

'I was doing well back then,' Vijay recalls. 'I had no health problems. So, I just took the pain medication my family physician prescribed. It gave me temporary relief.' However, the pain soon began to intrude into various aspects of his daily life.

At work, sitting for long hours became increasingly uncomfortable, and he found it difficult to concentrate. The constant ache gnawed at his focus, making it hard to maintain his usual productivity. Simple tasks that once seemed effortless, like lifting objects or bending over, now required careful consideration and often resulted in sharp pain.

Despite his efforts to manage the pain with medication, the lack of a permanent solution began to weigh on him. The temporary relief offered by the painkillers was just that – temporary. Each day became a struggle to maintain his normal routine while coping with the persistent discomfort. Since he worked in the medical field, Vijay knew the importance of caution. He decided to consult an orthopaedic surgeon, eager to rule out any potential complications and ensure his health was in top shape.

The surgeon instructed Vijay to get an X-ray to investigate any changes in his hip bones. The results were shocking: the femoral head was flattened, a clear sign of advanced Avascular Necrosis (AVN).

'I was stunned,' Vijay says. 'How could my hip have deteriorated so rapidly in just one month since I first felt the pain?'

The surgeon explained that AVN is often a silent attacker, with many patients not experiencing symptoms until the disease is well advanced.

'Hip pain is usually the first sign,' the doctor told him. 'The condition can progress slowly over months or even years. Unfortunately, in your case, you've already reached stage three AVN.'

Vijay was taken aback.

'Hearing that was a punch to the gut,' he says. 'I had no idea something so serious was happening inside my body. It was a lot to process.'

To treat the condition, the surgeon recommended bone grafting to decompress the femoral head, considering Vijay's young age.

'He said bone grafting was the best option for me, and ruled out a hip replacement surgery,' Vijay explains. 'He mentioned that younger patients tend to have a better chance of bone regrowth and that I should just stick to bone grafting.'

In July 2007, Vijay underwent the bone grafting procedure. He was informed that the graft would take about three months or a little longer to heal. The recovery went well, and everything seemed fine for the first twelve months. However, the pain in his hip returned, and he started walking with a limp. His physical activities became grossly restricted.

'It was frustrating,' Vijay admits. 'I had hoped the surgery would solve the problem, but instead, I found myself dealing with the same pain and limitations. It felt like a never-ending struggle.'

The bone grafting procedure had failed miserably, leaving Vijay in agony and his work performance plummeting.

'For six months, the pain was excruciating,' he recalls. Desperate for relief, Vijay sought out another top specialist in Mumbai.

This new surgeon, renowned in his field, quickly identified the problem and recommended an immediate total hip replacement. He suggested the ASR XL.

'He assured me that I'd be able to live a normal life again – free from limping and pain,' Vijay says, his voice tinged with hope.

On 17 July 2008, Vijay went under the knife in Mumbai, clinging to the promise of a pain-free future. But this hope was short-lived. Within a few months, the searing pain returned. It wasn't just the physical torment that plagued him; it was the crushing weight of disappointment and the frustration of feeling trapped in a cycle of unending pain.

After his total hip replacement surgery, Vijay had diligently taken his prescribed pain medication and followed the rehabilitation exercises to the letter. He knew that a full recovery would take time. His surgeon had warned him about the discomfort he would experience in the weeks following the surgery, and Vijay braced himself for the challenge.

A few months later, when pain first flared in his hip and groin, Vijay reminded himself of the surgeon's words and tried not to worry. He stayed positive, believing that each day of discomfort was a step towards regaining his strength. However, as the months passed, his optimism waned. Nearly six months after the surgery, he found himself still struggling to return to his normal activities. The frustration was palpable.

'I thought maybe it was because I had undergone two surgeries in just two years that my recovery was taking longer than expected,' he reflects.

Gradually, the pain became so severe that Vijay found it difficult to walk or even stand. This was far from what his surgeon had promised – that he would be able to return to his job within a couple of months. As a result, at work, he couldn't make sales like he used to, and his frustration grew.

But it wasn't just the pain and discomfort that troubled him. Vijay's body started flashing more warning signs. Every time he moved, a clunking and popping sound emanated from his right hip. While this noise didn't conclusively mean that the metal implant was failing, such sounds are often linked to the loosening of a hip implant, signalling that his hip needed further investigation. Vijay knew he had to consult his surgeon. To his dismay, the surgeon dismissed his concerns, attributing them to psychological factors.

'He said it was all in my head,' Vijay recounts.

Vijay did not feel quite right about his hip. He experienced a dull, persistent ache that nagged at him daily. However, his surgeon insisted that these symptoms were not a cause for concern.

'Instead, the doctor said: "You are not suffering from anything." He kept repeating the same thing to convince me that I was doing perfectly fine,' Vijay recalls, frustration evident in his voice.

As time passed, the pain and discomfort only grew worse.

'Suddenly, when I would walk, it felt like my hip was getting locked,' Vijay says, describing the alarming sensation. By this time, he was convinced that the pain had nothing to do with his post-operative recovery. Each step became a grim reminder that something was amiss.

Soon, there were changes in Vijay's general health that could not be ignored.

'I started experiencing intermittent palpitations. I had difficulty urinating,' he says, recounting the distressing symptoms. These issues compounded his worries. His symptoms got worse. He grew too fatigued and weak to perform the duties expected of his role. And it was not just his body – he began finding it difficult to remember things.

'Every problem was unexplained. It continued to remain a mystery,' Vijay says, his despair surfacing. His once-sharp mind now felt clouded, and the simplest tasks became burdens.

Despite these escalating symptoms, his doctors did not pay heed to the red flags. No MRI tests to ascertain possible tissue damage were recommended. No blood tests to check if he had elevated metal ion levels in his blood. Instead, they asked him to do a routine check-up.

'But the results did not reveal anything. It was all normal,' Vijay says, recalling his disbelief.

Days turned into months, and Vijay's condition deteriorated further. He felt trapped in his own body. The fatigue became overwhelming, and the pain was his constant companion. His job performance suffered, and his personal life began to crumble under the weight of his unrelenting symptoms. Ultimately, in September 2011, Vijay discovered the truth behind the inexplicable pain and poor health through an unexpected turn of events.

―――

Medical conferences provide a unique opportunity for surgeons to meet their peers in a relaxed and informal atmosphere. Doctors present scientific papers on the latest trends and challenges in their field. But these medical conferences are probably most valuable for medical device manufacturers. The branding opportunities they get at these events are precious, as they can showcase their latest technology and products to a broad audience, including, most importantly, the region's top surgeons.

Manufacturers set up elaborate booths, eager to attract the attention of the medical community with demonstrations and promotional materials. Reps hand out brochures and free samples, hoping to catch the eye of a prominent surgeon. As part of his core role to hit the annual sales target, Vijay also had to attend medical conferences. He had participated in many of these events over the years – it was almost as important as going to hospitals to make pitches. Each conference was a battleground for brand visibility and client engagement, demanding his full attention and effort.

In September 2011, Vijay attended a high-profile orthopaedic conference in Nagpur. The venue was abuzz with excitement, the air thick with the mingling scents of coffee and freshly printed pamphlets. Top surgeons from across the region converged to exchange their experiences in the field of orthopaedics, with their discussions ranging from advanced surgical techniques to the latest medical breakthroughs.

Vijay navigated through the crowd, shaking hands with old

The Industry Insider: From Victim to Fighter

acquaintances and making new connections. He listened intently to presentations, noting down key points that might align with his products. Amidst the backdrop of cutting-edge presentations, product demonstrations and the hum of professional networking, he seized every opportunity to engage with doctors. The conference hall, with its mix of serious conversation, flashy exhibits and the occasional burst of laughter, illustrated the intersection of medicine and commerce.

For Vijay and many of his competitors, the goal was clear: to persuade potential clients to choose their products. However, during his pitch, it wasn't just his product that caught the surgeons' attention – it was Vijay himself.

'When I walked up to the stage with the aid of my cane and a noticeable limp, the surgeons took notice,' he recalls.

The primary cause of limping in younger people is usually physical trauma, often from sports injuries or accidents. However, in Vijay's case, he hadn't experienced any such trauma. A group of doctors gathered around him, concerned. Vijay explained his situation in detail, mentioning that he had undergone a total hip replacement surgery with a MoM implant from Johnson & Johnson. One of the surgeons, with a sudden look of alarm, interrupted him.

'Did the doctor implant the ASR XL? Is the ASR XL in your right hip?' the surgeon asked, his voice tinged with urgency.

Vijay, taken aback, said he wasn't certain about the specific model. The surgeon's face grew more serious as he delivered the troubling news.

'If it's the ASR XL 50, you need to get tested for cobalt and chromium immediately. This implant has been recalled by the company,' he said, his concern evident.

Though Vijay was unsure about the exact implant model inside him, the surgeons at the conference were concerned. They probed further into his symptoms, questioning him about issues beyond the persistent hip pain. Vijay described additional troubling signs, including the drowsiness he had started to experience at work, which he hadn't connected to the hip implant until now.

The surgeons' urgency intensified. They strongly recommended that Vijay undergo blood tests to check for metal ions. But even before the results were in, they urged him to mentally prepare for another critical procedure: revision surgery to remove the faulty implant. The seriousness in their voices and the gravity of their recommendations left Vijay with a sinking feeling.

Immersed in the medical sales industry for years, Vijay was no stranger to the nature of business in this field. He was well aware of the shadowy tactics employed by manufacturers to shield their strategies from competitors and the undue influence they wielded over surgeons. But nothing could have prepared him for the shock of stumbling upon the news of the ASR recall.

The revelation that a critical issue linked directly to patient safety had been concealed was startling enough. Yet what left Vijay reeling was the fact that, despite being an insider in the orthopaedic industry, he had been completely unaware of the recall of an implant by a major global medical device company.

Day after day, Vijay rubbed shoulders with orthopaedic surgeons. He sold them high-end medical equipments. His job required him to engage in detailed discussions about various implants and surgical needs. These conversations were often extensive, and he prided himself on being a trusted partner to these medical professionals. Despite this, he never heard a whisper about the recall.

'The surgeons were all tight-lipped, revealing just how far they would go to protect the company's interests. It was a jarring reminder of how insulated we were from the truth. Outside the company and its circle of doctors, no one had a clue about the recall,' Vijay says.

The shock deepened when Vijay saw his own surgeon at the conference. He hoped this would be the moment to get some answers. Yet, when he approached his surgeon, the response was evasive.

'I had met with my surgeon several times. He always dismissed my concerns about pain with vague assurances that it was psychological,' Vijay recounts. 'But the real issue was the secrecy. Why did the medical community want to keep this recall under wraps? It felt like this crucial piece of the information was deliberately withheld from us, leaving me questioning the integrity of the entire industry.'

The experience left Vijay angry, grappling with the stark reality of a system that seemed more interested in protecting its own interests than in safeguarding patient well-being.

After the doctors delivered the news about the recall at the medical conference, Vijay returned home with his mind racing. Sitting at his desk, he frantically began researching online, his hands trembling as he read each headline that seemed more unbelievable than the last.

'Faulty artificial hip points to broken implant system,' one article screamed. Another detailed the heartbreaking story of a patient affected by the faulty implant. Vijay's disbelief quickly turned to dread as he grasped the full impact of the recall. Lives had been irreversibly changed; each story was a blow to his already reeling mind. A cold sweat broke out as he imagined the potential consequences he might face during the painful revision surgery.

The implant, which was meant to enhance his life, now threatened to shatter it. The thought of undergoing a painful and risky revision surgery filled him with crippling anxiety. What if the surgery went wrong? His professional career, built over the years, hung in the balance. Each scenario played out in his head, feeding his growing fear.

Simultaneously, he was struck by a deep unease – how could such a crucial development regarding a product recall have escaped the notice of distributors in the medical device industry? Desperate for answers, he frantically dialled the dealers. Each unanswered ring amplified his anxiety until he finally connected with someone. When he did, their casual acknowledgment of the product recall stunned him. They were well-informed, almost relaxed, while he, an industry insider, had been completely in the dark. This revelation hit him hard. It was more than a lapse in communication; it was a glaring oversight.

'If even a well-connected person in the medical device industry did not know about the recall, imagine the others who were suffering,' Vijay says.

At that moment, Vijay felt compelled to bring this issue into the public eye. Yet, he held back due to his own dire situation. He faced the daunting prospect of revision surgery, fraught with financial and health complications. He knew that as he moved forward, he could encounter new challenges – mounting medical costs and an unclear path for recovery, making the overall situation complex and stressful.

The first step was to get in touch with Puri Crawford, a firm appointed by the manufacturer to process claims related to revision surgeries. This was uncharted territory for Vijay and the doctors who had implanted the devices. Typically, once the doctor advises the patients, the hospital and insurers step in, ensuring everything is handled smoothly. But this time, the company had introduced a new process. As Vijay began this process, he had no idea that he would face a daunting maze of paperwork, tests and follow-ups seemingly designed to complicate matters.

After extensively researching about the recall online, Vijay pored over numerous articles and blogs. He consulted specialists in Mumbai for expert advice. Each discussion was detailed and thorough. After these conversations, his primary concern remained the unknown complications that he might potentially face. Anxiety plagued him constantly, an invisible threat lurking in the back of his mind. This time, his worry was exacerbated by memories of doctors previously dismissing his symptoms as psychological. The sting of being ignored and misunderstood had left deep scars.

He couldn't shake the fear that long-term symptoms might be just as elusive, silently causing damage inside him. Each twinge and strange sensation sent his mind spiralling into dark possibilities. The thought of something faulty inside his body felt like a ticking time bomb – one he couldn't defuse.

'No one can truly understand what a patient goes through when they're told something faulty is inside their body. You feel like your life is at stake,' he recalls, his voice trembling.

At the same time, he was apprehensive about the revision surgery. The thought of it haunted him. What immediate medical complications might he face because of this procedure? Infections, blood clots, muscle loss – each possibility sent a shiver down his spine. How long would recovery take? Would he ever walk without pain again? Would he regain any semblance of his old life, or was he trapped in an agonising limbo?

The uncertainty about his career added to his sleepless nights. As a product manager, his performance was constantly evaluated and he felt the pressure mounting.

'I worried about what would happen at work,' he says. His limp was already affecting his ability to meet his sales targets. 'If I took another six months off, would I become a liability for the company?' The fear of being deemed replaceable consumed him, adding to the weight of his anxiety.

The fear, apprehension and anxiety weren't just Vijay's story; they reflected the experiences of other patients facing revision surgery. When they heard about the recall, a wave of dread washed over them as they grappled with the terrifying unknowns of their future. One would expect that, given the emotional state of the patients, the company would have established a system showing genuine concern and empathy. The process for revision surgery and reimbursement should have been seamless and straightforward. Instead, Vijay found himself trapped in a convoluted reimbursement maze.

'Each step was a battle of its own. The process was not only complicated but downright infuriating,' Vijay recounts. 'One day, they'd demand one set of documents, and just when I thought I was making progress, the next day they'd request an entirely different set. It felt like a never-ending ordeal.'

Things took a dramatic turn when Vijay decided to seek a different specialist for his revision surgery.

'I was too young to be facing revision surgery,' Vijay explains. 'After everything I'd endured with the first surgery, I couldn't afford any complications this time. My fears were consuming me.' Determined to avoid further health-related complications, Vijay decided to seek the expertise of a renowned surgeon outside India. He believed an international specialist was crucial due to the cobalt–chromium poisoning he had suffered.

'The release of metal ions into the blood would have definitely damaged my hip. But we did not know how bad it was. I could not risk it. Hence, to avoid any further complications, I wanted the best possible care,' he says.

But Puri Crawford, the company's representatives, were anything but accommodating in their response. They flatly refused Vijay's request, citing their policy against sponsoring surgeries abroad.

'They told me, "As per our policy, we can't cover a revision surgery in the US or any other foreign country,"' Vijay recounts, his frustration evident. The disagreement quickly escalated into confrontation.

'They kept insisting that the revision surgery was a minor procedure,' Vijay recalls. 'I knew full[y] well it was a major operation. I challenged them, asking, "How can you claim it's a simple surgery? Are you a doctor? What clinical evidence do you have to back up your assertion that it will go smoothly?'"

After the company refused Vijay's request for surgery outside India, he seethed with anger. He did not want to let the conversation end there. He made another demand: that the company provide him with insurance coverage. This would be for any unforeseen complications during the revision surgery.

'I need you to provide some form of safety cover for my revision surgery,' Vijay firmly told the company representative at Puri Crawford. 'The surgery is complex, and the potential complications could be severe. You can't guarantee a smooth process or that there won't be issues afterward.'

The representative, with an air of practised calm, leaned back in his chair.

'We are the only company that truly cares about its patients,' he replied, his tone almost dismissive. 'We were the only ones to recall the metal-on-metal implant. Other companies didn't even bother.'

Vijay's jaw tightened.

'That's not good enough. I've been in this industry for years, and I only found out about the recall two years after it happened. How does that reflect care? You're talking about patient safety, but I was left in the dark.'

The representative's face remained impassive.

'We've done more than others. We're proud of that.'

At this point, Vijay's frustration boiled over.

'Pride doesn't fix my problem. I need reassurance. You're asking me to trust that everything will be fine, but how can I when you can't even offer support?' When the representative remained unmoved, Vijay pressed on. 'I'm asking for insurance coverage for any serious complications. The doctors have made it clear this is a high-risk surgery. They can't rule out complications. My family is dependent on me – what happens to them if something goes wrong?' However, the company did not offer any assurance, flatly replying that no special arrangements would be made in Vijay's case.

Despite having two of his requests rejected by the company, Vijay was not one to back down easily. Determined to undergo the complex revision surgery at a chosen hospital with a preferred surgeon, he decided to look in Mumbai. He began by researching the top surgeons in the city and gathering recommendations. After compiling a shortlist, he scheduled consultations with three surgeons.

'They all sat down and explained my situation in detail,' Vijay recalls. During these important interactions, he listened attentively, occasionally nodding and taking notes. 'Everyone made it very clear that the revision surgery was going to be complex,' he says.

In his second meeting, a surgeon recommended that Vijay follow a straightforward approach: first, finalize a hospital with the necessary infrastructure, such as a state-of-the-art operating theatre.

'Every surgery has its risks, but advancements in the field have significantly improved outcomes. With careful planning and the right team, we can manage this. But first, you need to finalize a hospital equipped with facilities that can handle any complications,' the surgeon advised. This discussion gave Vijay a clearer understanding of the challenges and possibilities ahead.

'Within weeks, after evaluating various options, I zeroed in on one of the best in Mumbai,' he recounts.

As the next step, Vijay communicated his decision to Puri Crawford which stood in for the company: he would be undergoing revision surgery at a different hospital from where the primary surgery had taken place. Confident that there would be no obstacles and that the company would readily approve his request, he prepared for the process. However, he was in for a surprise – the process proved to be far more complicated than he had anticipated. Each negotiation was an uphill battle, marked by tense phone calls and heated meetings that left him drained. The company resisted hard, their objections centred on the high costs associated with Vijay's chosen surgeon and hospital. The company kept insisting that Vijay's demand was unreasonable.

However, even after almost five months of heated arguments, Vijay did not let the company have their way.

'They kept telling me that the cost of my revision was the highest they had estimated yet. They also made an insensitive remark about how I would not have been able to afford the hospital if I were spending money from my own pocket,' Vijay says. After multiple rounds of back and forth, the company finally relented. It agreed to cover the cost of Vijay's revision surgery at the hospital of his choice.

Once Vijay had chosen his surgeon and hospital for the complex revision surgery, he plunged into preparation mode. He gathered all his medical records, including the latest X-rays of his right hip, which had become a source of constant discomfort. Anxiety tightened in his stomach as he approached his surgeon's consultation room for their crucial meeting.

Vijay carefully described the pain and the unsettling snapping sensation that had plagued his right hip for over a year. The surgeon listened intently, his face revealing professional concern.

'It's like walking a tightrope,' the surgeon said, the gravity of his words hanging in the air. 'Neither you nor I fully know the extent of the damage the defective device might have caused inside your body.'

The surgeon examined Vijay and reviewed his X-rays with a critical eye. He pointed out worrying signs of edge loading – a term that made Vijay's heart drop.

'My heart just sank,' Vijay recalls. The images revealed that the metal components of the implant were grinding against each other, causing excessive wear. This could lead to the formation of abnormal growths known as pseudotumors, a complication Vijay feared the most.

The surgeon's voice was stern.

'Vijay, we need to act quickly,' he said, recommending an MRI examination. This test would rule out metallosis, a condition where metal debris accumulates around the joint. Vijay nodded, his anxiety mounting.

'What else should I do?'

'We also need a cobalt-chromium blood test to check for elevated metal ions,' the doctor explained. 'It's crucial we assess these levels'

Vijay underwent the MRI, feeling a mix of fear and anticipation. On 27 February 2012, he gave his blood for the cobalt–chromium test, his mind racing with anxious thoughts. What if the results were bad? A week later, the confirmation came. The results were stark: cobalt at 171.8 micrograms per litre and chromium at 85.76 micrograms per litre. The levels were alarmingly high.

On 31 March 2012, when Vijay could finally get an appointment, the surgeon's face was serious as he delivered the news.

'Vijay, your blood tests show high levels of metal. The MRI scans reveal significant inflammation and fluid buildup around your hip joint.' Vijay's stomach dropped. The metal debris was causing a severe inflammatory response.

'The revision surgery will be complex,' the surgeon warned. 'Recovery will take at least three months. It won't be easy.' Vijay took a deep breath, trying to steady himself. With a mix of anxiety and hope, he braced himself for the revision surgery.

On 13 June 2012, the doctors were set to perform the life-changing operation on Vijay. He entered the cold, sterile environment of the operating room, where the surgical team awaited him, their faces partially hidden behind masks, eyes sharp with concentration.

As he lay on the table, Vijay felt the prick of the needle as the anesthesiologist administered the anaesthesia. A wave of drowsiness washed over him, and he felt a deep sense of resignation mixed with a glimmer of hope, knowing this major surgery was his only shot at retrieving his life.

The hours in the operating room blurred together. The surgical team worked with focused precision, their hands moving skillfully amidst the constant hum of medical equipment and the low murmurs of conversation. Their goal was clear: to correct the metallosis that had plagued Vijay's right hip and surrounding tissue, causing him relentless discomfort.

Finally, after what seemed like an eternity, the surgery was complete. The lead surgeon emerged from the operating room, removing his mask to reveal a tired but triumphant smile. He approached Vijay's anxious family, who had been waiting for news with bated breath.

'The operation was a success,' he announced.

Relief washed over them, and tears of joy filled their eyes. Vijay's journey wasn't over, but the first crucial step towards recovery had been taken.

Post-surgery, Vijay was carefully moved to the recovery room. Nurses and doctors monitored him closely, ensuring that his vital signs were stable and that there were no immediate complications. He was put on a regimen of medicines to manage pain and prevent infection, while the medical team kept a vigilant eye on his progress.

As days turned into nights, Vijay's strength began to return. The nurses were a constant presence, checking his wounds, adjusting his medications and offering words of encouragement. Each day brought a small victory, a sign that he was on the mend.

Twelve days later, Vijay left the hospital, his body exhausted but his spirit buoyed by the successful surgery. The discharge brought a moment of revelation as the top surgeon delivered the final diagnosis: metallosis had been the root cause of the unusual neurological symptoms he had suffered for the past two years. This diagnosis provided clarity, finally unravelling the mysteries of his condition.

'Vijay,' the surgeon said with a reassuring smile, 'we've addressed the main issue, and you should begin to see improvements in your symptoms. Recovery will take time, but you're on the right path now.'

Vijay nodded, a mixture of relief and gratitude in his eyes. He knew the road ahead would be challenging, but for the first time in years, he felt a sense of hope. As he left the hospital, supported by his family, he looked forward to a future free from the pain and confusion that had shadowed his life for the last few years.

―――

Vijay took six months of complete rest after the high-risk revision surgery. Despite his best efforts to regain a semblance of normalcy, the process was excruciatingly slow. The relentless cycle of recovery, with its constant battles against pain and fatigue, weighed heavily on Vijay's spirit. Each day seemed like a test of endurance, where hope and frustration often collided.

Vijay's family became his lifeline during this challenging period. His wife meticulously prepared nutritious meals to aid his healing. She ensured he never missed a dose of his medications. His children, too, played their part in his recovery. His elder son and younger daughter brought him small joys – sometimes just sitting quietly with him, their presence a soothing balm. During this time, his work had to take a backseat as he focused entirely on regaining his physical strength.

Vijay engaged in exercises prescribed by his physiotherapist, each movement a step towards reclaiming his mobility. The days slipped into weeks, yet Vijay saw little sign of change. The simple acts of walking or standing were marred by persistent discomfort. His limping gait became a symbol of his ongoing battle. Mentally, the prolonged recovery was a harsh trial. The anticipation of regaining his former life was often overshadowed by the grim reality of his physical limitations.

'Each day brought its own set of challenges,' Vijay recalls.

At the same time, he did not have the respite he had been seeking from the unusual neurological symptoms. In fact, there was now another problem to contend with: hearing impairment in his right ear.

'This was followed by dizziness and muscle myalgia,' Vijay says.

In April 2013, the situation grew worse when he experienced a sudden difficulty in breathing.

'My pulse rate came down. I was rushed to the hospital,' Vijay recalls. The doctor conducted several routine tests but, keeping in mind Vijay's history of metallosis triggered by the failure of the implant, recommended another blood test to check the levels of metal ions in his bloodstream.

Vijay assumed the metal ions in his blood would have returned to normal levels now that the implant had been removed. To his shock, despite it being a year after his revision surgery, metal ions continued to remain at elevated levels in his blood. Specifically, the chromium level in his blood was still worryingly high: 25.44 micrograms per litre.

These results were a stark testimony to the grim reality that the revision surgery had not fully remedied the damage inflicted by the faulty implant. The high metal ion levels in his bloodstream revealed a disturbing truth: even after the implant's removal, the residual metal ions in the blood continued to wreak havoc on his body. But it was not just about the negative health impact. The barrage of health investigations and doctor's appointments drained Vijay's finances more than he had anticipated, and left him struggling to keep his head above water.

Vijay's worst fears materialized when his health continued to falter despite a six-month recuperative break. His inability to perform at work led to a painful outcome: he was asked to resign from his position at Philips India in December 2013. The resignation felt like the final blow to a once-promising career.

Months later, Vijay managed to secure a new position at a different medical device manufacturer.

'This role involved less travelling,' he reflects. 'I thought things would slowly improve, both with my health and my career.' But his hopes were quickly dashed as even the short trips within Mumbai proved too taxing. His deteriorating mobility forced him to resign once more, this time after less than a year.

The financial strain was becoming unbearable. As the sole

breadwinner, Vijay was the linchpin of his family's financial stability. With his daughter about to enter high school, the pressure was mounting. School fees, once manageable, now loomed as an insurmountable hurdle. The loss of two jobs in such quick succession left him grappling with stress and uncertainty, and his dreams of making it big in the lucrative medical device industry seemed to slip through his fingers.

At home, the conversations were fraught with anxiety and strained hopes. Vijay's family was deeply concerned about the mounting bills and the precarious future they faced. His friends, seeing the strain he was under and his indomitable spirit, rallied to his side. They offered both moral support and practical help, encouraging him to explore new avenues. With their backing, Vijay took a bold step into uncharted territory.

'Eventually, we started a small-scale metal fabrication and chemical trading business,' he says. It was a venture born out of necessity. This new beginning, though fraught with challenges, held a glimmer of hope in a period of profound struggle.

But before he could turn the page to a new chapter in his professional life, Vijay made another important decision.

'The company was legally bound to uphold patient safety, and they failed badly. I demanded accountability,' he says, indignant. 'They didn't do more than reimburse the cost of the revision surgeries, leaving patients to grapple with mounting financial burdens. All this suffering, caused by a defective implant. So, I took a stand and decided to send a legal notice to the company.'

Vijay says. His decision wasn't just about seeking justice for himself, but about challenging a system that had failed thousands of others.

Vijay sat at his cluttered desk, the glow of his laptop casting a faint light across the room. Over two dozen medical reports, legal documents and news clippings were scattered around. Months after his revision surgery, Vijay was gearing up to visit the lawyer to discuss filing a case against the company that had manufactured his faulty hip implant.

He scanned the screen, absorbing the stories of patients outside India who had successfully filed product liability cases in the US.

Headlines screamed of multimillion dollar settlements. One article detailed how a sixty-five-year-old man in Los Angeles County had won his case in the California Superior Court after suffering years of pain and multiple surgeries due to the implant. His lawyer had argued that the company had known about the flaws but had continued to sell the product anyway, prioritizing profit over patient safety.

Vijay felt a surge of hope. Could he, too, hold the company accountable for his suffering? He clicked on another link, a detailed investigation from a prestigious medical journal. The story revealed how pharma giants essentially control the destiny of their products, wielding excessive influence over surgeons. Vijay scribbled down notes, trying to wrap his mind around the findings of the investigation.

Vijay knew that filing a case in India might be different, perhaps even more challenging, but he was prepared to fight. The meeting with the lawyer was just the first step, but he felt ready.

'For an ordinary person, sending a legal notice to a pharmaceutical giant is a daunting task. But I knew I had a strong legal case. I knew almost everything that had happened outside India and how patients were fighting for justice there,' Vijay says.

He went to the lawyer armed with all the documents he had gathered over months – and with a mix of hope and apprehension.

'I've been struggling with this device for years,' Vijay explained to the lawyer, who could see the frustration and urgency in the man before him. Vijay then described almost every detail about his painful journey over the last few years.

'Even after it had been removed from my body, my symptoms persisted. It's like no one is taking my suffering seriously.'

The lawyer listened intently, jotting down notes and occasionally asking for clarification.

'Can you detail the timeline of your symptoms and the recall process?' the lawyer inquired, focused and professional.

Vijay nodded, his eyes reflecting the depth of his ordeal.

'The recall was announced, but it was months before I heard about it. By then, I was already experiencing severe complications.' The lawyer's questions and Vijay's answers began to build a clear picture of the progression of his medical struggles, and the complex recall and reimbursement process. After a thorough discussion, the lawyer began drafting the legal notice. Important details of Vijay's case were incorporated into the document. This marked the beginning of a formal effort to address Vijay's grievances and seek justice for his ongoing suffering.

On 9 September 2014, Vijay took a bold step by sending DePuy a legal notice demanding a compensation of Rs 80 million. His action was not just a routine legal manoeuvre; it was a calculated risk aimed at holding the company accountable. However, the response from the company was swift and uncompromising. The company dismissed Vijay's claim as entirely untenable, baseless and bad in law. They asserted that their recall of the ASR was a precautionary measure driven by a higher-than-expected revision rate, not due to any inherent defect in the product.

'Our clients have responsibly demonstrated their commitment towards care of patients and have accordingly supported your (Vijay) client for the revision surgery,' the company's lawyer replied.

However, Vijay wasn't at all surprised by the company's response. He had worked closely with big medical device companies and knew their tactics. These multinational giants would spend millions to crush anyone who dared to challenge them. It was like taking on Goliath with a slingshot.

'Sending the legal notice wasn't just about compensation. It was about justice for Indian patients,' Vijay says. He knew the grim reality of battling a corporate behemoth.

'I knew how these companies operated. I didn't have the legal resources. They'd unleash an army of lawyers. The psychological pressure would be immense.'

So, he chose a different path.

Undeterred, Vijay embarked on the next stage of his journey. His mission: getting the government to wake from its slumber and respond to patient concerns. All his hopes rested on the government stepping up for Indian patients. He knew he had to be meticulous and persuasive to make any impact.

Vijay spent hours drafting each email, ensuring his message was clear, compelling and impossible to ignore. He laboured over every word, knowing that his plea needed to cut through the bureaucratic noise.

The Industry Insider: From Victim to Fighter

On 9 October 2014, after multiple revisions, he began sending his passionate appeals for justice for everyone affected.

One by one, he sent emails to the senior officials of the health ministry, the offices of the Chief Minister of Maharashtra, the Prime Minister's Office (PMO), members of the law ministry and those in the National Human Rights Commission. In these emails, Vijay specifically highlighted the stark contrast between the US and India. In the US, the company had paid billions of dollars as part of their settlement with patients. But in India, the company had no intention of paying anything in the form of compensation. 'The company says it will pay only for revision surgery. This is unacceptable because patients continue to suffer,' he wrote, his outrage palpable in every line.[1]

By this time, through the Right to Information Act, Vijay had managed to get his hands on some key documents related to the local criminal investigation jointly launched by the Maharashtra FDA and the Mumbai police. These documents were a treasure trove of information, and Vijay knew their potential impact. He wrote in his emails that he could immediately forward all the documents to the central government authorities for further action. In addition, he included all the international literature on the product that he had painstakingly gathered over two years of relentless research.

Vijay left no stone unturned. Two weeks later, he fired off reminder emails to all the officials. 'Awaiting your response,' he wrote, each word a calculated nudge, a reminder of the urgency of the situation. With each sent email, Vijay felt a surge of emotions: hope, tinged with anxiety. The stakes were high, and he knew this was just the beginning of a long battle. But he was determined to fight for justice, one email at a time.

'I told myself that I will never give up. Never stop trying,' Vijay recalls. Vijay's efforts began to show results. On 21 October 2014, the health minister's office finally replied, requesting the documents mentioned in the series of emails.

With a surge of hope, Vijay swiftly gathered the voluminous documents, ensuring every page was in order. He meticulously made photocopies, just in case, and neatly organized them into a thick envelope. The next morning, Vijay hurried to the nearest courier service. With a final, steadying breath, he handed over the package. His heart pounded with excitement and hope, as he watched the clerk weigh the manila envelope full of documents and print the label. It felt like there was some progress when they were sealed and sent off to the minister's office.

Meanwhile, Vijay's emails, which initially landed in the health minister's inbox, were sent on for action to the DCGI. This was the first sign that the government could no longer afford to ignore his urgent plea for justice. It became clear that this wasn't just about Vijay but about thousands of other patients who were implanted with these recalled devices, and were suffering in silence.

The pressure was mounting, and Vijay's persistence was starting to pay off. On 15 December 2014, the DCGI officially communicated to the company that it had received a detailed email from Vijay. His email underscored the critical issue of the absence of compensation in the country for those affected by recalled implants. This acknowledgment from the authorities hinted at a glimmer of hope for Indian patients who had long felt abandoned.

―――

The middle of that winter saw the lighting of a flame of hope – 15 December 2014, was an important moment in the ASR saga in India. On this day, the national regulator, driven by a heartfelt plea from a patient, demanded answers from the company about compensation for Indian patients. Acting on Vijay's relentless emails, the regulator issued a directive to the company.

'You are requested to take necessary action in the matter in the similar line as taken by you in other countries. The action taken in this regard may be intimated to this Directorate on an urgent basis,' the Drugs Controller General of India wrote.[2]

Two weeks dragged by. Finally, the company submitted its reply to the regulator.

The company reiterated its stance. They had been covering reasonable costs – testing, monitoring, revision surgery and loss of wages. The claims, they said, ranged from Rs 500,000 to Rs 2.5 million – which was nowhere near what they actually paid up.

Nearly four years after the global recall, the company at last disclosed the compensation amounts given to Indian patients. They had settled four ASR cases in India, with settlements between

Rs 250,000 and Rs 750,000. This was in stark contrast to the much higher sums offered in the US. The company's glaring double standards were evident.

The numbers spoke volumes. The compensation offered to Indian patients was embarrassingly low. Yet, the company failed to explain its methods for such minimal settlements. Instead, they argued that legal systems and case specifics varied by country.

From the reply, it was evident that the company would offer compensation only if the affected patient proactively reached out. However, the process was far from simple. The company's legal team would meticulously examine all the documents submitted by the patients, and, in accordance with the prevailing local laws, determine what the company deemed a 'reasonable settlement'.[3] The company also assured the regulator that its team considered all 'applicable factors' in their assessment.[4] Unfortunately, they fell short in clarifying what exactly constituted a 'reasonable settlement' and withheld details on the specific factors influencing their decisions, leaving many questions unanswered.

'...The company is continuing to appropriately address the litigation in a manner that is consistent with that country's legal system,' the company told the regulator. By sending this strong message, the company made it unequivocally clear that no matter how much it was compensating the US patients, in India, it would determine compensation strictly based on local laws.

For Indian patients, this was nothing short of a devastating blow. Unlike in the US, where robust laws ensured fair compensation for medical device recalls, India's lack of specific legislation left patients in a precarious position. Each person, already burdened by their medical plight, now faced the daunting prospect of fighting individual legal battles.

Days turned into weeks, and weeks into months, yet Vijay still hadn't heard anything from the regulator regarding his plea for compensation. The silence was deafening. The responses to his initial emails had seemed promising, perhaps even stirring the regulator into action and pressing the crucial question of compensation for Indian patients. However, that momentum quickly fizzled out, leaving Vijay in a limbo of uncertainty.

'After receiving a reply from the company, the regulator did nothing for months,' he recounts with frustration. He immersed himself in running his new business, but amidst the flurry of new tasks and responsibilities, he often found his thoughts drift back to the unresolved plea for compensation. 'How long can they ignore this?' he wondered.

Vijay did not give up.

'This time, I went to Delhi; met the officials,' he recalls. With his file of documents clutched tightly in his hand, he walked into the office of the regulator. He waited patiently, watching as officials moved about with an air of indifference. When his turn came, he presented his case with fervour, detailing the financial losses he had incurred and the urgency of his plea.

'But the response was underwhelming. The officials listened with calm, nodding occasionally, but offering little assurance,' he recalls. Within a few hours, he left the office with a heavy heart. 'I discovered that there was so much red tape,' he confides. The lack of clear answers left him frustrated. He realized just how much the government was dragging its feet.

However, after this meeting, he also learnt of something perplexing. 'I found out that my emails had been sent straight to the company by the regulator,' Vijay recounts. 'It was utterly bizarre. I couldn't grasp why the regulator used my name to extract answers from the company on compensation. They should have sought an independent explanation rather than shuffling my personal correspondence.'

Yet, despite these efforts, nothing substantial emerged.

'The entire process felt like another layer of bureaucratic red tape, complicating rather than resolving the issue,' Vijay says. Returning home, he felt a sense of disappointment. The journey had been long and the outcome disheartening. Yet, amidst another setback, a spark of resilience persisted.

'I knew I would continue to fight, no matter how many obstacles stood in my way,' he says. He bided his time.

In 2016, Vijay decided to take a different approach. In India, ordinary citizens can communicate with the highest office – the Prime Minister's Office (PMO) – to address public grievances related to various central ministries. These grievances are then forwarded by the PMO's public wing to the relevant ministry for action. On 7 October

2016, filled with a mix of hope and determination, Vijay carefully drafted and sent a grievance to this office, seeking compensation for Indian patients. His heart raced as he hit send.

'I knew this was my last chance,' Vijay recalls.

By 25 November 2016, Vijay's grievance had been forwarded to the health ministry, which promptly communicated with the drug regulator, urging swift action. 'It is requested that the grievance of the petitioner be redressed,' the health ministry wrote to the drug regulator.[5] The real surprise came on 23 December 2016. Vijay's hands trembled as he opened a letter from India's Deputy Drugs Controller General. As he unfolded the letter, his eyes skimmed over the text with anticipation and his heart raced with hope. But as he read on, his excitement turned to confusion and then to disappointment.

The letter began by stating that, according to Indian law, compensation was only available for patients who suffered injuries or death during clinical trials. Vijay's case, involving a recalled product that had been approved and was not in the clinical trial stage, seemed to fall outside this provision.

'When I read this, I was deeply disappointed,' Vijay recalls dejectedly.

But the news grew even worse. The drug regulator explicitly stated that there was no compensation procedure under the Drugs and Cosmetics Act for injuries or deaths occurring during routine surgeries with already approved devices.

'Essentially, the drug regulator conveyed that its hands were tied. At that point, I felt shattered. This meant the government could do nothing about compensation for Indian patients,' he says. The words were a crushing blow to his hopes.

Then, as Vijay sat with his head in his hands, the last few lines of the letter caught his eye. A sudden glimmer of hope pierced through his despair.

'Further, the Ministry of Health and Family Welfare has recommended constituting a high-powered committee to examine the issues regarding the faulty ASR implants,' the letter revealed.[6] Vijay's breath caught in his throat. The possibility of further action, contingent on the expert committee's recommendations, offered a chance of relief. He exhaled deeply, a sigh of cautious optimism replacing the waves of frustration.

'Ultimately, almost seven years after the recall, the process of addressing the issue of compensation to Indian patients kicked off,' he says.

For the first time in the history of India's drug regulatory system, an expert body was established to meticulously scrutinize the evidence in a case of medical device recall – and recommend compensation for the affected patients. The wheels of justice, long stagnant, began to turn slowly – thanks to the impassioned pleas of patients like Vijay.

On 8 March 2017, Vijay boarded a flight to the national capital, filled with hope. His mission: to stand before the expert committee and deliver a compelling presentation of his harrowing struggle – marking another historic first in India's drug regulatory system.

Part V

Part V

12

The Scrutiny

In 2011, Johnson & Johnson should have been basking in the glow of its 125th anniversary – a century and a quarter of medical breakthroughs and corporate success. But instead of champagne toasts and glowing headlines, the occasion was overshadowed by economic challenges. The mood was sombre. After two tough years, the company clawed its way back to operational sales growth in 2011, but even then, its medical devices division – the largest in the world – limped forward with growth just under 2 per cent.[1]

Yet, on 14 March 2012, the company's CEO struck a different chord. In a letter to the investors, his words brimmed with optimism. He painted vivid pictures of lives transformed by Johnson & Johnson's innovations – a patient, once paralysed by a stroke, now walking again thanks to a new clot-removal device; an oncologist, whose work helped bring a new prostate cancer therapy into existence.

But beneath the surface of this glowing narrative, a storm was brewing. The CEO's upbeat tone couldn't fully muffle the creakings of a foundering behemoth. Beyond the economic downturn and shrinking consumer wallets, Johnson & Johnson was reeling from crises it hadn't anticipated. At McNeil Consumer Healthcare, quality issues plagued its over-the-counter products. Even more troubling was the monumental challenge posed by the ASR Hip System recall.

'Our company was severely tested,' William C. Weldon, Chairman of the Board of Directors and Chief Executive Officer, admitted in his letter to investors in the company's annual report.

In frank terms, the company didn't shy away from the truth. It flagged these challenges to investors, acknowledging the toll on its operating profit margin. The ASR Hip System recall, with its spiralling product liability costs, was a financial haemorrhage that hit the Medical Devices and Diagnostics segment the hardest.

Still, as 2011 drew to a close, the CEO clung to a spark of hope. The litigation, while far from over, was being managed. The DePuy ASR recall – the company's deepest wound – was being addressed. Nearly two years later, in November 2013, a breakthrough arrived. Johnson & Johnson struck a monumental deal with a court-appointed committee of lawyers representing thousands of ASR Hip System plaintiffs. The staggering $2.5 billion settlement – meant to compensate around 8,000 ASR patients in the US – was not just a financial resolution. It was a chance to close one of the darkest chapters in the company's storied history.

By early 2017, Johnson & Johnson had more optimistic numbers to show its investors. The scale of legal claims against the ASR had shrunk dramatically. From 10,750 lawsuits in the US alone in 2012, the number had dwindled to just 2,000 by 2017.[2] It was a sign of the company's aggressive effort to put the past behind it. That same year, it announced a significant development in Australia – a $250 million settlement with a class-action lawsuit. The Federal Court of New South Wales approved the deal, marking another milestone in Johnson & Johnson's efforts to clean up the ASR mess.

But even as the company made strides in the US and Australia, there was a glaring omission: India. Investors were informed about the progress in Canada, Ireland, Germany and Italy. But when it came to India, there was a thick wall of silence. It was as if the thousands of ASR patients in India barely existed. For seven long years, Indian patients waited, hoping for a compensation plan that seemed to be forever on the horizon. Their cases, a trickle compared to the torrent seen elsewhere, were stuck in a bureaucratic limbo – endlessly adjourned, slowly suffocating in the country's consumer forums. When settlements finally did come, they were almost insultingly low, ranging from Rs 250,000 to Rs 750,000 – mere crumbs compared to the amounts offered elsewhere.

The company's disinterested silence was deafening, a stark contrast to the high-profile settlements in other countries. In India, it was as if these patients – left in pain, waiting for relief – had slipped far down the priority list. Their suffering was a footnote, almost forgotten amidst the company's efforts to clean up its global image.

Then, in 2017, after years of neglect, the Indian government finally took a stand. It wasn't a perfect solution, and it came far too late for many. But it was something – a significant moment in the long, painful ASR saga in India. For thousands of Indian patients, it was a light at the end of the tunnel of a long fight for justice.

For years, the regulator and the company were locked in a frustrating game of back-and-forth, exchanging multiple communications about the recall – compensation, safety concerns and more. On the surface, the drug regulator seemed to be fulfilling its duty, asking questions and demanding answers. But the company's responses were nothing more than vague reassurances, skillfully crafted to avoid real accountability. Thus, the cycle continued, with nothing substantial coming to light.

What was truly alarming in this drawn-out process was the glaring gap in clinical expertise. The officials in charge, seasoned in drug regulations, were thrust into unfamiliar territory, dealing with a medical device recall they barely understood. They lacked the real grasp of what could go wrong with such a device or the impact it could have on patients. However, at the start of 2017, some hope dawned for Indian patients.

It seemed the government was finally on the verge of taking meaningful action on compensation for ASR patients, having decided to form an expert committee. This group would consist of specialists from various fields – medical science, law, consumer affairs and toxicology – each bringing a unique perspective crucial to understanding the case. On 8 February 2017, the ministry quietly issued an internal order to form a committee – no public announcement, no press release.

In a situation that clearly involved public interest, one would have expected a more transparent approach. An open announcement through the media could have allowed patients to step forward and share their stories, but that didn't happen. Instead, only Vijay received an invitation, making him the sole patient to have a voice in the proceedings. Dr Arun Kumar Agarwal, a professor of ENT at New Delhi's Maulana Azad Medical College, was appointed to lead the nine-member team. The government set a strict deadline, demanding the committee's recommendations within just two months.

Two weeks later, on 22 February 2017, the expert committee gathered at the FDA Bhavan in New Delhi for a first meeting that would set the course of their scientific scrutiny. As the members settled into their seats, a sense of urgency filled the room. Among them were three orthopaedic surgeons who, even before the meeting began, knew the gravity of the issue. They had seen the writing on the wall – thanks to data from the UK and Australia, where orthopaedic registries had raised alarms about the safety of the implant. Peer-reviewed clinical studies from the US had further fuelled their concerns. Yet, despite this wealth of information from abroad, India was in the dark, lacking the crucial data needed to assess the situation at home.

Recognizing this glaring gap, the committee decided to focus on three critical areas: first, pressing the hospitals for patient data and adverse events, which would also uncover the alarming trend of revision surgeries, as the company had not provided the complete data to the regulator.

Second, the team needed to understand the potential harm the implant might be causing – specifically, the release of metal ions into the blood. There was a growing suspicion that the design itself might be the culprit behind its failure. To find answers, they decided to collate and review global scientific literature and meticulously piece together the scientific evidence.

Third, the most crucial task was to look into the issue of compensation. News reports about millions of dollars being given to US patients were widely known, but how did the company decide on these amounts and what was the formula behind them? The committee chose to find out by examining the legal actions taken outside India, which would help them create a plan for compensating Indian patients as well.

For the second meeting, to be held on 8 March 2017, the committee decided to invite three main stakeholders. First, they decided to invite two leading surgeons to share their first-hand experiences and insights about the implant's performance and complications. A company representative was called upon to give a detailed technical presentation. But perhaps the most poignant decision was to invite Vijay, the only patient to testify before the expert committee. His story, laden with personal struggles and pain, would provide a human face to the data.

The committee had decided at its first meeting that first of all, it needed the patient data and revision surgery records, buried in hospital files. The regulator finally took action. For the first time since the 2010 recall, the regulator directly reached out to hospitals. This was a step that should have come years earlier, back when it became clear that the company wasn't giving them the whole story.

On 2 March 2017, the regulator sent an urgent message to the hospitals. This message was significant because it disclosed, for the first time, that the expert committee had been formed due to mounting pressure from patients. These patients, frustrated by the lack of compensation for Indian victims, had sent complaints to the government.

After years of delay, this critical action was finally taken – not voluntarily, but because the voices of the affected could no longer be ignored. It was a message the regulator would never dare to make public. Yet, behind closed doors, they made this clear to the hospitals. It was a candid admission of the growing pressure they could no longer ignore. 'In light of the complaints from patients, it has been decided to review medical management, adverse reports and CAPA taken by the firm by a high-powered committee,' the Deputy Drugs Controller wrote to the hospitals.[3]

The regulator informed the hospitals about the first meeting of the expert committee and its intent to review the details of affected patients and any revision surgeries before making a decision, all in public interest. By emphasizing public interest, the regulator compelled the hospitals to share this information – something they might have otherwise refused to do, citing patient confidentiality.

The regulator also painted a vivid picture of the recall situation in the country, explaining why they had to take the unusual step of contacting hospitals directly. '… Affected patients who have been identified in India through the ASR helpline constitute roughly 25% of the total affected patients. Hence, the remaining 75% of the affected patients are still unaware and need to be identified for any adverse consequences,' the regulator urged the hospitals, underscoring the urgency of the situation.

It wasn't just that most patients were unaware of the recall. The regulator also pointed out that, in the first meeting, the committee had flagged the company's failure to provide details of all patients who had undergone the ASR surgery.

Consequently, the regulator requested six crucial pieces of information from the hospitals: (i) the total number of ASR surgeries performed between 2006 and 2012, (ii) detailed patient information, such as contact details, (iii) the number of revision surgeries, (iv) any reported adverse events or health issues post-surgery, (v) discharge reports and (vi) the medical management provided in these cases. The regulator imposed a strict ten-day deadline for this information.

'This matter must be treated with priority,' the regulator wrote.

Although this was an internal communication rather than a public notice, it marked a significant development: for the first time, key stakeholders outside the regulatory office – in this case, the hospitals and indirectly, doctors – were made aware of the regulator's struggle to access even basic patient details from the firm. This revelation highlighted two important issues. First, the weak regulatory medical device ecosystem allowed medical device manufacturers to potentially exploit the system.

Second, this communication made it clear that if the regulator truly wanted to address patient safety, it had the power to act. It could have reached out to hospitals directly, cutting through the red tape. It eventually did – though not until March 2017. But this should have happened as early as August 2010, or shortly after, when the company announced the global recall.

When the ASR was launched, it was aggressively marketed as a unique hip implant, one that claimed to outshine all others. The key selling point? A hip implant design that featured an extra-large-diameter bearing technology.[4] According to the company, this was a breakthrough. The company claimed it was introducing a groundbreaking 'concept' of 'fluid film bearing lubrication'. Imagine the precision needed to maintain the perfect balance between two moving parts – like the careful alignment of a door hinge that ensures smooth movement without excessive wear.

In other words, just as a well-oiled hinge works more smoothly and lasts longer, 'DePuy ASR XL is designed and manufactured to ensure optimal clearance to allow a film of [the body's natural] joint fluid to flow across, and lubricate, the entire bearing surface – measurably lowering wearing rates', the company claimed. It claimed that with the large head fitting comfortably into the cup, the implant would minimize wear, offering patients a hip implant that was longer-lasting than anything seen before.

On 8 March 2017, the expert committee reconvened at the first floor of the conference room, FDA Bhawan. One of the first items on the agenda was the very design that had been hailed as groundbreaking. During their second meeting, two orthopaedic surgeons joined the discussion, invited specifically to shed light on the issue. One of these surgeons, who had personally implanted this device in several patients, sounded the alarm. He pointed directly to the oversized head of the implant, a feature that was supposed to be its strength, and argued that it was, in fact, its flaw.

The surgeon described how the large head, rather than fitting perfectly into the acetabular cup – the component meant to fit inside the hip socket – was instead causing significant problems. This design made it difficult for the cup to fit properly. The very feature that was supposed to prolong the life of the implant was, ironically, the reason it was faulty. This implied that for a patient, such an implant inside the body could potentially lead to pain, reduced mobility and, as seen in many cases, a need for complicated revision surgery.

The second expert delved into the MoM hip implants, noting their long-standing use since the 1950s. However, despite this history of reliability, the ASR hip implant, along with a few other MoM implants in the market, proved to be a troubling outlier, falling short of expectations. This suggested that the design of an implant, not just the material, could be a critical factor in premature failure.

The discussion then turned to a crucial topic: compensation. At this point, the committee did not delve deeply into the issue, but it was a necessary first step towards understanding how to address it for Indian patients. The second expert referred to the US ASR reimbursement programme and why it could be one of the templates that could be looked at to create a fair compensation system for Indian patients. This was particularly important, because it directly impacted the patients.

After this, the two most important stakeholders met with the committee: the company representatives and Vijay, the sole patient who had been invited. The company's director of Medical Affairs and Device Safety was tasked with making the crucial presentation. The first two topics covered were fairly generic – an overview of hip implants and the evolution of MoM hip replacements. However, during this presentation, the company highlighted two key issues. First, it said that at the time of speaking, there was 'insufficient scientific data' to confidently make a 'science-based' recommendation on what specific metal ion levels in the blood should trigger doctors to take action or consider replacing the MoM hip implant.[5]

By making this submission, it appeared that the company was using the lack of definitive scientific evidence as a defence, arguing that the situation was complex and that the risks associated with the ASR implant might not be as straightforward as perceived. They also seemed intent on emphasizing that if the scientific community hadn't agreed on what level of metal ions is dangerous, then it would be unfair to hold the company entirely responsible for the revision surgeries. This seemed like a well-thought-out strategy aimed at positioning the recall as a responsible action taken in an ambiguous situation, rather than an admission of fault. In addition, the company drew the committee's attention to two other recalls by its competitors, both involving MoM hip implants listed by the US FDA. It seemed as though the company was eager to shift the spotlight, subtly suggesting that it wasn't just their product underperforming, but that other MoM implants in the market were also plagued with flaws.

Next came the moment everyone in the room had been waiting for: the company's presentation on the ASR recall. They started with a recap of everything they had done so far in India – something that felt like a rerun of what had already been communicated to the regulator and was well known by the government. Then, they got to the heart of the matter: the recall data. Nearly seven years after the recall, only 1,028 ASR patients had registered through the company's helpline, with 253 of them undergoing revision surgeries.[6]

This shocking data revealed that nearly 70 per cent of Indian patients were still untraced – a number that should have set off alarm bells. Yet, as they wrapped up, the company made four points: first, that the recalled implant wasn't defective or faulty; second, that the recall hadn't been forced by any regulator; third, that not every patient needed revision surgery; and finally, that they were covering the reasonable and customary costs of testing, treatment and revision surgery.

In essence, the company, through the presentation, made a calculated effort to convince everyone that despite the recall, there was nothing fundamentally wrong with the implant. They portrayed themselves as responsible, assuring the room that the situation was well under control. Every word was carefully chosen to create a sense of calm, to suggest that they had done everything required, leaving no room for doubt. But as the presentation concluded, there was one glaring omission – the complete absence of any mention of compensation for Indian patients. The silence on this issue was deafening.

Before the committee wrapped up the second meeting, they met Vijay, the lone patient invited, yet perhaps the most crucial stakeholder they had yet to engage. Vijay had lived through the ordeal of ASR surgery, a revision surgery and a painful recovery, all while enduring a host of related health complications, both physical and mental. Every detail, big or small, was etched into his memory. He arrived fully prepared, armed with a detailed presentation. Yet, as he began speaking, it became clear that his firsthand experiences were more compelling than any slides could be. In a calm, resolute voice, he walked the committee through the sequence of events in his medical history, painting a vivid picture of the challenges he had faced.

When the committee inquired about his symptoms post-ASR surgery, Vijay responded with precision. He didn't just describe his pain – he conveyed the gravity of the situation, the uncertainty that haunted him and the hundreds of young patients like him who lived with the same fear and frustration. At this moment, the committee specifically requested that Vijay provide medical records to support his case. Without hesitation, he agreed, understanding that every piece of evidence could be crucial to their scrutiny.

Though Vijay was not an orthopaedic surgeon, his search for justice had turned him into a researcher of sorts. Over the years, he had meticulously collected a vast array of documents on the ASR case – from news articles and investigative reports to global scientific literature. These were not just papers; they were threads of a larger narrative that he hoped would bring the truth to light. Vijay decided to hand over copies of these critical documents to the committee, believing they would bolster the committee's scrutiny and drive them closer to the truth.

As the meeting drew to a close, Vijay made two heartfelt pleas to the committee. First, he emphasized that despite his suffering, he had not yet taken legal action. This, he implied, was because he placed his trust in this scientific process, hoping it would deliver the justice he so desperately sought. Second, he urged the committee to conduct a thorough investigation and ensure fair compensation for all Indian patients who had endured similar hardships. His words resonated deeply. Though Vijay was the only patient present, he stood as a representative of thousands who suffered in silence across the country.

In that conference room, his voice might have been just one, but it carried the weight of many, and it was heard loud and clear.

Following the crucial interaction with the three key stakeholders, the committee engaged in a detailed deliberation at the close of their second meeting. The two orthopaedic surgeons had presented vital insights from their experience with the ASR implant. Yet, the expert committee was unwilling to limit its understanding to just these two voices. These men of science knew that a thorough and objective assessment was critical, so they resolved to broaden their scope. They asked the regulator to contact three more top orthopaedic surgeons as special invitees, with the aim to seek their opinion. Among the new experts were two high-volume surgeons who had performed far more hip replacements than their peers. These two surgeons also had extensive scientific insights into using various other hip implant models and were in the best position to compare their performance. This comparison would precisely explain why the ASR had performed poorly.

During the presentation, the company shared the data from the 2010 UK National Joint Registry, which had led to the decision to recall the ASR implant. This data revealed that within five years, 12 per cent of patients with ASR hip resurfacing and 13 per cent with the ASR XL required revision surgery. The figures were an indicator of the rate of failure of the implants. However, they did not provide any data specific to India. In contrast, data from the company's helpline in India presented a far grimmer picture. Out of 1,028 ASR patients, 253 had undergone revision surgeries, indicating a revision rate of 25 per cent in seven years after the recall. This alarming figure might be just the tip of the iceberg, as many Indian patients still remained untraced.

To obtain a clearer and more accurate assessment of revision surgeries in India, the expert committee chose a different approach. They decided to invite a surgeon from the All India Institute of Medical Sciences (AIIMS) in New Delhi, the country's premier medical institution, to the next meeting.

The second meeting concluded with the committee deciding to confront the company, demanding full transparency and a complete account of the recall. The company's presentation lingered in their minds – not for what was said, but for what was conspicuously absent. An unspoken tension filled the room as they wondered: Had the company overlooked important aspects directly affecting the patients, or were they deliberately hiding something? To uncover the truth, the committee decided to compile a questionnaire, giving the company a one-week deadline to respond. The company's reply would be crucial in determining the future course of the committee's scrutiny.

Exactly one week after the second meeting, late in the evening on 15 March 2017, the regulator sent the company a detailed questionnaire containing a staggering forty-one questions. The company missed the one-week deadline, eventually submitting a detailed reply on 30 March 2017. Meanwhile, the expert committee had reconvened for its third meeting on 22 March 2017. Due to the delay in DePuy's reply, they couldn't discuss the company's responses to the exhaustive questionnaire, but they proceeded with other crucial discussions on their agenda.

At the third meeting, the AIIMS surgeon arrived to present his findings. He began by explaining the implant to the committee through a detailed case study. Then, he shared a crucial piece of data: out of forty-six ASR surgeries at AIIMS, five had required revision – reflecting a 10 per cent revision rate. However, it was his next point that underscored the true gravity of the issue. He warned the committee that at AIIMS, likely the busiest hospital in the country, maintenance and availability of old records is a monumental challenge.

This wasn't just a technical concern; it suggested a deeper problem. First, the incomplete patient records implied that the numbers for revision surgeries might be significantly underreported due to a seven-year delay in data collection. Second, there was no evidence of how many patients might have sought revision surgery outside AIIMS, slipping through the cracks of the hospital's records. Third, without access to complete patient records, it would be nearly impossible to reach out to those affected, years later, to check if their health had deteriorated and if they needed revision surgery.

The AIIMS surgeon's presentation exposed the critical gaps in patient data management at the hospital level. The committee members, once merely concerned, now confronted the grim reality that the scale of the problem might be far greater than anticipated – and this could be the case at other major hospitals as well.

Following the AIIMS surgeon's presentation, the committee began examining the available clinical literature on the ASR revision rates. The emerging scientific literature from outside India painted a dramatically different picture, revealing that the revision rate could soar as high as 30 per cent within just five years. This was a stark contrast to the reassuring claims made by DePuy at the previous meeting. Additionally, it indicated that, in the absence of complete patient data, it was almost impossible to determine the exact revision rate – just as the AIIMS surgeon's presentation had suggested.

By this point, it was clear that only countries like Australia and the UK had caught on to the unusually high failure rate of the ASR implant. The reason? They had robust orthopaedic registries in place. Besides keeping tabs on the performance of implants, these systems offered crucial insights that made all the difference. They highlighted which products were performing well, helping surgeons make smarter choices when recommending hip replacements. Just as importantly, they flagged failures early, enabling doctors to track down affected patients and monitor their health closely.

As a result, the committee broadened its discussion during the third meeting to encompass not just the company, but the entire medical device ecosystem in India. First, the committee discussed the processes and mechanisms for supporting a registry for tracking medical devices. For this, they studied countries that were already excelling at this – how their systems worked, who the key players were and why these registries are so crucial for patient safety.

The committee's next topic of discussion was a system already in place in India – a potential lifeline for patients dealing with faulty medical devices. This initiative, officially known as the Materiovigilance Programme of India (MvPI), was quietly launched in July 2015. But what exactly does it do? In theory, it's a well-coordinated system: it collects data on adverse events related to medical devices, subjects them to scientific analysis and then relays this crucial information to the regulator. The goal is to warn patients about medical devices that may be dangerous.

On paper, it sounds like a solid plan. But there was a problem. At the very moment the expert committee was investigating the ASR, almost no one knew about this initiative. There was barely a whisper of awareness. The ASR patients suffering from the painful consequences of faulty implants weren't informed that they could report their issues. The government also kept the public largely in the dark about the adverse events being reported across the country. And then, there was the silence from the doctors. Many feared that submitting a report might land them in trouble, possibly even implicate them.[7]

The discussion then shifted to the two other alarming gaps in the system – loopholes so wide they were almost impossible to ignore. Take the case of the ASR, for instance. The company had issued a voluntary recall on 24 August 2010. But this crucial recall went unlisted on the regulator's website for nearly three years – an oversight unheard of in countries like the US, Australia or the UK. It wasn't until 9 December 2013, that a medical device alert was finally issued for the ASR in India.

Why the delay? Because under Indian law at the time, there was simply no requirement to notify medical device recalls in the public domain or even on the regulator's own website. Picture this: had the recall been promptly and widely publicized back in 2010, and with a swift issuance of a medical device alert, the outcome in India could have been drastically different. More patients might have come forward, more lives might have been protected. This very issue – whether to introduce mandatory provisions for notifying recalls – became a focal point of discussion within the committee.

Next, the expert committee turned their attention to another crucial system for monitoring device safety: periodic safety update reports. Under current laws, as part of post-marketing surveillance, drug companies must submit these reports to the regulator after their new drug receives approval. These periodic reports play a vital role in tracking the ongoing safety of a medicine once it's on the market. They assess whether the benefits still outweigh the risks by scrutinizing new safety information and all data accumulated since the drug was first approved. These reports are filed at regular intervals, ensuring that the product remains safe over time.

During the committee's discussions, it noted that the existing law required companies to submit periodic safety update reports for only four years. This timeframe, however, was not long enough for implants. The ASR recall had shown that a device could begin to fail after the four-year mark. If there had been no cap on the duration of the safety update report submissions, the company would have been obligated to provide data beyond the fourth year, which might have alerted regulators sooner and potentially prevented further issues. Therefore, the committee discussed the need to re-evaluate the safety report submission duration, considering whether to extend or remove the current cap.

In their discussion, they also explored the possibility of implementing legal provisions to mandate post-marketing surveillance submissions for all implants. This was particularly important given that, unlike in the UK, there was a noticeable lack of domestic post-marketing surveillance data on ASR in India; and even if such data existed, it was rarely made public to Indian patients.

As the third meeting drew to a close, they shifted from broad discussions about medical device safety to focus squarely on the implant in question. They made two key decisions. First, they recognized the need to delve deeper into the experiences of Indian surgeons who had worked with the implant, a move designed to add scientific rigour to their scrutiny. One expert committee member was tasked with gathering both technical feedback and personal insights from these surgeons.

Second, the committee took another important step: they asked the Indian regulator to directly reach out to national regulators from leading countries such as the US, the UK, Australia, the European Union, Japan, Canada and Brazil, known for their rigorous medical device oversight. Their aim was twofold: first, to understand the legal measures these countries had implemented to support and compensate patients affected by the ASR device recall; and second, to see if these regulators had responded with new policy recommendations aimed at tightening patient safety standards and ensuring future medical devices are more secure. By doing so, the committee sought to learn from global best practices and possibly influence broader, more robust safety regulations.

―

The committee gathered for its fourth meeting on 19 April 2017. The primary agenda was to dissect the company's much-anticipated reply to a detailed questionnaire. The committee had asked for a blow-by-blow account of the steps taken to implement the recall, how patients were being reached, the exact scientific cause for the voluntary recall, the role of Puri Crawford and the post-recall support given to patients affected by the faulty ASR implants.

Many of the answers weren't new – most were already in the regulator's hands. Further, several key issues remained unanswered. The expert committee wasn't going to let the company off the hook so easily. They zeroed in on critical areas where even the Indian regulators had been left in the dark, despite having multiple discussions with the company about the ASR recall. What came next was telling.

During the company's presentation, the committee had realized the company had quietly made the decision to phase out reimbursement for revision surgeries. The committee knew that for many untraced patients – those who had yet to realize their implants were part of a massive recall – this could be devastating. Imagine someone, years after surgery, finally discovering that their implant had been recalled, only to find out that they were no longer eligible for any financial help.

The committee wasn't going to let this slide.

'Till what period ASR reimbursement programme at global level and India is going to continue. Provide objective evidence,' they pressed.

The company's response was initially coated in concern. It explained that it faced unique challenges in certain countries – though it never mentioned India by name, the implications were clear. These challenges, it claimed, had made it difficult to find and notify all patients. To address this, they said, they had extended the reimbursement time limit, so that even delayed cases could still access compensation. It almost sounded reassuring at first.

But then came the real news – a twist that undermined the earlier sentiment.

The company highlighted two key details. First, they said that the company would reimburse the costs of medical tests, including the cobalt–chromium blood tests – a key test linked to the recall – only if the expenses were incurred on or before 24 August 2017 in India. But the second detail was even more concerning: the reimbursement for revision surgeries would be considered on a case-by-case basis, and only if the surgery took place within ten years of the original ASR implant.

Picture this: a patient has ASR surgery in 2006, thinking everything's going to get better. Then, out of nowhere in 2017, the patient hears there had been a recall of the implant, of which the patient was not informed. Now, this patient is not only ineligible for any reimbursement, but is also stuck with a massive medical bill for the complex revision surgery, since it is after the arbitrary ten-year time limit.

In other words, it meant that if a patient learnt about the recall more than ten years after the primary surgery, they would not qualify for any reimbursement. In India, where little effort was made to inform patients, this left many of them unknowingly facing a growing health crisis, without financial support.

The message was clear: the window for help was closing fast, and many might find themselves out of luck.

The company's next set of responses addressed the regulator's pressing questions regarding the issues surrounding revision surgeries.

First, they were asked to provide the number of patients who had undergone revision surgery. In response, the company cited data from its ASR helpline: 1,032 patients had registered, with 254 having undergone revision surgery. However, they offered no insight into the status of the remaining 778 patients – 75 per cent of those who registered. Instead, the company provided a vague defence: 'DePuy is unable to provide information on all revision surgeries because not all patients are registered with the ASR Help Line and not all revision surgeries are reported to the company.' This response was significant.

From this reply, two unsettling conclusions emerged.

First, it suggested that far more revision surgeries were occurring across India than the company was aware of. Many patients, flying under the company's radar, were likely bearing the hefty costs of these procedures despite the existence of a supposed reimbursement system.

Imagine the frustration of a patient already grappling with the physical and emotional toll of surgery, as well as an unexpected financial burden.

Second, there were contradictory claims made by the company. If, as DePuy claimed here, not all surgeries were being reported to it, this was at odds with its claims of having made a comprehensive outreach to surgeons to ensure they informed patients undergoing revision surgery that they were eligible for reimbursement. If the company's latter claim was true, how could these procedures slip through the cracks? Were doctors intentionally withholding information, leaving patients to cover their expenses? Why would they do that? The entire situation was perplexing, as if a crucial piece of the puzzle was missing, and the answers simply didn't add up.

According to the company's own helpline data, a staggering 778 patients who had registered never underwent revision surgery. Was this because some ASR patients were healthy and merely signing up out of caution? Or was it that their surgeons, after assessing the risks, decided against removing the faulty implants altogether? The company, predictably, came forward with a defence. They claimed that not every patient with an ASR hip implant would need revision surgery, emphasizing that the final call was up to the surgeons. But this explanation felt hollow – an empty reassurance with no real evidence. If they wanted to back up their claim, all they needed to do was ask the doctors how many of those 778 patients had normal levels of cobalt and chromium in their blood. But they didn't. Instead, they crafted a narrative that placed the burden on the surgeons, quietly sidestepping the company's own responsibility.

The committee had anticipated that the company would respond in this manner. To uncover the truth, they pressed the company for data on patients who chose not to undergo revision surgery. This information would reveal the ground reality of the ASR revision surgeries in India.

For a moment, you'd expect this number to be quite large, given that 778 patients had registered on the company's helpline but had not undergone revision surgery. But the actual number was surprisingly low: only twelve patients had informed the helpline that they didn't opt for the revision.

The company's response was vague, almost rehearsed. They quickly deflected any blame, pointing fingers squarely at the surgeons. 'It is important to understand,' they said, 'that the ASR helpline is merely providing reimbursement support to patients, not clinical management.' It was a polished statement, designed to create distance between the company and the decisions that surgeons were left to make on their own.

'As a result,' they continued, 'we are unable to provide exact information on how many patients in India chose not to undergo revision surgery because not all patients are registered with the ASR Helpline, and not all such cases are reported to the company.' The defence was clear: they were washing their hands of the issue, leaving patients and their doctors to deal with the fallout. You could sense the defensiveness in every word, as if they were desperately trying to shield themselves from the issue.

The committee had also anticipated the company's response regarding the mere 22 per cent of Indian patients who had registered on the company's helpline, despite claims of extensive patient outreach. That's why, in their questionnaire, they specifically asked why only 1,058 Indian patients were registered, when a staggering 4,700 surgeries had been performed.

The company offered six carefully crafted excuses why, 'despite the best [of] efforts', it couldn't register all ASR patients to the helpline. Each reason pointed a finger elsewhere, painting a picture of a company that had done everything right, only to be thwarted by external forces.

First, many patient medical records were 'not available' with surgeons and hospitals, implying the lack of centralized or easily accessible documentation. Second, it said some surgeons 'prefer to inform patients on their own', indicating a desire to handle the matter privately rather than involve external entities. Third, there were patients who simply did not want to register, perhaps unsure about the process.

Then came the fourth excuse: some surgeons outright refused to share patient information. Again, the company shifted the blame onto the doctors, as if this alone could explain the dismal registration numbers. Fifth, they pointed to unreachable surgeons – those who had retired, moved abroad or simply disappeared. But this reason was flimsy too, as hospitals, not surgeons, usually hold patient records. And finally, they discounted international patients, claiming they were beyond reach because they lived outside India.

As the excuses piled up, it became clear that DePuy was weaving a web of deflection. Instead of owning its failure, it crafted a defence that squarely blamed surgeons, hospitals and the system – with reasons that could not be verified. It wanted to sweep away any paper trail leading to it.

Then came one of the most important questions from the committee: where were the preclinical and clinical data for the ASR? You'd expect the company to submit the results of simulator tests – the kind engineers run to stress-test a device's durability and performance. After all, these tests likely shaped the final design of the implant. In India, this crucial information was never handed over to the regulators. Why? Because, at the time, there wasn't even a regulatory requirement for such data.

However, in its reply, the company confidently assured the committee that it had conducted 'dozens' of preclinical studies on the ASR system's design, materials and performance. These, they claimed, were all submitted to US regulators when the device was approved through the 510(k) route, a statement meant to sound reassuring.

But there was a catch – a few, actually. First off, the ASR system came in two versions: the ASR XL and the ASR Hip Resurfacing. Only the ASR XL received US FDA approval through this 510(k) process, while the ASR Hip Resurfacing was never even approved in the US. Now, for most of us, this technical stuff can feel like being stuck in a medical jargon maze. So, what exactly is this 510(k) route the company kept referring to? Imagine this: you're buying a new gadget, but instead of going through rigorous tests to ensure it works safely, it's approved simply because it's similar to something already on the market. That's the 510(k) process in a nutshell. It allows new medical devices to enter the market if they're considered 'substantially equivalent' to an older product. The problem? Sometimes, the older product it's compared to may never have been properly tested or may have even been recalled for failing miserably. But because the new device looks close enough like a passed product, it gets a free pass.

Here's what the company conveniently left out when responding to the committee: the ASR XL's 510(k) approval had a bizarre backstory. The approval was based on it being made of parts originating from ninety-five other approved devices, some of which had subsequently been pulled off the market. And if that wasn't alarming enough, the MoM components of the ASR XL were cleared based on prostheses from the 1970s – ones that were abandoned years ago because they performed poorly. Yet, despite this track record, the ASR XL was rubber-stamped by the USFDA in 2005.[8]

Now, how did this happen? It all goes back to 1976, when the Medical Device Amendments were passed to regulate medical devices in the US. To keep things simple, devices were categorized into three classes based on risk: Class I for low-risk, Class II for moderate-risk and Class III for high-risk devices like implants. However, since there were already many devices on the market at the time, lawmakers allowed some high-risk devices, known as 'preamendment' devices, to be reviewed under a shortcut process – the 510(k). This meant these devices didn't have to undergo the more thorough premarket approval (PMA) process, which would require actual clinical trial data to prove they worked safely. So, instead of proving these devices were safe through hard evidence, companies could slide through on the basis of 'substantial equivalence'.

So when the company talked about 'dozens' of preclinical studies to the committee, what studies were they really referring to? It's anyone's guess. In reality, the ASR XL got its green light because it was deemed 'substantially equivalent' to something else that had been on the market. And that was that – no thorough testing, just a nod to the past.

As for the ASR Hip Resurfacing model, it never received US FDA approval. US surgeons never implanted it, simply because it didn't meet the necessary requirements to even make it through the door.

The committee continued to sift through each of the company's replies. It was like trying to piece together a puzzle with too many missing parts – vital details were either vague or completely absent. The committee wasn't buying the company's incomplete responses. Determined to get real answers, they decided to send one final questionnaire – a last chance for the company to come clean.

At the end of the meeting, another important step was taken. The company had provided the committee with addresses of 1,032 ASR patients registered on its helpline. This was their golden opportunity to hear directly from the patients. The committee decided to randomly select 100 patients (eventually it was 101), sending them a questionnaire asking about their personal experiences with the implant, the challenges they faced and how – if at all – the company had addressed their health concerns.

On 6 May 2017, the company submitted a detailed response to the final questionnaire. Three days later, the expert committee reconvened for its fifth meeting, with the key agenda being a review of the company's submission.

The first major issue raised in the questionnaire was the discrepancy in time limit for reimbursing patients affected by the recalled ASR hip implant. The expert committee pointed out something unusual: in the US, the company promised to cover revision surgeries for up to seven years after the initial implant, but outside the US, including India, this coverage extended to ten years.

However, when it came to covering medical tests related to the recall, the company only provided support in India until 24 August 2017. This raised a crucial question for the expert committee: if revision surgeries in India were covered for ten years, why weren't the necessary tests and exams covered for the same duration? After all, these tests, especially cobalt–chromium testing, were critical for monitoring potential complications with the faulty implants, which could arise over time. The committee was concerned that, after the 2017 deadline, Indian patients would have to bear the cost of these important medical tests themselves. They argued that this was unfair – if revision surgeries were covered for ten years, shouldn't the tests and exams be included within that same timeframe?

In its response, the company argued that its reimbursement programme was based on medical standards and practices available at the time of the recall in 2010. Back then, no clear protocols existed for the long-term monitoring or treatment of patients with MoM implants. As the first company to offer such a reimbursement programme, they set specific time limits for coverage.

The company further claimed that since then, medical associations and regulatory bodies had 'published' standards of care for patients implanted with MoM implants. 'Ongoing monitoring and treatment of such patients is now accepted practice, which was not the case in the early period following the voluntary recall in 2010,' DePuy replied. Their response implied that the ongoing cobalt–chromium testing had become part of the standard care of patients with MoM hip implants, which was why they set the 24 August 2017 deadline for reimbursement.

However, for India, this was far from the truth. Neither the major orthopaedic associations in the country nor the national regulator had issued any specific guidelines for monitoring patients with MoM hip implants, especially after concerns about the performance of these devices following the 2010 recall. According to the company's own data, it had already shelled out Rs 176,076,656 in testing reimbursements. The data made one thing clear: if the company stopped paying for these, the patients would be left shouldering a crushing financial burden, with many unable to afford the care they desperately needed.

In the last round of questioning, the expert committee once again zeroed in on the preclinical data surrounding the ASR hip implant. This time, however, they asked the company to produce the exact preclinical and clinical data submitted during the ASR's approval process in the European Union.

The company responded by explaining how the ASR hip implant was introduced to the EU market through a process known as CE marking. Governed by the Medical Devices Directive, this process acts like a green light for medical devices in the EU.

To secure that CE mark, the company submitted what they called a 'clinical literature evaluation'. After sifting through this material, the notified body British Standards Institute (BSI) granted approval, signifying that the ASR met the necessary standards for sale across Europe. This BSI approval got the device its CE mark.

At first glance, it seemed as if the company implied they had run rigorous clinical trials to win over the BSI. But dig a little deeper, and that assumption falls apart.

A clinical literature evaluation is not the same as hard clinical trial data. It doesn't necessarily mean the company conducted its own human clinical trials. Instead, it's more akin to compiling studies and scientific data already available to demonstrate the device's safety, without the company having to provide its own clinical trial evidence.

However, it's not just about the company not being required to submit clinical trial data. Critics have argued that this system, designed to protect consumers, has instead let them down, raising concerns about the transparency of the approvals that affect countless lives.

So, what exactly is the CE marking? 'CE' stands for 'Conformité Européenne', or European Conformity, and it's more than just a label. You've probably seen it on everything from medical devices to children's toys. It's a small logo with a big responsibility. For medical devices like implants or life-saving equipment, the CE mark signals that the company has done its homework. They've ensured the product won't jeopardize patient safety, and any risks involved are carefully balanced against the potential benefits. It's a seal of trust that what's inside the box won't just work, but will work safely, keeping patients' well-being front and centre.

In the CE approval system for hip implants, think of the notified bodies as quality control inspectors at a factory. These inspectors review the technical details – essentially, the blueprints of the device to ensure it meets all safety and performance standards. Once everything checks out, they place the CE mark on the product, signalling that it is compliant and ready for market. These notified bodies are chosen by specific EU member states, somewhat like independent auditors hired to oversee certain processes.

However, this fast-tracked approval system for medical devices has faced several criticisms. The notified bodies responsible for approving these devices are private companies, and their competence and transparency have been questioned. Clinicians have raised concerns that 'nobody knows the make-up of notified bodies or their skill base, and nobody knows their [...] process of approving.'[9]

More alarmingly, concerns have been raised about the practice of seeking approval from a notified body perceived as more likely to give a favourable opinion, known as 'forum shopping'. In fact, the BSI was 'aware of situations' where a manufacturer had withdrawn an application from the BSI and had 'been successful just a few months later, clearly without any further clinical data, to gain certification through another (notified body)'.[10]

And that's not all.

In 2012, the prestigious *British Medical Journal (BMJ)* teamed up with *The Daily Telegraph* for an undercover investigation that laid bare the shocking loopholes in this approval system.[11]

In this investigation, they crafted an application for a large-diameter MoM hip implant – essentially designing a product on paper with specifications similar to the DePuy ASR XL acetabular system, which had already been recalled in August 2010. Despite the real-life product having been pulled from the market for safety concerns, the team submitted an almost identical device for approval to a notified body in Slovakia. What happened next was jaw-dropping: the body provisionally gave the green light, allowing the device to move towards certification.

Imagine that a recalled implant slipped right through the cracks because the system relied on private companies that barely raised an eyebrow. This exposed just how dangerously easy it could be for faulty devices to gain approval and enter the market.

The expert committee also revisited another issue regarding the clinical data on the device – this time focusing on the performance of the ASR after it had been introduced into the market.

In the first round of questioning, the committee demanded answers about the company's internal findings from its root cause analysis of the ASR failure. The company's response felt rehearsed, blaming three factors: the patient, the surgeon and the implant's design or material, as if reading from a script.

'Each of these three categories can contribute to the mechanism leading to revision,' the company stated blandly. But for the experts across the table, this was déjà vu – the same response the company had given regulators years earlier. However, this time, it was different. Now, the company was facing specialists who lived and breathed the science of hip replacements. These weren't just bureaucrats; they were experts who knew that poor patient selection or surgical techniques weren't to blame for the ASR failures. They saw right through the company's carefully worded statement.

When the committee sent a second questionnaire, they reminded the company that the three factors – patient, surgeon and design – are standard in any implant failure or revision surgery. This wasn't new information to anyone in the room. What they wanted, and demanded, was a direct explanation of the design and material flaws specific to the ASR implant. No distractions.

Instead of providing clarity, the company dodged the issue. They claimed there was no definitive product design or material root cause for the increased revision rates, thus avoiding any admission of fault. Then they tried to deflect, suggesting that all MoM implants, including the ASR, had more problems than metal-on-polyethylene ones, in an attempt to broaden the conversation. They argued that each implant failure was unique and required individual analysis. Some factors could increase revision rates, they admitted, but they dismissed others as mere 'theories or speculation' needing further research.

What should have been a straightforward response turned into a maze of vague statements and circular reasoning. The company's reluctance to acknowledge flaws in the ASR's design was glaringly obvious. They had turned a simple question into a complex riddle, all while avoiding the real issue at hand. Instead, in the response, they highlighted various factors influencing revision rates, such as patient activity levels and surgical techniques – these points served to dilute the focus on the ASR's design.

The company also emphasized that it was currently unclear how individual patients reacted to metal debris from implants, and while some patients might experience a strong negative reaction to even small amounts of debris (hypersensitivity), others might have a different response based on how much debris is present. This variability had not been linked to any specific design of the implant, the company argued.

It was puzzling that, even seven years after the recall, the company still struggled to provide a clear explanation for the higher revision rates of the ASR implant. As patients continued to share their stories of pain and disappointment, one could not help but wonder how a major corporation could remain so vague about such a critical issue. It seemed almost surreal that, after so much time, the company hadn't been able to definitively identify whether the design flaws or the materials used in the implant were at the heart of these complications.

Not surprisingly, the committee followed up with another related question, pressing the company to explain the published studies that reported failure rates higher than DePuy's own claim of 11–13 per cent revisions over five years. These studies were linked to an investigation in the *British Medical Journal*, which had cast serious doubt on the safety of the ASR implant.

The company's response was swift but calculated. They argued that the article in question relied on statements from specific individuals, and these needed to be considered alongside the full range of data available to DePuy at the time of the recall. It was clear they were trying to shift focus away from those damning statistics.

The investigation had also brought up the work of Nargol and Langton, two prominent figures whose research had raised red flags about the ASR. The company was quick to go on the offensive, suggesting that both Nargol and Langton were being paid by personal injury lawyers from around the globe who were suing DePuy. They didn't stop there, adding that both men had personally sued the company, seeking millions in damages.

Yes, it was true that Nargol and Langton had testified as expert witnesses in a handful of ASR-related cases. In fact, many other specialists had also served as expert witnesses in ASR cases. But here's where the company's defence faltered – the whistleblower lawsuit they were trying to pin on Nargol and Langton had nothing to do with the ASR at all. It was tied to a completely different DePuy model, unrelated to the matter at hand.

―――

The most important question raised by the expert committee in the final questionnaire concerned developments related to the ASR recall in Australia. The committee questioned why, if the company had voluntarily recalled the ASR in Australia in 2009, only a warning was issued in India in March 2010, and why the recall was delayed until August 2010. Essentially, the committee was highlighting the delay between these key events in different regions and seeking an explanation: why lives were potentially left at risk in one region while swift action was taken elsewhere.

'There was no recall in Australia in 2009,' the company replied. It clarified that the decision wasn't a recall but was made for commercial reasons: the use of the products at that time in Australia was limited.

'In Australia, the decision to discontinue ASR sales was announced in letters to customers in late 2009 and was communicated in writing to the Therapeutic Goods Association (TGA) in early December 2009,' DePuy explained.

Technically, they were correct – it wasn't a formal voluntary recall. But was this decision solely driven by commercial factors? The full picture wasn't conveyed to the expert committee. The company presented a one-sided narrative to the committee, painting the discontinuation as purely a commercial decision.

Here's why that was only part of the story:

In Australia, the Australian Orthopaedic Association National Joint Replacement Registry (NJRR), funded by the Commonwealth Department of Health, monitors each device meticulously. Whenever the NJRR flags an implant as an outlier, the TGA jumps into action, notifying the manufacturer and demanding detailed explanations. An implant is considered an outlier when its revision rate is at least double that of other devices.[12] These responses are scrutinized by the Orthopaedic Expert Working Group (OEWG), an independent team of specialists who provide scientific advice to the TGA, which then makes a decision based on this guidance.

In 2006, the Birmingham Hip Replacement (BHR) was the gold standard in Australia, with the lowest revision rates among resurfacing hip implants. That same year, the NJRR noted that the ASR had a higher revision rate compared to the BHR, but the difference wasn't statistically significant – yet.

However, the NJRR's 2007 report sounded alarm bells. It revealed that 31 out of 753 ASR resurfacing hips had been revised, translating to a 4.1 per cent revision rate. In stark contrast, only 218 out of 8,192 other resurfacing hips had been revised, representing a 2.7 per cent revision rate. In response, the TGA convened the OEWG to sift through the NJRR data.

At their first meeting on 8 August 2007, the OEWG speculated that the higher revision rates might be due to the ASR's technical complexity. They recommended that Australian surgeons receive additional training to handle the device properly.

In September 2007, the Australian regulator held a meeting with DePuy officials to address the high revision rates. The company claimed it had already implemented mandatory training for surgeons to curb revision surgeries. By May 2008, the company's status report to the regulator revealed an important data: sales of the ASR implants had plummeted following the introduction of the training programme, with fifteen surgeons abandoning the device.

In October 2008, the NJRR uncovered another issue – the ASR XL cup was also showing higher-than-expected revision rates, but only when used with a specific femoral stem model, the Corail component. In these cases, the revision rate climbed to 4.5 per cent three years after the initial surgery.[13]

The following year, in October 2009, the NJRR data painted a grimmer picture: the ASR XL exhibited a higher-than-expected revision rate of 5.4 per cent three years after surgery, regardless of the femoral stem used.[14]

The TGA and DePuy held another round of discussions about the

ASR at this point. The TGA indicated that, given the 2009 NJRR data, the company needed to explain why it continued to supply the ASR. DePuy responded that sales had drastically fallen, making the product commercially unviable.

Two months later, on 8 December 2009, the company formally notified the regulator of its decision to discontinue the ASR. The very next day, the OEWG took up the matter. Their minutes recorded that the TGA had reported a concerning rate of ASR revisions due to metal sensitivity. The OEWG unanimously agreed that the ASR should no longer be available on the market.

The expert committee had one key goal: to find out if Indian patients affected by the ASR hip implant failure would be compensated fairly. This issue was at the core of everything. In their final questionnaire, the committee once again asked for specific details about the compensation paid to Indian patients who had called the ASR helpline, hoping for help. But the company's response was surprising and confusing. They provided a figure: Rs 142,072,014. However, this wasn't actual compensation. It was simply the amount they had reimbursed for revision surgeries and related costs, like out-of-pocket expenses and loss of wages. They seemed to be dodging the real question – this wasn't the compensation the patients deserved.

Not willing to settle for half-answers, the committee pressed on, asking for details about the company's compensation policy – both globally and in India.

The company reiterated that their policy depended on the legal system of each country. They explained that compensation sought by patients were handled on a case-by-case basis, according to local laws. The company also mentioned that some patients in India had taken their cases to court, but the outcomes were still pending.

'In India, there are some patients who have preferred to assert their claim before the courts of law ... Whenever an ASR patient brings a claim for compensation, DePuy will assess the specific facts and background with its legal advisors in India based on prevailing local laws by taking into account all the applicable factors and where appropriate, seek to reach a reasonable settlement by mutual agreement with the patient,' DePuy replied to the committee.

The company's approach to compensation felt distant and impersonal. For each Indian patient who filed a claim, their case was thoroughly examined through a legal lens – every surgery, every failed implant, all measured against what the law allowed. While the company hinted at a willingness to settle claims, it was far from a guarantee. Their assurances of reasonable settlements felt more like empty words, with no certainty that patients would actually receive anything substantial.

Previously, the company had told the committee that thirteen court cases had been filed by ASR patients in India. At that time, only one case had been settled between a patient and the company, and another had been decided by the court. In their most recent update, they quietly mentioned that two cases had now been settled through court orders.

But what really stood out was the shockingly low number of cases. Out of 4,700 ASR surgeries performed in India, only a handful of patients – barely in the single digits – had taken the step to file a court case. This was a clear sign of a much bigger problem. Many Indian patients simply weren't aware of their legal rights, and even if they were, the cost of pursuing such cases was too high for most to afford. Taking on the company in court was an uphill battle, one that many couldn't even consider.

This situation worked out perfectly for DePuy. With only a few patients going to court and the settlements being relatively small compared to what patients were receiving in places like the US, it was facing little financial or legal pressure. Fewer claims meant fewer payouts, and the company could avoid the bigger financial hits happening abroad.

Thus, during the sixth meeting, when the committee reconvened on 5 September 2017, finally, it was time to tackle the pressing issue of compensation. The expert committee decided that a compensation amount would be allocated to affected Indian ASR patients. It was the first formal step towards addressing the grievances of those who had suffered since the August 2010 recall. Although it came nearly seven years too late, it was a significant and necessary development that many had thought would never come.

Next, the committee decided to develop a formula for determining the compensation. In a landscape where no legal precedent existed for compensating patients affected by a medical device recall of this magnitude, the task seemed daunting. Yet, the committee decided that compensation would be based on the percentage of disability each patient experienced. This was a major breakthrough, a step towards acknowledging the real impact of these devices on lives once lived in hope and health.

The committee also decided to form a panel dedicated to assessing each patient's percentage of disability. This panel would consist of three orthopaedic experts, tasked with evaluating the patients. They would be joined by a member from the regulatory body, a legal expert and a representative from a consumer affairs NGO. At the end of the meeting, the committee decided on an important time limit: ASR patients who had received the implant within fifteen years of their initial surgery would be eligible to claim compensation.

On 10 January 2018, the committee gathered for its seventh meeting.

The very formation of this expert committee was unprecedented. Imagine a room filled with seasoned doctors, people who had spent their careers in scrubs and stethoscopes, now in an unfamiliar role – as investigators. For many, this was uncharted territory; their daily work was about mending lives, not unearthing corporate failures. Yet, here they sat, poring over documents, analysing charts and retracing the experiences of patients whose lives had been painfully altered by these implants.

As they combed through each piece of evidence, the seriousness of the situation weighed on them. This wasn't just about malfunctioning technology – it was about real people, their lives affected in ways that couldn't be undone. The government's delayed action increased the gravity of their task, but even so, their late intervention sent a clear message: when patient safety is at stake, action becomes not only essential but inevitable. With each recommendation they carefully crafted, the experts took one more step towards safeguarding future patients and nudging justice forward, driven by the collective realization that this crisis couldn't be ignored any longer.

On 10 January 2018, the expert committee came together for its seventh and most crucial meeting. The atmosphere was grave, with an undercurrent of satisfaction, as members reviewed the final report – a document that held recommendations poised to impact the lives of hundreds of ASR patients. It was an epoch-making report, but the journey to reach this point had been equally important. Months of tough discussions and relentless questions had pushed them to consider every angle. At last, they had reached a shared conclusion, underscoring how vital each step of this long process had been. And with each recommendation forwarded to the government, these experts took one more step towards safeguarding patients and setting the wheels of justice in motion.

13

The Indictment

On 19 February 2018, an important communication arrived at the Union Health Secretary's desk. The subject of the communication was 'Submission of ASR Report'.* Inside was a report that had been the subject of endless anticipation and no small amount of anxiety. Dr Arun Kumar Aggarwal, head of the expert committee, had finally sent the report the government had been waiting for, containing crucial findings on the faulty ASR hip implants and the vital issue of compensation for Indian patients. For hundreds of patients and families across the country, this report carried hope for justice, for some relief from the pain they'd endured for too long.

This report was the result of seven crucial meetings that began almost a year earlier, on 22 February 2017, and stretched to 10 January 2018. Each session required the committee to dig through reams of documents and firsthand accounts. Surgeons, patients, hospitals, court records and the company, DePuy, all added layers to the story. It was an unprecedented process, with each record underscoring the very human cost of medical oversight.

'The finalization of the report as such had taken some time owing to the ... complex nature of the subject,' Dr Aggarwal explained to the health secretary in the 19 February 2018 communication, acknowledging the months of work that led to this moment. But for those whose lives had been shattered by the ASR implants, this

---

* This Report of the Expert Committee was generated to address the issue of faulty ASR hip implants. It can be accessed through the following link: https://cdsco.gov.in/opencms/opencms/system/modules/CDSCO.WEB/elements/common_download.jsp?num_id_pk=ODQ0.

report was more than a government document – it was a long-awaited glimmer of hope. 'After detailed deliberation and looking into the entire gamut and array of issues ... the committee makes the following observations,' the report stated.

At the outset, the expert committee focused on two key issues: the scientific evidence surrounding the early failures of the ASR implant and the severe impact of the faulty device on patients' health.

The expert committee's report opened with an urgent matter of patient safety: a critical piece of information was still glaringly missing, even seven years after the global recall. Despite the urgency and the thousands of lives impacted, this vital detail had somehow slipped through the cracks.

When a medical device is recalled, it rings a loud alarm, signalling that something has gone terribly wrong. Whether it poses a direct threat to patient safety or reflects a flaw that undermines the product's effectiveness, a recall sets off a cascade of investigations. Manufacturers are then obligated to dive deep, uncovering the root cause as part of their corrective and preventive actions (CAPA) process. This isn't just about solving the immediate issue; it's about ensuring that the same mistake doesn't happen again.

The key question was: What exactly went wrong, and why? Was it a design flaw? A manufacturing error? Inferior materials? Or perhaps even an issue with how surgeons handled the implant during surgery?

In India, nearly seven years after the ASR recall, the expert committee convened to scrutinise the implant's failure. Given the severity of the issue – thousands of patients needing painful revision surgeries – the expert committee expected a comprehensive root cause analysis by now, especially considering how much time had passed since the recall.

But what they received felt scripted – like rehearsed lines. The company pointed fingers at three factors: the patient, the surgeon and the implant's design or materials.

Imagine sitting in that room, expecting hard data and in-depth reports, only to hear vague explanations that shifted blame without offering real answers. The committee wasn't looking for generalities – they wanted specifics. What exactly about the ASR's design caused so many patients to suffer? What material flaw led to its rapid failure? Yet, the company sidestepped these questions, offering no substantial or clear findings.

Previously, DePuy had assured regulators that their experts were conducting a scientific investigation on the explanted devices at the London Implant Retrieval Centre. Yet, despite these claims, the Indian regulator remained in the dark about the results.

Frustrated, the expert committee's first major finding was this: the company had 'failed' to provide a detailed root cause analysis explaining why the ASR implants had such a high revision rate. 'The firm has also not provided CDSCO the details of investigation, despite being asked on several occasions,' the committee noted.

Although the company didn't provide clear answers on the root cause of the higher revision rates, the expert committee members had pieced together the reason by the end of their deliberations, thanks to the surgeons' firsthand experiences and international literature on the device's clinical performance.

During their discussions, these surgeons had highlighted a crucial design flaw: the femoral head – the ball-shaped part of the implant – was noticeably larger than usual, but the acetabular cup, in which the ball rests, didn't fit properly. This poor fit wasn't just a minor inconvenience; it caused a serious issue. The surgeons explained that the design of the implant caused an uneven distribution of forces between the ball and the cup. Instead of spreading the pressure evenly, the forces were concentrated at the edge of the cup, leading to excessive wear. Worse, it released tiny particles of metal debris – cobalt and chromium – which in turn released toxic ions into the bloodstream, far exceeding safe levels. As a result, patients who had hoped the surgery would bring relief found themselves back in hospitals, undergoing revision surgeries to replace the failing implants. 'This could be one of the reasons for the higher rate of revision surgeries,' the committee observed.

The committee then looked into whether the faulty design of MoM hip implants was harming patients by releasing toxic metal ions into their bodies. They had reviewed research and alerts from regulatory authorities around the world, all pointing to the same issue: ASR implants had a flawed design. Because of this, metal particles, especially cobalt and chromium, were being released into patients' bodies, the committee observed. The committee also pointed out that the amount of metal released varied from person to person, but it was still a serious concern. If the body couldn't rid itself of these metal ions, they could damage tissue and even affect other organs. The poor design not only caused the implants to wear out faster but also led to health problems, forcing patients to undergo more revision surgeries than they would have with better-designed implants, the committee emphasized.

The committee went on to describe the far-reaching impact of the faulty design, highlighting how it affects patients not just physically, but in nearly every aspect of their lives. They explained that the ASR implant, because of the excessive release of metal ions, doesn't just damage the hip – it can lead to a host of other health problems, from dizziness and hearing loss to cognitive decline, heart issues and even organ failure. The committee emphasized that this kind of suffering spills over into every corner of patients' lives. It affects their ability to work, robs them of the joy they once found in hobbies, and strains relationships with family and friends. For many, it shatters their self-esteem and deteriorates their mental health.

Then came the first major revelation. The committee had randomly selected 101 patients and sent them letters, hoping to uncover the true depth of their struggles. Out of those, forty-four patients chose not to respond, while only twenty-two bravely opened up about their experiences. However, even the responses from these twenty-two patients were deeply unsettling. The committee revealed that some had undergone multiple revision surgeries, while others shared tales of excruciating pain that had shadowed them for years. Many reported feelings of relentless fatigue that sapped their energy, alongside a host of alarming issues: pseudo-tumors, pain while walking, reduced sperm motility, kidney cysts and high cobalt–chromium levels. 'The committee feels that these possible adverse events needed to be followed by way of an appropriate investigation at appropriate frequency by the firm,' the committee observed.

The committee then vividly described the emotional struggles these patients faced. Some were still grappling with the inability to carry out their daily activities, confined to their beds, which led to a spiral of mental anguish.

The committee also emphasized that many patients had suffered similar – and in some cases, identical – injuries. The committee detailed the physical and emotional impacts: the crushing pain and suffering, the effects of high levels of metal ions coursing through their blood, the loss of mobility that turned simple tasks into monumental challenges and the loosening of implants that had once held the promise of relief.

Next, the committee highlighted a unique and important issue tied to the silent struggle of the ASR patients: how difficult it was for them to make sense of their pain. Imagine enduring constant discomfort and not knowing whether it's caused by the hip implant meant to improve your life, or by a new injury resulting from its failure. The committee observed that patients often find it challenging to determine the source of their pain, as it can be difficult to distinguish between problems caused by the ASR implant itself and injuries related to its use.

At the heart of the ASR recall lay a troubling reality: patients were undergoing revision surgeries far earlier than anyone had anticipated. This unsettling trend highlighted a range of serious issues that demanded careful scrutiny. In response, the expert committee members rolled up their sleeves and delved into the complexities of the situation, examining it layer by layer.

First, the expert committee laid out just how serious the threat of revision surgeries was for ASR patients, making it clear how many risks and challenges they could face ahead. They stressed that a revision surgery isn't just another procedure but a 'major' one fraught with dangers like 'infection, loss of bone and other serious complications'. Imagine the frustration of patients who, after enduring the gruelling hours of surgery, are forced into bed rest for weeks. The committee noted how, during this time, '... apart from enduring pain, patients are unable to work or engage in their daily activities', leaving them trapped in a cycle of discomfort and helplessness.

The expert committee then turned its attention to an issue that weighed heavily on their minds: the revision surgeries data of Indian ASR patients. They highlighted that, based on data submitted by DePuy in 2014, the rate of revision surgeries had reached an alarming 35 per cent. While the latest figures from 2017 showed a lower but still concerning revision rate of 25 per cent. The committee stressed that even if they accepted this more recent figure, the revision rate was still 'startling'. They also cautioned that this data represented only those patients who had reached out to the registry established by the company, leaving a majority of others with ASR implants unaccounted for – patients who may still be grappling with the implications of their faulty devices in silence.

The committee then pointed out that while the firm had initiated outreach efforts to connect with doctors and patients, the results were disheartening. The committee observed a 'lack of seriousness' in these attempts, as evidenced by the mere 1,032 ASR patients successfully traced – most of whom had contacted the helpline themselves – the committee painted a bleak picture of the situation. 'Therefore, the committee is of the considered view that the steps taken by the firm are inadequate,' it observed.

As if that wasn't enough, the committee peeled back another layer and found gaping discrepancies in how the company reported adverse events – data directly linked to revision surgeries. The company had provided data between January 2014 and June 2017 – that 121 serious problems had cropped up with the ASR implant.* But by March 2017, 254 patients had already undergone revision surgeries due to complications with the ASR implant. 'Both figures stand in contradiction with each other regarding the number of revision surgeries and reported adverse events to CDSCO,' the committee emphasized, highlighting a glaring mismatch in the data. The numbers simply didn't add up.

But here's where it got tricky: 'As per the available records, only 48 of such reports are available with CDSCO (the regulator),' the committee pointed out. That meant there were far fewer reports on record than the company had led everyone to believe.

The committee's frustration mounted as it pored over the company's adverse event reports. These reports were all tagged as 'initial adverse event reports', but CDSCO hadn't received any final updates, leaving the case wide open. The company claimed it was 'awaiting the resolution of the patient', but the follow-up never came. '... So far, no final information in this regard had been submitted to CDSCO [the regulator],' the committee noted.

The committee then drew attention to the inconsistencies and glaring lack of clarity on linking these adverse events to the device. Their concerns deepened when they noted that 'in a couple of earlier reports', the company had acknowledged that 'serious adverse events are device related'. Yet, when reviewing the 'majority' of these cases,

---

* All data in this chapter has been taken from the report of the expert committee which addressed the issue of faulty ASR hip implants. I was the first journalist to access this report and make findings public.

the company simply cited 'pain' as the reason for revision surgeries, sidestepping the role of the poor performance of the device. The committee wasn't buying it. Pain, they pointed out, is a 'symptom', and 'pain alone cannot be considered as a basis for performing revision surgery'. The room must have felt tense as they concluded that this vague argument was a deliberate attempt to dodge accountability. The committee went further, asserting, 'Therefore, the firm had not reported to CDSCO the detailed reasons due to which revision surgeries were performed.'

Then came the hard evidence. In forty-eight reports, metallosis – a condition caused by metal debris accumulating in the body – had been flagged as a symptom. In 'a few cases', this toxic build-up of metal ions in the blood was identified as the reason for patients undergoing painful and complicated revision surgeries. It was now clear: the implants were breaking down inside patients, triggering a chain reaction of harm that forced them back into surgery.

The committee's attention turned to the gravest outcome of all: death. On 12 June 2014, the company reported four deaths of patients who had previously undergone ASR surgery. While it's understood that not all deaths were directly tied to the device, the committee was shocked by the company's handling of this sensitive issue. Instead of a thorough investigation, the firm had provided only 'a brief paragraph' outlining the deaths and their 'possible cause'. The committee wasn't having it, noting, 'The committee feels that the information is quite brief, and such serious events of death ought to have been investigated and informed with all relevant data by the firm.' Their disapproval was clear, as they called out the company for failing to fully disclose the true risks faced by patients.

The committee then highlighted another troubling trend regarding revision surgeries. India found itself in a unique situation: while the global recall of the ASR hip implant was announced on 24 August 2010, the regulator in India didn't issue a medical device alert until 9 December 2013 – more than three years later.

The committee noted that 'available records' revealed a concerning timeline: most of the revision surgeries took place in 2014, only two in 2016 and the rest in 2017. The committee highlighted this critical issue – although the product was recalled in 2010, 'revision surgery in India started only in the year 2014'. This delay implied that many patients endured pain and complications for years before undergoing a revision surgery.

What followed was even more alarming. 'The firm has not informed about the status of the patient,' the committee remarked, and there was no evidence that the company had attempted to reach out to patients during this period.

The committee did not hold back in criticizing the company's failures, particularly regarding adverse event reporting and patient safety. 'This is a clear abdication of responsibilities with respect to reporting serious adverse events on behalf of the firm and also not approaching the patients,' they stated. They also noted that the company's actions 'indicate suppression of material facts' when 'providing relevant information relating to patient safety during this period.'

The committee, after closely examining the data, made two important scientific inferences based on the adverse event reports. First, it pointed out something startling: the company had repeatedly provided 'identical reasons in almost all of the reports', claiming that medical or surgical interventions were needed 'to prevent permanent impairment to a body function'. The committee's observation was clear: 'There is a clear admission on the part of the firm stating that the ASR surgery has resulted in a permanent impairment to a body function, and it needed a revision surgery.'

The second finding was equally concerning. The committee noted that 'almost all the revision surgeries' were happening, on average, within seven years of the original surgery. Imagine expecting a hip implant to last you fifteen years, only to find yourself back in surgery halfway through that time. 'This indicated premature revision surgeries solely because of ASR,' the committee remarked, leaving no doubt that patients were undergoing early and unexpected surgical fixes.

As the scrutiny on adverse event reports drew to a close, the committee couldn't ignore the stark contrast between India and other countries. Outside India, the committee highlighted, patients typically had their revision surgeries within two to four years of the original procedure. But in India, it took an alarming seven years for most patients to undergo revision surgeries. The committee expressed its distress: 'The committee notes with concern that a lot of patients might be experiencing aggravated problems due to delayed revision surgeries. The firm should have ideally approached all such patients and ensured proper medical care,' they concluded. The image of patients suffering silently, their conditions worsening while waiting for revision surgeries, cast a heavy shadow over the findings.

The committee then decided to tackle a critical issue linked to low or delayed rates of revision surgeries in India. With most Indian ASR patients still untraced, the committee prioritized ensuring these individuals when located be given access to financial protection from the company, despite any delays. A key concern for the committee was a startling disclosure – the company had informed them that the ASR reimbursement programme was set to end on 24 August 2017. Aware of the lasting impact on patients, the committee urged an extension. They argued that since the ASR was recalled in August 2010, and considering the average hip implant lifespan of about fifteen years, the programme should be extended until at least August 2025. For many untraced ASR patients, this was a lifeline.

The expert committee's attention then turned to a troubling silence from DePuy – a deliberate withholding of critical information with potentially grave consequences for patient safety.

On 5 April 2017, the expert committee had reached out to the Australian regulator through the Drugs Controller General of India, to understand precisely how Australia had handled the ASR device and what protections it had put in place. Australia's reply revealed that in the face of the high revision rates, the ASR had been 'removed' from the Australian market in December 2009 – almost eight months before the global recall of the implant.

As the expert committee pieced together Australia's timeline, they realized DePuy had been silent on this score as well.

In India, the rules were clear: any company holding a registration certificate to sell medical devices was expected to act swiftly if issues cropped up. They were legally bound to inform authorities without delay – whether the device was malfunctioning or even pulled from a foreign market. The ASR licence granted in India came with the same strict condition.

In effect, this meant DePuy should have informed India's regulator about the ASR's discontinuation in Australia and the rising revision rates reported there. But instead, they kept a critical development hidden away – a gamble with potential life-altering consequences for countless patients.

The revelation was shocking in itself, but there was more. On 11 January 2010, the company applied for the renewal of its ASR import licence in India, all while withholding the Australian developments. Here was a company asking for renewed permissions, yet never once disclosing that the device had already been pulled from the Australian market months prior.

During the licence renewal process, the then Global Vice President of Regulatory Affairs at DePuy Orthopaedics, assured Indian regulators that DePuy would report any administrative actions taken due to adverse reactions, like market withdrawals or cancellations of authorization, in any country where the device was marketed, sold or distributed.

Yet, the company never disclosed that the ASR had been discontinued in Australia in December 2009. What's more, during this renewal process, DePuy took on yet another legal commitment: if any regulatory body deemed the product 'not of standard quality,' they would pull it from the Indian market within forty-eight hours.

And still, the committee found, the Indian regulator remained uninformed about the ASR's fate overseas, even as the 2010 application went through. The expert committee expressed it plainly: '... the committee observes that there appears to be suppression of material facts by the firm to the CDSCO. This is construed as a serious breach of condition of approval.'

The most important task before the expert committee was to craft a fair compensation formula for Indian ASR patients whose lives had been drastically changed by faulty implants. At first glance, this task seemed straightforward – after all, there was plenty of evidence showing just how deeply these patients were suffering. But as the committee dug deeper, they encountered a complex reality: there was no explicit legal provision to compel the company to pay compensation. For the committee, coming to the final conclusion on compensation felt like walking a tightrope, as they navigated uncharted legal ground, knowing their decision could set a powerful precedent.

In examining the issue of compensation, the expert committee began by scrutinizing the company's position on the matter. Throughout the scrutiny, the committee repeatedly sought details on whether, and how, the company intended to compensate Indian patients. Yet, as the company's responses trickled in, the committee's frustration grew – there were no clear answers from DePuy. When the committee finally unveiled their findings, the weight of their concerns was unmistakable.

The expert committee's first observation was about the data provided by the firm – Rs 142,072,014, reimbursed for revision surgeries and associated costs, including out-of-pocket expenses and lost wages. On paper, it looked like a large figure, but the committee's dissatisfaction was immediate. The committee observed that what they had demanded was compensation details, not reimbursement. The distinction was significant. The committee didn't mince words: 'It is clear that the firm has not paid any compensation.'

As they delved deeper, the committee's tone sharpened. They remarked that the company's reply on compensation was 'evasive' and that, in a 'strange way' it seemed to be blurring the line between compensation and reimbursement. The firm likely hoped no one would notice. But the committee saw through this tactic. 'It is observed by the committee that the firm has not provided any compensation to any of the patients for disability and suffering,' the expert committee noted.

The committee kept pressing on the issue of compensation to get clarity if, in the future, it would provide compensation to Indian patients. What stung the most for the committee was the firm's reluctance to provide 'any conclusive response'. The committee said that the company, instead, hid behind 'the camouflage of pending litigations'. But the committee wasn't buying it. 'It is well known that the firm has paid compensation in countries like the US, Australia and Canada, whereas they have not committed for any compensation in India,' they pointed out, highlighting the stark contrast with the situation in India. Offering to cover travel, food, accommodation and surgeries wasn't enough – 'This cannot be construed as compensation,' the committee asserted.

The committee could feel the burden of the patients' suffering. 'The fact remains that no compensation ever has been made by the firm in

India to any patient, despite the fact that the implant is faulty,' they stated. The committee then highlighted Vijay's case. His testimony laid bare the human toll behind the statistics. The committee saw his case as a stark example of how 'multiple surgeries have affected the lifestyle of not only the patients but also the dependent family members'. They emphasized that his family, like many others, was caught in a web of 'enormous physical, mental, sociological, psychological and financial burden', their annoyance growing as the company continued to hide behind the word 'reimbursement'.

DePuy had also failed to provide any information about the compensation paid in other countries. The committee had expected details – a blueprint of how justice was delivered elsewhere – but the company remained silent. 'The firm has never clearly stated the amount of compensation paid in other countries or the terms of settlement,' the committee noted, exasperated by the lack of transparency. Forced to rely on external sources, the committee confirmed that compensation had indeed been paid in places like the US, Australia and Canada. Yet, in India, the story remained starkly different.

On this issue, the committee's observation was scathing: 'The firm had failed in its responsibilities in providing these basic documents despite being asked and tried to colour compensation with reimbursement.' Their dissatisfaction was evident, and their anger justified.

The expert committee then delivered its most crucial recommendation – compensation for Indian patients. By making these recommendations, the committee wasn't just offering a solution – it was offering a lifeline to thousands who had been left to navigate this ordeal on their own. It wasn't just about financial reparation – it was about justice for those whose lives had been turned upside down by a faulty medical device. The decision started with a strong statement on why these patients deserved compensation. There was no room for doubt. 'The committee is of the considered view that the revision surgeries were necessitated due to the faulty ASR as well as negligence of the firm in approaching patients, and therefore, it is the responsibility of the firm to compensate all the affected patients,' the committee recommended.

The committee didn't stop at just pointing out the firm's responsibility. It outlined three vital factors to be considered when determining compensation, addressing the very real pain and suffering these patients had endured: '... the firm be made liable to pay adequate and just compensation commensurate with the severity of the pain, the resultant disability, suffering (both mental and physical), and the loss of wages for each of the patients who had received ASR,' the committee recommended.

But the path ahead wasn't simple. This was uncharted territory. Indian law had no explicit provisions for compensating patients affected by a medical device recall. For many, the legal system felt like a maze – while they could approach the courts under the Consumer Protection Act, doing so individually meant facing a long, uncertain battle. With over 4,000 patients affected, how could each one fight for justice alone? The lack of clear guidelines on determining the amount of compensation only made matters more complicated. 'At present, there are no specific legal provisions to provide compensation to patients in such cases. The committee feels that the object of awarding damages is to compensate for the loss suffered as a result of wrong done, as far as money can do so, in a fair, reasonable and equitable manner, for which a provision needs to be made and recommended,' the committee emphasized.

As a first step towards achieving justice, the committee turned to the Rights of Persons with Disabilities Act, 2016, and the rules to define the concept of 'disability', aiming to find a way to measure the impact of this disaster on the lives of the patients. The committee then shifted its focus to a crucial task – establishing a mechanism to calculate compensation for affected patients. To do this, it proposed a two-tier system: a regional expert panel and a central expert panel. These panels, made up of specialists, would evaluate the claims of patients who suffered disabilities and pain from the faulty ASR hip implants.

Picture the regional expert panel as a team of four: three specialists – two orthopaedic surgeons, with experience in joint surgeries, and a radiologist skilled in interpreting the X-rays and scans – and a representative from the CDSCO zonal office. These experts would conduct physical and clinical examinations. The committee recommended setting up these teams across the country, so patients everywhere could access them.

This is how the committee envisaged it would work:

When assessing a patient's case, the regional panel would examine four key areas. First, they would determine whether the disability was temporary or permanent. If it was permanent, they would then decide if it affected the whole body, leaving the patient with total disability, or only a part of the body, resulting in partial disability.

If the patient's disability was confirmed as permanent, the experts would analyse medical evidence to determine the extent of the damage. This panel would then carefully consider how the disability had reduced the person's ability to earn a living, impacting their financial future.

Once the regional panel submitted its findings, the central panel would step in as the final authority. It would be their job to determine just how much compensation each patient truly deserved.

The expert committee recommended that this amount be based on two key factors: the base amount and the patient's degree of disability.

They suggested setting the base compensation at Rs 2 million. Why Rs 2 million? Consider this: a patient with a lifelong disability puts that money in a bank as a fixed deposit. With an interest rate of 7 per cent per year, the monthly earnings from that interest alone would be similar to the minimum wage of an unskilled worker in Delhi, which stood at Rs 13,350 back in March 2017. The idea was that this amount would offer the patient some level of financial security, allowing them to at least cover basic needs.

But it didn't end there. The committee also advised the central panel should take into account two other crucial factors: how much the patient has suffered financially due to lost wages and other expenses, and the percentage of their disability. This added layer would ensure that the unique struggles of each patient are considered, making the compensation more personalized.

When it came to setting the maximum amount of compensation, the committee took a clear stance. Since there wasn't any other model available, they proposed aligning the maximum compensation with what's typically granted in cases of clinical trial-related death and permanent disability. However, they left room for flexibility, noting that the health ministry could make changes to this recommendation if necessary.

Lastly, the committee made it clear that financial compensation should go beyond just covering medical bills – it should provide the patient with the security they need to rebuild their lives after their suffering. This meant compensation on top of any expenses related to medical treatment and reimbursement.

The committee laid out a practical and detailed approach to assessing compensation for patients living with permanent disabilities, ensuring every aspect of their situation is carefully considered. First, they recommended looking at the patient's daily life – what activities can they still manage, and what simple tasks, like walking up the stairs or even holding a cup of coffee, have become impossible? Then, they suggested digging into the patient's work life before the surgery – whether they were a teacher, mechanic or office worker – and how the disability has affected their ability to earn a living. Next, the focus shifted to their ability to support themselves: Is the patient now completely unable to work or can they still manage parts of their previous job, like someone who can no longer run a business but can still handle small administrative tasks? Finally, the committee urged considering the financial impact – those mounting hospital bills, medicines, transportation for frequent doctor visits and the income they lost while being treated. This also includes the future financial strain, like any ongoing medical needs and the permanent reduction in earning power.

In the end, on the issue of compensation, the expert committee made an urgent and heartfelt appeal to the government. The central expert panel should therefore take an active role to ascertain the true and correct position so that it could assess the 'just compensation', the committee urged. By this appeal, the committee implicitly conveyed that compensation wasn't just about numbers but about justice – ensuring that each patient's suffering was recognized, and that they received compensation that genuinely reflected the depth of their physical limitations and financial burdens.

Most importantly, the expert committee's focus extended far beyond compensation. Comprising mostly medical experts, it voiced a concern that touched the very core of human dignity. This wasn't simply about financial redress for a faulty medical device; it struck at a larger, more profound issue – the fundamental right enshrined in the Indian Constitution to live with dignity. Imagine a patient who once led an active life, now confined by pain and limited mobility, struggling to do even the simplest things. The committee saw this loss as more than just physical; it was a violation of their right to live fully and freely.

'The committee also feels that the right to life to live with dignity has been compromised by use of faulty implants which also hampered their other fundamental rights to a great extent,' the committee emphasized. In making this statement, the committee underscored the emotional and physical toll that faulty implants had inflicted, reminding the government that this was about restoring a person's right to live without unnecessary suffering.

In their second recommendation, the committee pushed DePuy to take responsibility for patients beyond those who had come forward. There was a significant number of ASR patients out there, unregistered, and perhaps unaware of the full risks they were living with. 'Sincere efforts should be made by the firm to trace all patients ... and collect data related to their health status,' the committee stressed. The image of untraced patients, silently suffering, hovered behind the words. The urgency to find them and assess their health was paramount.

Equally important was the need for regular health check-ups. The committee didn't mince its words. It demanded that each ASR patient's health be checked annually until 2025, pushing for routine follow-ups. '... follow-up should also include soft tissue imaging, monitoring rising blood levels of cobalt and chromium,' it reiterated. The committee further insisted on compliance reports being sent to the health ministry every six months, ensuring no patient slipped through the cracks.

When it came to medical management, the committee didn't hold back. It recommended that the company provide free, complete care for all ASR patients who had undergone revision surgery, as well as those who still needed it. This was a call to prioritize patient safety. From metal ion tests to systemic toxicity checks, the committee recommended comprehensive care. Most notably, it insisted that even patients without symptoms receive regular follow-ups. The silent dangers lurking within – the possibility of metal poisoning or tissue damage – required vigilance. Each follow-up would include clinical, radiological and laboratory tests, ensuring no stone was left unturned.

As the expert committee wrapped up, it put the spotlight on preventing incidents like the ASR fiasco from happening again. For regulators, hospitals, surgeons and, above all, for the safety of patients, this recommendation felt paramount. It wasn't merely a list of solutions; it was a call for systemic reform, zeroing in on a pressing need to track the performance of medical devices in real time.

First, the committee recommended an 'independent registry', a proposed safeguard for tracking high-risk medical devices across India. The suggestion was preventative, drawing inspiration from global standards. 'The same should be worked out taking reference of [the] international scenario so that such events can be prevented soon before it arises from the manufacturer's end,' the committee emphasized, painting a picture of vigilance long before a product ever reaches a patient.

The committee also urged the government to create legal provisions that would empower authorities to issue immediate alerts and warnings to manufacturers when concerns arise. It cited Australia's early actions against the ASR hip implants, noting how the country's registry system allowed swift regulatory intervention as soon as evidence mounted. 'The first instance of ASR withdrawal was from Australia as they have in place a registry ... to monitor the performance of ... orthopaedic implants ... This allowed the TGA to take prompt regulatory action against the firm as soon as the evidence were found,' the committee stressed, underscoring the power of proactive monitoring.

Turning back to India, the committee critically examined the existing Materiovigilance Programme of India (MvPI), a system for tracking adverse events in medical device usage. It flagged a missing link – the need for a real-time mechanism that alerts both regulators and the public of any device recalls, whether prompted by international agencies or voluntary actions from manufacturers. 'This will enable the regulatory agency to take immediate review of the situation and take remedial action well in time,' it noted, sketching out a future where the public and authorities are informed, prepared and swift to act.

In a final, crucial recommendation, the committee addressed a glaring gap in India's laws: compensation for patients harmed by faulty medical devices. This very committee might never have been formed if laws already existed to protect those affected. The solution it observed was clear: 'provisions related to payment of compensation and medical management, to the patient or his legal heirs for any serious adverse event or death caused due to the sole use of a medical device approved by the licensing authority, should be included in the Medical Devices Rules, 2017.'

With these final recommendations, the report became a milestone – a powerful reminder to government authorities that as India advances in medical device innovation, patient safety must be prioritized in regulation. This was more than a report; it was a blueprint for a reformed medical device ecosystem, one that demands accountability and centres on the well-being of every patient.

For Indian ASR patients, this report wasn't just about immediate relief; it was about building a foundation for justice. The observations made by medical experts became lifelines for future legal battles. In courtrooms, lawyers representing ASR patients used this report as essential evidence, transforming these pages into powerful tools for patients seeking fair compensation and justice.

In the saga of India's ASR implant crisis, the submission of the Expert Committee Report marked a turning point, finally nudging the slow wheels of justice into motion. For years, ASR patients had struggled, waiting for someone to listen, to act. Now, the government's adoption of these recommendations wasn't merely a formality; it was a long-overdue step towards accountability. Yet, it took months for the government to act on these recommendations – a stark reminder of how red tape can slow down even the most urgent issues. For the patients who had already spent years waiting in pain, this delay wasn't just frustrating; it was a bitter reminder of a system that seemed to ignore their struggles.

14

The Tide Turns: Patients Fight Back

On 19 February 2018, Dr Arun Kumar Agarwal, the chairman of the expert committee, handed over a report that could have changed the lives of hundreds of ASR patients. Packed with crucial recommendations, it was a blueprint for action. In the report, Dr Agarwal urged the health ministry to chart out the 'future course of action', leaving no room for doubt about the urgency. One might imagine the health ministry springing into action, calling emergency meetings and rolling out plans to compensate the patients who had already endured so much.

Oddly enough, hints of what the Agarwal Committee Report contained had already trickled out almost a month earlier. News reports painted a troubling picture: Johnson and Johnson and its subsidiary DePuy, the company behind the faulty implants, had been described as evasive, dodging the committee's repeated requests for information.[1] There were also talks of forming a new committee to calculate compensation and assess the pain, disability and suffering these implants had caused. These revelations should have been enough to trigger alarm bells and push the government into overdrive.

Yet, nothing happened. Picture this: as patients across the country waited anxiously, clutching their medical files and hoping for relief, the government simply sat on the report, buried under layers of bureaucracy. Days turned into weeks, and weeks into months, with no explanation for the inaction. For the patients who had pinned their hopes on this moment, it must have felt like a cruel joke – one that left them grappling not only with their pain but also with a system that seemed to have forgotten them.

Then, in August 2018, the tide finally turned. The media picked up the stories of the patients who had suffered due to the faulty ASR implant, shining a spotlight on what had been hidden for far too long. The first breakthrough came with *Mint*, where journalist Teena Thacker, who had been tracking the case closely, published a damning report on 23 August 2018.[2] Titled 'How Pharma MNC Johnson and Johnson Is Scooting from the Hip', it laid bare the struggles of patients like Vijay, who had suffered because of the faulty implants. Most notably, the report revealed that the expert committee's findings had been 'accepted by the government in principle'. 'There have been strong recommendations which will be implemented,' it quoted a senior health ministry official as saying. The use of the word 'strong' underscored just how critical these recommendations were.

The following day, *The Indian Express* joined the fray with a searing headline: 'Johnson & Johnson buried key facts on faulty hip implant surgeries, kept regulator in dark'. According to the report, Johnson & Johnson had 'suppressed' key information about the harm caused by its implants.[3]

'In a "clear abdication of responsibility", it did not inform the national regulator about the exact number of patients who used these devices, the adverse reports following such surgeries, and the corrective operations subsequently conducted. It also "did not provide any compensation" to those affected,' the *Express* report stated.

The revelations didn't stop there. The next day, the *Express* published another explosive piece: 'Govt panel findings: "Its hip implant recalled in Australia, in same month Johnson & Johnson got registration certificate in India"'.[4] This report exposed a shocking timeline: on 23 December 2009, Johnson & Johnson's Indian arm obtained a registration certificate for its ASR hip implants from the regulator, and weeks later, on 11 January 2010, it applied for an import license.

'However, the company did not inform authorities at the time that the product had been recalled in Australia in December 2009,' the report revealed, quoting the findings of the health ministry's committee.

As if these disclosures weren't damning enough, the *Express* published yet another report titled: 'Johnson & Johnson admitted: Many young patients were affected by faulty hip implants'.[5] This article detailed the adverse reactions suffered by patients, some as young as thirty-two.

'Two out of ten patients who reported adverse reactions to "faulty" hip implants manufactured by a subsidiary of Johnson & Johnson and underwent revision surgeries were under the age of forty; severe pain in the hip, inability to walk, destruction of bone, and deposition of harmful metal debris in body tissue were the reasons behind these surgeries,' the report stated.

The findings were shocking. According to the *Express* report, 32 per cent of patients who underwent revision surgeries were in the forty to fifty age group, while 20 per cent were under forty. The youngest patients affected were two thirty-two-year-old men.

For the first time, the key details of the expert committee's findings were coming to light – not through official channels but courtesy of investigative journalism. The media coverage marked a defining moment in India, bringing unprecedented attention to a medical device recall. The pressure on the government was mounting – not just to publish the full Expert Committee Report but also to begin compensating the affected patients.

Finally, on the evening of 28 August, the CDSCO uploaded the report on its website. That same day, news broke that ASR-affected patients had demanded 'participation in any further deliberations' regarding 'action to be taken' based on the report. For the first time in nearly eight years, patients and their families who had been excluded from the compensation process demanded a seat at the table. Though it came late, this was an important moment – a long-overdue acknowledgment of their suffering and a critical step toward justice.

Two days later, on 30 August 2018, the health ministry passed two important notifications. First, Dr R.K. Arya, the then Director at the Sports Injury Centre in Safdarjung Hospital, was appointed to lead a Central Expert Committee. This committee, which would decide how much compensation affected patients should get, included a mix of experts: two orthopaedic doctors, a pharmacology professor and a law professor.

The second notification brought more clarity to who would be eligible for compensation. The government accepted most of the recommendations of the Agarwal Committee, which had identified six types of patients who should be compensated. However, the government went a step further by adding a seventh category. This included patients who had received the faulty ASR implants but hadn't yet undergone – or been advised to undergo – revision surgery. For many, this was a huge relief, as it acknowledged their struggles even without the need for additional surgery.

The government also made changes to how committees would be organized. While the Agarwal Committee had suggested forming regional committees, the Ministry of Health and Family Welfare decided on state-level ones instead. The reason? State committees would make the process easier for patients. 'State Level Committees, instead of Regional Committees, should be formed to enable hassle-free access to the patients as they can easily approach the State Level Committee in their respective States,' the government said.[6] Patients were also given the option to approach either a state-level or central committee, whichever suited them better.

The process for deciding compensation was straightforward. The Central Expert Committee would consider three main factors: 1) degree of disability – how much the implant had affected the patient's ability to function; 2) patient's suffering and financial loss – including things like lost wages or other hardships caused by the faulty implant; 3) percentage of disability – a way to measure the severity of the problem. The compensation would be decided according to these factors, and the starting point would be a base amount of Rs 2 million, to ensure all patients got fair compensation.

On 4 September 2018, the Drugs Controller General of India finally communicated to the company that it was liable to compensate the ASR patients. This communication, arriving eight years and eleven days after the company's global recall announcement, was a glaring reminder of the excruciating delay. Yet, for thousands of Indian patients who had suffered in silence, it was the first glimmer of hope, signalling the beginning of long-overdue justice.

The communication from the regulator came packed with six recommendations from the Agarwal Committee, each offering a pathway towards relief for patients.[7]

First, the company was told to extend the ASR reimbursement programme until 2025, ensuring patients had enough time to seek the financial support they desperately needed.

Second, the government demanded a comprehensive effort to conduct health assessments for patients. The instructions were clear:

leave no one behind. Those unregistered with the helpline had to be found. The company was asked to 'give due diligence' and make 'sincere efforts' to trace every single affected individual. It was a call for action to track down the missing, to knock on every door and ensure no patient was overlooked.

'The Committee has also recommended performing health assessments of the patients for the laboratory tests specified in this report, at least once a year based on the advice of the clinician till the year 2025,' the regulator informed the company.

Third, medical management for affected patients was mandated, in line with the Agarwal Committee's guidelines, ensuring those suffering could access the care they needed.

Fourth, the company was instructed to issue regular advisories for medical professionals. These advisories, the regulator noted, would help orthopaedic surgeons manage patients better, including through regular follow-ups.

Fifth, the company was tasked with spreading awareness. Through periodic advertisements, the company was required to ensure every affected patient knew about the support available to them.

But the most important order came last: compensation.

'It is the responsibility of the firm to compensate all the patients. The firm be made liable to pay adequate compensation commensurate with the severity of the pain, the resultant disability, sufferings (both mental and physical) and the loss of wages of each of the patients who had received ASR,' the regulator wrote. The regulator emphasized that the union health ministry would determine the quantum of compensation.

This order, though delayed, set the wheels of justice in motion, offering a sense of accountability, which had eluded Indian patients for far too long.

On 6 September 2018, the company responded to the regulator's communication of 4 September.

For years, it had sidestepped the term 'compensation', navigating every inquiry with carefully crafted responses. When the regulator had repeatedly pressed for clarity on whether Indian patients would be compensated, the company leaned on a strategy that felt almost evasive – insisting that it would handle claims individually, guided by local laws, and negotiate settlements only when approached by patients. A uniform compensation plan? That was simply off the table all these years.

Given this history, one might have expected the reply of 6 September to echo the same steadfast refusal. But what came next caught everyone off guard.

The company began with a familiar tone, stating that it had 'reviewed' the Agarwal Committee Report. The phrasing was deliberate and measured. 'We do have concerns and observations about the factual basis of conclusions drawn in the Expert Committee Report, and we would like the opportunity to formally respond to the Report so that you have all the relevant facts and context,' it stated.[8]

But then, the reply took an unexpected turn – one that seemed almost uncharacteristic of the company's prior stance. 'As the report recommends, we are agreeable to working with DCGI [Drugs Controller General of India] to compensate ASR patients in India based on appropriate criteria that we would like to work with DCGI to define based on other programs with similar goals in other countries,' the company said.

It was a seismic moment: signs of the first crack in the armour of a company that had resisted bending to the regulator's demands for years. This was a stark departure from its earlier insistence that 'legal systems in different countries function differently according to their own applicable laws and the individual facts and circumstances of a specific case'.

The company's previous stance, as presented in Chapter 10, had been one of calculated caution. 'Whenever an ASR patient brings a claim for compensation,' it had stated, 'DePuy will assess the specific facts and background with its legal advisors in India based on prevailing local laws by taking into account all the applicable factors and, where appropriate, seek to reach a reasonable settlement by mutual agreement with the patient.'

But now, under the glare of public scrutiny and mounting regulatory pressure – nearly eight years after the recall – it was as if the company had been backed into a corner. And for the first time, it appeared willing to compromise.

The shift was significant. The language in this new reply signalled a move away from a rigid, localised legal approach to something more collaborative, even globally inspired. The company, which once clung to Indian legal frameworks as its shield, now spoke of defining compensation criteria alongside the DCGI, drawing lessons from programmes in other countries. This wasn't just a change in wording – it was a concession, an acknowledgment that the old playbook was no longer sufficient.

'We believe that our active involvement in establishing the necessary criteria and implementation will help establish an effective and efficient framework for compensating ASR patients,' the company said.

It wasn't just what was said – it was how. The tone seemed less defensive and more conciliatory, with the company emphasizing its desire to 'closely' work with the Central Expert Committee. 'We also believe it would be important for us to jointly work out and agree the details ahead of any regional roll-out,' it added.

This moment illustrated that when governments confront even the most powerful corporations with hard facts and unrelenting scrutiny, accountability can be achieved. Yes, it came late, but it was proof that no company, no matter how influential, can forever dodge its responsibility to the patients it claims to serve.

On 11 September 2018, the company sent another important communication to the regulator. The timing was significant – it came just days after an exclusive closed-door meeting of Johnson & Johnson's top officials who handled regulatory affairs. What exactly transpired in that room remained shrouded in mystery, but the softened, even unctuous, tone of the follow-up communication hinted at a calculated effort to appease growing scrutiny.

'We thank you for the kind courtesies extended to us last week at our meeting,' the company began, its words polished and formal, like a carefully written invitation to rebuild trust.[9]

In the letter, the company offered a summary of their 'discussion' at the meeting. 'We are grateful for providing us the opportunity to work with you to design a framework for an appropriate compensation protocol for ASR patients in India,' it stated. Then came an announcement: the company was 'ready to organize and place advertising to create further patient awareness on ASR'. These ads, it proposed, would appear in two major national newspapers once a year for the next three years.

But the most consequential part of the letter was yet to come. 'Since we would be working together to arrive at compensations for patients on a case-by-case basis, we believe this compensation should cover the costs of annual health check-ups of ASR patients, and we shall not be required to provide or assist further medical management of ASR patients,' the company wrote.

The real revelation, however, was attached to the letter. 'Attached to this letter we would like to provide a proposed ASR protocol, outlining eligibility and compensation criteria for ASR patients in India. This proposal ... is based on similar programs that were implemented to resolve legal claims in other countries,' the company wrote.

The attached compensation formula revolved around two factors. The first factor was how long the faulty ASR implant had been in the patient's body before it was replaced with revision surgery:

1. For implantation lasting between 180 days to five years: Maximum compensation (let's call it Rs. X).
2. 5 years ≤ X ≤ 6 years: 90 per cent of the maximum compensation.
3. 6 years ≤ X ≤ 7 years: 80 per cent of the maximum compensation.
4. 7 years ≤ X ≤ 8 years: 60 per cent of the maximum compensation.
5. 8 years ≤ X ≤ 9 years: 40 per cent of the maximum compensation.
6. 9 years ≤ X ≤ 10 years: 20 per cent of the maximum compensation.

The proposition was simple: the longer the defective implant stayed in the body, the lower the payout.

The second factor added another layer of reduction, this time based on the patient's age at the time of the original surgery:

1. Age ≥ 70 years: Compensation reduced by 4 per cent.
2. Age ≥ 75 years: Compensation reduced by 8 per cent.
3. Age ≥ 80 years: Compensation reduced by 12 per cent.
4. Age ≥ 85 years: Compensation reduced by 15 per cent.

However, this approach didn't take into account a critical situation unique to India. Many patients in India retained the defective implants not because these implants were functioning properly but because they were unaware that these implants had been recalled. This lack of awareness occurred because Johnson & Johnson failed to proactively notify all the patients about the recall. As a result, the compensation formula appeared inherently unfair. It penalized Indian patients who suffered longer simply due to the company's inadequate communication, which delayed their ability to take corrective action. The proposal seemed too little, too late and deliberately designed to reduce expenditure.

This proposal also revealed a stark truth: Although the company had the tools to offer compensation in India as early as 2013, it chose to act only when public and regulatory pressure became unavoidable. There had been an egregious delay in the turnaround, and now there was a blatant shift in tone. Suddenly, the company's language had turned deeply empathetic.

'… We are here to help patients, serve the community and care for the well-being of the people in India. We are pained for any patient who has concerns about the outcomes of their treatment,' it wrote, projecting itself as a compassionate ally.

'We hope the above proposal will facilitate a centralized process that results in an efficient and expeditious structure that further provides support for ASR patients in India. We are truly committed to ensuring that ASR patients in India are well served and supported out of this process,' the company concluded, its words carefully crafted to exude sincerity.

On the same day, the proposed compensation formula was sent to the regulator, the Drugs Controller General of India issued a public notice that caught everyone's attention. It was a lifeline for Indian patients waiting for justice. The notice from the Central Drugs Standard Control Organisation announced, '… The Central Government has now constituted a Central Expert Committee chaired by Dr R.K. Arya to determine the quantum of compensation "as admissible under appropriate law" for the affected ASR patients.'[10]

The notice further stated, 'The Govt. has also requested the Principal/Health Secretaries of all States/UTs to constitute the State Level Committee to examine the affected patient's details in their respective states.' Patients now had the option to seek help close to home or approach the central committee directly. The message was clear: 'In case the affected patients intend to approach the State Level Committee, they may write to the concerned State Drugs Controller.'

For many patients and their families, this was a crucial moment.

Finally, they were officially told they could reach out and seek the compensation they had been longing for. Yet, as the spotlight turned to the committee led by Dr R.K. Arya, a glow of anticipation filled the air. This committee held the power to define the compensation formula, a decision that could either provide long-overdue justice or leave patients feeling betrayed once again.

Would the committee craft a formula that reflected the pain and suffering of those who lived through failed implants? Or would it simply rubber-stamp the company's proposal? These questions lingered heavily.

Amid this unfolding drama, one glaring omission couldn't be ignored – the very people most affected by the decisions, the patients themselves, had been completely sidelined. No calls for their opinions, no attempts to understand their lived realities. But then, the tide began to turn. Patients started raising their voices, demanding to be heard. After years of silence, the people who had endured unimaginable pain and uncertainty were stepping forward, ready to fight for their place in the ASR saga.

In May 2015, the Maharashtra state drug regulator had sounded an alarm. After uncovering a scandal involving the import of cardiac stents, it wrote to the National Pharmaceutical Pricing Authority (NPPA), urging swift action to bring stents under the Essential Commodities Act. The findings were alarming – these vital, life-saving devices were being sold at prices inflated by as much as 300 to 700 per cent over their import cost. It was a scheme that preyed on vulnerable heart patients and their families, who were already grappling with life-and-death decisions in hospital corridors.

The Maharashtra FDA didn't stop there. It pushed NPPA to include cardiac stents in the National List of Essential Medicines (NLEM), a move designed to curb exorbitant pricing and ensure fair profit margins. Around the same time, a Public Interest Litigation (PIL) was filed in the Delhi High Court, calling for coronary stents to be added to the NLEM, a crucial step to control their spiralling prices.

By February 2017, the pressure had peaked. After months of intense consultations with manufacturers, industry leaders, health activists and civil society groups, the NPPA finally set a ceiling on coronary stent prices. Among those at the table was Malini Aisola, co-convener of the All India Drug Action Network (AIDAN), which predominantly works for increasing access and improving the rational use of essential medicines.

During this period, Malini spent hours poring over documents, attending meetings and engaging with key stakeholders – from government officials to industry representatives. She sought to understand the intricacies of medical device regulations and price capping. Shortly after the February 2017 decision on cardiac stents, her focus expanded – she delved into cochlear implants and other important medical devices.

'As the demand to regulate various devices grew, I found myself drawn deeper into the world of medical devices,' Malini explains.

Her advocacy brought her into contact with journalists covering these public health developments. During one such interaction, a journalist tipped her off about Maharashtra's FDA probe into the ASR case unfolding in Mumbai under Mahesh Zagade. It was a piece of news that piqued her curiosity, though she hadn't yet connected with any ASR patients.

'Even though I wasn't in touch with the affected ASR patients then, those early conversations made me realize the gravity of the situation,' Malini recalls.

Then, in 2018, everything changed. A series of news reports about the ASR recall began surfacing, finally exposing the painful struggles of patients affected by the faulty device. It was a rare moment, as stories of poor medical device regulations took centre stage. Because AIDAN had previously worked extensively on medical device regulations, Malini decided to connect directly with these patients, hearing their stories firsthand, no longer just an observer from the sidelines.

At that time, ASR patients, including Vijay, had formed a small WhatsApp group, a tight-knit circle of just a few patients desperate for answers. Malini was soon added to the group, and as she started interacting, everything became clearer.

'What we quickly realized,' Malini recalls, her voice tinged with frustration, 'was that the patients directly affected by the ASR were completely in the dark. They didn't even have access to the expert committee report that had been submitted to the government.' It felt as though the government was guarding the report like a state secret.

No one in the government seemed willing to share the report with the patients. Frustrated but determined, the small group made a decision: they would draft a letter to the central government, demanding a copy of the Expert Committee Report on behalf of all ASR patients.

'Back then, there were only about five of us,' Malini recalls. 'The first letter came from this tiny group, just a few people vaguely connected through WhatsApp.' It felt like a long shot, but within twenty-four hours, the Expert Committee Report was suddenly public.

'That letter actually worked,' Malini says, still amazed at how their small, united effort had broken through the silence.

The real turning point came in September 2018, when the small patient group, alongside AIDAN, decided to organize a press conference on the ASR recall. For the first time in India, ASR patients were about to publicly share their stories of pain and struggle. The event was like a last-minute scramble.

'Even though we had very little time, we dug deep into the research. The patients had no choice but to make their demands known,' Malini recalls.

In the days leading up to the conference, Malini and the patient group turned to a few orthopaedic surgeons for help. Late-night discussions followed. They talked in detail about the ASR's flaws, how it paled in comparison to its competitor, the Birmingham hip, and the long, complicated history of hip implants.

'We were like detectives, piecing everything together. By then, we knew the regulatory approval process inside-out – how this faulty implant slipped into India, the timeline, and, most shockingly, how so many patients had been completely left out of the conversation,' Malini says.

The press conference was their chance to be heard, to finally shine a light on a problem to which no one had paid attention for too long.

On 15 September 2018, thirty-five patients and families affected by the ASR hip implant gathered in Delhi, many of them meeting face to face for the first time. They arrived with a sense of shared purpose, driven by a straightforward but deeply personal mission: to ensure their voices – voices that had long been ignored – were finally heard. The Press Club of India buzzed with quiet determination as they took their seats, ready to tell their stories.

The timing of the press conference couldn't have been more crucial. In just a few days, on 18 September, the central committee responsible for determining compensation for ASR patients was set to meet for the first time. But what worried the patients most was that the government had completely excluded them from any consultation. They felt invisible in a process that directly affected their lives. The press conference was their moment to change that – to publicly demand their rightful place at the table and ensure they were directly involved in the compensation process. The room held a tension of urgency and hope, as they prepared to make their stand.

At the press conference, they argued that compensation shouldn't be reduced to cold, clinical assessments of physical disability. This wasn't just about a revision surgery. Many of them had lost so much more – jobs, peace of mind, their social standing. In such an unprecedented situation, they insisted the government needed to consider the full picture: the physical pain, the mental trauma, the social isolation and the economic toll they had suffered. They demanded a compensation process that reflected the full scope of their suffering.

'What are the checks or balances on the working of the committees? What is the guarantee that the committees will be fair, just, equitable and reasonable in determining compensation?' Vijay asked the audience, his frustration clear.*

'We know the government has been in constant talks with J&J,' he began, his voice sharp with displeasure, 'but what about the people who've been seriously hurt? It's like they don't even have a place at the table.'

Vijay paused for a moment.

'I was the only patient who got to speak in front of the Central Expert Committee,' he said, shaking his head. 'How can they possibly understand the pain and suffering of so many others if they've only heard from me?' It was a question that left everyone thinking, as the scale of the issue became clear.

---

* The quotes have been taken from the press conference jointly issued by ASR patients and AIDAN, which I attended and recorded for my reference.

He then leaned forward, his voice growing stronger.

'Every single patient needs a voice in this,' he insisted. 'It's the only way to make sure their concerns are actually taken seriously.'

Next, Mahesh Zagade stepped up to the podium. Zagade wasn't just any speaker – he was the first official in the country's regulatory ecosystem to stand toe-to-toe with the powerful medical giant, demanding answers that no one else had dared to. During his time as the head of Maharashtra FDA, he'd relentlessly pursued the company, questioning their negligence in tracing all ASR patients. Now, though he was retired, his determination hadn't wavered. His voice was calm but carried the unmistakable edge of someone still fighting for a cause that mattered.

'The J&J hip implant issue,' he began, his words cutting through the silence, 'once again reminds us of the grim reality that in today's world, all stakeholders must remain alert. We cannot allow the commercial interests of pharmaceutical and medical device corporations to come before human lives.' He paused, letting the gravity of the situation settle over the room.

Zagade's tone sharpened. He turned his attention to the role of the regulatory bodies.

'The regulator – the Drugs Controller General of India and the Central Drugs Standards Control Organisation has a statutory responsibility. It is their duty to act decisively to prevent disasters like the ASR hip implant failure. And when they do happen, no matter how rare, action must be immediate.' He shook his head slightly. 'The law is already there – criminal prosecution, patient relief. It should have been used the moment this issue came to light.'

Malini then stepped forward to address the press. She called out the company's refusal to disclose complete patient data on the ASR device, hiding behind claims of confidentiality. To her, this was more than a legal loophole – it was an unacceptable excuse in the face of human suffering.

'How can they hide behind confidentiality,' she asked, 'when lives are at stake?'

She made it clear: the priority should be public safety, not corporate secrecy. Transparency, she argued, was the only way to stop more patients from becoming victims of faulty implants.

'What the company has done – knowingly providing harmful implants – is a strict liability offence,' she continued, her words sharp with conviction. 'And criminal action should be taken against everyone involved, including government officials who stood by and did nothing.'

Malini then raised a red flag that left the audience in stunned silence.

'While the ASR device was pulled off the market in Australia, the company applied for a fresh licence to sell it in India.' The shock in the room was palpable.

'The company knew,' she pressed on. 'They had internal data showing the device's high failure rate and its harmful impact on patients. Australian regulators forced it out of their market in 2009. So why, knowing this, did they [the company] still seek a licence to sell it in India? Are they claiming that the information behind the so-called voluntary recall appeared overnight?' Her words lingered, making it clear the calculated decisions were driven by profit, not concern for patients.

As the press conference wrapped up, the patients' concerns echoed throughout the room, resonating deeply with everyone present. This was no ordinary event. Rarely are the hidden cracks in medical device regulation thrust so boldly into the public spotlight, but on that day, they were. The speakers hammered home a vital point: patient safety is not just an afterthought – it is the foundation that must never be ignored. What made the moment even more significant was the unprecedented alliance that had formed – patient support groups and civil society standing shoulder to shoulder for the first time to demand accountability on important issues related to medical device safety.

The patients left the event hopeful, thinking they'd finally have a seat at the table for the critical discussions about compensation. But that invitation never came. Disappointment hung in the air, but they refused to back down. In the weeks and months that followed, they bonded together, working tirelessly to push forward. Their collaboration grew stronger as they took their fight to the government, determined to address not only compensation but also the safety of medical devices that had been ignored for too long.

On 5 October 2018, a thick envelope landed on the desk of the Union Health Secretary, its weight hinting at the storm of arguments it carried within. The sender? The Vice President of Regulatory Affairs at Johnson & Johnson Pvt. Ltd., Mumbai. Inside was a detailed, 41-page document with the subject line: 'Response to observations and recommendation of the ASR Hip implant'.[11]

The communication was anything but conciliatory. It argued that the company did 'not agree with the recommendations provided by the Committee specific to the ASR matter'. As one leafed through the pages, it became clear that the document was meticulously crafted, with objections laid out paragraph by paragraph. Each rebuttal seemed to act as a shield against the committee's observations, painting a picture of a company unwilling to accept fault. The tone was defensive, even self-assured, as it claimed yet again that 'the implant was never faulty'. Instead, the company portrayed the product as a marvel of innovation: 'developed after years of research and testing'.

The rhetoric grew bolder:

'We reiterate that the voluntary recall of any product does not necessarily translate into [the] product being labelled faulty as has been wrongly held in the Report. The Report has not taken cognizance of the fact that the Company has voluntarily recalled the Implant due to higher than expected revision surgery rates,' the company argued.

Yet, amidst this defiance, it struck a softer note: 'We would however like to reiterate our ongoing commitment in finding an effective way to compensate eligible ASR patients in India and look forward to working closely with you in this.'

But the most striking part of the communication concerned the very formation of the expert committee itself. Having participated in and presented its case before the expert committee, the company now claimed that the very foundation of the committee was flawed. It was as though a chess player, cornered after a series of missteps, suddenly questioned the legitimacy of the board itself. This new argument – one that seemed absent from earlier communications – felt like an afterthought, brought up only because the final recommendations were damning.

'We submit that the very incorporation of the Committee is *vires* the provisions of the Drugs and Cosmetics Act, 1940, read with the Drugs and Cosmetics Rules, 1945, and as the same does not have the requisite jurisdiction and powers to act in the matter as envisaged. We have made our presentations to the Committee and cooperate with the same notwithstanding this foundational objection which is reiterated as is,' the company wrote.

The timing of this argument raised eyebrows. Was it a desperate move to discredit the committee now that its conclusions painted a critical picture?

This communication came while Dr R.K. Arya Committee was engaged in crucial discussions about the compensation formula. Ten days later, on 15 October 2018, another letter reached the health ministry – this time, it was the patients who voiced their concerns.[12]

Thirty-five patients came together to write an important letter to the government. Addressed to the Union Health Minister, the letter expressed their concerns about how the government was handling compensation for ASR patients. They were frustrated to see the government talking closely with the company responsible for their problems, while they themselves hadn't even been consulted once.

The patients made it clear they were aware of the Central Expert Committee led by Dr R.K. Arya, which had met a few times and started accepting applications for compensation. However, they raised three key worries that weighed heavily on their minds. First, there was confusion about which ASR cases would actually be considered for compensation. Second, they were unsure about the documents they needed to submit their claims, feeling like they were trying to solve a puzzle without any clues. Third, they were concerned that the committee didn't have the expertise to recognize the broader impact on patients, including mental pain, suffering and trauma. They also pointed out that no patient representatives were involved in the entire process, making them feel sidelined and unheard.

'Given the lack of transparency and any guidelines, there are grave concerns about whether the committee will be fair, just, equitable and reasonable in determining compensation,' they wrote. They were also worried that patients were being pressured to submit applications without any clear understanding of how the committee was operating. In a situation filled with uncertainty, they just wanted a little clarity and support to help them navigate their path forward.

The patients voiced their unhappiness with the company's statement that was appearing in the media. They expressed their concerns that the company was trying to shift the narrative and appeared to challenge the findings of the Agarwal Committee, casting doubt on the very facts that exposed the harm done. What frustrated them even more was the company's brazen demand to be part of the decision-making process for compensating ASR patients.

'We are unaware of the outcomes of any discussions between the government and J&J ... we remain perplexed over the apparent inaction of the government to hold J&J accountable for the harm they have caused to patients, including through criminal proceedings,' they wrote.

On 18 October, media outlets buzzed with reports that the expert panel had devised a compensation formula for Indian ASR patients, with amounts ranging from Rs 3.3 million to Rs 120 million. The news spread quickly, raising both hope and pessimism among the affected patients. By 20 October, this group of patients, still burdened with uncertainty, wrote once again to the health minister, voicing their growing concerns.[13] In their letter, they stressed their dissatisfaction with the ongoing lack of transparency surrounding the compensation process.

The letter opened with a pointed question: How could a formula be created without consulting the very patients who had endured years of suffering? The faulty hip implants had wreaked havoc in their lives, intensifying their pain, delaying essential medical care and leaving them to grapple with the physical and emotional toll of the implants' failures. Yet, no one had asked them about the full range of their suffering, making the compensation formula feel distant and disconnected from their reality.

'We question why we have to rely on media reports ... for information about an issue that is directly related to our pain and suffering,' the letter read, each word echoing their frustration. 'We are surprised that it is not more obvious that transparency in the working of the committee and the compensation mechanism, which we have been asking for, is also needed to prevent immense confusion from arising in the future.' With growing desperation, they demanded an official explanation, seeking clarity about how the compensation was determined and the details of the formula itself.

The patients, many still grappling with the lasting effects of their failed surgeries, were not just seeking compensation – they were pleading for transparency, hoping the government would finally hear their voices. However, the government continued to ignore their concerns.

A few days later, on 30 October 2018, the company sent another crucial communication to the regulator. The executive director (government affairs and policy) of Johnson & Johnson informed the regulator that the company was 'introducing' an India-specific 'reimbursement program' called the ASR India Patient Assistance Program. 'This program will support Indian patients who have been implanted in India with the ASR hip system between June 2004 and August 2010 and provide for the reimbursement of eligible tests and revision surgery upon advice from their orthopedic surgeon, up to 15 years from the date of primary surgery,' the company wrote.[14]

This move came as a lifeline for many. It was an acceptance of a major recommendation of the Agarwal Committee, and for patients who had been in the dark about the recall for years, it was a welcome relief. This ensured that even those who remained unaware of the recall could still claim reimbursement for crucial tests and revision surgeries – costs that could otherwise have weighed heavily on them.

Behind closed doors, the Arya Committee was holding internal deliberations, ironing out the final details of the compensation formula. Yet, the final call lay in the hands of the health ministry. Then came 29 November 2018. The health ministry issued a press release announcing the compensation formula – marking a critical landmark in the ASR saga.

On 29 November 2018, the health ministry finally broke its long silence, and for many, it was a moment of relief. After years of uncertainty, a compensation formula for ASR patients was officially approved. For the 4,700 Indians enduring the painful consequences of faulty hip implants, it was a glimmer of hope after years of waiting and unanswered questions.

The government explained that the compensation formula was finalized by the Arya Committee after five rounds of discussions. This highlighted just how complicated the issue was.

To help patients, all state governments were instructed to form State-Level Committees. These committees would evaluate the affected patients in their regions and then send their recommendations to the Central Committee, which would decide the final compensation amounts. To ensure no patient missed out, state governments were asked to run newspaper ads encouraging patients to come forward and contact either the Central Expert Committee or their local State-Level Committees.

This step showed something important: when the government truly wanted to connect with patients, it could do so efficiently. But from this arose a troubling question: What if this had been done back in August 2010 when the faulty implant was first recalled? If the government had acted decisively then, urging state governments to spread the word about the recall, how many patients could have been saved from years of suffering? Perhaps more patients could have been traced, and the company might have been pushed to act quickly, prioritizing safety instead of dragging its feet.

In the press release, the government provided a mathematical formula along with illustrative cases showing the compensation amounts payable to patients with ASR hip implants, based on their age and percentage of disability.[15]

According to the formula, compensation is calculated by multiplying the base amount (B) by the age factor (R) and the disability factor (F), and then dividing the result by 99.37. To this, an additional Rs 1 million is added for non-pecuniary damages. The base amount for the compensation formula starts at Rs 2 million.

The disability factor takes into account the severity of the patient's condition. A higher level of disability results in a higher risk factor. For example, a disability between 20 and 30 per cent gives a risk factor of 1, while a disability of 50 per cent or more raises the risk factor to 2.5. The age factor varies depending on how young or old the patient is. Younger patients receive a higher age factor since their disabilities are likely to affect them for a longer period. For instance, if the patient is sixteen years old, the age factor is 228.54. For patients aged sixty-five or older, the age factor drops to 99.37.

Now, let's walk through how this formula applies in real cases.

For a forty-five-year-old patient with an ASR hip implant, the age factor is 169.44. If their level of disability is between 30 and 40 per cent, they would receive Rs 6.115 million in compensation. If their disability is more severe, between 40 and 50 per cent, their compensation would increase to Rs 7.821 million. For disabilities above 50 per cent, they could receive up to Rs 9.526 million.

For patients aged 65 or older, the age factor reduces to 99.37. In this case, a disability between 20 and 30 per cent would result in Rs 3 million in compensation. If the disability is between 30 and 40 per cent, the compensation rises to Rs 4 million. Disabilities between 40 and 50 per cent would entitle them to Rs 5 million, and for disabilities above 50 per cent, the compensation could reach Rs 6 million.

In essence, younger patients receive a significantly higher age factor, which results in a larger compensation. This is because the impact of a disability at a younger age is expected to last longer, leading to a higher payout.

The health ministry's approval of the compensation formula for ASR patients marked a major turning point in India's ASR saga. Imagine the relief for patients who had been living with the painful aftermath of faulty implants, watching billions in compensation being paid to victims abroad while they were left to struggle alone. This was proof that their voices, long ignored, were finally being heard.

For years, many felt abandoned, knowing the government was aware of the payouts happening in other countries but did nothing to help its own people. That realization was as frustrating as it was heartbreaking. But this decision brought a sense of validation, a long-awaited acknowledgment of their pain and suffering. For those who had endured both physical and emotional trauma, it felt like a breath of fresh air – a glimmer of hope that things might finally start to change.

However, beneath this glimmer of optimism lay unresolved concerns, which the patient group urgently communicated to the government in a heartfelt letter dated 6 December 2018.[16]

In their letter, they shared their diverse experiences as patients. They represented a wide range of ages, from twenty-one to seventy-five, at the time of their first implant. Many of them had dealt with the frustrating reality of having multiple ASR implants – some had one, while others had had, over a course of time, two or even three faulty devices (including the revision implants) installed into their bodies. Each person had their own unique story, filled with different health challenges and medical issues over the years, and these struggles had affected every part of their lives, stalled careers and put dreams on hold.

They expressed their concerns that the proposed compensation formula didn't take into account individual circumstances. For those who had experienced multiple faulty implants or had complicated medical histories, the formula felt insufficient and out of touch with their realities. 'Its poor formulation renders it incomplete and riddled with ambiguities,' they wrote, emphasizing that the complexities of their lives weren't reflected in the proposed numbers.

They also pointed out that ongoing medical management was crucial for ASR patients, but this important aspect had been overlooked. Despite the Expert Committee's recommendations highlighting the need for continued care, it seemed like the support they desperately needed was ignored, leaving patients to navigate their health journeys on their own.

In conclusion, they once again urged the government to listen to the voices of the patients, emphasizing that the outcomes of the compensation process would profoundly affect their lives. 'Given the urgency of this issue, we hope you will take the necessary steps to convene a meeting as soon as possible,' they wrote. This communication finally broke through the bureaucratic walls.

Nearly a decade after the global recall of the ASR implants, on 28 December 2018, the government finally took a meaningful step – it invited patients to discuss the long-overdue issue of compensation.

On 9 January 2019, a group of patients gathered, their emotions a mix of hope and nervousness, for a meeting with the Central Expert Committee. This was a rare chance for them to share their stories directly with high-ranking officials who, for once, seemed ready to listen.

One by one, patients spoke, their voices trembling with emotion as they described how the ASR implants had turned their lives upside down. They talked about the relentless pain they endured every day and the mysterious medical complications that seemed to follow them like a shadow. For many, this was the first time anyone in power had truly heard the depth of their struggles.

As their stories unfolded, the room's atmosphere began to shift. This wasn't just about policies or compensation amounts anymore – it became a deeply human conversation about suffering and accountability. For the first time, patients, government officials and civil society members sat together, united by a shared determination to address critical issues around patient safety and faulty medical devices.

The meeting that day was a moment of hope. It showed that when patients raised their voices together, change was possible – and it felt within reach.

However, weeks before the government had an interaction with the patients, another new twist had emerged. The government had gone ahead and announced the compensation formula. It had drawn a line in the sand, making it clear who was in charge. The company's response was just as predictable. They weren't about to let the government's plan take off without a fight. Everyone knew what was coming next – the company would challenge the government's formula in court.

―――

As the government finalized its compensation formula, it cleared the way for central and state committees to begin determining the amount of compensation for individual patients. The government's decision to reject the company's proposed formula in favour of its own sent an unmistakable message: this wasn't open for negotiation; it was a directive. For the company, it must have felt like standing at a critical crossroad, forced to choose between complying with the government's orders or challenging them in court.

Although the company had fiercely opposed the findings of the Agarwal Committee, it had assured the government that it would provide compensation. However, those assurances came with numerous conditions, much like the fine print in a contract. With pressure mounting and time running out, the company was left with only two options: accept the government's formula or take the fight to court. Ultimately, it chose the latter.

On 10 December 2018, Johnson & Johnson Pvt. Ltd. filed a plea in the Delhi High Court, seeking directions to quash the reports and findings of the Agarwal and Arya Committees, the health ministry's press release of 29 November 2018, and the government's letter of 30 November 2018, which directed the company to compensate ASR patients.

The company presented six broad arguments. First, the company argued that the two committee reports, the press release and the letter were issued without giving it 'any opportunity of hearing, without any application of mind, in an arbitrary and unilateral manner under a wrongful assumption that the ASR implants in question are faulty, in a hasty and haphazard manner and most importantly without any legal basis or statutory foundation.'[17] Nevertheless, it assured the government it was 'ready and willing' to collaborate in 'arriving at not only a just and proper compensation formula for all affected patients but also a proper and effective mechanism by which such compensation can be paid to affected patients'.

Second, the company argued that the Agarwal Committee itself had acknowledged a major gap in the law. The company flagged that the committee noted in its report, 'There was no legal provision in relation to determination of or giving of compensation in the present case.' Building on this, the company argued, 'Therefore the term of reference qua recommending a quantum of compensation as given unto the Arya Committee was without any legal basis whatsoever.'

The company went on to argue that there was no law in place at the time that gave the authorities the power to demand compensation in cases involving medical devices. It stated, 'It is submitted that there is no statutory law in existence as on date which specifically empowers the Respondents to mandate payment of compensation in cases pertaining to medical devices.'

Referring to the Drugs and Cosmetics Act and its Rules, the company explained, 'The D&C Act and the D&C Rules, which are applicable in the current case, do not contain any such provision providing for payment of compensation to users of medical devices.' Essentially, the company claimed that the legal framework simply didn't allow for compensation in situations like this.

Third, the company strongly criticized the government, accusing it of overstepping its authority by 'unilaterally making modifications to the Agarwal Committee Report'. This change, the company claimed, expanded eligibility to all patients with ASR hip implants, whether or not they had undergone revision surgeries.

'It is respectfully submitted that only those patients who had undergone revision surgeries had been deemed eligible in the Agarwal Committee Report. The unilateral decision to change the eligibility criteria was an absolute abuse of power by Respondent No.1,' the company argued. The company also took issue with the government's approach, saying it had 'no legal sanction' to modify the report. It emphasized that this was 'a technical matter', one that only the Drugs

Technical Advisory Board (DTAB), the designated expert body, had the authority to handle.

Fourth, it argued that both the Agarwal Committee and the Arya Committee were set up 'without any legal basis, as neither of the two are statutory committees under the D&C Act and Rules'. It claimed that these committees were formed without the legal backing they needed. It then emphasized that the DTAB is 'the proper authority' under the D&C Act to 'advise' the government on technical issues. The company argued that the 'evaluation of the Hip Implants was a technical exercise that could only be conducted by the DTAB, as per established procedures'. It stated that only the DTAB had the expertise to properly handle such a detailed and technical matter. 'It is respectfully submitted that the DTAB is the only statutory body that can address the multitude of technical issues in the present matter, as these issues are central to the controversy at hand. As such, reports issued by both these committees are untenable, illegal, and devoid of any legal sanction,' it argued. In essence, it was saying that the reports from the committees were not valid and should be dismissed because they didn't have the right legal foundation.

Fifth, the company expressed concerns about the formula being used, highlighting that it came from the draft New Drugs and Clinical Trial Rules (NDCT Rules). It pointed out that they were published in draft format in the *Gazette* on 1 February 2018 for public feedback but were not finalized when the formula was adopted. 'The said NDCT Rules do not have any legal force and as such cannot be relied upon in any manner,' the company argued.

The company further argued that the formula relied on the draft NDCT rules designed specifically for cases involving 'death or permanent disability in clinical trials or bioavailability and bioequivalence studies'. It emphasized, 'It is submitted that this is neither a case of clinical trial nor a case of bioequivalence studies ... this is at best a case of product liability, which is outside the scope and purview of action by the Respondents.'

Additionally, the company said that the formula in the draft NDCT Rules was created for clinical trials and did not fit the unique nature of medical devices. It stated, 'The formula prescribed in the said NDCT Rules as applicable to clinical trials cannot be made applicable in the case of medical devices as medical devices are different.'

The company also stressed that the consumer forum was the correct platform for addressing such claims, arguing, 'The consumer forum is the appropriate forum for any determination of compensation claims, and the Respondents cannot assume this judicial power by crossing the lines of the D&C Act and Consumer Protection Act, 1986.'

The company further accused the government of misusing the formula by applying it to all ASR cases. 'There is no logical basis for applying a formula designed to calculate compensation in cases of death, to a situation involving much lesser injury or disability, and the same is unjust, inequitable, and completely arbitrary,' it argued.

Sixth, the company argued that the Arya Committee had made an arbitrary decision by increasing the base amount for compensation calculations from Rs 800,000 to Rs 2 million. It claimed this change was made 'without assigning any logical reason or explanation for the same'. The company also argued that the committee added an extra Rs 1 million for non-pecuniary damages without providing any justification.

On 12 December 2018, the Delhi High Court opened its doors to hear the petition filed by Johnson & Johnson Pvt. Ltd. In the first hearing, the Delhi High Court refused to stay the government's compensation formula.[18] This decision effectively allowed the Central Expert Committee to continue determining compensation amounts on a case-by-case basis, even though the formula was still under legal challenge.

By March 2019, the central and state committees had begun assessing compensation amounts for patients who had suffered due to faulty ASR implants. The first case was that of a sixty-two-year-old woman. At fifty-two, she had received a primary ASR implant, only to face the agony of a revision surgery five years later. The Maharashtra state committee, after a thorough evaluation, determined she had 53 per cent locomotor disability. Her case was then passed to the Central Expert Committee, which, on 6 March 2019, decided on a compensation sum of Rs 7,457,180. Just two days later, on 8 March, the CDSCO issued an order, demanding that the company pay this amount within thirty days.

Similarly, there was the case of a sixty-three-year-old man, whose active life had been marred by dual ASR implants. At the age of fifty-three, he received implants in both hips, and by sixty-one, he was forced to undergo revision surgery on one. The committee found him to have 67 per cent locomotor disability, and on 28 March 2019, the CDSCO approved compensation of Rs 6,724,565 for his suffering.

In a particularly striking case, a forty-three-year-old woman, who had received her ASR implants at just thirty-one, was found to have 83 per cent locomotor disability after a painful revision surgery at forty-one. The scale of her suffering was reflected in the staggering compensation amount of Rs 10,125,993, which the CDSCO approved on 26 April 2019. That same day, the CDSCO also granted a compensation of Rs 9,026,567 to a thirty-six-year-old woman who faced a similar fate.

By 3 May 2019, the number of patients seeking compensation had grown to 289. The central committee was preparing to recommend compensation for many more cases in the coming weeks, each patient's story more heartbreaking than the last.

But just when it seemed like the momentum was building, an unexpected twist emerged on 2 May 2019. In the midst of the ongoing legal battle, with the Delhi High Court still hearing Johnson & Johnson's plea against the compensation formula, the company made a surprising move. It offered to pay Rs 2.5 million to every patient who had undergone revision surgery. It was an unexpected gesture – one that no one saw coming.

With this new development, the company presented another stand on the issue of compensation. Because it had not followed this template elsewhere in the world, it left both patients and the government questioning what this offer truly meant. Would it be enough to settle the growing number of claims, or was this just the beginning of an even bigger battle ahead?

More clarity emerged on 30 May 2019. The Delhi High Court took up for hearing a petition filed by the company asking the court to clarify parts of its earlier order from 2 May 2019, when the company had voluntarily offered to pay Rs 2.5 million to each patient who had undergone a revision surgery. In its plea, the company requested the court that this payment should be treated as a 'without prejudice' offer. This meant that the payment would be made without admitting they are at fault or liable. They also wanted it clarified that this payment shouldn't be seen as proof that they were responsible for any wrongdoing.

After the hearing, the court made important observations. First, if the patients accepted the Rs 2.5 million offered voluntarily by the company, it wouldn't harm their rights. They, or the government, could still ask for additional compensation later.

Next, the court said that if the patients or the government won the case and were awarded a higher compensation amount, the Rs 2.5 million already paid voluntarily by the company would be subtracted from that higher amount. 'The petitioner will not be called upon to pay the same twice over,' the court said.[19]

Third, the court clarified that if the company successfully defended itself and proved it was not liable, the Rs 2.5 million it voluntarily paid would not be returned to them. This meant the payment was irreversible, regardless of the case outcome. 'It is further clarified that all other rights and contentions of the petitioner are reserved,' the court observed.

Fourth, the court clarified that it had not decided yet who was right or wrong in this case, and the voluntary payment did not mean the company accepted responsibility.

Importantly, during this court hearing, the lawyer representing the company informed the court that they had received a list of 289 claimants from the government. Out of these, the government had verified ninety-three people as eligible for compensation. The company then reviewed this list further and found that only sixty-seven of these individuals had actually undergone revision surgeries.

'He [the lawyer representing the company] states that the petitioner has brought cheques for a sum of ₹25 lakhs each in favour of those 67 persons in the Court today. The petitioner shall deliver the cheques to the said claimants within a period of two weeks, from today,' the court ordered.

This directive marked a turning point in the ASR saga, like the first crack in a fortress long defended. Johnson & Johnson, which had staunchly resisted the idea of blanket compensation, suddenly announced it would voluntarily pay Rs 2.5 million to all Indian ASR patients who had undergone revision surgery. This move was deeply symbolic.

For many patients, this announcement felt like a bittersweet moment. After years of pain and struggle, the gesture hinted at acknowledgment – but it came wrapped in the company's carefully chosen language. They didn't call it 'compensation'. Yet, for those who had endured faulty implants and revision surgeries, this payment stood out as a rare ray of hope, however modest, in a saga defined by defiance and delay. The voluntary payment, though symbolic, spoke louder than words, suggesting the company could no longer ignore the suffering etched in the lives of its patients.

Interestingly, the important hearing on 30 May 2019 came just five days after the Joint Drugs Controller from the CDSCO filed a detailed counter affidavit. In it, the government firmly pushed back, breaking down the company's petition point by point and opposing its attempt to scrap the compensation formula and dismiss the findings of two expert committees. The timing felt significant, setting the stage for a legal battle that had everyone watching closely.

―⁓―

The government first focused on the timing of the company's plea opposing the compensation formula, raising an eyebrow at its intentions. It pointed out that Dr R.K. Arya Committee 'had already commenced its working and had held several meetings' to finalize the quantum of compensation for Indian patients. With the committee diligently working, even bringing in 'some other subject experts to assist them in their deliberations and working',[20] the government's concern over the plea's timing seemed more than justified.

Then came the government's pointed observation about the company's prior behaviour. For months, the company had been 'actively' participating in the process, giving every impression of cooperation. It had even 'showed his willingness to compensate the suffering patients'. The government reminded the court of the company's public outreach: 'The Petitioner in fact took out advertisement asking patients to approach Central Expert Committee or concerned State Level Committee if they have received implant between June 2004 and August 2010.'[21]

The government then homed in on a key document: a communication from the company dated 9 September 2018. In it, the government highlighted that the company had clearly stated that 'on the basis of the recommendations of the Agarwal Committee Report, they are agreeable to working with DCGI to compensate ASR patients in India'. It went further, highlighting the company's direct involvement: 'The petitioner had requested for their involvement and to work closely with the respondents in this regard.' The statement stood as a stark reminder of the company's earlier promises to stand by patients, and that it had recognized the committees as legitimate.

Finally, the government spotlighted one concrete action already taken by the company, exposing its selective compliance. 'Vide letter dated 30.10.2018, the petitioner had informed that they will be introducing the ASR India Patient Assistance Program till 2015,' it noted. The government pointed out that this step was 'also one of the recommendations of the Agarwal Committee which has been accepted by the petitioner'. This detail served as a reminder that the company was capable of action, raising questions about the motives behind its resistance to other recommendations.

Through these details, the government painted a vivid picture of a company that seemed, at best, inconsistent, and at worst, calculated in its approach to compensating patients.

The government then laid out its case before the court, weaving together with meticulous detail the rationale behind the compensation formula. It explained how the Central Expert Committee, over a series of meetings, had pored over various options, debating the suitability of the Motor Vehicles Act framework and the clinical trial formula. 'The committee, after examining these formulas, noted that the clinical trial formula under the Drugs and Cosmetics Rules, 1945, as formulated in 2013, is working fine with regard to the payment of compensation in cases of death and permanent disability,' the government stated. The explanation unfolded further, with the government adding that the expert committee had 'further' dissected the clinical trial formula, eventually deciding to 'adopt this formula with modifications' for ASR compensation.

'The committee, during its meetings, worked out a formula to govern compensation payable to victims of ASR Hip Implants, taking into account pecuniary and non-pecuniary elements necessary for determining appropriate and just compensation,' the government said.

Returning its focus to Johnson & Johnson, the government underscored that the company had been given ample room to express its stance. 'The company was given the opportunity for a personal hearing on 21 February 2019, as per their request,' the government stated. The government also revealed how Johnson & Johnson Pvt. Ltd. had been 'requested to submit a detailed proposal in writing on the above-mentioned issues and other related matters as well'.

Finally, the argument shifted to the company's response. The government pointed out how Johnson & Johnson had stepped forward with its own ideas. 'The company submitted a detailed proposal for a compensation formula and a fast-track settlement process to make it easy and simple for patients to receive compensation promptly, through a unique transparent manner,' the government recounted.

But above all, the government raised a red flag about India being kept in the dark by the company about the patient safety issues related to the ASR, and only to be informed just months before the recall.

To drive its point home, the government drew a detailed timeline. It started with 30 April 2009, when the company submitted an application to renew its Registration Certificate for the ASR implant with the CDSCO. A few months later, the government highlighted, on 1 September 2009, the CDSCO asked the company to provide an 'undertaking stating that they have not received any complaint regarding the sub-standard quality' of the ASR in the last three years.

On 23 September 2009, the company replied. In its response, it assured the CDSCO that they have 'not received any complaint regarding sub-standard quality of the devices during the last three years'. Based on this assurance, the government renewed the Registration Certificate on 23 December 2009, thinking everything was in order.

In court, the government explained that manufacturers in India are required to report certain issues immediately. For instance, if a medical device is withdrawn from a market, faces regulatory restrictions or is declared substandard by authorities in any country, this information must be shared with the licensing authority in India right away. The law is clear: manufacturers 'shall inform the licencing authority forthwith'.

But here's where the problem came to light. The government pointed out that the ASR implant had been 'already withdrawn' from Australia in December 2009. This was crucial information, yet it 'was not informed to the CDSCO even at the time of application for import licence and this vital information was withheld by the petitioner'.[22]

Above all, the government presented a pivotal piece of evidence. It pointed to an important communication, stating that the regulator was 'informed' by the company 'for the first time' on 8 March 2010, through a Field Safety Notice (FSN) about the dangers linked to the faulty implant. The government didn't mince words, emphasizing, 'They [the company] had themselves admitted that the patients on whom this product has been implanted are undergoing revision surgeries which are more than normal.'

But as India prepared to step into the legal battle, its regulators were left grappling with a grim reality – they had no access to additional evidence beyond what the company chose to disclose. Abroad, a different picture had emerged, one that painted the company's top management in a harsh light. Red flags had been raised repeatedly, their warnings sharp and glaring, like alarms blaring in the dead of night. Yet, the company brushed them aside, choosing to safeguard its profits over the lives of patients. These shocking details came to light during the first ASR trial in the United States, where damning evidence unveiled how the storm had been brewing long before the recall.

Had Indian regulators been armed with the same arsenal of information, the ASR saga here could have unfolded very differently. The delays, the lack of accountability – perhaps they could have been replaced with swifter action, stronger measures and justice delivered more speedily.

Part VI

15

Courtroom, California – Loren Kransky vs. DePuy

On 25 January 2013, *The New York Times* published a report titled 'Maker Hid Data About Design Flaw in Hip Implant, Records Show'.[1] The revelations were damning: Johnson & Johnson executives had known 'years before' the 2010 recall that their ASR hip implant had a 'critical design flaw'. Yet, this vital information was kept hidden from doctors and patients alike. The report cast a harsh spotlight on what many would come to see as a betrayal of trust, with the shocking details emerging not in quiet boardrooms but in the dramatic setting of a Los Angeles courtroom, in the case of Kransky vs. DePuy.

Inside the courtroom, tension crackled in the air like before a thunderstorm. The first ASR-related lawsuit had gone to trial, and the plaintiff's lawyers wasted no time in presenting damning internal documents.[2] The walls of the courtroom seemed to echo with a silent question: How could a company prioritize profits over people?

The case revolved around sixty-five-year-old Loren Kransky, a Vietnam War veteran and former prison guard who had suffered severely because of the ASR. The patient's lawyer stood before the jury, his voice steady but resonant with outrage.

'What did they [DePuy] do? They wanted to continue selling its newest, most expensive product. For DePuy, it was all about business, not the patients. It was obvious in this case,' he said. 'Look at this.' He held up the evidence: internal documents that laid bare the company's decisions.

The room seemed to hold its breath as he continued.

'They are getting warnings right away ... then they get warnings about the pain ... then there is a doctor, who says he is appalled. He is a key opinion leader, a surgeon; [he] writes a letter that he is appalled. Did they [DePuy] do anything? No. ... That's a company that cares about patient safety? This is a company that needs a solid message sent to them, and you are the only one who could do it, ladies and gentlemen,' he implored the jury, pointing to letters from surgeons as far back as 2005 and 2007.

By the time the verdict was announced on 8 March 2013, the case had already captured attention in the United States. In a groundbreaking decision, the California State jury found that DePuy had defectively designed the ASR hip and acted negligently in manufacturing it. The ruling sent shockwaves through the industry: DePuy was ordered to pay a staggering $8.3 million in damages for Kransky's pain and suffering. For many, the verdict was an uncompromising message that companies could no longer brush aside the safety of their patients in favour of profit.

Just hours after the courtroom emptied following the verdict, DePuy doubled down on its stance, releasing a statement that sounded both calculated and defiant. The company reiterated its belief that the ASR hip implant was 'properly designed', that physicians had been adequately informed of its risks, and that all its actions concerning the product were 'appropriate'.[3] But their reaction didn't end there – DePuy swiftly appealed the 2013 judgement, setting the stage for yet another legal battle. It would take three long years, during which time 'Bill' Loren Kransky had died of 'metalosis due to metal hip prosthesis' (as his autopsy report stated) on 26 February 2014, and his widow and estate carried on with the case. Finally, the Court of Appeal reaffirmed the jury's decision, cementing the landmark ruling.

The original 2013 verdict on Kransky vs. DePuy was the culmination of an exhaustive five-week trial that unfolded like a TV drama. Kransky's lawyers called an array of key witnesses to the stand, each testimony adding weight to their case. The jury heard from the ASR's product manager, a biomedical engineer who conducted the implant's risk analysis, and orthopaedic surgeons who had firsthand experience with the ASR. Every piece of evidence – from internal company documents to video depositions of pivotal employees – painted a clearer, more chilling picture of what had gone wrong.

For the first time, the truth was laid bare in the public eye. Internal company communications, once hidden behind closed doors, revealed a damning paper trail exposing their knowledge about the ASR's safety issues. The jury was confronted with evidence that showed the company had not conducted adequate testing of the implant before launching it into the market. The documents were unrelenting in their exposure, showing how DePuy had been aware of the ASR's early failures long before the recall in 2010.

Even more damning, the evidence revealed that DePuy had quietly initiated a project to redesign the implant – a tacit acknowledgment of its flaws. But instead of pausing sales or informing surgeons, the company pushed forward with selling the flawed implant. Meanwhile, behind closed doors, it worked on potential safety changes, keeping implanting surgeons and their patients in the dark.

Among the most striking moments of the trial was the deposition of Andrew Ekdahl, the leader of DePuy's influential marketing team that had spearheaded the ASR XL's introduction into the US.[4] When the first warnings about the ASR surfaced, Andrew Ekdahl was at the helm as the global president of Marketing and Strategy. By 2012, with the ASR recall causing ripples across the medical world, Johnson & Johnson handed him an even more powerful title: Worldwide President of Joint Reconstruction at DePuy Orthopaedics. Ekdahl wasn't just another executive – he was the nerve centre of the ASR saga. Every critical discussion about the troubled implant made its way to his desk. Decisions about what the public would learn and what would be buried in the shadows rested in his hands.

The jury watched intently as video footage showed Ekdahl confronted with damning documentary evidence. His deposition, followed by a grueling cross-examination, became a pivotal moment in the trial. It was a window into the company's internal workings – one that left the twelve jurors in the box with little doubt that the decisions had prioritized profit over safety.

Inside the Los Angeles courtroom, Ekdahl's name loomed large. Ekdahl had given his deposition earlier, which had been recorded for use in the court. Kransky's lawyers had come armed with a treasure trove of damning evidence: internal emails bristling with red flags, meeting minutes that hinted at buried truths, memos outlining mounting concerns and test results that couldn't be ignored. Each piece was a puzzle that pointed to a calculated effort to downplay the ASR's dangers.

The lawyers left no stone unturned, their questions precise and relentless. What unfolded wasn't just a deposition – it was a layer-by-layer unmasking, of the decisions and silence that had endangered so many lives.

Segments of Ekdahl's videotaped deposition were shown to the jurors. In the video, Ekdahl sat across the table, stony-faced, as the lawyer confronted him with an important email. It was sent on 30 April 2008 by a top engineer who had been instrumental in designing the ASR cups. His understanding of the ASR's intricate tribology ran deep, and even after the product hit the market, he had meticulously tracked its performance.

The lawyer began to read aloud: 'Yesterday, we were given some clinical data which compares metal ion levels between BHR and ASR.' The email, laced with technical jargon, pointed to a growing problem. The data from a surgeon working with both ASR and BHR revealed something alarming: the ASR implants were releasing significantly higher levels of metal ions in certain conditions compared to the BHR implants. The engineer reported that the BHR, used by the same surgeon, remained unscathed.

And that wasn't all. The lawyer continued, highlighting a critical pattern the engineer had noticed. The problem appeared to be worse for women and seemed to be correlated to the use of smaller ASR cups. This lined up perfectly with what Dr Nargol in the UK had been flagging. He'd been warning DePuy about the complications his patients were facing with the ASR implants.

Then came the part of the email that made the atmosphere in the room feel even more charged. The lawyer paused before reading the engineer's recommendation: 'I think this data has a bearing on the urgency of updating ASR.' On the surface, it sounded like a genuine call to fix the issue. But as the lawyer continued reading, it became clear that there was more to it than just patient safety.

'I believe that this data will appear in the journals in two parts in 6 months and 12 months, and has the potential to seriously affect our business,' the lawyer read. The engineer wasn't just concerned about the harm to patients – he was also worried about the impact this could have on the company's image and profits. 'We need to discuss this at the earliest possible opportunity as I believe it means that we need to start an ASR upgrade sooner than our previous plan had suggested,' the email concluded.

The email's contents were damning. It revealed that the ASR implant, when positioned at certain angles, unleashed extreme levels of metal ions. The revelation raised an unsettling question: had the company even tested the implant at these angles in their lab before launching it? This critical oversight, if true, painted a grim picture of negligence. For the first time, in a public forum, lawyers grilled the company's top official on this shocking issue, ensuring that it couldn't be swept under the carpet any longer.

'In 2008, when your leading engineer sent you an email saying that at certain placements and angles, there are extreme levels of ions in ASR patients, did you ask him whether or not any testing had been done at these angles on the ASR, prior to having been put onto market? Did you ask [the engineer] at that time?' the lawyer questioned.

Ekdahl hesitated, offering an evasive response.

'I don't remember what we asked him. What I do know is that, as I look at the conclusion of what drove ... [the engineer's] commentary, ... you come to the conclusion that this does not appear to be implant specific.'

But the lawyer wasn't easily deflected. He read out the email, leaving no room for ambiguity.

'It is very clear that the extreme levels are specific to ASR and not the BHR. Correct? He specifically states in the email that this does not occur in the BHR, does he not?' The lawyer's relentless questioning left no room for escape. Ekdahl reluctantly agreed, acknowledging that the engineer indeed 'states that in his email'.

But the grilling didn't stop there.

'And up till today, they have not told you anything about whether or not this product was tested in this fashion, prior to putting it on the market?'

Ekdahl's response was as unsettling as it was revealing.

'To my recall, they have not.'

Next, the lawyers confronted Ekdahl with an email exchange

about the ASR between senior marketing executives and powerful key opinion leaders (KOLs) – the rock stars of orthopaedics – discussing the ASR.

But who are these KOLs? They are the most sought-after surgeons, their calendars packed with surgeries and lectures, shaping the future of orthopaedics. These influencers don't just perform surgery; they design cutting-edge devices for it. Some worked hand-in-hand with DePuy, crafting hip implants. Their words, backed by years in the operating room, carried the weight of authority, pushing others to adopt new technology without hesitation.

An email, dated 19 December 2008, was read aloud by the lawyer in portentous tones. It wasn't just any holiday greeting; it was a carefully crafted Christmas message directed at a select group of elite surgeons – the KOLs, considered the crème de la crème of the world of joint replacement. These specialists were highly skilled doctors who pushed the boundaries of medical science, shaping the future of implant technology. What made this particular email even more striking was that the thread contained the reply from one of its recipients: a surgeon chosen by the company to design another flagship MoM hip implant. Though he hadn't used the ASR implant himself, this surgeon had been diligently studying it in his lab, alongside other one-piece metal cups, trying to understand their nuances.

The lawyer's voice rang out as he turned to Ekdahl, a pointed finger highlighting the significance of the email.

'He writes to you and says that he has concerns about the design of the ASR, doesn't he?' the lawyer asked.

Ekdahl nodded slowly. He replied:

'He writes about his concerns about the design of the product.'

The lawyer pressed on:

'He tells you that "I have concerns about the design and have started to see failures consistent with my concerns". Did I read that correctly?' He scanned the email again for dramatic effect, his finger resting on the key phrase.

'Yes.' Ekdahl nodded

The lawyer zeroed in on another crucial detail in the email. He highlighted a specific red flag raised by the surgeon.

'One, "the inferior bone ingrowth surface, and the less than hemispheric shape make it less likely to obtain bone ingrowth". Did I read that correctly?'

The lawyers homed in on the issue of bone ingrowth because it was absolutely critical for the ASR implant to stay securely fixed within the patient's bone. Imagine the implant as a new leg on a chair – if it is not properly fixed to the chair, it wobbles, making it unsteady, and the leg is liable to break off when weight is put on it. Similarly, an implant needs a solid, stable connection to the bone to function correctly. This connection is achieved through bone ingrowth, where the bone literally grows into the porous surface of the implant, forming a strong bond that keeps it in place.

When the company launched the ASR cups, they made bold claims about their advanced technology. They promised that the implant would not only fix securely from the start but also maintain that strong connection over time. In other words, they assured that once the implant was in place, it would stay there, providing long-term support. But for this to happen, the implant needed to be firmly attached right from the beginning. This was where bone ingrowth became so important.

If the bone didn't grow properly into the surface of the ASR implant, the result was weak fixation. In the case of the ASR cups, this poor bone growth could cause the implant to loosen, leading to painful complications and, in some cases, requiring another surgery to fix it. Surgeons, therefore, were always on the lookout for implants that encouraged strong, healthy bone growth. These were the implants that provided both a solid initial fix and long-term stability.

The surgeon's concern, as highlighted in the email, was that the ASR cups weren't achieving that crucial strong initial fixation. His worry was that the design of the cup, specifically its less-than-ideal shape, was preventing proper bone growth. This flawed design meant that the cup didn't sit properly in the hip, making it harder for the bone to grow into it. As a result, the implant was more likely to loosen, leading to the dreaded need for revision surgery much sooner than expected.

The lawyer then turned Ekdahl's attention to a section of the email that carried a warning too conspicuous to ignore.

'I want you to look at the middle of the document,' the lawyer said. 'Specifically, I want to go to number 2: "the articular surface is too small".' Ekdahl's eyes flicked to the document, and he barely nodded – an unwilling acknowledgement. The lawyer didn't hesitate. He read aloud the next damning piece of the puzzle:

'The 160-degree low profile shape, the increased dome thickness, and the recessed rim of the articular surface all combine to dramatically decrease the effective articular surface. This leads to edge loading.'

Ekdahl's response came quickly, though his voice lacked any of the confidence he might have once felt:

'Yes. That is his impression of the device.'

It was clear now. The surgeon wasn't just voicing a concern – he was ringing an alarm. His communication laid out a striking flaw in the design: sharp edges that could tear into the soft tissue surrounding the hip, a potential disaster for any patient. Worse still, the cup's design was making it more like a vertical cup, increasing wear and accelerating its failure.

The lawyer leaned forward, sensing Ekdahl's growing unease.

'When you saw this, you would have been completely shocked because you have never heard this before? Right?'

'I don't even recall my reaction to this particular email other than what I have got here; which is, we need to get onto the phone, as soon as possible, and have a conversation about that with the team,' Ekdahl said flatly.

The lawyer wasn't done.

'Certainly you would be concerned that a key opinion leader was having problems that you have never heard before?' he pressed.

'Yes,' Ekdahl responded.

The lawyer's questions came faster now, relentless, like a drumbeat.

'Because this kind of report suggests, first of all you have enough experience to know that you want maximum bone growth and good initial fixation. Right?'

'Correct,' Ekdahl replied.

'You wanted a good long-term fixation?' the lawyer continued.

'Yes,' Ekdahl said again.

'And because the last thing you want are premature revisions?' The lawyer's voice seemed to harden.

'That would be the last thing that we would want for our patients,' Ekdahl responded.

Now, the lawyer's questions turned personal.

'So when he [the top surgeon] communicates to you his concerns about problems with ASR, you understand that he is writing to you as a knowledgeable and scholarly friend? Right?'

'He is a knowledgeable and scholarly surgeon. That is correct,' Ekdahl agreed.

The lawyer didn't let up.

'He has devoted his life to relieving pain and restoring mobility, in getting the best possible result for his hip replacement patients. Correct?'

'Yes,' Ekdahl affirmed.

The lawyer's final question was clear, as if cutting through the fog of ambiguity.

'You have to take into consideration his background, education, training, knowledge when you read this, don't you?'

'Yes,' Ekdahl replied.

There it was: a recognition that the company had a glaring red flag waved before its eyes – one it could not ignore. And yet, when the lawyer asked what action the company had taken after receiving this urgent message, Ekdahl's answers grew more evasive, and each one exposed another layer of indecision.

'Did you immediately call the clinical and regulatory people to see what the reports you had to date of inferior bone growth were?' the lawyer asked, his voice rising in expectation.

'I don't recall exactly what I did following receiving this email,' Ekdahl responded, his hesitation palpable, as if the memory had slipped through his fingers.

'Did you at least immediately forward this to the clinical [team] to make sure that they knew what was going on so that they could open clinical files?' the lawyer pressed.

'I don't recall if I did that,' Ekdahl admitted.

'You had the obligation to directly report this message to the clinical. Didn't you?' the lawyer pressed one final time.

'We should have reported this. One of us. I don't know if it happened as a result of our phone call, or if one of us did eventually report this to the clinical. I don't know the answer to that ...' Ekdahl replied, his voice trailing off into silence.

In that silence, the weight of Ekdahl's evasiveness had left ripples that spoke volumes – it was an unmistakable sign that the company's response to a critical concern had been far from immediate, far from adequate.

The lawyer then drew Ekdahl's attention to a particularly damning observation made by the surgeon.

In July 2008, Zimmer, a leading orthopaedic device manufacturer in the US, voluntarily halted the marketing and distribution of its Durom Acetabular Component (also known as the Durom Cup). The decision was prompted by reports of unusually high revision rates. Zimmer claimed their investigation revealed the need for updated surgical techniques and enhanced training programmes to ensure better outcomes. Yet, the aftermath was far from smooth. Patients flooded Zimmer with claims for reimbursement, citing pain and suffering linked to the Durom Cup.

The email at the centre of this case drew a parallel between Zimmer's Durom Cup and the ASR implant. As the lawyer highlighted, the surgeon's words carried a warning: history might be on the verge of repeating itself.

'Personally,' the surgeon had written, 'I think we would be dealing with a Durom situation in the near future, and the one-piece cup should be redesigned.'

'Did you understand the sentence?' the lawyer pressed Ekdahl.

'I understand his personal statement,' Ekdahl, outwardly composed, replied.

The lawyer didn't let up.

'When you saw this, you understood that what he is saying, he is concerned that is going to happen with you with ASR, right?'

Ekdahl hesitated, his words carefully measured.

'I believe there was a great deal of conversation around Durom, and whether there was the opportunity to educate surgeons about cup placements around one-piece acetabular component.'

But the lawyer wasn't satisfied. He argued that the surgeon's statement went beyond discussing mere surgical training. It was a call for something far more urgent – a redesign of the ASR.

'When you read this, you didn't understand that he was saying, "I think we will be dealing with the Durom situation," to mean that this thing is going to be taken off the market?'

Ekdahl offered a carefully neutral response.

'Yes, and I believe that there is later a phone call with him that provides some clarity about his statement. I think it is one sentence of his personal impression.'

Courtroom, California – Loren Kransky vs. DePuy

The lawyer pressed further.

'At the end of this sentence, he says: "And the one-piece cup should be redesigned." You understood him to be telling you, in his opinion, the one-piece cup ASR cup should be redesigned. Right?'

'He is suggesting that there is a need for a one-piece cup redesign,' Ekdahl conceded.

This was no ordinary warning. This was a respected figure – a voice trusted and respected within the company – sounding an alarm that couldn't be ignored. However, this surgeon's cautionary note wasn't an isolated case. In fact, whispers of trouble with the ASR had been growing louder within the company as well as in the industry. A storm had been brewing all along, and the company had seen it coming.

This was revealed even as the lawyers confronted Ekdahl with another crucial piece of evidence – a high-stakes internal PowerPoint presentation.

The presentation delved into the perceived weaknesses of the ASR implant in the marketplace, unravelling a web of concerns that had surfaced years before the worldwide recall.

Ekdahl's gaze fell on the document, the culmination of a 'worldwide acetabular strategy meeting' that took place in the glittering heat of Las Vegas in May 2008. One could picture the scene: a conference room buzzing with the sharp energy of top marketing executives. The walls might have echoed with the click of laser pointers and the hum of laptops, as they dissected every angle of the ASR implant in a meticulous SWOT analysis – strengths, weaknesses, opportunities and threats.

The lawyers wasted no time, pointing directly to the presentation's damning revelations. Their questioning left Ekdahl with no choice but to confront the hard truths about the ASR's design flaws and the potential health risks they posed to patients.

The first slide came into focus.

'I am just looking here at the weakness of the ASR. The first one says: "susceptible to effects of vertical cup placement (ions)". Do you see that?' the lawyer asked.

'I do,' Ekdahl replied.

'That's a health risk, isn't it?' the lawyer pressed.

Ekdahl hesitated, choosing his words carefully.

'I think it demonstrates there is susceptibility to vertical cup placement. And then what follows from there – what are the issues around that.'

The lawyer leaned in, his tone sharper.

'The follow-on is ions. You understand what that means, correct?'

'That is what they put in,' Ekdahl replied. 'This team who did this. I don't know who did it. But the team who did this is saying: yes, ions are the issue there.'

'So, the notion of susceptibility to effects of vertical cup placement (ions) – that's a health risk, isn't it?' the lawyer repeated.

'Ions represent a potential health risk,' Ekdahl finally agreed.

The lawyer's pace quickened as he moved to the next slide.

'Let's talk about the next weakness: cup deformation. That's a health issue, isn't it?'

'Cup deformation has the potential to result in greater wear and ions,' Ekdahl replied.

'So when it says "perceived", that is a suggestion that the physicians, somebody, is talking about a perception of cup deformation. And that is a weakness. Right?' the lawyer questioned.

'Yes,' Ekdahl replied.

'And the potential to cause greater [release of] ions with cup deformation, as you have just told me, is a health issue?' the lawyer pursued.

'It could be among the issues created by cup deformation,' Ekdahl said.

The lawyer pressed on, pointing to another blatant flaw flagged in the document.

'Next, cup loosening – technique-related improper seating. That's listed as a weakness, isn't it?'

'The team that created this [presentation] ... classified it as a weakness,' Ekdahl confirmed.

'And a potentially loose cup is a health issue, isn't it?'

'Potential cup loosening is a health issue,' Ekdahl admitted.

But the most damning weakness was still to come. The lawyer turned to the slide highlighting the ASR's most prominent design flaw.

'Next, it says "sharp edge on head". That's a safety issue. And a health issue. Isn't it?'

'Sharp edges on the head could potentially be an issue in some patients,' Ekdahl agreed.

With each slide, the lawyer painted a grim picture: a product riddled with design vulnerabilities, each one a potential risk to patient safety. These glaring red flags should have set alarm bells ringing long before the ASR implant reached patients. Yet, here they were – buried in an internal document from a meeting held two years before the recall, unearthed only under the light of legal scrutiny.

During the trial, the lawyer approached the jury purposefully, holding up internal documents that pulled away the curtain on the company's secrets. These documents revealed that even as the ASR was being marketed with great fanfare, the company's experts were quietly grappling with the implant's flagrant design flaws. As early as 2007 – three years before the global recall – the company had quietly started discussing a redesign. Cloaked in secrecy, it was given a code name: Project Alpha.

To make this point, the lawyer zeroed in on a crucial piece of evidence: a PowerPoint presentation prepared by an engineer detailing the potential redesign of the ASR, even before the May 2008 Las Vegas presentation. This document, dated 27 September 2007, revealed that discussions about redesigning the ASR had started almost three years before the global recall in August 2010.

The lawyer's tone sharpened as he directed Ekdahl's attention to a specific slide.

'It says "potential solutions". Do you see that?' he asked.

'Yes,' Ekdahl replied.

'The first one says, correct me if I am wrong, "major redesign of the ASR acetabular component and associated instruments". Do you see that?' the lawyer asked.

'I do,' Ekdahl replied.

The lawyer pressed on.

'Do you know if there was ever a suggestion made to redesign the ASR acetabular component and remove the lateralization and the groove?'

Ekdahl answered hesitantly.

'I think ... there was a contemplation, over time, for what eventually was, what I would say, was early work, and early contemplation ... for what ... we called eventually Project Alpha.'

The lawyer leaned in.

'So do I understand this correctly that these recommendations made ... in this PowerPoint were essentially the suggestions and recommendations made in Project Alpha?'

Ekdahl, now visibly on edge, replied:

'These come up with options, which he then explores in the following slides, right. He continues to work his way through that ... He has laid out a potential solution.'

But the story didn't end there. The lawyer wasn't about to let the jury forget the role of the engineer, someone who had gone a step further by redesigning the ASR cup itself to address the issue of metal wear.

The lawyer confronted Ekdahl.

'Your very bright young engineer had in fact successfully drawn a redesign of the cup. You did know that? Correct?'

'He had drawn an alternative to the grooved design of the cup that was never tested in the hands of a clinician to see if it met the needs of the clinician,' Ekdahl, now on the defensive, replied.

Unrelenting, the lawyer pushed harder.

'You actually knew at that time that ... [the engineer] had successfully drawn a cup that would reduce metal wear. Isn't that true?'

'He drew a cup that didn't have a groove,' Ekdahl, cornered but careful, admitted, 'and the groove has the potential to increase metal wear. But I don't believe we tested it to say, "Does it truly reduce metal wear?"'

It wasn't just the engineers who were discussing the potential redesign of the ASR implant. The courtroom stirred as startling revelations from the lawyer unveiled a hidden layer of corporate decision-making. Internal communications dating back to June 2008 painted a vivid picture of high-stakes discussions in the top echelons of the company. These were pivotal gatherings, occurring nearly two years before the global recall of the ASR implant.

The lawyer presented minutes from key meetings held by the company's influential US Joints and Extremities Board, a powerhouse of decision-makers. This elite board was a melting pot of expertise, with representatives from medical affairs, research, marketing and sales, including the president and vice president of sales. Together, they controlled the pulse of the company's operations in the US, making decisions that rippled across the industry.

Zeroing in on the minutes, the lawyer commanded attention: 'Let's look at what these minutes state. It indicates that ... [a medical affairs official] presented this initiative and advised: "It was prioritized by the Hip Development Group as mission critical." We are talking about the redesign project: ASR 2. True?'

'Correct,' Ekdahl replied.

The lawyer sharpened the focus on an important exchange in those very minutes between a prominent marketing executive and the worldwide vice-president of Development. The executive had raised a question about why the redesign was classified as 'mission critical'. The response from the vice-president, in charge of product development, had been telling – he had emphasized the 'extreme sensitivity to malposition' in the ASR implant.

The lawyer turned to Ekdahl, probing further: 'He is talking about the cup and its extreme sensitivity with respect to ions, correct?'

Ekdahl hesitated before responding: 'Hmm ...'

This hesitation hung in the air, underscoring the weight of the evidence. The lawyer drove home the significance of the vice president's observation. As someone directly involved in implant design and performance evaluation, his statements carried the authority of a top-tier expert. His acknowledgment of the ASR's flaws laid bare the compelling scientific rationale for the redesign.

The lawyer didn't let this point slip past the jury.

'He is someone who is respected at DePuy for being accurate, thorough, and for understanding what he is talking about, right?' the lawyer pressed.

Ekdahl nodded, confirming the official's credibility and further solidifying the case.

Then came another revelation – a crucial email exchange from 25 March 2008, between Ekdahl and a high-ranking marketing executive. The email contained a detailed list of questions and answers about the ASR redesign project. The lawyer revealed that this information had been shared with a select team of specialists in Leeds, experts in tribology and engineering.

The jury's attention was drawn to a notification exclusively addressed to the Leeds team about a forthcoming meeting. It was a critical gathering to deliberate on the ASR project, bringing the weight of technical expertise to the table.

When the lawyer confronted Ekdahl with the internal email, he pointed to a specific question and its response. The email showed that a key marketing executive had made two things very clear. First, patient safety had to come first when introducing the redesigned ASR. Second, economic concerns should never outweigh the safety of the patient.

'I'm at question 6,' the lawyer said. 'It says: "What are the risks of starting such a project whilst the current implant is on the market?"' He glanced up at Ekdahl. 'You know what he's talking about here, right? The redesign of the cup?'

'Well, I think he's talking about a broader subject around redesigning or evolving the ASR platform,' Ekdahl replied. 'I don't think it's particularly the cup.'

'The ASR platform included the cup. Isn't it?' the lawyer pressed, not missing a beat.

'Yes,' Ekdahl replied.

The lawyer's gaze remained fixed on the email as he read the next section aloud.

'What he answered is: "Ethically, we would be doing the right thing." Correct?' he asked, turning back to Ekdahl.

'That is his answer,' Ekdahl replied.

'You're familiar with the concept of ethics, right?' the lawyer asked, his tone now almost a challenge.

'Yes,' Ekdahl said, nodding.

'Ethical implies what is good, honest and best for the patient. True?' the lawyer pressed, his words deliberate and weighty.

'Among other things, yes,' Ekdahl replied.

The lawyer's finger moved once again, pointing to another section.

'Independent of the ethical obligation, he talks about business implications by using the term "commercially". Right?' he said, as if placing the word under a magnifying glass.

'Correct,' Ekdahl replied.

'You recognize that when he talks about "commercially", he's referring to the potential risks of selling two products at once, don't you?' the lawyer asked.

Ekdahl hesitated before answering.

'You'd have to ask [the top marketing official] ... exactly what he means by that statement.'

The lawyer continued reading aloud, revealing the marketing executive's own words: that 'commercially', having two cups in the market 'would need to be managed', but that the 'risks would be limited'. It was clear – the implication was that patient safety must come first, but the company seemed to be hedging its bets on the economics of the situation.

Based on this email, it might seem that the company was placing patient safety above all else, but it didn't.

The lawyer placed an important piece of evidence – an email dated 28 September 2008. It was written by Ekdahl himself, where he had stated, in no uncertain terms, that selling two cups simultaneously was a path the company should never tread.

The lawyer turned to Ekdahl, his voice sharp.

'You actually sent an email, at some point, saying that we are not going to sell two cups at the same time. Do you remember that?' he asked.

Ekdahl hesitated for a moment before responding.

'Yes. You refreshed my memory,' he admitted.

The email, like an open diary entry, laid bare Ekdahl's stance.

'As you see here,' he began, scanning the words he himself had written years ago, 'I sent my opinion in an email about: I don't think we should have two cups in the marketplace, and that I don't think it would be the right thing to do.'

The lawyer's tone sharpened as he read aloud key excerpts that highlighted Ekdahl's resistance to the introduction of another redesigned ASR cup – not for patient safety reasons, but to safeguard the company's business interests.

'In order to make it clear to them that you were not going to sell two different cups on a worldwide basis, you told them that "financials will not fly". Correct?' the lawyer pressed.

'That is correct,' Ekdahl replied.

'And you said the competition will have a field day with this. Those are your words, right?'

'That is correct,' Ekdahl replied.

The lawyer leaned in, unrelenting:

'You chose those words in this email.'

'I was making a provocative statement to the team about my opinion,' Ekdahl countered, his tone defensive.

But the lawyer was unsparing.

'You were making an unequivocal statement about what is going to happen. True?'

'No. I was making my opinion known to the team, relative to conceptually selling multiple cups,' Ekdahl replied.

The lawyer's questions worked like a scalpel, cutting deeper into the company's motivations. Internal communications revealed that while the potential redesign of the ASR cup touched on patient safety, management's deliberations centred on competitive implications. They were acutely aware that any design changes could be exploited by rivals, a factor that loomed larger than safety in their decision-making process.

Finally, the lawyer delivered the final blow:

'And you never sold different cups. Did you?'

'I believe, later this year, we made a decision that we could not accomplish our goals technically – with another large cup,' Ekdahl replied.

The courtroom hung onto every word as the lawyer brought up the financial analysis Ekdahl had referenced in the email.

'Financially, what was going to be required to fix the cup and do the ASR Alpha cup project?' the lawyer asked.

But Ekdahl, like a man caught in quicksand, fumbled with his answers.

'I don't recall today,' he said evasively, dodging the lawyer's piercing questions.

'You say here that financials will not fly, which indicates that you had analysed them?' the lawyer pressed harder.

Ekdahl's reply was convoluted.

'To me, that is, when I say, financials, I mean it is business case that it will not fly – which is more than just numbers: it is the technical challenges of doing it; it is the clinical challenge of doing it; it is can we actually make something that much better than it is today. Financials and business cases are pretty much the same thing, in my opinion,' he rambled.

Courtroom, California – Loren Kransky vs. DePuy

The lawyer didn't let up.

'When you say that the competition will have a field day with this, you are talking about the makers of other hip products?'

'Yes,' Ekdahl replied.

'And those are your competition. Correct?'

'That is correct.'

In one final, damning question, the lawyer pointed to the heart of the issue:

'Would it be your practice, typically in marketing, to determine whether or not to make safety changes based upon how competition would react?'

Ekdahl floundered, his response a jumble of corporate jargon.

'No. I think this is a balance. I think I have also said that this will not be a business case. That is because of all the technical challenges, the clinical challenges, which I also make note of here relative to the regulatory pathway. So there are more challenges here than just two sentences laid out,' he said.

However, the lawyer had peeled back the layers of corporate rhetoric, exposing the uncomfortable truth: when it came to the ASR cup, financial interests had stood higher than patient safety ever could.

Even before the global recall of the ASR implant, the company had quietly decided to pull it from the Australian market. But what raised eyebrows was their calculated effort to avoid calling it a recall. As the trial unravelled the tangled web hiding the truth, this decision took on a sharper focus, exposing a significant link between the timing of the withdrawal and troubling data from the Australian registry.

During the trial, the lawyers presented crucial evidence directly linked to key events related to this controversial decision: internal documents from September 2009. They were minutes from the company's elite management board, the US Joints, Trauma, Extremity Board. Among the dense corporate jargon and routine agenda points, one item stood out: a specific mention of the ASR implant and the 'damaging' data soon to be released in Australia.

The lawyer directed Ekdahl's attention to an internal communication embedded in these minutes:

'It says: "Australian Registry will publish data next week very damaging to the ASR." Right?' he asked. Ekdahl acknowledged the sentence.

'You read that sentence correctly,' he replied.

This revelation was significant. It became clear that the company's top management knew the Australian registry's findings were not just bad – they were devastating. The report would lay bare the clinical failures of the ASR in Australian patients, and this was months before the company issued a global recall. The lawyer pressed further, zeroing in on Ekdahl's evasiveness.

'What does damaging to the ASR mean in this context?' the lawyer asked. Ekdahl hesitated, retreating into ambiguity.

'I don't know,' he replied.

The lawyer wasn't letting up.

'Didn't you understand at that time that it will be damaging to your sales?' he probed.

'Damaging to the image of the brand,' Ekdahl replied.

'Because it was going to report an unacceptably high revision rate? Isn't it true?' the lawyer asked. Ekdahl's response was a tangle of uncertainty.

'I don't know what it reported. I don't know if that is ASR or ASR XL. I am presuming that it is ASR,' he replied.

But the lawyer had facts to anchor his argument.

'Australian registry ultimately published data in the following week that showed unacceptable revision rates for both ASR and ASR XL. Didn't it?' he asked. Ekdahl's evasion was almost predictable now.

'I don't recall the date it was published the next week,' he said, deflecting from the main question.

The internal communication revealed a clear sense of concern among the top management regarding the impending public release of data on the alarmingly high revision ASR surgeries, as recorded by the Australian registry. What made this situation particularly critical was the fact that it marked the first instance of such significant adverse data on patient safety directly associated with the ASR being made available to both the public and the market.

The lawyer, in fact, questioned Ekdahl about the importance of the Australian registry data because it directly dealt with patient safety.

'Registry data involves the health of patients. Doesn't [it]?' the lawyer asked.

'Registry data is an important data that we look at among the other data. That is correct,' Ekdahl replied.

'But it relates to the health of the patients because it talks about revisions? Right?' the lawyer asked.

'It relates to the performance of the device,' Ekdahl replied.

'How could information on performance of a device, in people, be damaging?' the lawyer asked.

'I am presuming. Again, I don't have the data, I don't know who made this comment; I am presuming they are talking about data that is going to be published on the performance of the device,' Ekdahl said evasively.

The lawyer then turned to a particularly astounding piece of data.

'It says here: "revision rates with ASR XL are two–three times higher than Pinnacle [another MoM implant manufactured by DePuy]." Do you see that?' the lawyer asked.

'Again, I don't know who is quoting the data … I see that you have read that correctly,' Ekdahl responded.

The lawyer pressed on.

'Did you ever tell any of the doctors you were selling ASRs to that you knew your revision rate with ASR XL was two–three times higher than Pinnacle?'

'I don't know where these data comes from. Or whether these data eventually show up in the [Australian] registry,' Ekdahl replied.

The lawyer was not to be put off like this.

'That was not my question,' he said. 'My question was: Did you tell any of the doctors you were selling ASRs to that you actually knew that your revision rate with ASR XL was two–three times higher than the Pinnacle?'

Ekdahl paused, as if searching for the right words to sidestep the question.

'I don't recall what would have been communicated, at this point in time,' he said.

The lawyer, undeterred, moved on to a new revelation. He pointed to another section of the minutes.

'There was also somebody's comment that they believed the Australians would want the product removed from the market. Correct?'

'And I don't know who made that comment,' Ekdahl replied after a slight hesitation.

The lawyer pressed harder.

'I understand that, but it does say, someone at this high level of management, in an official company document, believed the Australians would want the product removed from the market. Correct?'

'They believed. Yes,' Ekdahl replied reluctantly. 'They didn't know for sure. It was a belief.'

The lawyer seized the opening.

'But the belief, as stated, clearly points to the Australian regulatory authorities, doesn't it?' he asked.

'Our Australian business people down there might have asked us to take the product off the market,' Ekdahl replied. 'They might make that decision to say: We have chosen not to sell this because it is something that is not efficient for them to sell. We have countries around the world that make a decision on what they can do or not on ways to sell.'

It was a careful pivot, but the lawyer wasn't letting him off the hook.

'Do you believe that this sentence – "believe they would want the product removed from the market" – refers to anyone other than the Australian regulatory agencies?' he asked.

Ekdahl's reply came slowly, his words carefully chosen.

'I am saying I don't have data to say, that is, that our own team is going to say we are not going to sell anymore, or whether it is the agency down there saying no.'

The lawyer repeated his question on this issue.

'Are you telling the jury and the judge that the sentence – "believe they would want the product removed from the market" – refers to anyone other than Australian regulatory personnel?'

Ekdahl's response remained evasive.

'I am saying here under oath that I would like more information about who "they" is and what "removed" means. I think that is very fair,' he said.

The lawyer then drew Ekdahl's attention to the minutes of another important meeting. In this meeting, one of the DePuy board members made a striking recommendation.

'Here what it says, "recommendation is to get out of ASR and ASR XL business". Did I read that correctly?' the lawyer asked, holding up a copy of the minutes for emphasis.

'I don't know who was the individual that made that recommendation or [if] that recommendation came from among the team,' Ekdahl replied, his voice careful, evasive.

The lawyer didn't relent. He pointed to another remark from the same meeting: a suggestion to swiftly withdraw from the Australian market if a recall wasn't deemed necessary.

'It says someone on the committee said, "If we don't need to recall, we will get out of Australia quickly." Right?'

'That is correct,' Ekdahl replied.

'You did get out of Australia quickly, didn't you?' the lawyer pressed, his tone sharp.

'I believe the business made that decision to exit Australia,' Ekdahl replied.

'Almost immediately after this meeting?' the lawyer asked.

'I don't know the time,' Ekdahl replied, his responses increasingly opaque.

The lawyer shifted gears, zeroing in on the most damning question yet: Why weren't surgeons outside Australia informed about this abrupt decision?

'When you got out of Australia, did you send a communication to all of your American surgeons saying, we are out of Australia. Did you tell them that?'

Ekdahl's response was the same hollow refrain: 'I don't know the answer to that.'

'Did you tell your sales personnel: I think it is important that you tell all doctors, who we are selling these hips to, that we have decided to leave Australia,' the lawyer asked.

Again, Ekdahl's reply was a deadpan: 'I don't know the answer to that.'

The lawyer, undeterred, continued to peel back the layers of the company's decisions, exposing yet another critical turning point. He read aloud from the minutes: the board's decision to 'rationalize' the ASR in the US.

'You made a decision to rationalize the product in the US on this day in September of 2009. Didn't you?'

'Over the ensuing six months,' Ekdahl answered.

'But the decision to rationalize was made in September 2009, wasn't it?'

'It was,' Ekdahl conceded.

The lawyer's questions turned sharper, zeroing in on what 'rationalization' truly meant.

'The process of rationalization? The plan was: we will use up all we have, and we won't sell any more. Correct?' the lawyer asked.

'That was not the point of rationalization,' Ekdahl countered. 'The point of rationalization was to allow surgeons to make other decisions, knowing that we are removing the product from the market. So they can make clinical decisions to use other devices.'

The lawyer then got straight to another important question that remained unanswered: If the product was taken off the market in Australia, why wasn't it done globally at the same time? Aren't all patients just as important? The lawyer's scepticism was palpable.

'What would have been the economic consequences of withdrawing the ASR in the US the same day you withdrew from Australia?'

'I don't know the answer to that,' Ekdahl replied.

The lawyer drove the point home with one final, damning question.

'This group had the power, on that very day, to say, "We are not going to sell any more ASRs anywhere." Didn't it?'

'This group had the ability to look at it and make a policy decision about rationalizing the product,' Ekdahl replied.

'That wasn't my question,' the lawyer shot back. 'That wasn't my question. This group had the power and the authority to decide, if they chose, to stop selling the product in the US immediately, didn't they?'

Ekdahl hesitated, then finally admitted: 'It could have.'

At its launch, the ASR implant was introduced with grand claims. But beneath the bold assertions lay a glaring omission – these assurances were built entirely on laboratory stimulator tests, not real-world clinical trials. The aftermath of the ASR saga would later reveal the price of this oversight: compromised patient safety that could have been prevented with rigorous pre-market clinical testing.

During the trial, the lawyers focused their cross-examination on this pivotal question – the necessity of clinical testing for implants.

The lawyer began with a pointed question: 'Do you agree that clinical testing is the ultimate test for the safety of a product?'

Ekdahl responded cautiously: 'I believe clinical testing, if you are gonna talk about the safety of the product, if the safety issue is the long-term survivorship of the implant – then clinical safety, if that is the end game – clinical safety is demonstrated, among other places, through a clinical trial.'

The line of questioning pressed further.

'Do you believe that laboratory testing mimics what happens in human beings?' The lawyer's tone was steady yet charged with the weight of implications.

'They don't,' Ekdahl replied.

The lawyer's questions grew sharper.

'Have you ever believed that what happens in laboratory testing mimics what happens in human beings?'

Ekdahl, measured but candid, replied: 'We do use it for guidance into how a product will perform.'

Each question seemed to strike at the heart of the case, bringing the jury closer to understanding the flawed foundation of the company's decision on testing the ASR.

'Have you ever been told by any DePuy tribology engineer that laboratory tests on stimulators exactly mimic what happens in human beings?'

Again, Ekdahl's answer was a blend of technicality and resignation:

'I have been told by our R&D team that it is among the surrogates, and it is something that they look at while testing an implant. You cannot mimic every human interaction with an implant on a stimulator.'

The lawyer's final thrust was a clincher, bringing the issue into stark clarity: 'The way to mimic and find out what exactly happens in human beings is by in-vivo clinical trials. Correct?'

'That would give a sample of how the product would perform in a subset of patients,' Ekdahl replied.

The lawyer then confronted Ekdahl with another important exchange related to the issue of pre-clinical testing of the ASR. He began by explaining the significance of the communication, dated 15 December 2008. The email involved a senior marketing executive and a prominent surgeon, one of the select few in the company's exclusive 'leadership council'. The lawyer also pointed out that Ekdahl had been copied on the email.

The lawyer didn't let the significance of this group escape

unnoticed. A membership to the leadership council, he pointed out, was a distinction granted to few surgeons. Ekdahl acknowledged the prestige of the council, an elite circle of surgeons brought together for their insights on orthopaedics.

The lawyer then drew attention to the surgeon's concerns raised in the email.

'He shared all the way back in 2008 ... the problems one of his fellows was having. That is correct?'

'That is correct,' Ekdahl said.

The lawyer then pointed to another line in the communication. 'In addition to the problems ... he notes "This is coupled with some of our local problems with our ASR implant." Did I read that accurately?'

'Yes,' Ekdahl said.

But the lawyer wasn't interested in simple confirmations. He went for the jugular.

'Did you yourself ... pick up the phone, try and find out what the problems were with ASR to which he is referring to?'

'I did not,' Ekdahl replied.

The lawyer then highlighted another excerpt from the surgeon's email: 'He says among other things: "We are anxious to look up these patients who have had ASRs placed, into a thoughtful, well-balanced evaluation of this system." Did I read that correctly?'

'Yes'.

'In fact, he ultimately did a thoughtful, well-balanced evaluation of the system, didn't he?' the lawyer asked.

Ekdahl deflected: 'I don't know if he did or didn't.'

At this point, the lawyer showed an important scientific paper to Ekdahl. The title was bold and damning: 'Early Failure of Articular Surface Replacement XL Total Hip Arthroplasty'. It was published in 2011 in the reputable *Journal of Arthroplasty*.[5]

Turning to Ekdahl, the lawyer delivered his next blow: 'After this was published, did you call [the surgeon]?'

'I don't remember calling ... at that point in time,' Ekdahl replied.

The lawyer pressed on, dissecting the paper piece-by-piece.

'When you read it, you would have read the conclusion, correct?' the lawyer asked.

'I would have read his conclusion, based on his patient group that he's evaluated – 120-odd patients,' Ekdahl replied.

'Under the heading "Conclusions", he wrote that "the purpose of our study was to determine the clinical and radiographic outcome of the ASR XL total hip system",' the lawyer said, pointing to the paper.

'Yes,' Ekdahl replied.

'Although the theoretical advantages of extra-large head are attractive, the 12 per cent early aseptic revision rate and 28 per cent combined clinical and radiographic failure rates are clearly unacceptable. That is the statement of his opinion. Correct?' the lawyer asked.

Ekdahl's response was measured.

'Well, it's a statement of his opinion based on the data he presents here in this paper.'

The lawyer didn't let him off the hook.

'Exactly. It is his opinion based upon his experience and the data he reviewed for this paper. Right?'

'Yes,' Ekdahl replied.

'This is actually a well-thought-of journal, isn't it?' the lawyer asked.

'Yes,' Ekdahl agreed.

'It is peer reviewed, right?' the lawyer asked.

'It is a peer review. Correct,' Ekdahl agreed.

'When you read that, did you agree, frankly, that an early 12 per cent aseptic revision rate and 28 per cent combined clinical and radiographic failure rate was clearly unacceptable?' the lawyer asked.

'I think we recalled the product based on, prior to this, based on data,' Ekdahl hedged.

'I know you recalled the product based on data. I am just asking if you agree with his specific conclusion,' the lawyer asked.

'I do agree with his specific conclusion that's not an acceptable outcome for our products,' Ekdahl agreed.

On this important issue, the lawyer then posed his final and perhaps most pivotal question. Referencing the last sentence of the paper's conclusion, he asked:

'The last sentence of his conclusion says: "Adequate pre-clinical trials may have identified some of the shortcomings of this class of implants before the marketing and widespread use of their implants ensued." Do you see that?'

'Yes,' Ekdahl replied.

'Do you agree with that?' the lawyer asked.

'He talks about the class of implants, which is a one-piece metal-on-metal product,' Ekdahl replied.
'Which includes the ASR?' the lawyer asked.
'Correct,' Ekdahl replied.
'Do you agree with the proposition that adequate preclinical trials of the ASR may have identified some of the shortcomings of the ASR, before its marketing and widespread use?' the lawyer asked.
'I think, probably yes. In retrospect, we agree with that,' Ekdahl admitted.

The ASR recall raised a critical question: was the decision truly about patient safety, or was it a masterstroke of corporate spin? Rather than admitting any flaws in the implant, the company leaned on revision rate data from the UK National Joint Registry to frame the issue. When the recall was announced, they carefully sidestepped responsibility, emphasizing instead that the product still performed well in some patients – a selective narrative that diffused the gravity of the situation.

This wasn't just damage control; it was a calculated move to shape the story. By deflecting attention from the real issue – serious concerns about patient safety – the company ensured its version of events dominated.

However, inside the courtroom, Kransky's lawyer sought to challenge this narrative by questioning Ekdahl on the fundamental question at the heart of the ASR recall: did the company recall the ASR because it was unsafe for patients?

'You recalled the product because it was unsafe and ineffective, right? Isn't that true?' the lawyer asked, his tone pointed, almost daring Ekdahl to admit what the company had worked hard to keep vague.

Ekdahl's reply was deliberate and evasive.

'We recalled the product because it did not meet what we believed were the clinical standards we wanted for the product. We acknowledge that.'

The lawyer pressed on, refusing to let Ekdahl's words go unchallenged.

'For the benefit of the twelve people sitting in this jury box in

California, or jurors in other states hearing this case, do you agree that you recalled this product because it was unsafe? Yes or no?'

Ekdahl's response was a masterclass in corporate deflection.

'I agree we recalled the product because it didn't meet the clinical standards of products we wished to sell in the marketplace,' he said, his tone steady.

The lawyer's impatience was palpable as he attempted to pin down an answer.

'I'm not using the term clinical standard in my question ... Do you agree that you recalled this product because it was unsafe?'

Ekdahl didn't waver.

'I would answer it again the same way I have answered it: we recalled the product because it didn't meet the clinical standards we wanted for a product in the marketplace.'

The lawyer pivoted, trying a different angle.

'Was there any concern whatsoever about the number of people who were being hurt when you recalled it?'

Ekdahl, unyielding, stuck to his script.

'We recalled the product because it didn't meet clinical standards that we wanted for a product in the marketplace.'

It was a battle of persistence versus obdurate precision, with the lawyer chipping away at Ekdahl's carefully constructed responses.

'The clinical requirements you are talking about – those were all established before it was ever first sold, right?'

'Yes,' Ekdahl replied.

'So, tell me,' the lawyer continued, his voice rising slightly, 'which of the clinical requirements, established before it was first sold, it was not meeting that required it to be taken off the market?'

Ekdahl hesitated, and then his response was a maze of circumlocutions.

'I have not read the documentation or reviewed the documents ... when they did that evaluation. The decision they made through that whole health hazard evaluation and the decision to recall – I wasn't part of the team. I am not sure how I can answer that, other than my general knowledge, which is – it had a revision rate, at that point in time, that was not something that we wanted for the product in the marketplace.'

The lawyer wasn't about to let up.

'Anything else that you understood was a clinical need in the marketplace that it was not meeting, other than the revision rate?'

'I have not seen the documentation that the team went through when they made that decision,' Ekdahl replied.

'I am asking only about your knowledge, sir,' the lawyer pressed.

'My knowledge,' Ekdahl repeated, as though clinging to a lifeboat of rehearsed answers, 'is that it was not meeting the clinical requirements in the marketplace and had a revision rate that we did not find acceptable.'

The company's legal defence revealed a calculated strategy: minimize the recall's impact by framing it as a matter of high revision rates. But the truth was far more unsettling. This wasn't just about high revision rates. The ASR hip recall was rooted in deeper issues – flawed design, insufficient testing and the insidious release of toxic metal ions into patients' bloodstreams. Each of these failures carried a dire risk to patient safety.

In the courtroom, Kransky's lawyer pursued the truth with relentless determination, focusing on one critical question: had the company ever defined a clear standard for what constituted an acceptable revision rate for the ASR?

Facing a barrage of pointed questions, Ekdahl faltered.

'What was the acceptable revision rate that was set for the product before it was sold?' the lawyer pressed.

Ekdahl hesitated.

'I don't know the answer; I don't think we put a revision rate down on paper and said that this is the revision rate that would be acceptable.'

The lawyer pushed further.

'Why not? Why wasn't it done?'

'I don't have an answer to that,' Ekdahl admitted. 'I wouldn't want to speculate.'

'Certainly something that could have been done?' the lawyer leaned in, sounding incredulous.

Ekdahl offered a weak concession.

'Could we have written down and said this is the number that we were willing to accept? Our acceptance would be that we want a product that meets our clinical aspirations in the market that is equal to or comparative to a product we already have in the market.'

'Yesterday,' the lawyer countered, 'you told me that if you're bringing something to market, it has to be at least as good, if not better, than [what] you are already selling.'

'Right,' Ekdahl admitted.

The Kransky trial, with its gripping courtroom drama, was nothing short of a turning point, but it was Ekdahl's deposition that was truly telling. It painted a damning picture of what went on behind the closed doors of the top management of the company.

Fast forward nearly a decade, and the ripples of that trial had reached far-off India. Patients here, many grappling with unbearable pain and shattered lives due to faulty ASR XL implants, clung to the truths unearthed in that courtroom. And in 2024, as Indian courts sought to deliver justice, they turned once again to Ekdahl's testimony that revealed what happened when the marketing team first learned about the devastating release of metal ions into patients' bodies.

16

Courtroom, New Delhi – Daisy Bharucha vs. DePuy

Daisy Bharucha's family often described her as the rock that held them together – strong, independent and unshakable. Coming from a middle-class family, Daisy had built an impressive career, having worked at top multinational companies. Even at sixty-seven, while many of her age embraced retirement, Daisy was still travelling to her office, proving that her dedication and resilience knew no bounds.

Daisy lived in Dadar, one of Mumbai's busiest neighbourhoods, and braved the city's chaotic local trains daily, commuting from Dadar to Bandra Kurla Complex, a bustling business hub. The crowded compartments, the constant jostling and the blistering heat of Mumbai summers didn't deter her. She had a purpose, a routine and a willpower that seemed unbreakable.

But on one fateful day in July 2007, everything changed. At the perpetually crowded Dadar Railway Station, where the cacophony of rushing trains and hurried footsteps filled the air, Daisy was making her way through the throng of commuters. Out of nowhere, someone carrying a long steel pipe rushed past, and it struck her lower body with brutal force.

'She was just walking down the platform when it happened. That pipe hit her hard,' recalls her daughter Jennifer, her voice trembling slightly as she relives the moment. Jennifer was in her thirties, working as an executive assistant at the pharma giant Pfizer when this happened.

What followed was a true testament to Daisy's strength. Despite the pain that gripped her, she didn't say a word to her family that evening. She came home, carried on with her usual chores and hid her discomfort behind a stoic face.

'That's who she was,' Daisy's daughter Jennifer says, her eyes glistening. 'She would never let us worry. Even when she was hurting, she'd always put on a brave front.'

It wasn't until the next day, when the pain became unbearable, that Daisy finally confided in her husband.

'She simply said, "The pain is getting worse," like it was nothing. But we knew. We could see it in her eyes,' Jennifer says, her voice breaking. 'She never pampered herself, never asked for help. She always carried the weight of the world on her shoulders, even when it hurt.'

Daisy consulted a renowned surgeon, seeking clarity about her injury. After a thorough examination, the doctor diagnosed her with secondary osteoarthritis, a condition that can result from an injury, infection or other diseases. In Daisy's case, the surgeon identified Avascular Necrosis (AVN) as the underlying cause – a condition where the bone tissue in the hip dies due to insufficient blood supply. The surgeon's verdict was clear – her right hip was severely damaged, and a total hip replacement was the only solution. But Daisy wasn't convinced.

'Mom didn't want it,' Jennifer explains, remembering everything ever so vividly. 'She was adamant. She kept saying, "After the implant, I won't be able to bend my leg or sit down properly. How can I live like that?" For her, being mobile wasn't just about getting around – it was freedom.'

The surgeon, however, offered a glimmer of hope, presenting an alternative – a new implant: the ASR.

'He assured her it was cutting-edge technology, something just launched by Johnson & Johnson,' Jennifer recalls. 'He promised it would allow at least 90 per cent of the mobility she cherished. We felt relieved. It was Johnson & Johnson, after all – a name we all trusted blindly. We thought, if anyone can deliver on such a promise, it's them. That day, we left the clinic feeling optimistic.'

In August 2007, Daisy underwent the primary total hip replacement surgery. The family clung to hope as she began her recovery, each small step bringing them closer to a semblance of normalcy. But by October, things took a sharp, unexpected turn. Daisy began complaining of strange sensations in her hip – an unsettling cracking and snapping sound that seemed to echo within her.

'She would sit quietly, then suddenly say, "It feels like my joint is coming apart." It was unnerving to hear that,' Jennifer says. 'We couldn't hear the sounds ourselves, but we could see her discomfort. She'd wince ever so slightly while walking, her usual determined gait faltering. Still, we tried to dismiss it, telling her, "It's probably just part of the healing process." But deep down, her words worried us.'

As days turned into weeks, Daisy's unease grew.

'She kept saying "I think my joint is dislocating again", but we struggled to believe her. How could this happen so soon after surgery?' Jennifer's voice softens, tinged with guilt. 'Looking back, I wish we had listened more closely.'

Daisy's struggles began to escalate; commuting to the office became a daunting challenge. By February 2008, the pain and discomfort had grown unbearable. Clinging to hope, she visited her surgeon.

'He assured Mom that she would be all right,' Jennifer recalls. But those words, meant to comfort, proved to be hollow assurances. Nothing changed.

By July, desperation drove Daisy back to the surgeon. This time, the examination revealed a tumour lurking on the inner side of her right thigh.

'He recommended immediate surgery,' Jennifer says, the urgency of that moment still vivid in her memory. In August 2008, Daisy was wheeled into the operating room again. The tumour was removed, but relief remained elusive.

In her discharge summary, the surgeon explained that they had removed an inflamed sac near the hip joint and observed a 'blackish' discoloration near the head of the joint. Most importantly, tissue samples were taken for examination under a microscope.

Two days later, the surgeon informed the family via email, along with pictures, that she had experienced clicking in her right leg and upon further exploration of the hip, they discovered metallosis. This was the first evidence that the ASR implant was releasing metal ions into the body. However, in August 2008, the family did not suspect anything unusual about the implant and instead focused on Daisy's recovery.

Within weeks, the pain returned, sharper than before.

'Mom couldn't sit for long, which made her office work nearly impossible. She had to rely on a walking stick, and travelling by train or bus was out of the question,' Jennifer recalls.

By 2009, the pain wasn't confined to her hip any more. It was as if her body was waging a silent rebellion. Doctors, unable to piece the puzzle together, failed to connect her symptoms to the ASR implant. New problems surfaced – headaches, unlike anything Daisy had ever experienced before.

'They weren't frequent, but when they came, they were unbearable,' Jennifer says, her eyes clouding at the memory. 'Mom would describe them as a throbbing pain, not like a normal headache. She said it felt so strange, almost like her head was being squeezed. Sometimes, she'd run cold water over her head just for a moment of relief.'

And then, as if her suffering wasn't enough, tragedy struck. Daisy lost her husband in 2009.

'Losing Dad was devastating. Mom's headaches worsened during that time. She was grieving too, but she had to keep going. We even did an MRI to figure out what was causing the constant pain,' Jennifer shares, her voice heavy with emotion.

Despite her deteriorating health, Daisy refused to give up. Financial pressure weighed heavily on her shoulders, pushing her to keep working.

'She stopped taking local trains and switched to taxis – it was the only way she could manage. That was in 2010,' Jennifer says.

By 2011, Daisy's troubles took a completely unexpected turn. In February, she got a call from her surgeon's assistant, asking her to come in for a check-up. Daisy thought it was just a routine visit. At the clinic, they took two X-rays of her hip, and everything seemed normal – until it wasn't.

The assistant dropped a bombshell: her hip implant had been recalled. Daisy could barely process the news when the surgeon recommended another surgery to fix the issue. He assured her the company would cover all the costs, but that didn't make it any easier to hear.

'Everything looked fine, or at least that's what he said,' Jennifer recalls. But then he suddenly added, 'We'll have to do another surgery.' I couldn't believe it. I just blurted out, 'Mom, why another surgery? Are you serious?" Jennifer's voice grew softer as she added, 'But the doctor warned us – if she didn't go through with it, she might end up bedridden, and things could get worse fast.'

The family left the clinic in a daze, overwhelmed by the thought of another surgery and all the risks it brought. Unsure of what to do next, they decided to get a second opinion, hoping for some clarity in the middle of all the confusion.

'We went to a senior surgeon,' Jennifer says. 'The moment we started speaking, he didn't even need to hear the full story. He asked, "Which hip implant? J&J? ASR? It's a faulty product. This is a recall. You have to get it removed." His words hit us like a thunderclap.'

The surgeon didn't mince his words. He explained how the ASR device, made entirely of metal, had corroded inside Daisy's body, releasing dangerous levels of chromium and cobalt. The toxic metals were wreaking havoc on her system.

'He urged us to act immediately. There wasn't any time to waste,' Jennifer recalls.

In March 2011, Daisy underwent revision surgery. The defective ASR implant was removed, but what the surgeons found during the procedure left the family shaken.

'They discovered a tumour filled with blackish liquid,' Jennifer says, her voice faltering. 'It was clear that the metal had corroded so badly that it poisoned her body.' On 2 April 2011, the results of the crucial blood tests arrived. They confirmed their worst fears – Daisy's blood showed dangerously high levels of chromium and cobalt. Despite the alarming findings, the family clung to the hope that removing the implant would bring her some relief.

But that hope was short-lived. The revision surgery didn't deliver the improvement they had desperately prayed for.

'She couldn't even sit for more than ten minutes,' Jennifer recalls. Frustration and desperation led the family to dig deeper. They scoured the internet for information about the ASR implant and its failures abroad. 'We found medical reports and stories from patients outside India. We even spoke to friends who could explain the clinical research. It was a grim picture,' Jennifer recounts.

In January 2012, Daisy decided enough was enough. She sent a legal notice to the company, demanding compensation of Rs 30 million. But her hopes were dashed in March when the company flatly refused to pay.

Daisy refused to let the setback crush her resolve. In March 2013, she took her fight to the National Consumer Disputes Redressal Commission (NCDRC), India's apex consumer forum. Her case was one of the first in India to challenge the company over the ASR implant. But life dealt Daisy another cruel blow – she was diagnosed with cancer. Despite the diagnosis, she fought bravely. Tragically, her battle ended on 29 April 2014.

Daisy's passing didn't end the fight. Her family vowed to carry forward her quest for justice. For over eleven years, they pursued her case relentlessly. Finally, in September 2024, the NCDRC delivered its verdict. The court acknowledged the truth that Daisy had long suspected: the ASR implant was 'defective'.

'In view of aforesaid evidence, we found that ASR hip implants, metal-on-metal manufactured by the OP suffer from inherent manufacturing defect and released a harmful amount of metal debris, which was poisonous. ASR hip implanted in right side of [the] hip of the complainant 09.08.2007, released metal debris of cobalt and chromium and due to Metallosis near the femur head, she had to go for surgery on 21.08.2008 and revision surgery on 29.03.2011,' the court ruled.[1]

The verdict was bittersweet. It came too late to change Daisy's fate, but it validated her struggle. This wasn't just any decision; it was a landmark ruling on a major medical device recall, carrying significant weight. The key questions were: what evidence did the court rely on to reach its decision? How did that evidence shape the final judgement? And, most importantly, how would this ruling impact other Indian patients who had filed similar cases and were still waiting for justice?

At the NCDRC, when patients seek compensation, the commission has significant powers to address consumer disputes. It's not just about reviewing papers – it can hold a full trial like in a civil court, where witnesses can be called in, questioned and even asked to present test reports from labs or other critical sources.

But in Daisy's case, things took a different turn. Neither side pushed for a full trial. Instead, they presented everything through written affidavits and documentary evidence. No one asked to cross-examine the individuals who gave sworn statements, nor did they request to bring in any additional witnesses to testify.

On 3 September 2024, the NCDRC finally delivered its verdict. It was a comprehensive ruling that carefully weighed every argument from Daisy and the company. The commission made important observations, shedding light on the nuances of the case, before ultimately delivering its final order.

One of the first legal issues examined by the apex consumer court was the company's argument that Daisy's case should be dismissed outright because it was filed too late. The company argued that her first surgery happened on 10 August 2007, and the revision surgery took place on 29 March 2011. However, the complaint seeking compensation was not filed until 11 April 2013. Its argument was that the complaint was 'time barred', meaning it was filed after the legal time limit under the Consumer Protection Act and, therefore, should be dismissed.

The court, however, pointed to the affidavit filed by Jennifer in April 2017. This document contained the crucial blood test report from 2 April 2011, which revealed her mother had very high levels of cobalt and chromium in the body. Daisy had undergone revision surgery and was discharged from the hospital on 1 May 2011. The court said that this blood test report provided at the time of discharge revealed 'latent defect in the implant'. It also said that the complaint was filed within two years of the discharge date, so it was within the time limit. Additionally, it pointed out that under Section 17 of the Limitation Act, 1963, if 'fraud or mistake' is involved, the time limit starts from when the affected person first becomes aware of the issue. 'Supreme Court ... held that where effect of medical negligence was manifest, cause of action arises on the date, when negligence was committed. However, where effect is latent, cause arises when harm or injury is discovered,' the court observed.[2]

Additionally, the court pointed out that the company had itself announced a reimbursement programme on 24 August 2010, which was initially valid for seven years and later extended by another five years. It also pointed out that in May 2019, the company also made a statement before the Delhi High Court, agreeing to pay Rs 2.5 million to all patients who had undergone revision surgery. 'Therefore, it cannot be said that this complaint is time barred,' the court ruled.

Next, the court looked into the company's argument that the blood test report, filed in 2017, could not be considered because it was not explicitly mentioned in the original complaint. They had cited legal precedents which required material facts, key details forming the basis of the case, to be stated in the pleadings; and without such pleading, evidence introduced later might be excluded.

The court reviewed the original complaint and noted that Daisy had indeed described relevant material facts, such as 'increased metal ion levels in the blood'. '[Her attending surgeon] advised that [the] ASR hip ... had corroded leading to a high level of chromium and cobalt ... that her tumour was full of blackish liquid which indicated all the metal pieces which had corroded,' the court pointed out.

That 'there was no relief to the patient from third surgery except that the tumour was again removed. The complainant still suffers from mouth ulcer[s] and unable to sit regularly for more than ten minutes,' the court pointed out, was among the key material facts placed by Daisy.

Based on these pleaded material facts, the court held that the blood test report could be considered as evidence, even though it was formally submitted later. In essence, the court concluded that since the complaint already included the key facts that the blood test report substantiated, the blood test report was admissible.

Next, the company had argued that under Section 13(1)(c) of the Consumer Protection Act, an 'analysis test' from an appropriate laboratory is necessary to prove that the ASR hip implant was defective. While making this argument, they relied on legal precedents, emphasizing that if the law specifies a particular way to do something, it must be done in 'that manner alone and in no other manner'. In response, firstly, the court emphasized that the legal principle in the cases mentioned by the company deals with how a government authority must follow procedures as required by law. Next, it said that Section 13(1)(c) of the Consumer Protection Act provides a rule about how evidence can be used by the parties involved.

The court pointed out that a laboratory report obtained under this section is not a 'conclusive proof' and can prove to be unreliable under Section 13(1)(f) of the Act. This section states that if either party disagrees with the findings of the laboratory or questions the methods used for testing or analysis, the court will ask that party to provide their objections in writing. Essentially, this allows both sides to formally challenge the laboratory report if they believe it is incorrect or the testing methods are flawed.

The court then emphasized that the patient 'can prove latent defect in ASR hip implant by other evidence'. The court made two important observations. First, that the Supreme Court has held that in the absence of expert evidence, courts can rely on standard literature; and second, that in civil cases, the courts are not strictly bound by the 'best evidence' rule. '...and the court is required to form its opinion of the evidence available on the record,' the court said.

The court ultimately held that the lack of a laboratory report does not prevent the patient from proving the defect. The complainant can rely on other evidence, and the court is empowered to assess and form an opinion based on the evidence available.

The company built a legal argument that the recall of the ASR hip implants was merely a precautionary step, not an acknowledgment of any defect in the product. They wanted to frame the recall as a responsible action, not an admission of fault.

Here's how the company's defence unfolded. First, the company highlighted the 'Information for Use' (IFU), which was provided to doctors and hospitals. The company argued that they had clearly listed the known risks of the implant. It argued that it mentioned possible issues that could arise, such as improper positioning, tissue reactions or choosing the wrong implant size. By making this argument, it wanted to claim that it had warned users about potential problems.

Next, it argued that the recall decision was based on data from external sources, such as joint replacement registries in Australia, England and Wales: these reports highlighted higher-than-expected failure rates, especially with smaller implant sizes and female patients. But the court was quick to note: '[The company] denies that the recall was due to any defect.'

The court, then, paid close attention to the instructions from the US Food and Drug Administration (FDA), which the company had itself included as part of its defence. The lawyers highlighted five crucial points from the FDA's instructions, which painted a clear picture of what patients and surgeons were up against.

First, while orthopaedic surgeons take multiple steps to ensure that the metal parts of the implant fit as smoothly as possible, it's impossible to 'fully avoid' metal particles from being produced when the parts rub against each other. Second, the lawyers pointed out the crucial part of the FDA instructions, which said these particles affect people differently, and it was 'not possible' to know who might experience a reaction, or when it could happen. Third, it is 'known' that these tiny metal particles can build up over time, slowly causing damage to the surrounding tissues; and that these particles can cause an adverse local tissue reaction (ALTR). Third, this tissue damage 'may cause' the implant to loosen or lead to pain, requiring revision surgery to fix the problem. Fourth, high levels of metal ions from the implants can end up in the bloodstream, leading to 'illnesses elsewhere in the body', including 'effects' on heart, nervous system and thyroid glands; however, these cases are rare. Fifth, patients with these implants need to be vigilant about certain symptoms, such as groin pain, swelling around the hip joint, difficulty walking or even a limp.

The court then made its observations on the company defence's claim that 'adverse effects' were due to improper positioning, tissue issues, or the wrong implant size. The court made it clear that the purpose of the hip implants was to help patients live pain-free lives – moving, sitting and sleeping without discomfort.

'In [a] metal-on-metal implant, in every movement of [the] implant, there will be friction and create metal particle(s). The reasons for friction as mentioned in the warning are not correct,' the court pointed out.

The court then emphasized that the US FDA 'clearly mentioned' that it was impossible to fully prevent metal particles from forming, and that, over time, these particles could cause harm to the bone or tissue around the implant, leading to painful conditions like ALTR.

'Such a reaction may cause the implant to become loose or cause pain. High levels of metal ions in the bloodstream in some patients may cause other types of symptoms or illnesses, including effects on the heart, nervous system and thyroid glands,' the court said.

The court also pointed out that the company had not only recalled the ASR implants but also created a remedial scheme. This scheme, as the court highlighted, included a letter with the heading 'Information for Patients', listing potential complications such as implant loosening, bone fractures, dislocation, metal sensitivity and pain caused by the metal debris from the implant, caused by its wear and tear.

This letter, the court pointed out, explained how, over time, the metal parts wear down, creating tiny particles too small to see, and how some patients might react to these particles. The court emphasized how the letter explained that this reaction could cause fluid buildup in the joint and surrounding muscles, which might not hurt at first but, over time, could lead to pain, swelling and damage to the muscles, bones and nerves around the hip.

The court also referred to a letter from 24 August 2010, which acknowledged similar issues, such as component loosening, infection, bone fractures, dislocation, metal sensitivity and pain.

Then the court made a crucial observation:

'If these reasons are correlated with the remedial measure and the instructions of the US Food and Drug Administration, then there appears to be no other conclusion except that the metal-on-metal implant was creating metal debris at the joint, which was the root cause for component loosening, component malignancy, infection, fracture of the bone, dislocation, metal sensitivity and pain in at least 13 per cent of patients, and mostly in females.'

The court made three more important observations linked to the company's defence. First, the 'Information for Use' about the implants, which the company had relied on, was supplied to doctors or hospitals, but it was never shared with the patients. Second, the court pointed out that the surgeries were performed by highly qualified and experienced doctors, and the company never claimed that the doctors were negligent in performing the surgeries or in choosing the correct implant size or positioning. The company didn't even question or cross-examine the doctors, the lawyers noted. Third, the court stressed that medical records could verify if there were any patient-specific (histological) issues with the implant.

Fourth, the court found it odd that the company had only considered the revision data without considering the reasons for the revision surgeries at the time of the recall.

'The OP [opposing party] adopted 'plea of not guilty and innocence', which is not applicable in civil proceeding(s). It is not a natural conduct that the OP considered only the revision data and not the reason for revision surgery, at the time of recall. But due to business strategy, the OP is now claiming that ASR hip implant was not defective as in more than 85 per cent patents, it had no side effect. If the evidence of the patient shows metal debris and complications and remains unrebutted, then it can be safely relied upon,' the court observed.

The consumer court then delved into the Kransky case in the US, a legal battle that had rippled across borders and served as the backbone of Daisy's fight in India. In that US courtroom, Kransky and his family had courageously taken on the corporate giant, exposing the devastating impact of the implant. The chilling accounts of pain and betrayal resonated deeply with Daisy's case as well. They pointed to the parallels – different continents, but the same suffering.

The consumer court first addressed the company's argument that Kransky's case 'is neither admissible nor reliable' because it did not involve the same parties and evidence. However, the consumer court disagreed. 'This judgement relates to ASR XL hip implant, metal-on-metal, manufactured by DePuy at the same time; as such, [it] is relevant and admissible under Section 13 of Evidence Act,' they observed, while referencing past rulings to support its decision, showing that such judgements can be used as evidence in similar cases.

Kransky filed the lawsuit with thirteen claims against DePuy. However, by the time the case went to trial, only three main issues remained against DePuy: negligent design, claiming the implant was poorly designed; liability for design defect, arguing the implant was defective and unsafe; and liability for failure to warn, accusing DePuy of not properly warning about the risks of the implant.

The consumer court specifically cited five key observations of the 21 July 2016 judgement of the Court of Appeals of State of California Appellate Court in Kransky's case.

First, the consumer court pointed out that on the 'recall form' DePuy submitted to the FDA, the company had 'checked' a box indicating that the recall was due to a 'defective product that would affect product performance and/or could cause health problems.'

Second, the consumer court highlighted a biomedical engineer's analysis, which revealed excessive metal wear and a critical design flaw. The court referred to the part of the order noting that the engineer, while analyzing Kransky's ASR XL implant, had 'found evidence' of 'much more than normal' metal wear than expected. Additionally, the analysis uncovered 'black-stained tissue' stuck to the back of the implant's cup. The engineer 'concluded' that the implant was defective due to its design, which caused the head of the implant to press excessively against the rim of the cup – a problem known as 'rim loading'. This defect resulted in the release of an unsafe amount of metal debris.

To drive home the fact that the ASR XL's design process had been 'inadequate' and the product itself was riddled with flaws, Kransky had brought forward a series of witnesses whose testimonies painted a damning picture. Among them was the project manager who had overseen the ASR XL's development. The consumer court highlighted a key observation from the US Court of Appeals regarding this witness's deposition. 'The project manager testified that he had never developed a hip implant before joining DePuy and he had no experience with orthopaedic devices before joining DePuy,' noted the Court of Appeals, as cited by the consumer court. The consumer court further referenced the US Court of Appeals order, which included a biomedical engineer. The engineer stated that DePuy's testing 'technique and its decisions based on premarket testing fell short of acceptable industry standards'. 'The engineer further testified that DePuy conducted a risk analysis that violated fundamental international consensus, downplayed the risks of the ASR XL's failure, and avoided fixing problems that would have prevented the implant's failure. He testified that DePuy violated the "rules of the road" of developing medical devices,' noted the US Court of Appeals, as cited by the consumer court.

Third, the consumer court drew attention to a crucial part of the US Court of Appeals' order on Kransky's evidence related to the higher revision rate and the unique design features that acted like a ticking time bomb – causing excessive wear and releasing toxic metal debris into patients' bodies. 'A toxic-chemicals specialist from the University of California, San Francisco, testified that metal ions released by the implant were toxic and could cause tissue damage. A key engineer of the ASR XL also testified that metal ions from the ASR XL could cause tissue damage,' noted the US Court of Appeals, as cited by the consumer court.

The consumer court further cited the testimony of an orthopaedic surgeon described as having 'extensive experience with the ASR XL implant'. This surgeon had brought the California courtroom to life with stark, visual evidence. 'He showed the jury pictures from five other revision surgeries that he had performed on other patients with the ASR XL implant. He used these pictures and information about these surgeries to explain to the jury how he believed the ASR XL failed and how it showed signs of such a failure,' noted the US Court of Appeals, as cited by the consumer court.

'After performing 207 surgeries to implant the ASR XL, and 70 revision surgeries to remove the ASR XL... [the doctor] testified that he saw "trends" in his experience [of] "taking care of this particular product". He testified that patients "start developing a local collection of metal ions and then the hip starts hurting and then they get this soft tissue mass that gets bigger and bigger and bigger and then to a varying degree it starts eating away soft tissue, muscle, bone and capsule. Their ion levels go up. We see them very frequently compared to other total hip replacements,"' noted the US Court of Appeals, as cited by the consumer court.

Fourth, the consumer court emphasized the testimony of two other experts. Dr John Dennis Bobyn, a professor and researcher in artificial joint replacement at McGill University, testified, as noted by the US Court of Appeals, 'that certain design features unique to the ASR XL caused increased wear.' The court further recorded that 'Dr Bobyn examined Kransky's explant (the implant after Kransky's surgeon removed it from his hip) and testified that it was defective. Dr Bobyn concluded Kransky's hip implant had worn excessively, "far beyond historical norms, far beyond expectations", which caused the implant to generate excessive amounts of cobalt and chromium.'

Robert Harrison, a toxic-chemicals specialist who had 'treated patients with high cobalt and chromium levels' from the ASR XL implant, also testified, as noted by the US Court of Appeals, that metal debris from a MoM hip implant like Kransky's caused 'destruction, inflammation, pain and disability'. Harrison stated that cobalt and chromium 'are most certainly poisonous' and 'toxic', adding that 'when they get out into the blood, [they] can cause really severe local tissue damage around hips.'

Fifth, and most strikingly, the consumer court drew attention to a pivotal finding from the US Court of Appeals order, which laid bare the reality that surgeons, like skilled craftsmen, had meticulously followed all the instructions and warnings provided by the company. Despite their precision, some implants were still placed at high angles – an outcome shaped more by the patient's unique anatomy than any lapse in the surgeon's expertise. 'Multiple witnesses testified that surgeons often insert implants at high angles, and that a patient's anatomical distinctions, rather than a surgeon's skill, primarily determine the angle at which implants are inserted,' noted the US Court of Appeals, as cited by the consumer court. 'There was no evidence that inserting a hip implant at a high angle was misuse of the product or malpractice by a surgeon, and DePuy admitted in its interrogatory responses that it was not contending that the surgeon who implanted Kransky's ASR XL failed to follow warnings or instructions, or acted negligently when inserting the hip implant at a high angle,' the US Court of Appeals further noted, as cited by the consumer court.

After reviewing the crucial details of the US case, the court made an important observation: 'California Court found that the ASR XL implant was defective because of excessive rim loading (the engineering term for when the head of the implant gets too close to the rim of the cup) that released a harmful amount of metal debris, which was poisonous.'

The consumer court then turned its attention to the fifteen key pieces of medical literature on MoM hip implants that Daisy had relied upon. Among these were research papers by Antoni Nargol and David Langton.

But it wasn't just the literature that grabbed the court's focus. It was also the Agarwal Committee Report that Daisy had relied on – expert opinions that painted a damning picture of the implant's flaws. The court carefully placed this on record, all while taking note of the company's objections.

Then, the court reached its final conclusion – a moment portentous with the weight of justice.

'In view of the aforesaid evidence, we found that ASR hip implants, metal-on-metal, manufactured by the OP, suffer from inherent manufacturing defects and released a harmful amount of metal debris, which was poisonous,' the court concluded, each word carrying the significance of what had been uncovered.

The words landed like heavy hammer blows, but this time, they carried justice behind them. Daisy's long ordeal, marked by surgeries and relentless pain, was finally validated, her suffering acknowledged in a way that no one could ignore.

The court continued, stating that the ASR hip implant in Daisy's right side had released toxic metal debris, cobalt and chromium, into her body. 'And due to Metallosis near the femur head, she had to go for surgery on 21.08.2008 and revision surgery on 29.03.2011,' the court noted, underlining the series of operations that had become her reality.

Then came another critical finding of the court. During the proceedings in 2014, Jennifer stepped forward with a heartbreaking claim: the cancer that had ravaged her mother, Daisy, was a direct result of the ASR hip implant. When this application was reviewed, the court found no evidence to prove a direct link between the ASR hip implant and the cancer. In February 2017, the court directed Jennifer to file an affidavit specifying when the cancer was first detected and where Daisy had undergone treatment.

In April 2017, Jennifer returned with a stack of medical reports. Among them was a blood test report revealing shockingly high levels of chromium and cobalt, and an MRI – with contrast and MR spectroscopy (MRS) – of the brain dated 26 November 2013. The MRI painted a grim picture – a tumour lurking on the right side of Daisy's brain. Just days later, on 29 November 2013, Daisy was admitted to the hospital. The next day, surgeons performed a right parietal craniotomy, delicately excising the tumour.

The company's lawyers, however, were quick to counter. They argued that the elevated chromium and cobalt levels in Daisy's blood could not be directly linked to the ASR hip implant. They reasoned that chromium and cobalt are also found in food and the environment, and can fluctuate due to various factors. The company further argued that Daisy's brain tumour was unrelated to the ASR hip implant and was a separate medical condition.

But the court wasn't convinced. Turning to the evidence, the court highlighted the alarming metal ion levels in Daisy's blood: chromium at 62.99 µg/L (far above the normal range of 0.7–28 µg/L) and cobalt at 95.11 µg/L. The court also pointed to the MRI report from 28 March 2011, which revealed troubling details: 'A gliotic right posterior frontal infarct is seen. Multiple ischaemic lesions are visualised within the cerebral white matter.' These findings painted a vivid picture of damage – scars in the brain's frontal lobe and tiny areas of reduced blood flow in the white matter, the brain's vital communication network.

Finally, the court concluded: 'Although her Brain MRI Report dated 28.03.2011 mentioned "A gliotic right posterior frontal infarct is seen. Multiple ischaemic lesions are visualised within the cerebral white matter," which resulted in a brain tumour, for which she had to undergo surgery on 26.11.2013, all these ailments had a causal connection with the excessive cobalt and chromium released from the metal-on-metal ASR hip implant. Ultimately, she died on 29.04.2014.' Jennifer's fight for her mother's justice had finally reached its poignant conclusion, shining a spotlight on the devastating effects of the faulty implant.

The court's ruling was a confirmation of her suffering, a legal acknowledgment of the horrors she had endured. In the end, the court addressed an important argument made by the company lawyers. They had argued that under the Consumer Protection Act, if a defective product is sold, the company should either fix the defect or replace the product. The company argued that they had already reimbursed the cost of the revision surgery and even paid Rs 2.5 million to patients who had undergone revision surgeries. The company believed no further compensation should be given.

But the court didn't buy this argument. It made it clear that when defective products cause harm to a person, the law requires that compensation be given for the injuries caused. The court explained that the Consumer Protection Act's role is to determine compensation that is 'just'. It pointed out that 'compensation for loss of limbs or life can hardly be weighed in golden scales. Bodily injury is nothing but a deprivation which entitles the claimant to damages. The quantum of damages fixed should be in accordance with the injury.'

The court went further to explain that injuries don't just affect the body. They can lead to a loss of income or cause emotional suffering. 'A person becomes entitled to damages for mental and physical loss, his or her life may have been shortened or … he or she cannot enjoy life, which has been curtailed because of physical handicap,' it emphasized.

The court also emphasized that determining what is 'just' compensation isn't easy. It's a complicated issue. 'What would be "just" compensation is a vexed question. There can be no golden rule applicable to all cases for measuring the value of human life or a limb,' the court said. 'The measure of damages cannot be arrived at by precise mathematical calculations. It would depend upon the particular facts and circumstances, and attending peculiar or special features, if any.' With these words, the court finally awarded Daisy a compensation of Rs 3.5 million.

But the wheels of justice, though turning, do not always move swiftly. Daisy, the woman who had suffered so much, wasn't alive to see the victory. Her case became a tragic reminder of how the pace of justice can be manipulated, especially by powerful companies.

'The company used patients as scapegoats,' her daughter Jennifer reflected. 'It was never about money; it was about justice. We knew we were fighting a huge company. But despite all the obstacles, a patient winning a case is symbolic. Mom had told the lawyer, "When will you do this after I die?" I had told her we would win it. And her wishes finally came true.'

In the larger picture, too, it was as Jennifer said: Daisy's fight for justice was not just about the money – it was about accountability, about ensuring that someone, somewhere, recognized the damage that had been done to her and so many others. Her victory, even posthumously, stands as a powerful testament to the resilience of those who seek justice, no matter how long it takes or how hard the fight.

The judgement in the Daisy case in 2024 marked a pivotal moment in the ASR saga. The apex consumer forum's findings are poised to send ripples through the other similar cases filed by Indian patients, including Vijay and Dinesh, who have been waiting for their voices to be heard. But the harsh reality is that not all patients have the means to fight these battles, especially in such a high-stakes arena. The company is acutely aware of this vulnerability, knowing that many patients simply don't have the resources or energy to keep pushing for justice.

For many, the only glimmer of hope had been the compensation plan crafted by the government, based on recommendations from two expert committees. It was supposed to be a lifeline, a way to right the wrongs. Yet, the company has thrown a wrench into this process, challenging the formula in the Delhi High Court. And so, the wait continues – like standing at the edge of a cliff.

Meanwhile, the Central Expert Committee, which had previously recommended compensation tailored to each patient's condition, has been halted in its tracks. It's a situation unlike any other – one that seems uniquely Indian. The company's voluntary offer of Rs 2.5 million to patients who underwent revision surgery might seem like a step in the right direction, but it fails to capture the true scale of the pain. Each patient's journey is different: some have battled years of agony, while others have had their lives completely shattered by the device and many have succumbed to it – with untold trauma and loss for all of them and their families. To reduce their suffering to a single, uniform sum feels not only unjust, but also deeply insulting.

A real sense of closure for these patients will only come when they receive compensation that acknowledges their individual stories, their personal struggles and the unique devastation that the ASR device has caused in their lives. Only then will the chapter truly be closed, with justice not just as a number on a cheque but as a recognition of their very human experience.

However, outside of India, especially in the United States, it is not just that the patients have received compensation, but the government has also held the company accountable.

After the recall, enforcement authorities in the US government took strong action against the company for engaging in deceptive marketing practices. In 2014, the Oregon Department of Justice reached a $4 million settlement with DePuy Orthopaedics Inc. This landmark settlement resolved claims that DePuy failed to inform doctors and patients that its ASR XL hip device had a high failure rate.

While announcing the settlement, Oregon Attorney General Ellen Rosenblum stressed the importance of transparency for patients and doctors. 'Doctors also need to know that the products they suggest to their patients meet certain standards, and no company should be permitted to exploit that basic tenet. I am proud that Oregon has once again taken the lead on deceptive marketing practices that hurt patients,' she said.[3]

DePuy faced allegations that it violated the law by making claims about the ASR XL that were 'false, unsubstantiated, or contradicted by other data'. According to the Oregon Department of Justice, 'Specifically, the claims were that DePuy represented to Oregon physicians and patients that the ASR XL hip functioned properly, when evidence showed the hip was failing at unusually high rates. Even as other evidence and indications pointed to a critical design flaw in the hip implants, DePuy publicly maintained that their product was fine.'[4]

As part of the settlement, DePuy not only agreed to pay $4 million to Oregon but was also prohibited from 'making any false, misleading, or deceptive representation when marketing or promoting its hip replacement products; or from representing that any hip replacement product has approval, uses, benefits or qualities that it does not have.'

However, it wasn't just Oregon.

In an investigation led by Texas and South Carolina, forty-six states in the United States accused Johnson & Johnson and DePuy of making false claims about the 'longevity' of their ASR XL and Pinnacle Ultamet MoM hip implant devices. In January 2019, the company ultimately reached a staggering $120 million multistate settlement to resolve allegations of unlawfully promoting these two devices.[5]

'Doctors and their patients need to have accurate and up-to-date information to ensure that patients are receiving appropriate healthcare,' Letitia James, New York State Attorney General, said during the announcement.[6] 'Companies should never be allowed to freely mislead the public, especially when there are health concerns involved. This settlement serves as an important message that deceptive and false medical practices will never be tolerated,' James added.

'Companies that falsely market their medical products dangerously jeopardize patients' health in order to increase profits,' Ken Paxton, Attorney General of Texas, stated.[7] 'Consumers must be able to trust that the advertised benefits of hip implant devices are backed by solid scientific evidence, not exaggerated claims,' Paxton emphasized.

The landmark legal settlement had far-reaching implications, particularly in ensuring that accurate, proven and up-to-date information is provided to doctors and patients about the performance of medical devices.

Under the settlement, Johnson & Johnson agreed to reform how it markets and promotes its hip implants, committing to four key reforms aimed at safeguarding patient safety: The company had to base claims about survivorship on scientific data and the most recent registry information. It was required to maintain a robust post-market surveillance and complaint-handling programme. The company also needed to update and improve internal product complaint-handling procedures, including training for complaint reviewers. Lastly, it had to perform quarterly reviews of complaints and, if a subgroup of patients exhibited a higher incidence of adverse events than the general patient population, identify the cause and adjust promotional practices accordingly.

'Patients put their trust in Johnson & Johnson and DePuy that the hip implants they were receiving were safe and reliable, and these manufacturers unconscionably and systematically violated that trust. The $120 million settlement today will help ensure that doctors and patients have access to the full facts and information they need to make informed medical choices,' William Tong, Attorney General of Connecticut, stated during the settlement announcement.[8]

The actions taken by enforcement authorities in the United States marked a major turning point – a moment when the company was finally held accountable for its deceptive practices. Think about it: a $120 million settlement, along with strict reforms, sent a loud and clear message that patient safety, honesty and scientific proof are non-negotiable.

But this wasn't just about legal penalties. It was about standing up for the patients and their families who had trusted the company's promises of 'long-lasting' implants, only to find themselves dealing with pain, risky surgeries and shattered faith. The settlement was a wake-up call, showing that no company, no matter how big, can put profits over people's lives without facing serious consequences.

Now contrast that with the situation in India. Here, the company is still locked in a drawn-out legal battle with the government over a compensation formula for victims. At the same time, the global giant's subsidiary in India generated a staggering Rs 35 billion in income for the financial year 2022–23, with profits after tax soaring to Rs 11.31 billion. While patients struggled to afford basic treatment, the company spent Rs 515 million on 'seminar conference expenses' and 'advertising promotional expenses'.

These aren't just cold numbers on a financial statement – they tell a stark story.

Perhaps the most glaring revelation lies in the company's own financial statements. It reassured investors about the Indian ASR compensation issue, stating: 'The matter is yet to be heard finally (by the Delhi High Court) and hence any liability arising on the Company, if at all, is presently unascertainable. All compensation payments will be borne by the Parent Company.'* Clearly, it's business as usual.

For many of these patients, this fight isn't just about money; it's about being seen and heard, about being acknowledged for the struggles they've faced. Yet, the delays leave us asking: is it fair that Indian patients are treated like they don't matter as much? Is this what happens when powerful companies hold too much sway over the system?

One day, there might finally be closure to this case. Perhaps, after years of frustrating delays, the government will win the legal battle and compel the company to compensate patients – each payment reflecting the personal struggles and pain these individuals have endured. But whenever that day comes, one truth will hang heavy in the air: as the saying goes, 'Justice delayed is justice denied.' For those whose lives have been upended, whose health and dreams have been shattered, the wait itself is yet another injustice. The ASR hip implant saga has exposed some hard truths about our healthcare system. It's shown us just how easily things can go wrong when patient safety takes a backseat. But the bigger question is, have we learned anything from this? Or are we still allowing the same mistakes to happen, leaving vulnerable patients to bear the brunt? Only time will tell.

---

* Information has been taken from the regulatory filing of Johnson & Johnson Pvt. Ltd. before the Ministry of Corporate Affairs.

Notes

1. The Billion-Dollar Baby

1. 'Annual Report', DePuy Inc., 1997, filed before Security and Exchange Commission (SEC), https://www.sec.gov/Archives/edgar/data/200406/0000200406-97-000009.txt.
2. LipinStaff, Steven. 'Medical Device Maker Stryker to Buy Pfizer's Howmedica for $1.9 Billion', *The Wall Street Journal*, 14 August 1998, www.wsj.com/articles/SB903050777988256500.
3. 'J&J Acquires DePuy', CNNMoney, CNN, 21 July 1998, money.cnn.com/1998/07/21/deals/johnson/.
4. 'Annual Report', DePuy Inc., 1998, filed before Security and Exchange Commission (SEC), https://www.sec.gov/Archives/edgar/data/200406/0000200406-97-000009.txt.
5. 'Annual Report', Johnson & Johnson, March 2004, filed before SEC, https://www.annualreports.co.uk/HostedData/AnnualReportArchive/j/NYSE_JNJ_2004.pdf.
6. Perman, Cindy. 'Stocks Log Best Year-End Rally Ever', CNBC, 31 December 2008, www.cnbc.com/2008/12/31/stocks-log-best-yearend-rally-ever.html.
7. Regulatory filing by Johnson & Johnson before SEC, February 2009, https://www.investor.jnj.com/financials/sec-filings/default.aspx.
8. Regulatory filing by Johnson & Johnson before SEC, March 2010, https://www.investor.jnj.com/financials/sec-filings/default.aspx.
9. Regulatory filing by Johnson & Johnson before SEC, February 2011, https://www.investor.jnj.com/financials/sec-filings/default.aspx.
10. 'Annual Report 2010', Johnson & Johnson, https://www.annualreports.com/HostedData/AnnualReportArchive/j/NYSE_JNJ_2010.pdf.
11. Ibid.
12. Knowledge Enterprises, Inc. 'The Worldwide Orthopaedic Market – 1999-2000', *The Medical and Healthcare Marketplace Guide 2000-2001*, November 2000.
13. '1st Annual Report', Australian Orthopaedic Association National Joint Replacement Registry, 2000, https://aoanjrr.sahmri.com/documents/10180/75186/Annual+Report+2000.
14. 'Osteoarthritis', Centers for Disease Control and Prevention (CDC), 10 June 2024, www.cdc.gov/arthritis/osteoarthritis/index.html.
15. '1st Annual Report', National Joint Registry (NJR) for England and Wales, September 2004.
16. Learmonth, Ian D., et al. 'The Operation of the Century: Total Hip Replacement', *The Lancet*, Vol. 370, No. 9597, 27 October 2007, pp. 1508–1519, https://doi.org/10.1016/S0140-6736(07)60457-7.
17. '4th Annual Report', NJR of England and Wales.
18. '2003 Annual Report', Zimmer Holdings Inc., https://investor.zimmerbiomet.com/~/media/Files/Z/ZimmerBiomet-IR/documents/annual-reports/2003ar.pdf.
19. '2003 Annual Report', Stryker Corporation, https://www.annualreports.co.uk/HostedData/AnnualReportArchive/s/NYSE_SYK_2003.pdf.
20. '2003 Annual Report', Johnson & Johnson, https://www.annualreports.com/HostedData/AnnualReportArchive/j/NYSE_JNJ_2003.pdf.

21. '2005 Annual Report', Johnson & Johnson, https://highline.huffingtonpost.com/miracleindustry/americas-most-admired-lawbreaker/assets/documents/7/JJ_annual_report_2005.pdf?build=02281049.
22. 'Annual Report 2006', Johnson & Johnson, https://www.annualreports.com/HostedData/AnnualReportArchive/j/NYSE_JNJ_2006.pdf.

2. The Live Surgery: A Gamble for Life

1. Biswas, Parthasarathi. 'Know Your City: How the Barren Pimpri-Chinchwad Zone Came to Be the Industrial Hub of Pune', *The Indian Express*, 10 April 2022, indianexpress.com/article/cities/pune/know-your-city-pimpri-chichwad-zone-pune-industrial-hub-7861103/lite/.
2. As told to the author on 4 September 2021 in Pune. Used with permission.
3. 'Annual Report', DePuy Inc., 1998, filed before Security and Exchange Commission (SEC), https://www.sec.gov/Archives/edgar/data/200406/0000200406-97-000009.txt.
4. 'Annual Report 2006', Johnson & Johnson, https://www.annualreports.com/HostedData/AnnualReportArchive/j/NYSE_JNJ_2006.pdf.
5. 'Annual Report 2011', Johnson & Johnson, https://www.annualreports.com/HostedData/AnnualReportArchive/j/NYSE_JNJ_2011.pdf.
6. Johnson & Johnson. 'ASR Hip System Recall', 24 August 2010, www.jnj.in/div-class-cms-textalign-center-b-asr-hip-system-recall-b-div.
7. DePuy Orthopaedics Inc. 'DePuy Orthopaedics Voluntarily Recalls ASR™ Hip System', PR Newswire, 26 August 2010, https://tinyurl.com/r68ucr7e.

3. Flying Halfway Across the Globe – For an Implant She Never Wanted

1. As told to the author on 10 October 2019 and 2 September 2021 over the phone. Used with permission.
2. Regulatory filing by Johnson & Johnson before SEC, March 2012, https://www.investor.jnj.com/financials/sec-filings/default.aspx.
3. Regulatory filing by Johnson & Johnson before SEC, February 2013, https://www.investor.jnj.com/financials/sec-filings/default.aspx.
4. Ibid.
5. Ibid.
6. Regulatory filing by Johnson & Johnson before SEC, February 2014, https://www.investor.jnj.com/financials/sec-filings/default.aspx.

4. The First Red Flag

1. M. Hopper, Jonathan, et al. 'An Investigation of the Performance of the 3M™ Capital™ Hip System', The Royal College of Surgeons of England, July 2001, https://www.rcseng.ac.uk/-/media/files/rcs/standards-and-research/research/an-investigation-of-the-performance-of-the-3m-capital-hip-system-report-2001.pdf.
2. '6th Annual Report', National Joint Registry (NJR) for England and Wales, 2009, pp. 96, https://www.rcseng.ac.uk/-/media/files/rcs/standards-and-research/research/national-joint-registry-report-2009.pdf.
3. '7th Annual Report', National Joint Registry (NJR) for England and Wales, 2010, pp. 18, https://www.researchgate.net/publication/320473957_Neuropathic_pain-like_symptoms_and_pre-surgery_radiographic_severity_contribute_to_patient_satisfaction_48_years_post-total_joint_replacement/fulltext/59e78ce10f7e9bc89b506dd4/Neuropathic-pain-like-symptoms-and-pre-surgery-radiographic-severity-contribute-to-patient-satisfaction-48-years-post-total-joint-replacement.pdf.

4. Personal data shared by Dr Antoni Nargol.
5. As told to the author on 16 July 2021 and 30 August 2021 via Zoom. Used with permission.
6. Smith & Nephew PLC. 'Smith & Nephew to Acquire Leading Hip Resurfacing Business', *GlobeNewswire*, 12 March 2004, www.globenewswire.com/news-release/2004/03/12/307615/54085/en/Smith-Nephew-To-Acquire-Leading-Hip-Resurfacing-Business.html.

5. Exposing the Scandal – Through Science

1. 'Annual Report', Australian Orthopaedic Association National Joint Replacement Registry, 2007, pp. 64, https://aoanjrr.sahmri.com/documents/10180/42612/Annual+Report+2007.pdf/e046948c-962b-4d46-abb4-de8b505d2ecf?t=1349440500550&download=false.
2. Langton, D. J., et al. 'Blood Metal Ion Concentrations after Hip Resurfacing Arthroplasty', *The Journal of Bone and Joint Surgery*, British Vol. 91-B, No. 10, October 2009, pp. 1287–1295, https://doi.org/10.1302/0301-620x.91b10.22308.
3. Jameson, S. S., et al. 'Articular Surface Replacement of the Hip: A Prospective Single-Surgeon Series', *The Journal of Bone and Joint Surgery*, British Vol. 92-B, No. 1, 1 January 2010, pp. 28–37, https://doi.org/10.1302/0301-620x.92b1.22769.
4. Langton, D. J., et al. 'Early Failure of Metal-On-Metal Bearings in Hip Resurfacing and Large-Diameter Total Hip Replacement', *The Journal of Bone and Joint Surgery*, British Vol. 92-B, No. 1, 1 January 2010, pp. 38–46, https://doi.org/10.1302/0301-620x.92b1.22770.

6. Recall and Beyond: Learning from the Crisis

1. 'Medical Device Alert', MHRA, 25 May 2010, https://www.mcminncentre.co.uk/pdf/asr-alert-2010.pdf.
2. 'Urgent Field Safety Notice', DePuy, Johnson & Johnson, 8 March 2010, https://research.ncl.ac.uk/metalhip/resources/gl%20DePuy%20Field%20Safety%20Notice%20ASR%20position%20mar%202010.pdf.
3. 'PIP Breast Implants', NHS, United Kingdom, 2010, www.nhs.uk/conditions/pip-implants/.
4. 'Science and Technology Committee - Fifth Report Regulation of Medical Implants in the EU and UK, 2012–2013', House of Commons, UK Parliament, 17 October 2012, publications.parliament.uk/pa/cm201213/cmselect/cmsctech/163/120523.htm.

7. A Doctor, Among the Youngest Victims

1. As told to the author on 26 February 2021 over the phone. Used with permission.

8. Zero Regulation, No Holds Barred

1. Mazoomdaar, Jay, and Kaunain Sheriff M. '#ImplantFiles: Pharma Majors Gave Freebies to Doctors, Claimed Tax Benefits', *The Indian Express*, 13 September 2020, indianexpress.com/article/express-exclusive/implant-files-pharma-majors-gave-freebies-to-doctors-claimed-tax-benefits-5473545/.
2. Information derived from records maintained by the Income Tax Appellate Tribunal.
3. 'Five Companies in Hip and Knee Replacement Industry Avoid Prosecution by Agreeing to Compliance Rules and Monitoring', Statement by Christopher J. Christie, U.S. Attorney, United States Department of Justice, 27 September 2007, https://www.justice.gov/sites/default/files/usao-nj/legacy/2013/11/29/hips0927.rel.pdf.
4. 'Health and Family Welfare Statistics in India 2019-20', Ministry of Health and Family Welfare, Statistics Division, Government of India, 2020, mohfw.gov.in/sites/default/files/HealthandFamilyWelfarestatisticsinIndia201920.pdf

5. 'National Health Accounts India 2004-05', People's Archive of Rural India, Ministry of Health and Family Welfare, Government of India, September 2009, ruralindiaonline.org/en/library/resource/national-health-accounts-2004-05/.
6. Export Import Data Bank (2003–2004 and 2010–2011), Department of Commerce.
7. 'Report of the Expert Committee on a Comprehensive Examination of Drug Regulatory Issues, Including the Problem of Spurious Drugs', Ministry of Health and Family Welfare, Government of India, November 2003, https://tinyurl.com/jmw36fvv.
8. 'Minutes of the Fiftyfourth Drugs Technical Advisory Board Meeting Held on August 2, 2005 at New Delhi', Central Drugs Standard Control Organisation (CDSCO), 2 August 2005, pp. 3, https://cdsco.gov.in/opencms/resources/UploadCDSCOWeb/2018/UploadCommitteeFiles/54tDTAb.pdf
9. 'Department-Related Parliamentary Standing Committee on Health and Family Welfare, Thirtieth Report on Drugs and Cosmetics (Amendment) Bill-2007', Rajya Sabha Secretariat, New Delhi, 2008, pp. 19, https://mohfw.gov.in/sites/default/files/570451569bill.pdf.

9. The Cover-Up

1. Registration Certificate issued by Licensing Authority, CDSCO, 29 November 2006.
2. 'Problems with Your DePuy Metal-On-Metal Hip Replacement?', Walkup, Melodia, Kelly & Schoenberger, 25 August 2022, www.walkuplawoffice.com/depuy-asr-hip-implant-failure/.
3. 'Report of the Expert Committee to Address the Issue of Faulty ASR™ Hip Implants', Ministry of Health and Family Welfare, Government of India, January 2018, www.cdsco.gov.in/opencms/resources/UploadCDSCOWeb/2018/UploadCommitteeFiles/9ASRReport.pdf.
4. Plouhar, Pamela L. 'Urgent Field Safety Notice', DePuy International Ltd., 8 March 2010, https://tinyurl.com/3yyrwzt5.
5. Official communication of DePuy Medical Pvt. Ltd., Mumbai, to the Drugs Controller General of India, 24 August 2010.
6. Official communication of Assistant Drugs Controller, Ministry of Health and Family Welfare, to DePuy Medical Pvt. Ltd., Mumbai, 12 November 2010.
7. Official communication of DePuy Medical Pvt. Ltd., Mumbai, to Assistant Drugs Controller, Ministry of Health and Family Welfare, 27 December 2010.
8. Official communication of the Assistant Drugs Controller, Ministry of Health and Family Welfare, to DePuy Medical Pvt. Ltd., Mumbai, 18 February 2011.
9. Official communication of DePuy Medical Pvt. Ltd., Mumbai, to Assistant Drug Controller, Ministry of Health and Family Welfare, 28 March 2011.
10. Ibid.
11. Official communication of Assistant Drugs Controller, Ministry of Health and Family Welfare, to DePuy Medical Pvt. Ltd., Mumbai, 24 May 2011.
12. Regulatory filing by Johnson & Johnson before SEC, 8 September 2012, https://www.investor.jnj.com/financials/sec-filings/default.aspx.
13. Official communication of DePuy Medical Pvt. Ltd., Mumbai, to Assistant Drug Controller, Ministry of Health and Family Welfare, 8 June 2011.
14. Official communication of DePuy Medical Pvt. Ltd., Mumbai, to Assistant Drug Controller, Ministry of Health and Family Welfare, 22 June 2011.
15. Ibid.
16. Ibid.
17. Ibid.
18. Ibid.
19. Official communication of Assistant Drugs Controller, Ministry of Health and Family Welfare, to DePuy Medical Pvt. Ltd., Mumbai, 28 September 2011.

20. Official presentation by DePuy Medical Pvt. Ltd., Mumbai, to the Drug Controller General of India, 13 October 2011.
21. Official communication of DePuy Medical Pvt. Ltd., Mumbai, to Assistant Drug Controller, Ministry of Health and Family Welfare, 14 October 2011.
22. Official communication of DePuy Medical Pvt. Ltd., Mumbai, to Assistant Drug Controller, Ministry of Health and Family Welfare, 9 December 2011.
23. Official communication of DePuy Medical Pvt. Ltd., Mumbai, to Assistant Drug Controller, Ministry of Health and Family Welfare, 21 December 2011.
24. Official communication of DePuy Medical Pvt. Ltd., Mumbai, to Assistant Drug Controller, Ministry of Health and Family Welfare, 21 December 2011.
25. Official communication of DePuy Medical Pvt. Ltd., Mumbai, to Assistant Drug Controller, Ministry of Health and Family Welfare, 21 December 2011.
26. Regulatory filing by Johnson & Johnson before SEC, 23 February 2012, https://www.investor.jnj.com/financials/sec-filings/default.aspx.
27. Official communication of Assistant Drugs Controller, Ministry of Health and Family Welfare to DePuy Medical Pvt. Ltd., Mumbai, 20 December 2011.

10. FIR: 435/2011

1. 'Housing Study for Pune Municipal Corporation 2009-2010', Maharashtra Social Housing and Action League (MASHAL), https://www.pmc.gov.in/informpdf/City%20Engineer%20office/Housing%20Report%20Final.pdf.
2. Jayan, Arun. 'Pune IT Exports to Cross Rs 30,000 Crore Mark', DNA India, 5 February 2011, www.dnaindia.com/mumbai/report-pune-it-exports-to-cross-rs-30000-crore-mark-1503381.
3. 'Zagade Mulls New Plan to Curb Illegal Construction', *The Indian Express*, 15 September 2010, indianexpress.com/article/cities/pune/zagade-mulls-new-plan-to-curb-illegal-constr/.
4. 'Activists Want Zagade to Be Given Back Charge', *The Times of India*, 20 April 2011, timesofindia.indiatimes.com/city/pune/activists-want-zagade-to-be-given-back-charge/articleshow/8031012.cms.
5. As told to the author on 5 September 2021 in Pune. Used with permission.
6. Criminal complaint filed by Rakesh Narayanrao Tirpude, Drug Inspector (Head Office), Mumbai, the Food and Drug Administration, state of Maharashtra.
7. Ibid.
8. Ibid.
9. Nagaranjan, Rema, and Sumitra Debroy. 'Untraceable Implants Adding to Woes', *The Times of India*, 23 July 2014, timesofindia.indiatimes.com/india/untraceable-implants-adding-to-woes/articleshow/38899802.cms.
10. Official communication of Drugs Controller General (I) to DePuy Medical Pvt. Ltd., Mumbai, 24 July 2014.
11. Official communication of DePuy Medical Pvt. Ltd., Mumbai, to Drugs Controller General (I), 4 August 2014.
12. Ibid.
13. Patel, Deepak. 'Top Official Sought CBI Probe into Hip Implants Sold by Indian Arm of Johnson & Johnson: "Failure of Govt."' *The Indian Express*, 25 August 2018, indianexpress.com/article/india/top-official-sought-cbi-probe-failure-of-govt-5323983/.

11. The Industry Insider: From Victim to Fighter

1. Vijay's email to the government, 9 October 2014.
2. Official communication of Drug Controller General of India, Ministry of Health and Family Welfare, to Johnson & Johnson Pvt. Ltd., Mumbai, 15 December 2014.
3. Official communication of Johnson & Johnson Pvt. Ltd., Mumbai, to

Drug Controller General of India, Ministry of Health and Family Welfare, 30 December 2014.
4. Ibid.
5. Official communication of Ministry of Health and Family Welfare to Drugs Controller General of India, 25 November 2016.
6. Communication of Drug Controller General of India to Vijay, 23 December 2016.

12. The Scrutiny

1. 'Annual Report 2011', Johnson & Johnson, https://www.annualreports.com/HostedData/AnnualReportArchive/j/NYSE_JNJ_2011.pdf.
2. Regulatory filing by Johnson & Johnson before SEC, 2018, https://www.investor.jnj.com/financials/sec-filings/default.aspx
3. Official communication of Deputy Drugs Controller (India), Ministry of Health and Family Welfare, 2 March 2017.
4. Marketing materials of DePuy ASR XL.
5. Presentation made by DePuy before the expert committee.
6. Presentation made by DePuy before the expert committee.
7. Sarin, Ritu. '#ImplantFiles – First Official Red Flags: Over 500 Adverse Events', *The Indian Express*, 26 November 2018, indianexpress.com/article/express-exclusive/implant-files-first-official-red-flags-over-500-adverse-events-5463990/.
8. Starkman, Dean, and Delphine Reuter. 'Patient Hopes Rise and Fall as an Industry Balances Progress and Profit', International Consortium of Investigative Journalists (ICIJ), 25 November 2018, www.icij.org/investigations/implant-files/patient-hopes-rise-and-fall-as-an-industry-balances-progress-and-profit/.
9. 'Science and Technology Committee - Fifth Report Regulation of Medical Implants in the EU and UK, 2012–2013', House of Commons, UK Parliament, 17 October 2012, publications.parliament.uk/pa/cm201213/cmselect/cmsctech/163/120523.htm.
10. Ibid.
11. Cohen, Deborah. 'Faulty Hip Implant Shows Up Failings of EU Regulation', *The British Medical Journal*, Vol. 345, 23 October 2012, https://doi.org/10.1136/bmj.e7163.
12. 'Annual Report', Australian Orthopaedic Association National Joint Replacement Registry, 2007, pp. 64, https://aoanjrr.sahmri.com/documents/10180/42612/Annual+Report+2007.pdf/e046948c-962b-4d46-abb4-de8b505d2ecf?t=1349440500550&download=false.
13. 'Annual Report', Australian Orthopaedic Association National Joint Replacement Registry, 2008, https://aoanjrr.sahmri.com/documents/10180/42662/Annual+Report+2008.pdf/119c6d7e-e3cf-47b7-b774-273a64fc8349?t=1349440477970&download=false.
14. 'Annual Report', Australian Orthopaedic Association National Joint Replacement Registry, 2009, https://aoanjrr.sahmri.com/documents/10180/42728/Annual+Report+2009.pdf/972c42c5-f2cd-408b-b7cb-76b67eee9b93?t=1349440443326&download=false.

14. The Tide Turns: Patients Fight Back

1. Thacker, Teena. 'Faulty Hip Implants: Johnson & Johnson May Have to Pay Each Patient Rs 20 Lakh.' *Mint*, 20 November 2017, www.livemint.com/Companies/45x5h9TJGlzfC3QiavoowN/Faulty-hip-implants-Johnson--Johnson-may-have-to-pay-each.html.
2. Thacker, Teena. 'How Johnson and Johnson Is Scooting from the Hip', *Mint*, 23 August 2018, www.livemint.com/Companies/fLVkS9qlrpwUilcaMLxBaO/How-Johnson-and-Johnson-is-scooting-from-the-hip.html.

3. Sheriff M., Kaunain. '"Johnson & Johnson Buried Key Facts on Faulty Hip Implant Surgeries, Kept Regulator in Dark"', *The Indian Express*, 24 August 2018, indianexpress. com/article/india/johnson-johnson-buried-key-facts-on-faulty-hip-implant-surgeries-kept-regulator-in-dark-5322149/.
4. Sheriff M., Kaunain. 'Govt Panel Findings: "Its Hip Implant Recalled in Australia, in Same Month Johnson & Johnson Got Registration Certificate in India"', *The Indian Express*, 25 August 2018, indianexpress.com/article/india/its-hip-implant-recalled-in-australia-in-same-month-johnson-johnson-got-registration-certificate-in-india/.
5. Sheriff M., Kaunain. 'Johnson & Johnson Admitted: Many Young Patients Were Affected by Faulty Hip Implants', *The Indian Express*, 29 August 2018, indianexpress. com/article/india/johnson-johnson-admitted-many-young-patients-were-affected-by-faulty-hip-implants-5331864/.
6. Official communication of Ministry of Health and Family Welfare (Drugs Regulation Section) to Principal/Health Secretaries of all States/UTs, 30 August 2018.
7. Official communication of Drugs Controller General of India to the Managing Director, DePuy Medical Pvt. Ltd. (now Johnson & Johnson Pvt. Ltd.), Gurgaon, 4 September 2018.
8. Official communication of Johnson & Johnson Pvt. Ltd. to Drugs Controller General of India, 6 September 2018.
9. Official communication of Johnson & Johnson Pvt. Ltd. to Drugs Controller General of India, 11 September 2018.
10. Public notice issued by Drugs Controller General of India, 11 September 2018.
11. Official communication from Vice President of Regulatory Affairs, Johnson & Johnson Pvt. Ltd., Mumbai, to Secretary, Ministry of Health and Family Welfare, 5 October 2018.
12. Patients' collective letter addressed to the Ministry of Health and Family Welfare, 15 October 2018.
13. Patients' collective letter addressed to Union Minister of Health and Family Welfare, 20 October 2018.
14. Official communication of Executive Director, Government Affairs and Policy, Johnson & Johnson India, to Drugs Controller General of India, 30 October 2018.
15. 'Health Ministry Approves Compensation Formula for Hip Implant Cases', Press Information Bureau, Ministry of Health and Family Welfare, Government of India, 29 November 2018, pib.gov.in/Pressreleaseshare.aspx?PRID=1554266.
16. Patients' letter to the Ministry of Health and Family Welfare, 6 December 2018.
17. W.P.(C) 13395/2018, *Johnson & Johnson Private Limited vs. Union Of India & Anr*, filed in Delhi High Court.
18. Singh, Pritam Pal. 'Delhi HC Refuses to Stay Compensation Formula for Johnson and Johnson Faulty Implants', *The Indian Express*, 13 December 2018, indianexpress. com/article/india/delhi-hc-refuses-to-stay-compensation-formula-for-johnson-and-johnson-faulty-implants-5491096/.
19. Order passed by Delhi High Court (W.P.[C] 13395/2018 and CM [case management] application number 52177/2018) on 30 May 2019.
20. Counter affidavit filed by Joint Drugs Controller (India), CDSCO, before the Delhi High Court, 28 May 2019.
21. Ibid.
22. Ibid.

15. Courtroom, California – Loren Kransky vs. DePuy

1. Meier, Barry. 'Maker Hid Data About Design Flaw in Hip Implant, Records Show', *The New York Times*, 26 January 2013, www.nytimes.com/2013/01/26/business/johnson-johnson-hid-flaw-in-artificial-hip-documents-show.html.

2. 'Sandra Ellis, Loren Kransky, et Al. V. DePuy Inc., et Al', Courtroom View Network (CVN), 2013, cvn.com/proceedings/sandra-ellis-loren-kransky-et-al-v-depy-inc-et-al-trial-2013-01-22.
3. 'Failed Medical Devices Win $8.3 M Jury Award', The Cartwright Law Firm, Inc., 11 March 2013, cartwrightlaw.com/depuy-asr-verdict-failed-medical-devices-win-83-m-jury-award/.
4. 'Andrew Ekdahl Testifies', The New York Times, 31 January 2013, www.nytimes.com/video/business/100000002035365/andrew-ekdahl-testifies.html.
5. Steele, Garen D., et al. 'Early Failure of Articular Surface Replacement XL Total Hip Arthroplasty', *The Journal of Arthroplasty*, vol. 26, no. 6, 1 September 2011, pp. 14–18, www.arthroplastyjournal.org/article/S0883-5403(11)00126-4/fulltext, https://doi.org/10.1016/j.arth.2011.03.027.

16. Courtroom, New Delhi – Daisy Bharucha vs. DePuy

1. Order passed by the National Consumer Disputes Redressal Commission (NCDRC) in Consumer Case No. 89 of 2013, 3 September 2024.
2. Ibid.
3. 'Oregon Settles with Artificial Hip Manufacturer DePuy for $4 Million', Oregon Department of Justice, 2 July 2014, www.doj.state.or.us/media-home/news-media-releases/oregon-settles-with-artificial-hip-manufacturer-depuy-for-4-million/.
4. Ibid.
5. 'AG Paxton Announces $120 Million Settlement with Johnson & Johnson for Falsely Marketing Hip Replacement Devices', Texas Office of the Attorney General, 22 January 2019, www.texasattorneygeneral.gov/news/releases/ag-paxton-announces-120-million-settlement-johnson-johnson-falsely-marketing-hip-replacement-devices.
6. 'Attorney General James and 45 Attorneys General Nationwide Reach $120 Million Settlement with Johnson & Johnson and DePuy Inc. Over Misleading Information about Hip Replacement Devices', New York State Attorney General, Office of the New York State Attorney General, 22 January 2019, ag.ny.gov/press-release/2019/attorney-general-james-and-45-attorneys-general-nationwide-reach-120-million.
7. 'AG Paxton Announces $120 Million Settlement with Johnson & Johnson for Falsely Marketing Hip Replacement Devices', Texas Office of the Attorney General, 22 January 2019, www.texasattorneygeneral.gov/news/releases/ag-paxton-announces-120-million-settlement-johnson-johnson-falsely-marketing-hip-replacement-devices.
8. 'AG Tong Announces Multistate Settlement Regarding Deceptive Marketing of Hip Implant Devices', CT.gov – Connecticut's Official State Website, The Office of the Attorney General William Tong, 22 January 2019, portal.ct.gov/ag/press-releases/2019-press-releases/ag-tong-announces-multistate-settlement-regarding--deceptive-marketing-of-hip-implant-devices.

A Note on the Author

Kaunain Sheriff M. is the national health editor at *The Indian Express*, where he leads the newsroom's in-depth coverage of critical health issues. With more than a decade of experience, he brings expertise in two key areas: law and health. His outstanding investigative journalism has earned him an impressive array of accolades, including the prestigious Ramnath Goenka Award for Excellence in Journalism, the Society of Publishers in Asia (SOPA) Award, and the Mumbai Press Club's Red Ink Award. Kaunain was part of a three-member team that collaborated with the International Consortium of Investigative Journalists (ICIJ) on The Implant Files, a global investigation in 2018 that exposed irregularities and malpractice in the medical device industry.